An Invitation to
PLYMOUTH

By Joy David

Leisure in Print Publications

PLYMOUTH

ACKNOWLEDGEMENTS

The author would like to thank Adrian Carey, Hassina Carder, Anne Naughton, Hilary Kent, Sue Dymock, Tony Parr and Jamie Macleod for their devoted and determined research and support. Rose Dennis for the delightful illustrations and the design of the cover. Trevor Burrows for the photograph on the front cover.

I would thank also the hundreds of people who generously gave me their time and help in the compilation of this book, with a special thank you to the Western Morning News and the Western Evening Herald whose editors not only gave me their time but also permission to use their archive photographs.

ISBN 1 873491-25-5
First published in 1993
Copyright Joy David
All rights reserved

Typeset, printed and bound in Great Britain by Troutbeck Press a subsidiary of R. Booth (Bookbinder) Ltd. Cornwall. Tel: (0326) 373226

CONTENTS

An Invitation to

PLYMOUTH

YELVERTON

D A R T M O O R

Shaugh Prior

Bickleigh

Lee Moor

Plym Forest

Cornwood

onhill

Sparkwell

IVYBRIDGE

YMOUTH

Plympton

Plymstock

Westlake

Hooe

Brixton

Yealmpton

Knighton

NEWTON FERRERS

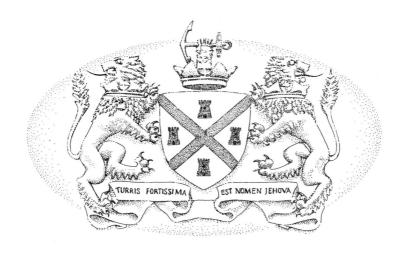

TURRIS FORTISSIMA EST NOMEN JEHOVA

FOREWORD

Some are Plymothians by birth and others by adoption - I fall into the latter category but I hope that does not disqualify me from writing the Foreword to a most unusual and fascinating book.

Straightforward guide books are two a penny, to use an old fashioned phrase and they can quickly bore even the most ardent seeker of knowledge, let alone the casual visitor. What lifts this book out of the ordinary is Joy David's touching affection for the City combined with a deep knowledge of both its past and its present. As she disarmingly acknowledges her own son finds history difficult to stomach, but many like him do want to know about the present and what the future may hold. The author supplies that need in chapters devoted to each aspect of the City's life in turn.

There are two features of the book that especially appeal to me. One is the author's willingness to give her own opinions, how refreshing to be told that one hotel, before its change in ownership, used to remind her of a vast box with compartments; and to see with what enthusiasm she espouses the ambitious scheme to build an international aquarium.

The second is her understanding that a city is more than the sum of its buildings and panoramic views - people matter. There are some delightful cameos of some of the City's lively personalities but I won't court disaster by singling any out for special mention!

Suffice it to say that whether you read this book from cover to cover or dip into those chapters of special interest to you, you will emerge much better informed and vastly entertained.

Do not refuse the "Invitation to Plymouth".

Dame Janet Fookes, D.B.E., M.P.
Deputy Speaker
House of Commons
London SW1A 0AA

April 1993

Smeaton's Tower

CHAPTER ONE

First Impressions

Plymouth has the largest population and is undoubtedly the most important place in Devon. Frequently under-rated and at one time considered a backwater this city has witnessed some of the greatest moments in history, and has suffered the ignominy of destruction under the weight of German bombers in World War II. Today it is a shining example to the world of what has been achieved by Plymothians and those who have adopted us. We have risen from the ashes and adapted ourselves to the present day and so taken a firm hold on the future.

In the space of two months in 1941 the people of Plymouth saw twenty thousand buildings, twenty four schools, eight cinemas, one hundred pubs, six hotels and forty two churches turn to rubble. Its loved ones were killed and buried in mass graves and yet survivors found the courage to go to Plymouth Hoe at night and dance in defiance of the worst that Hitler could do to us.

There was not a single part of the city which was not touched to a greater or lesser degree. Fire caused by incendiary bombs was the greatest destroyer. It was estimated that 75% of the loss in property was due to fire. No fire fighting force could possibly have prevented the wholesale damage. Firemen from Plymouth and other places who came to help worked gallantly but a great deal of Plymouth just had to be left to burn itself out. Looking back it is apparent that the more modern buildings were the survivors, built of fire resisting steel and concrete. Leicester Harmsworth House in Frankfort Street, that is now New George Street is, a prime example. It housed the Western Morning News and the Evening Herald until the end of 1992 when the magnificent purpose built building at Derriford came into being.

In spite of all this devastation and disorganisation the threads were quickly gathered and homeless businesses searched everywhere for premises. The retailers moved to Mutley and Mannamead into small shops, private house; anywhere that could be used. Some of them set up shop only to be bombed out again. Yet the work of the city never faltered, we walked to work climbing over the rubble frequently, wondering if we would find our workplace still in existence. I used to firefight - as we all did - in the Bank of England building opposite Derry's Cross Clock and there were some nights when the whole of Plymouth seemed to be on fire. Nonetheless the people never doubted that the Germans would be defeated.

It is the new Plymouth I want to introduce you to whilst making sure that we all remember that the city could not be as it is today without the glory of its past. I want you to take an imaginary step ashore in Plymouth whether it is from car, sea, train, coach or air and then pretend that you have been wafted by a magic carpet to the Plymouth Moat House, not the most architecturally pleasing building in Plymouth, nor one that in this instance I want to talk about but because from its Terrace Bar and Blue Riband Restaurant on the very top of the hotel you will see a view that, unless you are without soul, will make you addicted to this great city. stunning, unforgettable and panoramic view of the whole of Plymouth. You have an uninterrupted view of Plymouth Hoe guarded by Sir Francis Drake's statue gazing down at the greensward on which he would have played his famous game of bowls whilst awaiting the approach up Channel of the Spanish Armada. Thence to Plymouth Sound, surely the loveliest and most spectacular harbour in the world, to a bird's eye view of the glories of Mount Edgcumbe, and an enquiring look at what is still the Royal Air Force Station at Mount Batten where the legendary Lawrence of Arabia was once stationed, and from which the great Sunderland flying boats used to sweep clumsily across the water only to rise into the air like graceful swans.

Behind you are the waters of the Cattedown and the lower reaches of the River Plym, below the outstretched arms of the City centre with its pedestrianised shopping centre, flanked by the modern Theatre Royal, the not quite so modern but very tall Civic Centre, the old Guildhall and the mother church of St Andrews, where Drake knelt for blessing before his voyages, and in thanksgiving on his return. You can catch glimpses of the sprawling extremities of Plymouth as they reach the outskirts of the residential areas of Plympton and Plymstock. To your right lies Drake's Island and beyond, upstream in the River Tamar, the Dockyard and the ships of Her Majesty's Royal Navy. The tall tower of Plymouth station momentarily dulls your view but past it and outwards towards the industrial areas, are the giant factories of Plesseys and British Aerospace, signalling the new industrial wealth of Plymouth and then in the distance you can see the timeless tors of Dartmoor.

The excitement and magic of the city grips me every time I go to The Moat House. The hotel deserves extolling for its many virtues but that I will leave for a later chapter. For now I would challenge anyone who sees this view not to appreciate it and yearn to know more about the city that Plymothians have tried to hide for centuries - Drake was probably the first person who tried, and succeeded, in putting it on the map since when it has grown steadily until approaching the 21st century it has a new- found energy and a rapidly changing way of life.

Plymothians have an inbred modesty which has never allowed them to sing the praises of, nor recognise, the incredible potential of this unique place. It has taken the imagination, dedication and application, in the main, of outsiders who have come to the city and savoured its phenomenal beauty, to thrust it under the noses of industry, education and tourism and now you can begin to appreciate the sweet smell of success which will make sure the world of the 21st century will never forget the city of Plymouth, for all the right reasons.

In this decade we are witnessing a total change of direction. This was once a city whose main employer was the Dockyard caring for the needs of the Royal Navy. With the shrinking number of ships at sea has come the redundancy of many of its highly skilled labour force. On the plus side it was the availability of this skilled workforce that tempted major employers to come to Plymouth. The reduction in the numbers of men and women serving in the Armed Forces has lessened the retail power of the city, the accommodation required and all the ancillary services which were geared to produce goods and chattels for their needs.

We might have become a ghost city in winter and reliant on tourism for work in the summer but for the courage of a number of companies both from the United Kingdom and from overseas who, encouraged by the hard- working efforts of people like Graham Jones of the City Estates Department and his right hand man, Peter Burrows, together with the Devon and Cornwall Development Bureau, beat a path throughout the world and found Americans, Germans, Japanese and British industrialists and persuaded them to come and take a look at this so called backwater, Plymouth.

They liked what they saw, and listened to some of the earlier immigrants such as Toshiba, Wrigleys and Gleasons.

So, in spite of a world recession, Plymouth is able to say: here we are, try us out, work in buildings which look out over green fields, the river or the sea, come and stay in our hotels, have your conferences here, send your children to school in a healthy environment. Eat in our excellent restaurants, spend your leisure time pursuing your favourite sport. Soak up our fascinating history.

I have not met a family yet who have objected to living here once they got over the shock of being uprooted. Frequently they grow to love it so much that any kind of promotion which demands a move away, possibly back to the Midlands or the South East, is turned down because no member of the family can bear the idea of leaving all that we have to offer.

You may hear terrible moans from people who commute from outside Plymouth - it takes them all of twenty minutes to reach the city! How many of us have worked in London or Manchester or any vast city and spent hours travelling to and fro from work. Housing is comparatively cheap here. You can live overlooking the sea or the moors, at the very worst no more than fifteen minutes away from them. The range of schools offers anything from Public Schools, Comprehensives, Junior, Primary and Grammar Schools, to the smaller independents. There are Sixth Form Colleges, Language schools and now our Polytechnic, one of the finest in the country, has been given the status of a University. Adult education offers a range of courses that are unequalled anywhere else.

What do you like to do in your leisure time? Are you sports orientated or do you prefer the theatre, the concert hall You name it, we have it. Within easy reach of the city there are five golf courses, one of which, St Mellion, is championship standard and annually hosts major tournaments. Tennis thrives in local clubs and on municipal courts. We have swimming pools, bowls, cricket, squash, badminton. Football enthusiasts will know that Plymouth Argyle, known as The Pilgrims, are playing in the Second Division. The internationally famous Peter Shilton became Manager just before the end of the 1991 season and his skill and enthusiasm is just what they need. Plymouth Albion leads the rugger clubs and spawns, regularly, able players who take part at County level. The modern Theatre Royal stands proudly in Royal Parade in the centre of the city and puts on shows that attract people from all over the South West. Plymouth Pavilions is a new venture. This massive place houses an auditorium which will take thousands and is a venue for all the leading names in the country. It is a concert hall for Symphony Orchestras, a stage for the Ballet and a superb site for massive pop concerts. The swimming pool, which is largely a fun place, is busy all the year round, and the ice skating rink is so busy that it opens at 6.30am for dedicated skaters who need room on the ice to practice.

Plymouth does not have a beach but within less than an hour's drive are some of the finest beaches you will find anywhere. It is the home of several marinas, the Royal Western Yacht Club who play host to major events like the Transatlantic Race, the Royal Corinthian Yacht Club and the Mayflower Sailing Club which arranges regattas for smaller boats. I asked one solicitor why he chose to come and practice in Plymouth. 'For the sailing, of course.' he said with surprise in his voice. What a stupid question!

Of course Plymouth is not perfect. There is still much to be achieved. Our Derriford Hospital has been extended and encompasses a post-graduate teaching department. We hope soon to be able to undertake major heart surgery. Housing for the homeless is still a priority although we do not suffer from this tragedy of the nineties as much as many places. We can do with more businesses coming here especially those employing white collar workers. It would be splendid if we could be the national base for one of the big insurance companies for example.

You need to know a bit more about the history of Plymouth to understand its present circumstances. I am always arguing with my son who has no love of history and lives for the present and the future: he cannot understand my love of the past but for me how can you have a present or a future without the past?

Plymouth is the mother of many cities and small towns bearing the same name : look at the map and you will see there are 47 of them throughout the world. No one forgets her once they have her firmly in their memory. She is a city of three communities in one, Plymouth, Stonehouse and Devonport. She rises on a rock 150 feet above the waves and the waters which gather into two rivers finding their way to the sea enfolding in their arms this place that goes back in time before history when there were settlers here and Phoenicians traded with them for tin. The Romans worked the tin mines and fished in these waters and then came the Saxons. Thirteen centuries ago they fought a great battle with the Danes at one end of the Sound and all the time the little settlement grew. The Saxons built the forerunner of St Andrew's Church which dominates the city centre and is one of the best loved architectural sights of the city.

It took centuries before the town was given a charter for a market and eventually representatives in the first English Parliament. Plymouth has had many famous members of Parliament from the man who founded our first colony, Sir Humphrey Gilbert, the dashing Sir John Hawkins who founded the dreadful slave trade and then the incomparable Francis Drake who became Mayor of Plymouth, gave the city its water supply and made sure that even until this day our officials are clad in scarlet robes. In time Sir Joshua Reynolds, the famous portrait painter became our Member and in this century a remarkable list of names comes to mind: Waldorf and Nancy Astor, Lucy Middleton, Dame Joan Vickers, Dame Janet Fookes, Michael Foot, Leslie Hore-Belisha, Randolph Churchill, David Owen and Alan Clark not to mention the two new members, Gary Streeter, a solicitor with Foot and Bowden and David Jamieson, an ex school teacher. Sitting on opposite sides of the House, they are both doughty fighters intent on fighting Plymouth's corner.

Looking down upon the green and flower-bedded plateau that is Plymouth Hoe and in turn beyond to the Sound one wonders how the Pilgrim Fathers felt as they sailed out on the Mayflower to write their own pages of history in a far off land that we know as America. The adrenalin must have flowed through Captain Cook's veins as he upped anchor and sailed on his immortal voyage in which he found Australia and claimed it for his country. Did Captain Scott think of his birthplace and the town in which he spent all his young life and schooling at Stoke Damerel, when he lay facing death in the wastes of Antarctica? Men and women still play bowls on the same green sward where Drake played with Walter Raleigh, Martin Frobisher, Richard Grenville, John Davis and Lord Howard of Effingham until Spain's Armada was sighted from the Sound; they finished their game and then ran down the hill to their ships waiting below, to destroy the Spanish fleet. It was to Plymouth they returned in victory and bowed their knees in St Andrew's Church to a merciful God who had 'blown with his winds and scattered the foe'.

Golden Hind

Plymothians stood on the Hoe and watched the French ship, Bellerophon come to anchor with Napoleon on board, a captive on his way to exile. That great Italian, Garibaldi, was a welcome guest when he was hailed as a hero for giving freedom to the Italian people. They would have stood back quietly watching the arrival of the shy and bewildered Catherine of Aragon when she first set foot on the land where she was to spend the rest of her unhappy life. Widowed first in childhood, and then married to Henry VIII who all the world knows treated her disgracefully. Margaret of Anjou's ship brought her to Plymouth in 1470 to marry the weak Henry VI, leaving her virtually the ruler of England fighting the Wars of the Roses. The one who intrigues me most is Philip of Spain, who came as an honoured guest, and yet I think he was already planning his great Armada. He certainly promised his Admiral, the Duke of Medina Sidonia, the lovely estate of Mount Edgcumbe as a reward for conquering the English fleet. The Admiral was to be disappointed.

It is not only centuries ago that the rich and famous landed in Plymouth. In this century Royalty has mixed with film stars as they came ashore from the great liners that regularly anchored in the

Sound before World War II. Edward VIII, then Prince of Wales, Noel Coward, the mysterious Greta Garbo and many more. More quietly came the explorer Sir Edward Shackleton in 1921 when his ship, the Quest, called in before his last voyage. I do not remember him but I do remember the majesty of the liners, the Ile de France, the Mauretania, the Normandie, the Queen Mary and the Dutch Viendam, Vollendam and Rotterdam.

The might of the Royal Navy used to lie at anchor in the Sound or up the Hamoaze: the battleships, Rodney, Nelson, Hood, surrounded by their busy escorting destroyers. I knew every ship by name - Jane's Fighting Ships was my annual Christmas present. Plymouth has always been touched by events at sea which have brought glory and tragedy to its people. No one of my generation will ever forget the emotion and pride experienced at the homecoming of the cruisers Ajax and Exeter after their victory over the German pocket-battleship Graf Spee in the Battle of the River Plate. Winston Churchill was not yet Prime Minister but First Lord of the Admiralty. He came especially to the city and made one of his great speeches, standing on the battle scarred quarter deck of H.M.S. Exeter. He reminded the crew and anyone else who could hear his words, that even Drake, Raleigh and Hawkins never honoured their country more than in the glorious result of this battle which had come 'like a flash of light and colour on the scene, carrying with it encouragement to all who are fighting.' He ended his speech saying ' In the hearts of your fellow countrymen you have come back with your work nobly and faithfully accomplished, with your honours gathered, and your duty done.'

I remember too watching Mountbatten bring a war torn destroyer around Penlee Point, limping back to the safety of the Tamar. Round the same headland some years later came the little Gypsy Moth with Sir Francis Chichester aboard returning from his epic, single-handed round-the-world voyage.

Plymouth Hoe is no less appealing today as a ringside seat from which to watch the comings and goings of shipping. Some of it ships of the Royal Navy, more regularly the sailing from Millbay Docks of the Brittany Ferry ships going to Roscoff or Santander. They weave their way through the myriad of small sailing boats that bob on the water with their multicoloured sails. Sometimes it may be a great American aircraft carrier carrying thousands of men, as it was recently. They were on a courtesy visit to the port after a NATO exercise. Girls from all over the country had arrived to greet them, all hoping apparently to meet the man of their dreams! Sometimes it is cruise ships who anchor just inside the Breakwater allowing their passengers a chance to come ashore and seek out the treasures of the city.

In this decade Plymothians have seen the Armada of ships sailing for the Falklands conflict and within the last three years the build up for the Gulf War. It is not always peaceful.

A walk across the Hoe will not only please the eye and blow the cobwebs away, it will give you the opportunity to see the breakwater across the harbour, three miles offshore and two miles long. It leaves a passage of half a mile wide on the shore side and far, far wider on the west making the anchorage one of the safest in the world. What a feat it was to build it. John Rennie began it in 1812 and from day one until it was completed a generation later it was a fight by man against nature. Five million tons of limestone was poured into the sea until the great wall rose above sea level.

As you walk along the Hoe you will see the great white War Memorial, standing tall, proud and solemn. Four bronze figures at the top of the column hold aloft a copper globe. On each of the four buttresses supporting the base is a great lion, and on the panels between the lions are scenes of naval actions and the names of the thousands of men of the Plymouth Division who were lost in the

Royal Marines Memorial

two wars. It is the site for a moving Remembrance Day service every November. I like the smaller memorial to the Royal Marines which stands nearer to Charles II's Citadel. It was designed by one of their number, made of granite and has a marine standing on each side, and above them is a symbolical figure battling with an eagle. Their motto is there and so, too, are the poignant words of John Bunyan, ' So he passed over, and all the trumpets sounded for him on the other side.'

It takes the little red granite obelisk lower on the hillside to remind one that men of the West Country fought, too, in the Boer War. All the while the imposing statue of Francis Drake looks over us. A commanding presence. This is not the original statue but a replica of the one that stands in Tavistock, his place of birth.

Plymouth was not always as enthusiastically pro-Royal as it is today and it is no surprise, after the appalling time they had when the Stuarts were on the throne, that they declared for Parliament and Cromwell. It was because of this lapse that within five years of his Restoration, King Charles, built the massive Citadel on the east side of the Hoe. It was said to have been built to defend the port but more realistically the King had had enough of disloyal Plymothians and it was there to keep an eye on any possible sign of sedition.

The Citadel has recently had a face lift and its re opening of the barracks to troops was an opportunity for Plymouth to put on 'Music of the Night' a pageant in celebration which was nothing less than spectacular, directed by Plymouth's luckiest find, Roger Redfarn, whose artistic direction of the Theatre Royal has brought world recognition.

Many people find that the most exciting thing on Plymouth Hoe is the 18th-century Smeaton's Tower, a lighthouse which once stood on the treacherous Eddystone Rocks, 14 miles out at sea to the south west of Plymouth, and then in 1882, after the unrelenting wind and tide had begun to erode the foundation, it was taken down stone by stone and brought ashore to be rebuilt on its present site.

Smeaton's Tower has been Plymouth's most famous landmark ever since. If you are brave you will climb the 93 steps up the spiral staircase to the top; your reward will be a spectacular panoramic view which extends over the city and Plymouth Sound to Dartmoor, Devon and Cornwall. It is not always open so it would be a good idea to ring 0752 600608 to get admission details.

The new Eddystone lighthouse flashes its warning message out at every half minute and can be seen from the shore and ships for 17 miles.

Tucked into the Hoe where it joins the cliff road is one of the most interesting and award winning places to visit, **Plymouth Dome**. It is a very good idea to spend some time here before venturing any further into Plymouth's past.

It was completed in 1989 at a cost of £3 million, an investment the city has never regretted. Inside you will find a wide range of atmospheric constructions and high-tech equipment which will take you on an exhilarating journey back in time to the sights and smells of Elizabethan Plymouth, the excitement, sea-sickness, hardship and death on the voyages of Drake, Cook and the Pilgrim Fathers, and the mustering of troops for the Civil War siege of Plymouth. You will find it hard to believe that the people of Plymouth could have lived through the horrors and hardships and devastation wrought by Hitler's Luftwaffe on the city and then in calmer times, the rebuilding of this great city.

The high-tech observation gallery gives you hands-on control allowing you to guide in the TV camera and zoom in on ships and the shoreline. You can use the computers to call up data on naval shipping. It is an amazing experience which can be rounded off by a pleasant cup of tea or coffee in the little cafeteria or a browse in the shop downstairs which sells all manner of items from books to bangles.

This is a place not only for the visitor to Plymouth but for parties, whether they are schools or clubs, who will benefit enormously from the material that is available and from the very helpful and knowledgeable staff. You should allow at least 1½ hours for your visit. Special discounts are offered to group bookings, school parties and coaches. There is wheelchair access throughout the building.

The opening hours are from 9am daily except Christmas Day and it is open late on summer evenings. If you want more information prior to your visit then ring (0752) 600608. It is easy to find. Follow the signs to the City Centre and then to the Hoe. Plymouth Dome is sited on Hoe Road which runs along the seafront.

Plymouth Dome

One of the best restaurants in Plymouth is just down the road from Plymouth Dome. Somewhere I would recommend to anyone for several reasons. It is called **The Waterfront** and sits tucked away right on the seashore. It is young and vibrant, furnished simply but with an enormous number of fascinating paraphernalia on the walls and lying around.

Car parking is easy there - an important factor. In summer you can drink and eat sitting at tables outside looking right over Plymouth Sound. From inside almost every table has a good sea view too. It is a place that is open all day every day from mid-day to at least 11pm. The staff are all young and attractive, trained to care for you. If you are eating you will be allotted a waiter or waitress who introduces himself or herself to you with an engaging informality.

I like it at anytime of the day but I suppose my favourite times are in the morning before the luncheon rush starts when you can sit gazing out across the water and put the world to rights whilst you drink a cup of coffee. The food is American in style but the range is more than acceptable. If I had any criticism it would be that the portions are too generous but as my personal waiter said to me the other day. 'It is better this way - you will not go away hungry and you can always leave what you do not want.'

The Waterfront is particularly to be recommended to people with young families. My daughter and her husband were there quite recently with their three young ones - the eldest is seven - and she could not speak highly enough of the way in which the children were cared for. Special menus, games to amuse them and other small attentions to detail which are missing in many places.

It is not a place to go if you are in a hurry but then who would want to rush away from any restaurant situated in such an unequalled setting. Many people go there just to drink and in the evenings it tends to be exceedingly busy catering for people up to the age of thirty five I would say in general.

If I were a visitor I would walk up the road from the Waterfront passing Plymouth Dome and go into the **Aquarium**, with a wealth of marine life in its display tanks, each of which is devoted to fish which live in the waters around Plymouth. It is so easy for anyone to understand with simple and illustrated explanations. Children love the place and schools maximise this interest with the encouragement of Dr. Geoffrey Potts, the Curator and his staff. What is frustrating is that so much more could be seen, and a greater knowledge of the importance of marine life described, if there were more room.

The Aquarium

A recent Plymouth Visitor Survey shows that the Aquarium attracts more repeat visits than any other facility, more overseas visitors and is of great appeal to younger persons. It leads me to tell you about the Marine Biological Association (MBA) who own and run the Aquarium, and if the funds are available what the proposals are for the future.

First let me introduce you to Geoffrey Potts, who has devoted the last twenty years of his life to his work as a biologist and behaviourist, to the promotion of the MBA and the improvement of the Aquarium.

A man for all seasons is perhaps how I would describe this very likeable man. Not because he is remotely like Thomas More, but because this is a man who has the ability to be all things to all people in the world of Marine Biology. His role demands that he is centre stage most of the time whether it is in the day to day running of the Plymouth Aquarium or the world - wide part he plays in the fight to conserve marine life. He dons many mantles, that of lecturer in far distant countries, as a provider of data for eminent scientists around the world and a host to the distinguished visitors who come to research a specific subject.

His deep commitment to his job is legendary. I suggested to him that he must wake up in the morning to find the adrenalin flowing immediately; the response was that the same adrenalin stops him sleeping. He is a man of tremendous vision and courage. Unafraid to tackle the world of commerce with his begging bowl in order to get sponsorship for projects, he has gained the respect of the top people in his own profession both here and abroad and those in the world of commerce and industry who can understand what he is trying to do.

Just after I had been to see him he was awarded grants by the computer software firm Oracle UK and the Fisheries Society of the British Isles. This will pay for a complex database that, eventually, will provide a full annotated list of Britain's estimated 330 species of marine fish. This will add even more prestige to the Institution, which is already seen as a world leader in marine science. The fish database will be a valuable research tool and of great interest to other researchers from home and abroad as well as the UK fishing industry. Experts hope the detailed list of fish species will indicate how the seas around Britain are being affected by global warming.

Already fish have been found in our waters which are usually found in far warmer seas. In addition the grants will provide computer programmers and a part-time research assistant, Silja Swaby.

You probably do not know anymore than I did that the scientific work carried out in the Marine Laboratories in Plymouth has produced no less than seven Nobel Prize winners since 1888. What an achievement and what a good reason to see that this continues which it will do if the funding can be found to build the National Marine Aquarium of Geoffrey Pott's dreams. So far no comparable facility exists in Europe so what an opportunity for Plymouth.

The feasibility study has been done, and there is room at Coxside for the development which would do much for the city beyond the prestige. Such Aquaria become major tourist attractions and one here would bring something like half a million visitors to Plymouth every year. Just think what that would do for the economy, an increased visitor spending of some £10 million a year. Between 728 and 1118 jobs directly and indirectly would be created, new roads would open up and it would certainly be a catalyst for a regeneration programme in what is one of Plymouth's run down areas. This is not living in cloud cuckoo land but in reality based on what is happening in Aquaria around the world. Each one has produced significant social, cultural and economic benefits without there being a down side. All of this adds substance to Geoffrey's dream which is to create a National Marine Aquarium here in Plymouth, not unlike the aquaria to be found in North America, Australia and Japan, which are enormously successful.

What does it take to build and operate such a place? First of all it cannot be done without an army of biologists to keep the livestock in good condition. This Plymouth can provide. Secondly it must be in a recognised centre of excellence in marine science - again Plymouth qualifies because of the Marine Biological Association, the Plymouth Marine Laboratory and the University Of Plymouth with its extensive marine interests. It must be sited somewhere that will attract visitors; Plymouth has a strong maritime tradition and historic links going back to Sir Francis Drake and the Armada and the Pilgrim Fathers. It must be somewhere that is not a backwater; we know that the Plymouth of today is dynamic, modern, attractive and right at the heart of the United Kingdom's largest tourist region from which the primary market for the National Marine Aquarium would come.

The site that has been identified is within 100 metres of the Pilgrims' Steps on a natural promontory overlooking Plymouth Sound. It is within a hand's reach of the Barbican, soon to be linked to Coxside by a pedestrian lock. An independent survey of the Barbican area carried out by the Civic Trust says,

'There is no other attraction that would entail such a mix of cultural prestige, international research, educational excitement, genuine quality and straightforward crowd-pulling appeal as the National Marine Aquarium'.

We are talking megabucks here when it comes to building the NMA, far more than Plymouth can provide, although they are expected to help with grants and in building the infrastructure, and the government, it is hoped, will make a contribution. In addition, Geoffrey Potts is seeking funding from individuals with the vision and influence to support this project. There is this sort of money available and I just hope that it will be pinpointed to allow this great scheme to come to fruition by 1996.

"What will the public see and what will be the objectives? ", was a question I asked. First of all the building will be quite remarkable. It will have the drama of a modern theatre with the servicing complexity of a chemical factory. I am promised that it will be a building of architectural merit and not one that will cause Prince Charles to have apoplexy. It will also be designed with care to retain synergy with the Barbican and the foreshore position.

Inside there will be spectacular presentations of marine animals and plants in two exhibition halls; the first committed to temperate species with an estuarine diorama, touch pool and shore exhibit, and a dramatic seven metre high reef tank; the second, a tropical hall which will contain a brilliant coral reef exhibit, open ocean tank and a dramatic 'walk through' shark tank. Between the halls an open fisheries exhibition will provide information on the fishing port and allow visitors to learn something of commercial fishing operations. There will also be many smaller and ever changing exhibits. And there's more! The restaurant and cafeteria will provide good food at sensible prices, shops will offer all sorts of goods and the concourse provides a high spacious area capable of staging concerts - Handel's Water Music perhaps! Corporate functions would be held here too and a whole host of other activities. Educational and specialist groups will have priority with the use of an education suite, auditorium and functions facility.

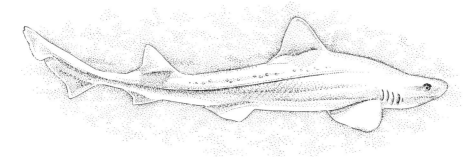

Hound Shark

One of the prime interests is Conservation, a subject on which Geoffrey Potts speaks passionately, and is an authority. Everything that is displayed and every piece of scientific research carried out is for the well being of the animals.

I listened whilst Geoffrey Potts unfolded his plan to me, and here we were talking about one of the most major projects this country has ever seen, yet the telephone was constantly ringing whilst we were speaking and he was patiently answering queries from the public. What to do with a toad that had been found abandoned was just one of the questions. He treated this as seriously as he does his dream project.

The Marine Biological Association produces The Journal of the Marine Biological Association virtually singlehanded and one that is foremost in sea life. It is produced quarterly, typeset using desk top publishing facilities within the laboratory, and is an international scientific journal with a world-wide distribution and one of the leading journals in marine biology. It publishes papers on research done at the Plymouth Laboratory, and also includes numerous papers by authors from other scientific institutions in this country and overseas.

An amazing man and one who will not rest until he has established his National Marine Aquarium. He deserves every bit of support he can get. It would be wonderful for Plymouth, the South West and the United Kingdom.

In the meantime the day to day work of the Aquarium continues and anyone wanting to take a look at the marine life will delight in what is there. What do I like best ? Possibly the Starfish and Sea Urchins the Sea Anemones and Corals, which I find fascinating and beautiful but it is all exciting.

Finally the story of Sneaky and Snappy has a fairytale quality. These two loggerhead turtles were saved from almost certain death after the nest containing their eggs was disturbed by dogs on a Greek beach. The eggs were hatched at Southampton University and the baby turtles sent to Plymouth Aquarium. Over the last two years they have flourished and the largest now weighs 50lbs. Throughout this time they have become a star attraction at the Aquarium but it was never Geoffrey Potts intention to keep them in tanks; his purpose was to rear them and return them to their native Aegean waters. This has now been achieved. Sneaky and Snappy were packed into specially designed foam-lined crates to keep them permanently wet with temperature controlled sea water for the flight home to Greece.

Could they cope with life in the wild after so much care and human attention? Geoffrey is confident. He says that they have been training them to forage for food and matched the water temperature in their tank to that in the sea where they will be going. They also reduced their contact with humans. The Aquarium staff will miss these great characters and so will the many visitors who have watched their progress.

The Aquarium is open throughout the year from 10am to 6pm in summer months and from 10am to 5pm in winter. It closes on Good Friday, Christmas Day and Boxing Day. The aquarium is to be found at the east end of Plymouth Hoe on a beautiful site overlooking Plymouth's historic Sound. There are special rates for group bookings and if you need more information or wish to book a visit, then ring 0752 22772.

CHAPTER TWO

The Barbican

Plymouth has a wealth of interesting places to see and none more so than the historic Barbican, slightly tarnished in this decade by the intrusion of far too many bars, cafes and restaurants taking away its village appeal but nonetheless it is still a mecca for people visiting the city and for locals.

Had you strolled down the hill in front of the Aquarium you would have come to the beginning of the Barbican and to the **Mayflower Steps** from which the Pilgrim Fathers set sail. For centuries this spot had nothing to state what a giant step for mankind had been taken when these intrepid people embarked on this voyage. This was rectified in 1891, not by Plymothians, but by descendants of the Pilgrim Fathers who paid tribute to the last bit of terra firma in England on which their illustrious feet had stepped. As travel became easier so more and more visitors flocked to look at this famous stone and in 1934 the Mayor of Plymouth, Sir Frederick Winnicott, decided that the Mayflower Stone was insufficient by itself. He generously presented the city with a stone gateway to highlight the hallowed place and called it 'The White Gateway to the Ocean'.

The busy Fish Market is close by sheltered from the elements by a building designed by Isambard Kingdom Brunel who would

The Fishmarket

be mortified if he knew that the corrosive action of the sea has eaten into his cast-iron posts and they are in danger of collapsing. This has confirmed the decision to move the market to the opposite side of the water where no doubt the new facilities and easier access will be great for the fishing fraternity but it will definitely take away a large chunk of the character of the Barbican.

We are promised that the Barbican will have a new lease of life and that ten million pounds will be invested to bring back its old charm and the first step is to improve the tidal defences. This is a project that is due to be completed by July 1993 and involves converting the harbour into a permanent 'wet dock', creating a new lock and incorporating the new fish market complex.

The scheme is promoted by the National Rivers Authority and the Sutton Harbour Company whose first aim will be the construction of the lock and emergency gate between the east and west piers of Sutton Harbour.

The lock will allow water to be kept in the harbour during the whole of the tide cycle, keeping out the sea and ensuring that the water level in the harbour is kept at a safe level when there are exceptionally high tides. The gates will be high enough to protect the harbour against a future rise in sea level which could occur because of the greenhouse effect.

Hopefully the Barbican will be pedestrianised which will make it much easier for people to wander along and enjoy the beauty of the old buildings. It still has its medieval street pattern and a number of buildings dating from that time. A walk down New Street will confirm this. Here you will find a delightful Elizabethan House at number 32 which has been superbly restored. A feeling of Elizabethan England touches your heart as you take in the oriel windows, the low ceilings, the roofs and floors of massive timbers. An old stairway winds round the weathered oak-mast of an old ship. As I climb up I am reminded of a true story told to me by Wynn Scutt, one of the City Museum curators who has a wealth of knowledge about Plymouth at his fingertips.

One day he was in the house waiting for a group of people. Never a man to stand idle he decided to climb to the top of the house. The early evening was still, there was no wind but as he approached a room at the top he could hear something creaking rhythmically. He could also feel the hairs at the back of his neck coming to attention! Quietly he slipped into the room expecting to surprise an intruder, he could feel a presence but all he saw was a low slung baby's cradle rocking gently to and fro. What had started it? Unseen hands from the past?

Wander through the house enjoying the beautiful fireplaces with pebble-patterned hearths and see if the cradle is still rocking! The narrow garden behind the house is planted with old English herbs, and flowers, a cutting of rue from Shakespeare's garden. Sage, thyme, and sweet scented balm, lavender, sweetbriar, golden rod and the simple wallflower, all striving to reach up for the sun that shines down upon this hidden treasure.

Many of the old warehouses in New Street have been converted into business premises housing a host of different activities. No longer needed for storage this has to be the best use for them rather than letting them fall into decay. In one building there is the well established Eating House, **The Green Lanterns** where meals are served virtually all day. It is very olde worlde and charming.

Number 27 is especially interesting. The building is 400 years old. Great deference has been paid to its venerability but nonetheless it has become **The Barbican Centre** containing over 30 crafts and design studios, small shops, boutiques, jewellers together with antique dealers and booksellers. Two restaurants, offering disparate food, flourish. One is a Vegetarian wholefood business and the other, **Rachel's Attic**, has established itself as the place to be to enjoy Devon home cooking. The building is open from 10am-5pm daily.

Most Plymouth people, and many from around the world, have reason to be grateful to Chris Robinson whose shop, **Plymouth Prints**, is at Number 34. This is a man who has evoked feelings of nostalgia amongst so many with his beautifully drawn pictures of Plymouth. His three books written about the City are gems. Go in there and you will be thrilled with the hundreds of local views, framed and un-framed and cards, all of them originating from his pen.

It seems fitting somehow for someone with as much love for Plymouth to be housed in a building dating back to 1650. It has a fine timber-framed structure and its back is one of the most delightful architectural features in the City.

Down on the quayside you should seek out **The Dolphin**, an inn that goes back further in time than almost any hostelry in Plymouth. Behind the bar you will no longer find Bette Holmes pulling the pints, a task she first did when she was just eleven years old; she has handed over the reins to her stepson but she is still to be seen on the other side of the bar amongst her regulars. Her Grandparents had the pub at the end of World War II and it has remained in the family ever since.

The most famous landlord was Charles Morgan, who in 1838 entertained the returning 'Tolpuddle Martyrs', Thomas and John Stanfield, James Brind and James Loveless, from Australia's Botany Bay.

Do not expect any frills in this pub which has become one of the unchanging features of the Barbican. The beer comes straight from the barrel, the floors are bare, in fact there are still those who use it who can remember the days when the smell of newly strewn sawdust assailed their nostrils as they walked in. There is no pub-grub, just good old fashioned drinking in an atmosphere created by the characters of the past and in which the art of conversation has not been lost.

Visitors are regarded with a certain amount of suspicion but if you are accepted you will be regaled with tales of life on the Barbican going back generations. Two splendid sisters, well in their eighties, and still running their fish stall, are regulars. They have lived on the Barbican all their lives and never been out of the city. There is nothing that they do not know about this historic spot. You will probably meet Gypsy Acora, too, a man who has made a name for himself with his uncanny predictions. If you want a palm read or something deeper he will whisk you off to his lair in Southside Street and tell you things about yourself that will astound you I know of one lady who comes every year, all the way from Guernsey, to visit this clairvoyant. He must have something to offer.

You may run into Fred Brimacombe, the undisputed king of the Fish Market, in the bar. He has been handling fish ever since he was a nipper of seven or so. He will tell you that he was always in trouble with his teachers at school, not because of his lack of attention to learning but because of the smell of fish that lingered on his person and in the air around him. He is quite glad that the Fish Market is to have a new home but he too realises that with the absence of the incoming trawlers and the men of the market in their new position, much of the character of the Barbican will be lost and the bar of the Dolphin will be deprived of many of its most colourful regulars.

The Dolphin

Nothing will ever manage to destroy the overall atmosphere. The cobbled streets have not changed in centuries. People will always want to come here to stroll along enjoying the many shops offering a wealth of goods. One or two antique shops still remain including one that is run by an extraordinary woman. Her shop is like walking into Miss Haversham's house in Dicken's Great Expectations. The dust of years is everywhere and if you want to look at anything in particular it takes a Herculean task to unearth the piece from the tentacles of other items curling around it. There are stone pigs of all sorts shapes and size, cherubs from cemeteries, vast fireplaces from the remains of old houses. Small dainty pieces of porcelain languish uncared for in a cheap rush basket. It is a wonderful place, full of the excitement of the unknown. You just never know what you will find there.

The Barbican Gallery is a different kettle of fish. Run by Bill and Sheila Hodges and their son, Robert, it has a treasure trove of another kind. The delightful old Georgian warehouse was converted in 1970 and the Hodges specialise in the sale of watercolours by living painters. The range also includes oil paintings by Gerry Hillman and Clem Spencer together with other West Country artists one of whom I love. His name is Nicholas St John Rosse and it is his ability to communicate a delightful escape from reality to his viewers that is so appealing. He makes you feel good and on a grey day puts a smile on your face. I could become addicted to his paintings quite easily.

A find for the Hodges was a doctor, Brian Pollard, from the Midlands, who has made Plymouth his home and even though he is extremely busy as a General Practitioner he finds time to paint. His work is better than any medicine he prescribes. He is self taught and untutored but he has developed a remarkable style all of his own. The paintings are bright, cheerful and with that degree of simplicity that only the great can achieve. Look out for his work, it is a joy to look at and won't be a bad investment either.

One of his paintings 'The Dolphin' is available in a limited edition of 450 prints, each one signed by the artist. The image size is 480mm x 358mm with an overall paper size of 610mm x 500mm. It will cost you £50 plus VAT but what a tonic to see this on your wall. Prints have become a part of life at the Barbican Gallery for they became publishing members of the Fine Art Trade Guild last year and intend to publish paintings by artists whose work has a particular interest or appeal to people living, working or visiting the West of England. Much of the work load on this side falls to Robert Hodges. In his own right he is the agent for Beryl Cook's Limited edition prints and books.

Bill Hodges is always on the look out for new artists and not so long ago he discovered London - born Maureen Walker who now lives in Newton Abbot. Her talent lies in fun paintings which need to be studied for about half an hour because there is so much activity, detail, and laughter depicted in what are ordinary scenes of life. Maureen had an exhibition in the gallery a little while ago which was amazingly successful. Some of her work is now available in print and if you happen to stop at Cap'n Jasper's Tea Bar, just by the Fish Market, you will find he has prints of the painting she did of his extraordinary establishment, which he intends to sell whilst feeding his customers with vast bacon butties, Fishermen's breakfasts or steaming hot mugs of tea. Standing room only but this is compensated for by the fantastic atmosphere.

The Gallery is a centre for prints by Britain's most popular artist, Beryl Cook who lives in Plymouth. Her latest Limited Edition and a selection of her famous prints are always on show and you are welcome to come and browse. Bill is a mine of information about the Barbican which he loves and mourns over. He feels a deep sense of bereavement that it no longer feels like a village; that went with the disappearance of the Post Office, the chemist and the butcher. There is still a general shop and a baker's where the bread comes fresh from the shop's ovens every day.

I wonder how Puritanical Plymouth came to be blessed with such out of the ordinary artistic talent. Not only do we have Beryl Cook, we have also Robert Lenkiewicz a man of infinite ability who is regularly to be seen striding across the Barbican from his studio on the Parade. His mane of greying hair frames a slightly austere face, his long scarf protects his neck and frequently his sensuous mouth leaving only his piercing eyes on view. They miss nothing; his observation of life, people, and in particular the underprivileged, emerges every time he paints. Sometimes his work is sensitive, sometimes creating pathos but more often sinister undertones. A strange man who has led an unusual life. Take a look at his vast mural on the Parade which depicts an Elizabethan scene and make your own judgment. Whatever my opinion may be I would never doubt his talent nor the sincerity with which he works and cares for those less fortunate than himself.

When I visited the **Armada Gallery** in Citadel Ope, Robert Lenkiewicz was there signing an enormous canvas, some 4ft high by 7ft wide depicting the starving children of Somalia. He is a man with the most enormous compassion for suffering humanity. Sonia Donovan owns the Gallery and likes whenever possible to specialise in 18th and 19th century watercolours. This interesting lady came into the art world havinq been a bursar in a private school at Mothecombe. She was born in Oreston in Lucas Boatyard, I am told. Her parents were well known licensees for many years of The Royal Oak at Hooe, and her grandfather a ferryman plying between Oreston, Turnchapel and the Barbican.

Her first venture was in 1985 when she opened a shop, called Connections selling gifts, jewellery and paintings. Her ambition was to have a gallery where she could handle lots of large and dramatic oils. This she has achieved and spending time in the

Gallery with so much colour, strength and beauty around you is something not to be missed. As well as the Gallery she also found a small shop in Southside Street from which she sold prints. Now she has the Pilgrim Gallery instead of the shop, in New Street. This is another place of delight for art lovers dealing with all kinds of pictures and limited edition prints.

Sonia Donovan exhibits many of the works of Albert George Bardsley, who studied at the Plymouth College of Art, and worked as a commercial artist with a local newspaper in which he ran a regular series of cartoons on prominent local people entitled 'As seen by Bardsley'. Unfortunately these cartoons have disappeared. Not even his neighbours ever suspected him of being a serious artist. It was not until after his death that his niece, Jill Sherwood, discovered among her uncle's belongings, around 500 paintings - all landscapes and with the exception of a few, all in watercolour. Jill Sherwood had no idea what to do with them. She was refused by many public and private organisations to buy off the entire collection. Sonia Donovan, belonging to Plymouth herself was thrilled when she saw the landscapes and was able to identify places where she had lived for many years and so enthusiastic did she become that she took the plunge and bought up all his works. What is so important is that he has left a record of a bygone Plymouth.

Here is a man who painted because he enjoyed it. He couldn't help himself. He didn't paint for fame or money and in fact was so modest about his God-given talent that he frequently painted on both sides of a canvas.

Sonia will tell you that many of his paintings form a documentary of changing times in the Westcountry, where the post war development has brought dramatic alteration.

Since nearly all of Albert Bardsley's work is unsigned and undated and the many local scenes are not identified, it must have been a daunting task for the Armada Gallery to sort out this prodigious painter's work spanning some sixty years. Luckily, the Donovans are both local people and were able to identify many of the scenes themselves. One of the very first Sonia came across was a view of Oreston and her parent's house. One Barbican fisherman recognised his father's boat in a view of the harbour, and that doyen of Western Evening Herald columnists, Crispin Gill, wrote an article which brought a response from various people in the city who had known him and were able to give the Donovans more details. Many of his pictures are seascapes, painted from the Rame Peninsula in which he captured that wonderful light beloved by artists, Turner among them. You will feel privileged when you have seen some of his work.

Another famous artist, George, of Gilbert and George fame whose 'living artworks' are known worldwide, was born in Plymouth. His surname is Passmore and although the family was poor, his mother found money to send him to an art foundation course at Dartington, Totnes.

I have just discovered another young Plymouth born artist who I think is extremely talented. Karen Pawley paints flowers mainly in gorgeous, bold colours, so full of life that they seem to climb out of the frame. There is almost a three dimensional look about her work. Exciting and paintings that would lighten up any room. She had an exhibition at Barretts, in Princess Street, where the owner, Steve Barrett, runs one of Plymouth's most entertaining restaurants, at the same time giving the opportunity to lesser known artists to display their work. More of him later. The Armada Gallery also displays Karen's work.

There is another fascinating place that you can visit, with an entrance in Southside Street or from the Parade and that is **The House that Jack Built**, it is a maze of specialist shops offering a wide range of goods from clothes to art materials jewellery, stained glassware and a Chinese restaurant. My favourite is **Briar Patch** on the ground floor just as you enter from the Parade. Inside every inch is full of artist's materials and run by a lady who is so helpful. I went there searching for a birthday present for my daughter. I had no idea what I really wanted but eventually came away with an easel and some board. She was patience personified. Showed me all the easels and pointed out what each had to offer. Asked me sensible questions without being in the least patronising and when I finally left her she sped me on my way with the words, 'Don't worry if what you have bought is all wrong. Just get your daughter to come in and we will find something that will suit her.' Fortunately I had acquired what my daughter wanted and I had no need to take up her offer but Briar Patch has acquired a customer for life and I do not hesitate to tell other people about this wonderful shop. How I wish one could say that about every establishment.

Two Dubliners, David Doyle and Martina Rooney with dedication and a sense of humour operate the unusual business **Well Oiled** at 11, Southside Street. I have no idea what the name conjures up in your mind but I did not expect to find the shop the home of essential oils and aromatherapy. It sounded to me like the description of someone who had imbibed a little too much. It certainly did to their bankers when they told the Manager what they intended to do. Rumour has it that he thought they were both plastered let alone well oiled. Time has proved the bank wrong. This highly successful business has gained the respect of everyone who goes there.

David Doyle made it quite clear that they do not consider the use of Essential Oils and Aromatherapy an alternative to medicine but as a helping and complimentary factor.

It all started whilst David was still serving with the Royal Navy and stationed in Plymouth. He and Martina had always been interested in oils and aromatherapy for their own use and found the supply in Plymouth very limited. As their interest increased so they found it more and more difficult to get what they required and to find people to discuss it with them. Eventually it seemed that there was a niche in the market for a specialist shop so they took the plunge.

In the three years they have been open much has happened. A mail order service for people who have discovered them but cannot visit regularly, takes their products throughout the United Kingdom and beyond. David has trained staff in shops in other places to handle the oils.

It says much for the respect the business has achieved that Doctors, Nurses and Midwives are among David's many customers and he is much in demand in schools, old peoples homes and various clubs, to talk about Essential Oils and Aromatherapy.

Well Oiled is a happy shop and one in which you are encouraged to walk around, ask questions and return to.

Just before you come to the House that Jack Built, there is a little one way street that links the Parade with Southside Street and in it is a shop with a difference, **Barbican Whole Foods**, owned and run by the personable Mandy Wilson who is in her early thirties. This enterprising lady opened the doors five years ago and gave Plymouth a whole new meaning to the words 'whole foods'. It is almost like stepping back in time when you shop here for almost nothing is prepacked. The window is full of open sacks showing whole foods of all kinds. Mandy has over a hundred spices with which intrepid cooks are encouraged to dabble and turn even the most unremarkable meal into a feast. A wonderful place in which to stock up your kitchen store cupboard.

It is Mandy's policy to use local produce wherever possible and that goes also for her range of cosmetics which comes from BREEZY BEAUTY BASICS, of Launceston just over the border into Cornwall. Her flour is milled locally and comes from DOVES COUDYMILL FARMS at Totnes. The most foreign import is a Macrobiotic diet from Japan which is reputed to remove all the toxins from your body. Certainly Mandy Wilson is a well versed lady in the subject of good health including the encouragement she gives to people with allergies. For example you can buy organic vegetables, wheatfree products, vegetable dishes and wholemeal breads.

Probably one of the best services she gives people is her advice on healthy eating which she makes attractive and takes any notion away that you might be dealing in something quackish.

One of the most distinguished members of the Barbican Guild of Traders and one who is deeply concerned about the future of the Barbican is Mr Foxsmith who occupies the 17th-century merchant's house, 53, Southside Street and in it for 12 years has run the successful and internationally respected **Foxsmith Galleries**. What for him started off as a hobby collecting prints, maps and engravings many years ago has become a lifetime's work. After some years he began to buy and sell in a very small way taking stalls at craft fairs. Now he has one of the largest collections in one of the smallest galleries outside London.

Today Mr Foxsmith spends half his time seeking out, buying and selling and the other half renovating, restoring cleaning and framing works ready for sale. It is a labour of love. All his prints, maps and engravings are genuine antiques with guarantees of age. Do not be put off venturing into this wonderful place by the thought of the cost. Of course some are fabulously expensive but there are finds that will not hurt the bank balance too much. His primary interest is old maps and I get the feeling that he is reluctant to part with any of them. He will encourage you to browse because he wants you to share his enthusiasm and also because he believes people visiting adds to the atmosphere.

The Foxsmith trade comes not only from Plymouth and the South West but from all over the world. His busiest time of the year is not the summer as one might suppose but in the months leading up to Christmas.

Whilst I would love to see the Barbican pedestrianised it is something that makes all the Barbican traders anxious. Parking would be provided on the periphery but they all fear it would take trade away. I see their point but how much easier and pleasanter it would be if one could walk everywhere without fearing the onslaught of traffic or missing out on things because of vehicles parked. A simple example of this are the astonishing colours of the stones on the pavement when the rain falls. Much money is about to be spent on restoration of this historic area and I am quite sure there will be many debates, discussions and arguments before the issue is decided. Whatever the outcome I am quite sure that no Plymothian will allow their most historic possession to be harmed.

Something quite different on the same side of Southside Street at the junction of Black Friars Lane and closer to the Notte Street end is a unique building, **The Blackfriar's Distillery**, the home today of Plymouth Gin. What a fascinating place it is. The building stems from the 15th century when it housed one of the three monastic orders set up in Plymouth in 1425. This order was the Black Friars and the monastery subsequently served many purposes; a place of assembly for the Pilgrim fathers, a refuge of safety for the Huguenots, and a debtor's prison.

There is sometimes a conflict amongst historians when the Distillery insists that the building was a Dominican monastery. I am reliably informed that we never had Dominicans in Plymouth and if we had they would have lived in a friary not a monastery. There were Grey Friars, Franciscans, at the top of Friary Lane but no Dominicans. I am not convinced there were three orders set up and so who was the third in this case - Dominicans?

There is no argument that at the turn of the 18th century it became the permanent home of Plymouth Gin which has been distilled here ever since. The recipe is secret and is a combination of a unique formula and the pure, fresh waters from the Devon streams. Now it is a Gin drunk all over the world and especially by the Royal Navy who add a dash of Angostura bitters to get a true 'Pink Gin'.

The surroundings in which it is distilled are wonderful. It is one of the oldest buildings in Plymouth and is protected as a National Monument. Visitors are welcome to have a conducted tour of the Distillery and encouraged first to listen to, and view, an excellent video which tells the story of the past right through to the present. You will learn that the Dutch invented gin and served it to their troops before going into battle. It helped to calm their nerves and therefore gave them 'Dutch Courage'! There are all sorts of artefacts for you to see in this building steeped in history. You would find it very difficult not to absorb the atmosphere.

The Distillery

Desmond Payne, a charming man, has been the Distiller here for many years and he is a fitting person to carry on the tradition. It is he and his assistant who will escort you around the building and at the end of the tour encourage you to buy a tot or two in bottles or special presentation cases in the Plymouth Gin Shop. One of the things that he is very thankful for is the manner in which he is allowed to operate this business. Coates & Co. (Plymouth) Limited who were the original company are now part of one of the giants, Allied Lyons, but apart from the bottling which is no longer done in Plymouth, there have been few changes in the gentlemanly way this business is run. It reminds me somehow of the difference between the Clearing Banks like NatWest and Barclays and the very dignified Coutts or Hoares - not that Desmond Payne wears the black frock coat uniform of these two illustrious establishments. There is something very nice about it.

I spent a very happy couple of hours with him whilst we reminisced about Plymouth over the years, the change in drinking habits and ran a whole gamut of topics. Plymouth Gin will be celebrating its two hundredth birthday in 1993. It would be interesting to know how many gallons have been drunk in the ensuing years. Needless to say all the while we were sipping an excellent glass of Plymouth Gin - the sun was over the yard arm!

Part of this romantic building was hived off a few years ago and turned into a **Beefeater Steak House**. It has been cleverly done and has a wonderful atmosphere. Through a vast panelled screen which divides the two businesses you can actually watch the distilling of gin whilst you are eating.

Almost next door to Plymouth Gin is another old established Plymouth business which came into being in 1879 to provide blinds for industry and the general public. In those days there was no competition from South Wales downwards. Anyone who wanted a blind could choose from green or white but all of them inners. The 20th century changed things and gradually more and more competition has appeared but **Skinners** still survives basically because of their knowledge and their appreciation of the need to give good service.

The move to the present premises came in 1959, at a time when the Barbican had not changed a lot. It was Mr. Wallis who ripped out an old bakers at the side to build a light industrial unit to manufacture these blinds, which has had this purpose ever since. During this and subsequent excavations out at the rear of the building it was discovered that the factory was built on the site where Roman wells were discovered.

Notte Street which adjoins Southside Street, often feels it is not sufficiently involved with the Barbican. I suppose the busy main road which divides the two streets does form a kind of barrier. This should not be so because Notte Street is one of Plymouth's oldest streets and housed no less personages than

William Cookworthy, Captain Cook and more recently was much connected with Isaac Foot and his family.

At No.61 is **The Saddle Shop**, the only one of its kind between Plymouth and Bristol. It is a Mecca for everyone in the horsey world and carries a very large stock of everything for this ever growing sport. Malcolm Norman is the owner and there is little he does not know about making a first class saddle. Once a Mounted Policeman with the Royal Military Mounted Police Force, he knows the importance of sitting comfortably and safely astride a horse.

Visitors to Plymouth always seem to find their way here and some of them have even bought saddles to take back to the States. The Saddle Shop also has a mobile shop which travels around the yards, on Saturdays mainly, which is extremely helpful to the recipients.

Some of you will know Sally Kingdom, Malcolm's daughter who is a Three Day Eventer and trained with the well known, Olympic medal winner, Ginny Leng. Sally only just missed being picked for the British team.

The Barbican has always been the home of interesting places to eat going back centuries to the time when upwards of 200 vessels would crowd the small confines of Sutton Pool and their crew would come ashore wanting food and fun. It is different now and far more salubrious; you are not likely to meet the tough Scottish fishermen with their fish wives whose skilled use of knives was as sharp as their tongues. You are far more likely to rub shoulders with yachtsmen from around the world, young Naval Officers on a run ashore from the 'University of the Navy' H.M.S. Thunderer at Manadon, business people from who knows where and the hard core of Plymothians who dine out regularly and have their favourite haunts. The choice is wide. It depends how deep your wallet is frequently and also what sort of food you enjoy.

I had a splendid night out not long ago. It was my birthday and my family took me to the **Barbican Pasta and Pizza Restaurant** where in very pleasant surroundings you have a choice of dishes that are all mouthwatering. I love tagliatelli and my choice lived up to my expectations. It is a place that is always busy but the staff always have time for you. There are two other restaurants of the same name, one in Union Street just across from the Drake cinema and the other opposite the Market. They are all owned and run by the same Greek Cypriot family, part of the Hajiyiani clan whose patriarch is Steve Hajiyiani.

This remarkable man arrived in Plymouth some 30 years ago and opened a small cafe in King Street, not the most salubrious part of town. From that small beginning a mighty dynasty has grown dominating the hotel, club and catering world of the city. The Hajiyiani flagship is **The New Continental Hotel** which five years ago was the most run down hotel in Plymouth. It has been reborn and sited as it is alongside The Plymouth Pavilions it cannot fail to go from strength to strength. I have to admit to being slightly amused by the cheek of the management who applied to the council for a reduction in rates because of the mess around them whilst the Pavilions was being built. The fact that the advent of this colossus of entertainment will have almost trebled the value of the hotel somehow got forgotten. Needless to say the request was not granted!

That was a slight digression from the eating houses of the Barbican. For an Italian evening in all the best traditions and service you will not better **The Bella Napoli**. The food is delicious and the atmosphere relaxed. The owner is a charming man who makes every customer feel special.

Across the road from the Bella Napoli is **Piermasters**, where Stephen Williams is the chef. His love for his job oozes out of him. Fish takes pride of place on the menu which is changed every day and written up boldly on blackboards. The dishes depend largely on what is available from the Fish Market that morning. The informal and simple interior makes for relaxed conversation. Your fellow diners will be a mixture of the yachting fraternity and business people. At some point during your meal Stephen will emerge from the kitchens, looking immaculate in his chef's clothing. He will stop at your table and make you welcome if you are a stranger, passing on to talk to those who are quite obviously Piermaster habitues. I love going there and I find the atmosphere at lunchtime is totally different to the evening session. At night it can get a bit noisy particularly in the summer months or when there is a major race starting or finishing in Plymouth. Don't let that put you off it merely adds to the enjoyment of a Piermaster meal.

We have the newly opened **Buddy's American Diner** just a few doors along Southside Street. I haven't been there and know nothing of the food but I understand it is expected to draw large crowds. It is reputed to be lively, offering good service, fast food and acceptable prices.

What is traditional, and although it has not been established for very long, has already made its mark, is the **Tudor Rose Tea Rooms** at 36 New Street. Run by Nicola Haigh a young woman who gets joy out of seeing her customer's reaction to the food. This is definitely a Tea Room and not a Restaurant.

Before the doors could be opened on this venture, a tea room had to be created out of a shell of a building. It has been done with tremendous flair and skill. One doorway is made from an old ship's mast with a carving of a Tudor Rose on it. The aim was to bring back into being some of the character of New Street and this has certainly been achieved. It is charming and enhanced by the waitresses who wear long dresses and frilly aprons whilst in the background gentle classical music creates a sense of well being.

What is unexpected is the enclosed garden with its lawns and flowers. It is almost idyllic and totally peaceful. It does not lack for trade. Barbican residents use it and so do many Plymothians. The summer months bring the tourists and it is even busier but people are important and Nicola makes sure that whether you are a visitor or a regular you are cared for.

A Henry VIII All Day Breakfast tempts many people but for those keener to watch their diets the Blackadder Salad Platters are put together with skill and thought to give a wonderful array of colourful and flavoursome salads. There are Barbican Special Toasted Sandwiches, Elizabeth Open Sandwiches, Ann Boleyn Toasted Toppings and the Sir Walter Raleigh Potato Discovery. In the afternoon Tudor Rose Afternoon Tea with home made scones, Clotted Cream, Strawberry Jam and a Pot of Tea is always welcome especially if you go the whole hog and have a slice of one of the delicious cakes.

The Barbican has been missing a good Tea Room and I hope the Tudor Rose will flourish as it richly deserves to do.

Two more ports of call should be mentioned. The Ship Inn which suffered a horrendous fire recently but Phoenix - like has arisen from the ashes and it is back to its cheerful self. It is a good hostelry and the food served in the Carvery upstairs is extremely good value.

The second is a pub that frequently confuses strangers because it has an entrance in Southside Street and one on the Quay, is **The Maritime**. Strangers frequently think the two entrances lead to different pubs and they go out of one door, round the corner and into the other only to find it is the same hostelry. Something that causes much amusement to the staff and the regulars. Run by Keith Ashford, a cheerful and convivial host, who with his staff copes with a busy lunch time trade, it is the haunt for many different kinds of people of every age. They come to enjoy the good inexpensive food and the banter that goes on in the bar. You will frequently find the BBC's Craig Rich there. No one minds if you just drink coffee rather than alcohol. That is great because you can still enjoy the atmosphere of a good Barbican pub and not feel lethargic in the afternoon or worry about driving.

At night the pub undergoes a transformation, not in decor, not in staff but in the age group of the customers. The evenings are definitely for the 18-30 age group. Nonetheless whatever time of day you go there you will find the Maritime a happy establishment.

Mitre Court lies just behind Southside Street and you enter it from either side of shops facing onto the street. It is a place to browse in. Sadly the shops change hands with regularity because it does not attract enough trade but what is there is charming and worth looking at.

Before you go anywhere else take a quick look at number 54 Southside Street **'Dolls and Miniatures'**. The Millman family bought this 18th-century building at auction in 1864 and ran it as jewellers and pawnbrokers for many decades. Mrs Tarafader, the trader now there, has built up a wonderful collection of dolls and miniatures, as fine a collection as anyone in the country.

Crossing the road and cutting through one of the little streets will bring you back on to the Quay facing which is the Custom House which looks down onto the north west corner of Sutton Harbour. Somehow it managed to survive the bombing and still stands. It was built in 1820 impressing everyone who saw it. It lacked only a clock and that omission was rectified three years later

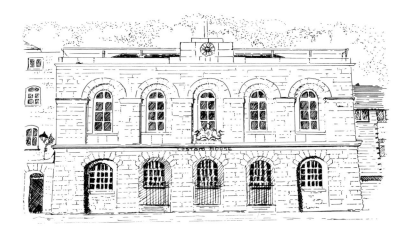

The Customs House

when one was installed of such magnificence that it almost belittled its bedfellow. Just next door is one of Plymouth's oldest pubs, **The Three Crowns**, which has remained much the same on the outside for centuries. Quite surprising really because persistent high tides have flooded the building almost every year since. Sadly it has lost much of its antiquity inside but I understand a new company has purchased it and are intent on restoring it to its former glory. I hope so, for it has a wonderful position.

With the new plans for the Barbican the Pool will not suffer from tidal changes and the smell will be a thing of the past. A century or two ago low water revealed 'gumphus' the Elizabethan word for raw sewage. Not only was it revealed but it had all the attendant repulsive stench. Children gathered where the sewage drain entered into Sutton Pool waiting for the waste to appear. They knew it would build up behind the flap controlling the flow and the natural gases would suddenly explode! Those days are gone but at low tide it is still neither pretty to look at nor devoid of smell.

If you walk around Sutton Harbour you will see that old warehouses have vanished and been replaced by luxury flats, small boutiques, health clubs, restaurants and workshops. Where once luggers would have tied up, yachts are berthed and their tinkling mast stays can be heard wherever you walk or live. It has changed considerably but with the influx of new people so has a demand for better conditions and facilities for the residents. It is almost as though history is repeating itself for once New Street - oddly named for the oldest street in Plymouth - was the home of notable and wealthy families whose lives are recorded in all the books on Plymouth. As Plymouth grew so these families moved further out and the street became less affluent. Now the newcomers who live around and about are bringing new wealth. New Street will never offer the same accommodation but its place in history will remain.

On the city centre side of Sutton Harbour is a unique family business, **Fox and Haggart**, established 60 years ago by Andrew Tait Haggart who came to Plymouth from Scotland looking for work. The year 1932 and a time of recession, if anything worse than the one we have been experiencing. In his search he met Arthur Fox, who had recently left the Royal Navy in which he had served as an Engine Room Artificer. They looked around and saw a niche for people able to repair steam trawlers and traction engines.

From small acorns oak trees grow and over the years the business has been developed to encompass all sorts of engineering repairs. The company works for the individual person or for the big boys, S.W.E.B. British Gas, Plymouth Co operative Society, British Aerospace, Brittany Ferries and the Department of the Environment. I discovered that they had built a mock section of a ship for the Fire Brigades Ships section to practice on. This is not only used here but by other Brigades as well. The firm is registered with Lloyds and the French equivalent, the Bureau Veritas. They have authority to work on foreign ships when in Plymouth or any other Devon port.

The Fox Haggart connection with the Barbican is even stronger than just the business. Andrew Tait Haggart brought up his two sons David and Andrew in a house on Lambhay Hill just below the Citadel. When the boys were old enough they joined the company and on the death of their father in 1955 took over the Haggart side of the business. Sadly David Haggart died young in 1984 but by this time Malcolm had qualified as a Mechanical

Engineer and took on his father's role. Andrew Haggart retired in 1991 but his son Andrew was also in the firm. Arthur Fox died in 1953 leaving no heir. Today Malcolm Haggart is the sole owner of this illustrious and respected company. His aim is to continue what the company has done for 60 years and that is to give fair, friendly service to their customers however big or small but for Malcolm he wants to acquire the ultimate accolade, membership of BS5750 which is the Gold Star of Engineering. An ambition I am sure he will achieve.

Tucked away in a corner close to the lively **Admiral McBride** pub and just below Lambhay Hill where the Haggarts lived is **The Barbican Theatre**, a little place with a great heart. In 1987 Rent-a-Role moved its headquarters to the theatre which it then began to develop as a regional Young People's Theatre, independent though complementary, to its work in schools. Financially it was shaky but in 1988 Plymouth City Council had the foresight to purchase the freehold, inviting Rent-A-Role to develop its programme and provide for the creative needs of young people in the region.

The Theatre has the full backing of teachers throughout the community who feel it gives them a helping hand in introducing pupils to the wider work of the theatre in general.

For the benefit of those who have never heard of the work of Rent-a-Role let me tell you that it was set up in 1980 by the present artistic Director, David Oddie, to establish drama as a vital part of learning, therapy and education. It develops approaches, techniques and structures that have made it unique in this field. David Oddie's enthusiasm for his project and his determination to acquire the backing he needed led him to pound on the doors of business and government until he got most of what he wanted. Rent-a-Role is now supported by the Arts Council, South West Arts, Devon County Council and various sponsors including the Gulbenkian Foundation, Christian Aid and Marks and Spencer. Thousands of young people are either involved in or watch the programmes and activities every year.

What and how does it achieve its aim every year? A 'Theatre in Education' service goes out to schools in Devon and Cornwall. A unique Actor-in Residence scheme for schools is available with the collaboration of the Devon and Cornwall Education Authorities.

Training is offered to teachers and bodies who have difficult tasks to perform such as the Plymouth Alcohol Advisory Centre, Plymouth Post Graduate Clinical Psychology Unit, Cancer Research etc. There are a range of Youth Theatre opportunities under professional guidance, for children of a wide age range.

The Barbican Young People's Festival of the Arts is a regular annual feature in the calendar. It is looked forward to with eager anticipation by the groups and individuals from schools, colleges, youth clubs etc who are able to use this professional theatre for their own work.

Regular contemporary dance classes are held with opportunities to work with visiting professional qroups such as the London Contemporary Dance Theatre, and the London Festival Ballet.

Throughout the year professional touring productions of special interest to young people come to the theatre. It is used too for local amateur groups and as a venue for national youth theatre companies coming to the South West.

I told you that it is a buzzing place with no time for anyone who does not have a positive mental attitude. If you go there without one you will certainly have been indoctrinated by the time you leave. It has this incredible sense of 'I'm going somewhere' about it. How lucky we are that David Oddie and his co-conspirators did not get put off by Plymouth's long time disenchantment with the theatre.

Rent-a-Role has much that it wants to do and most of it is very costly but with their enthusiasm I am sure they will rise to the challenges. However you can always do with a little help from your friends so if you feel you can contribute financially no matter how small the amount please step forward. The General Manager is Margaret Jones and the address is The Barbican Theatre, Castle Street, Plymouth PL1 2NJ. Telephone 267131. You will be in good company, The Prince's Trust which challenges young people to broaden their horizons creatively gave them £500 to help pay the production costs of the famous Brothers Grimm story, Rumpelstiltskin.

David Oddie summed it up rather well I thought. He said,

'Art is the process through which we express, share and come to understand our deepest feelings and responses. It belongs to all of us regardless of age, sex, race or class. In these times of division between people art can reach out, unite and remind us of our common heritage.'

Plymouth Moat House

CHAPTER 3

Lunch, Dine, Stay and Visit

I started this book by talking about the view from the Blue Riband Restaurant in **The Moat House** and that seems an equally good place to begin introducing you to the plethora of good places there are in which to Lunch, Dine and Stay in the City.

When the name 'Holiday Inn' disappeared and the welcoming sign of The Moat House took its place I was not at all sure that a change of name could alter how I felt about the Holiday Inn. This was a hotel that always seemed like a vast box with compartments. It had no soul, no spirit and was unwelcoming. With the arrival of the genial, interesting and dynamic Andrew Huckerby everything changed. This human dynamo set to with an energy that charged his staff as well as himself; the purpose to create from the box and compartments a first class hotel of which Plymouth could be proud. The process did not happen overnight but gradually the metamorphosis took place. It claims today to be Plymouth's leading hotel and the claim is justified.

The transformation of the two hundred and twelve bedrooms, many with breathtaking sea views across Plymouth Hoe, was one great benefit. The rooms now are luxuriously appointed, each with an en suite bathroom, colour television, direct dial telephones, in house movies, trouser press, hair dryer and tea and coffee making facilities, and have everything that you could possibly need.

At lunchtime if you go to the Blue Riband Restaurant you will discover how many of Plymouth's business fraternity eat there. Apart from it's having some of the finest cuisine in the west, thought has also been given to health, and the menu reflects this. The days of hefty eating at lunchtime have certainly gone; the afternoon is for working and not for the comatose state that too much wine or food engenders.

Sunday lunch is good fun in this restaurant. You can take as long as you wish, enjoy delicious food and wine and look out at the stunning vista of Plymouth Sound with all its colourful activity. Dining here is also a great experience. The Moat House has acquired a great reputation for its seafood dishes, quite natural really when you consider that they are prepared from the best of the catch brought fresh each day from the Barbican.

Close to the Blue Riband Restaurant is the Terrace Bar, beautifully appointed and with friendly, efficient bar staff. The drinks are good of course, but it is really the fabulous panoramic view that encourages me to go there. You look out either over the Sound or what seems to be the whole of the City. It is fabulous.

Many local people subscribe to the Metropolitan Health Club. Somewhere they can go to swim in the pool, use the steamroom or sauna or the sunbed and the mini gym and pay for the privilege on a monthly basis. The facilities are available, free of charge, too, for people staying in the hotel. One important point to emphasise about this club is the trouble they go to to work out a sensible exercising routine for each member. People tend to forget how dangerous a gym can be and what damage it can do to the human body if it is not used sensibly. The staff here are well trained, enthusiastic, polite and withstand the onslaught of children who delight in the swimming pool which they may use if accompanied by their parents.

A hotel of this size is obviously right for major functions. Under the firm reins of Andrew Huckerby, this side of the hotel has increased its business in the last couple of years. Quite remarkable in this time of recession. He was kind enough to give me lunch whilst we talked and he told me that he had increased his market share by a remarkable amount. More and more companies were using the hotel for their conferences, seminars and meetings and the spin off from that was an awareness of what the hotel had to offer, so that people enjoying business time spent in the hotel were equally happy to bring their wives and families back for a weekend break.

The hotel has always been a popular venue for wedding receptions, banquets and balls. I used to dread the dinners because the food was invariably cold by the time it was served. That is a thing of the past. A month or so ago I watched with a great deal of interest a meal for 200 people being served. It was fast, well presented, and piping hot. A triumph for any hotelier. I was equally impressed by the service and the quality of the food at The Breakfast Club meeting also held in the Moat House regularly. Light fluffy scrambled eggs, crisp bacon, flavoursome tomatoes and, bliss, some black pudding was on offer. There were probably a hundred of us and it is no mean feat to produce the right textured, scrambled egg for that number. The Moat House definitely has my vote.

Plymouth Moat House

When you meet a man with the ability to make things happen the energy invariably rubs off on other people, too. When Andrew Huckerby arrived in Plymouth he quite quickly forged a bond with his fellow hoteliers of comparable hotels. This group of owners and managers meets regularly, and it is their insight and drive which has made many things happen in the city to improve the outside world's awareness of what Plymouth and its hotels has to offer. Andrew Huckerby is a 'doer' and an achiever; the sort of man Plymouth needs to encourage more business and more visitors to the City.

I have sometimes been scathing about the building occupied by the **Forte Posthouse** on Plymouth Hoe. I will always wish it could be prettier but when you walk through the doors and into the main lounge the outside shell is forgotten. The view from the windows is breathtaking, especially on a sunny day when the sparkling blue sea stretching right across Plymouth Sound, tosses white spray gently up onto John Rennie's Breakwater two miles out, and you can see for miles, sometimes as far as the Eddystone Lighthouse. To the left the cliffs of Bovisand and Jennycliff, almost purple in hue, and to the right the green sward of Mount Edgcumbe and the far distant Penlee Point, create a semi circle protecting the harbour.

For me the lounge has become a place that answers a therapeutic need when I am grappling with a knotty problem of some kind. I can sit in a comfortable armchair, drink coffee served by a friendly waiter or waitress who always greet me like a long lost friend - very good for the ego. It does not cost me much and I leave refreshed. This is also an hotel to which I take friends and business colleagues to lunch in the Terrace restaurant. Another wonderful view - very good for the digestion and quite a help if you want to further a business cause!

The whole hotel has had a facelift recently and has a character of its own. Hotels which belong to big chains sometimes lose their individuality but not the Plymouth Forte Posthouse.

Functions of all kinds, large and small, are catered for extremely well. It is a delightful place for a wedding reception and children love it for Birthday parties. Many companies hold the Christmas 'do' there and on the more serious side, the facilities for conferences, seminars and small business meetings, complete with all the modern day equipment is second to none. Having explored the costs of these various occasions I was agreeably surprised. I thought it would be a great deal more.

One of the great assets of the Forte Empire is their ability and facility for training staff. They take youngsters from school and graduates and mould them into successful members of the company. The opportunity is there for anyone to reach the top. The Forte interests world wide enable many to travel extensively and get a wide ranging knowledge of the industry. The training scheme is impressive and pays dividends.

The current manager of the Plymouth Forte Posthouse, Andrew Whitlow, is young, enthusiastic and very much a 'hands on' man. He is almost always to be seen in the hotel somewhere. Obviously liked and respected by his staff he has also earned the respect of his fellow hoteliers in the City with his quick grasp of what is happening and what needs to be done to achieve the unending fight to ensure Plymouth is kept on the map strongly enough to increase its market share of visitors and business.

In the last two or three years **The Duke of Cornwall**, once the premier hotel in the City has emerged as something very special in hotel keeping. It is a building which stands out, turretted, castellated, it has a sense of grandeur from the outside and this restrained magnificence is repeated in the reception rooms, the elegant Dining Room with a superb, glistening chandelier that is the focal point of the room, and above all with the sweeping majesty of the staircase. The furnishings are rich in colour and the bedrooms individually decorated to continue this feeling of staying in a well to do castle, probably somewhere in Scotland! That is nonsense, of course, because the Duke is situated close to the City Centre and within striking distance of Millbay Docks where Brittany Ferries' ships tie up.

Duke of Cornwall Hotel

A little over fifty years ago the trade would have been very different. The hotel catered for people arriving in this country from the States and Europe on the liners that called in to Plymouth to disembark the famous and the immigrant. On the top of the building there is a look out from which the hall porters used to watch for the arrival of those great colossi of the ocean, the Queen Mary, Ile de France, Normandie, Mauretania and a host of lesser known passenger ships. The moment a ship was sighted it was helter skelter for the porters down to the docks, complete with their trolleys to await the arrival of the tenders bringing the passengers ashore. It was then their task to suggest - or perhaps fairly forcibly put across the idea - that the Duke of Cornwall was the best hotel in town for people to stay. The hotel must have seen more baggage with stick - on labels from across the world, than anyone can imagine. The aeroplane was a thing of the future whilst these great ocean liners ruled supreme.

In addition to the business from the sea it was also built to cater for the increasing number of people travelling by rail. It was advertised as such in one of its earliest brochures. 'It possesses the great advantage of being close in proximity to the Millbay Terminus of the Great Western Railway and also being within a short walk of the Great Western Docks, where the ocean liners embark and disembark passengers and merchandise from all parts of the world.'

Millbay Station was situated directly opposite the site for the hotel and was built in 1849. It was nicknamed the 'Shabby Shed' although if it still existed today, it would probably be considered a unique and ornate building. The stone pillars from its entrance have now been incorporated into the Pavilions which stands opposite the hotel.

Reading the records of the hotel you can see that when the need for the hotel was first recognised, a group of railway officials were appointed the original Board of Directors and selected 'Honest John' of Messrs Hall and Pethick to construct this large and luxurious building. The cost totalled £40,000 including the excavation work required to clear the site where the Saracen's Head Public House and Millbay Grove Terrace then stood. The hotel's function rooms are still named after some of the men originally involved in the design and running of The Duke of Cornwall. What intrigues me was that when I went to see Jeremy Palmer we were talking about the cost of cleaning the front of the building and he said that the scaffolding alone was quoted at over £60,000, a third more than the hotel cost to build.

Looking back through the first minute books written during the board meeting in 1862, it is fascinating to note the changes. The Bed and Breakfast tariff seems particularly reasonable at seven shillings and sixpence or 37p in todays money but a cold bath would cost you one shilling or 5p and your dog as much as three shillings and sixpence or 17p per day. The manager only earned £125.00 per annum!

Few of the places of interest advertised in that early brochure have altered. The Barbican, Burrator Reservoir, Eddystone Lighthouse, Mount Edgcumbe and the Dockyard were all featured although Plymouth Pier with its Pavilion has disappeared.

Throughout its history the hotel has always catered for the needs of Plymothians. Ballroom dancing was once a twice weekly feature in the lofty ballroom. Today it is still used for functions but for a different clientele. The hotel catered then for business as it does now. It does it with style, grace and a desire to ensure satisfaction. Because it is slightly to the rear of the City centre perhaps Plymothians have forgotten how pleasant it is to sit in its gracious rooms enjoying a coffee or a sandwich, something I can heartily recommended as I can a meal in the Dining Room. It has this old fashioned air about it that is stable and re-assuring. Probably the reason why the Americans love the hotel so much. They enthuse over its architecture and everything else. Not without reason did Sir John Betjeman call it the finest building in Plymouth.

Jeremy Palmer is the General Manager of the hotel. He spent some time in the hotel in his early days as a Manager and then took off for pastures new, only to return when he was offered by new owners the opportunity to take on the task of bringing the Duke of Cornwall back to its rightful place in Plymouth. A task he has relished and one that has proved successful. More and more people are discovering that the food is good, the wines excellent and the service a credit to the hotel.

I have always loved **The Grand Hotel** on the Hoe. This beautiful building stands a mere bowl's throw away from where Sir Francis Drake played his famous game. Built in 1879 by John Pethick, who was also the first owner of the hotel, it is of majestic proportions, delighting the eye from the outside, and decorated with charm and style inside. Like the Forte Posthouse and The Moat House it is unsurpassed in its views of the sea and Plymouth Sound. The bedrooms are distinctive, the restaurant a gem. Managed by Garth Powell and his wife Janet, it is a hotel that has grown in stature. It suffered a severe setback when it was taken over by the Berni group who almost destroyed its character, but thankfully that disaster was averted and for the last eight years these two have devoted just about their every waking hour to the reconstruction and the refurbishment of the hotel.

Stay here and you will find yourselves not only very comfortable but extremely well fed and all the time you have this wonderful bonus of views that have no equal anywhere in the world. It is a hotel that attracts many overseas visitors but it also has a healthy share of wedding receptions and business functions which are catered for with enormous care and attention.

The Grand offers some excellent weekend breaks with all kinds of interesting activities, such as clay pigeon shooting, hot air ballooning and dry slope skiing. Supper dances are held in the Promenade Restaurant on Saturday nights with live music from the Peter Hutchison trio, who alternate with The Cats Whiskers and Dave Hawkes Band.

I have always wondered what William Ewart Gladstone had that few others have ever achieved. Whatever it was made him capable of drawing 100,000 people to Plymouth Hoe in 1889. Here was a frail, old man of eighty, serving as Prime Minister for his third term in office, staying quietly in The Grand. The crowd, some of whom would have heard him address a meeting in the Drill Hall earlier in the evening, clamoured for his presence and finally he came out onto the balcony, on a cold, wet November evening and spoke to them. Whatever he said must almost have gone unheard for there were no such things as microphones or Public Address systems. His voice would have carried in the wind and his words been passed along from one row of people to another almost like a Chinese whisper. There is no way that John Major could conjure up that size audience anywhere, let alone Plymouth Hoe on a wintery night.

One Plymouth hotel I never expected to enjoy was **The Copthorne**. Situated right in the heart of the City at the top of Western Approach, it is architecturally unpleasing. Yet once inside it has an air of well being, somewhere that makes you feel at ease, yet remains efficient, capable of catering for people at any level. I was agreeably surprised on my first visit and have been going there ever since, particularly for a glass of wine after the trauma of doing the monthly shopping at Sainsbury's next door.

The Copthorne is part of a major group, each of which has a different character but offers throughout a standard of service that is hard to beat. It attracts its custom from businesses in the United Kingdom and from Europe. It is the ability to answer the needs of different nationalities that has made it such a success in Plymouth. Interesting and famous people stay here. Last year the hotel received a booking from France. It was for a coach load of people touring the gardens of Devon and Cornwall. Nothing very strange about that but when they arrived the staff realised it was very different. The coach had a large preponderance of millionaires including Baron de Rothschild. The guests were charming but in an unexpected way stretched the hotel. Everyone of them wanted/ breakfast in their rooms at exactly 8.15am! Imagine that number of breakfast trays. Needless to say the request was carried out on time as one would expect from the Copthorne. A totally different scenario appeared with the arrival of the Royal Ballet Company. They dined late, rose very late and needed pampering. Delightful to have them as guests but again a strain on almost every department in the hotel.

Those two incidents described how important it is for a hotel to be well run and that can only be so if the Management structure is of a high calibre. The Plymouth Copthorne has just had a new General Manager in place of the experienced, efficient and very human Patrick Maw, who has been appointed General Manager in the Copthorne at Slough. It is Slough's gain. Meanwhile Plymouth has been lucky enough to have the services of the internationally experienced Belgian, Louis van Heusden. He has been with the Group for some years and believes, as did his predecessor that efficiency and good management is all important to keep standards high.

I thoroughly enjoyed meeting Louis, who at thirty two, must be one of the youngest General Managers in the Copthorne Empire. From his childhood days he has always had the ability to learn a new language with comparative ease - how I wish I could say the same. His appointment to the Plymouth Copthorne is really a justified reward for the many successes he has had as he climbed the ladder of this demanding industry. He studied in Belgium before going to the acknowledged world leaders in hotel training, Ecole Hoteliere de Lausanne in Switzerland. The four years course is intensive, inspiring professionalism and dedication. It was whilst he was on this course that he had his first experience of working in England, at the Manor House Hotel, Morton in the Marsh, as Restaurant Manager.

Louis' compulsory military service was carried out in the Navy where his linguistic skills - he speaks French, English, Dutch and German - combined with his catering expertise, contributed to his appointment to the Belgian Royal household. After this he spent time in the Forum Hotel in Brussels - part of the

Intercontinental Group and then moved on to a five star hotel in Jeddah, Saudi Arabia.

Joining the Copthorne's Hotel Stephanie in Brussels was an exciting challenge followed by yet another when he was appointed to the new Copthorne Slough, Windsor. His brief here was to appoint staff, set up systems so that the hotel operated efficiently from the opening. This was entirely successful and the accolades rolled in. Building a strong team and getting a positive response from guests was his personal reward. It was from this strong platform that he was given his first General Manager's position at the Copthorne Plymouth.

Louis makes no secret of the fact that he is ambitious. He lives for his work, although his twinkling eyes tell me that he is not averse to a little fun from time to time providing it does not interfere with his first love. His hobbies reflect his lifestyle - travel, exploring new countries, languages, wine and gourmet food, music, cycling, walking and skiing. He told me he believes that everything stems from a happy staff of trained professionals who perform to the highest standards. He likes to create a team who will stay with him. In his mind this is the only way to establish consistency of standards.

Whilst I listened to him I absorbed how important little things are to the smooth running of a hotel. Louis van Heusden is a perfectionist and at the same time very human. This man will be good for the Copthorne and for Plymouth.

Whilst **The Moorland Links Hotel** is out of the City on the Plymouth to Yelverton road, I want to mention it here because it is so much part of the life of Plymouth. You come to it about half way from Roborough to Yelverton where you will see a sign telling you to turn off. It is a little way down this moorland road.

For me it is a place of nostalgia. During the war years and immediately afterwards it was the venue for the young set on a Saturday night. A place of fun and enchantment where the trauma of war was shelved. Evening dress was de riguer and somehow all the girls managed to find sufficient coupons to buy the pretty dresses that were a foil to the uniformed men. Frequently the dresses were made from gowns worn by their mothers and grandmothers, or even from materials found in the attic, old damask curtains or chintz that had lain mothballed in trunks for years. Sometimes one dined there, sometimes we went just to dance. Romance was always in the air, accentuated no doubt by the urgency of war. These were nights when we firmly shut out the thought that the very next day some of these men, and women, would be sailing or flying into battle perhaps never to return.

The gardens then were lovely in spite of the restrictions of the war and the digging up of lawns for vegetables. Today they are even lovelier with a wonderful variation of colour throughout the year and always the rich colours of the moor offering a backdrop. The foyer has not changed much in all those years but beyond that everything is different. Gone are the small sitting rooms that filled the space from the reception desk to the dining room and ballroom. Now there is a beautifully appointed restaurant immediately to your left looking out over the large lawn fringed with oak trees, and leading onto the ballroom. The Gunroom bar to the right of the entrance is a place of comfort in which you can sip a drink, enjoy a bar meal or just relax with coffee. The colour schemes have been carefully co-ordinated here and everywhere else which gives the whole hotel a sense of being cherished.

The bedrooms I found especially pleasing. Michael Jenkin, the General Manager, is responsible for the furnishings and it is his eye for detail that makes them so special. Some of the beds are crowned with pretty drapes that match those at the windows, and nice pieces of furniture dress each chamber, including comfortable chairs.

Who uses this hotel? Mainly business people who are relocating to Plymouth or down on business at one of the industrial estates which are a short drive away. If I had worked flat out all day, I can think of no more charming place to which to return than the Moorland Links. The food is excellent, the wine list intriguing and the staff are there to cosset you.

This is not the only use for the hotel. Many people have discovered the excellent weekend breaks that are available. It is so relaxing and of course the surrounding countryside offers a variety of choice. You can play golf, walk across the moors, ride, visit historic Tavistock or Plymouth, take a look at famous Buckland Abbey, home of Sir Francis Drake or just simply sit on the lawn and contemplate. I have discovered too that people from surrounding areas find that dinner here on a Saturday accompanied by a first class bottle of wine, or two, a stay overnight and a walk in the morning blows away the cobwebs. Then enjoy the traditional Sunday lunch in the hotel before returning home.

As in many good hotels today, great emphasis is put on the facilities for conferences and seminars. The excellent geographical situation of Plymouth, with its motorway connections across the West Country, and direct roads from all neighbouring counties: Cornwall, Somerset and Avon, makes the Moorland Links a natural venue. The efficient Irene Brown is the lady who will discuss this with you and ensure that any occasion you plan with her will run smoothly. She tells me that local companies regularly book rooms at the hotel for day meetings and every conceivable piece of equipment is available, including a helicopter landing facility. One must always remember that Plymouth Airport is only five minutes away.

I always regard the five General Managers I have just written about as the doyens of Plymouth Hotels, and in my mind I have christened them the five Musketeers, one for all and all for one - they are always prepared to do battle on behalf of their hotels, for other establishments and for the good of Plymouth. They certainly produce good and sound suggestions which are taken up by Plymouth Marketing Bureau and the City Council.

On the Plympton side of Plymouth there are three hotels of differing kinds. The first is **The Novotel**, at Marsh Mills roundabout - you take the slip road marked City Centre as you come into Plymouth on the A38, go round the roundabout and take the third exit signposted Plympton.

Jackie White is the General Manager of this 100 bedroomed hotel. This able lady arrived in Plymouth in November 1992 having been the deputy general manager for the Birmingham Airport Novotel from the time it was a building site until it became the successful hotel it is now.

Jackie told me quite a lot about her background which has covered running two successful pubs of her own, working for Brymon Airways and managing one or two private hotels. She has been with Novotel for five years and has benefited from their in - depth training. For example before becoming a general manager with them, she spent time at their training academy in Paris. Jackie has herself become a trainer, recently getting her Certificate for Food Handling and the Plymouth staff are undoubtedly benefiting greatly from her skills which in turn benefits the customer. Novotel are part of the Accor Group, which has recently acquired Wagon Lit (Pullmans) and with their other hotels now can boast of having the most hotel bedrooms worldwide.

Novotel is a corporate product which means that their staff can adapt easily when they are moved from one hotel to another. Jackie feels her task is to make Plymothians more aware of what the Novotel has to offer. Not from a business point of view because many local firms use the hotel regularly; Brittany Ferries and Silent Channel are two of their biggest customers. The fact that it is so easy to get to and the parking is easy should make it a good meeting point for people who just want to enjoy a coffee together or a sandwich. There is no need to buy a meal nor is there a cover charge. During Christmas when the local area was used for 'Park 'n' Ride' Jackie and her team put flyers on cars advertising the Novotel and what it offers and found she generated a lot of extra casual business.

This is not a hotel that acquires passing trade as most people come for a purpose. There are a lot of late arrivals using the hotel for a base prior to a meeting next day. For this reason the restaurant is open from 6am until midnight. The hotel also has an excellent conference trade due to its location.

Boringdon Hall is a magical place with a wonderful history. You reach it by taking the Plymouth Road towards Plympton at Marsh Mills, taking a left turn at Larkham Lane, just past the Unicorn Pub, continue along Crossway and at the junction turn left. You will find it clearly marked a little way up this road.

The small approach road lined with trees leads you to the house which was first mentioned in AD 956 when King Edgar granted the manor of Boringdon and Wembury to St Peter of Plympton. Henry VIII granted it to his friend, the Earl of Southampton, in AD 1539 at the dissolution of the Monasteries. Ten years later the Earl sold it to the Duke of Suffolk, father of the ill-fated Lady Jane Grey. Queen Elizabeth I slept in one of the bedrooms in 1588 by which time the house had come into the hands of John Parker.

John Parker spent a great deal of time and money in restyling the house and on completion he gave one of the greatest banquets ever seen in this part of the country. His guest of honour was Sir Francis Drake who brought with him Sir John Hawkins, Richard Grenville and Sir Walter Raleigh. A magnificent occasion and one you can recall when you dine here in the Gallery Restaurant which overlooks the Great Hall where these great men would have dined. A later Parker commissioned the magnificent Coat of Arms of King Charles I, which dominates the Great Hall to this day; the loyalty of the Parker family to the crown, however lost them the ownership of the house during the Civil Wars.

Boringdon Hall has had many changes of fortune in the ensuing centuries, and even today it is not simple running a hotel of this size and grandeur. Recently vast sums of money have been spent on it. Since 1989 £2 million has gone into the refurbishment of the sumptuously appointed bedrooms with their four posters and elegant furniture fit for a Queen. Every room and suite has all the modern comforts and luxuries you would expect from a four star hotel. In addition to this another £2 million went into the new leisure club and bedroom complex that surrounds a courtyard, perfect for open air events, perfect for conferences and seminars.

Because of the intricate nature of the building you can dine in a number of different settings, each beautiful and gracious, sometimes intimate, sometimes in the grand manner. An enchanting place. It is the most romantic place for a wedding reception, something that Boringdon Hall excels in.

The little plaque just to the right of the front door as you enter Boringdon Hall says, 'Please take care and note the unevenness of the floor.' Floors have been there since the day Boringdon Hall was first built and would give a spirit level apoplexy. Every large manor house throughout history has been very much a place of work as well as of gracious living; Boringdon Hall continues this tradition today.

Just up the road from Boringdon Hall is **The Elfordleigh**, where from the shell of the original hotel, Robert and Tina Palace have created a hotel, country club and leisure centre that many would love to copy but few would succeed. If you join Elfordleigh for leisure you will find it has every kind of sporting activity including an outdoor and indoor swimming pool, tennis courts, squash, snooker, and twelve piece gym where even the cushions on the machines are comfortably padded to take some of the pain out of exercising reluctant muscles. There is a solarium, a sauna, showers and changing rooms, all furnished comfortably and restful to the eyes.

It is a super place for business people in the local community. Here they may unwind after a hectic day, or bring their family for Sunday lunch and take in some exercise at the same time. The dining room is bright and has a rustic touch about it, the food is good, healthy, inexpensive and available on a daily basis.

More formally you can eat in the Churchill Restaurant which has rich mahogany panelling on its walls and bears some super prints, not only of Churchill but of elder statesmen of days gone by. A further dining room is set in a semi-circular conservatory which catches all the sun and is delightful for meals in the spring, summer and autumn.

Finally the function rooms are superb. The main room opens on to a patio with steps leading down into the grounds. What a glorious view there is from here. Wonderful for conference and seminar purposes with its own bar and ante-room and for which every modern training need is available, but on a lovely summer's morning when I was there my thoughts went to how super it would be for a wedding reception.

Grouped near Plymouth Hoe and equally close to the City Centre are many hotels and Guest Houses all of which have something to recommend them. I have tried to cover a number which I know personally or which have been recommended to me. They range in price and facility but there is not one of them from which you will not get a very warm welcome and be comfortable.

Parking facilities are always important and this is amply catered for in **The Imperial Hotel** in Lockyer Street which runs from just behind the Theatre Royal to the Hoe. Alan and Prue Jones are the resident proprietors of this elegant Victorian hotel which has been sympathetically modernised and now boasts twenty two bedrooms - sixteen en suite - and five at ground floor level. Every room has colour television, radio, direct-dial telephone and tea/coffee making facilities. There is a large comfortable sitting room with a roaring log fire in the winter months. This leads into a bar with a nautical flavour.The reason for this becomes obvious once you start talking to Alan Jones. This man of the sea spent many years afloat and has travelled the world. At one time he served in the old wooden training ship for Merchant Navy Cadets, the Worcester. He will tell you many tales of life at sea and you will not be unaware that he was the last cadet to scrub decks on the Cutty Sark! The discipline and strict standards of life at sea have been adapted to the smooth running of the hotel. It has a charming informality but underneath there are certain rules which he is insistent are adhered to. For example there is no swearing allowed in the bar. He has been known to ask people to leave the hotel because of offensive speech. No, he is not Captain Bligh but a man who believes that women on their own should be able to sit in his bar without being offended and to stay in his hotel without fear of intimidation. Something that many women have suffered from over the years, myself included. I would always choose to stay somewhere like the Imperial Hotel knowing that I was of some importance.

The Worcester

The clientele of the hotel is frequently made up of middle-management people staying from one or another of the big companies in the city. They may be of either sex but they always enjoy their stay. I noticed too that many couples from Devon and Cornwall come to the Imperial when they are visiting the city to shop or go to the theatre. Their names appear again and again in the register. Service families come to stay when they are visiting husbands in the port or perhaps waiting for a house to become available and many of Alan and Prue's seafaring friends make a beeline for Plymouth and the Imperial to reminisce.

At lunchtime bar snacks are available, as well as morning coffee and afternoon tea; the last orders for dinner are at 8.15pm. The standard of English fare is high and the substantial breakfast will leave you well set up for the day. There is a small conference room available for business meetings.

Alan Jones gave me a sensible piece of marketing advice. He gets a number of guests who choose the Imperial simply because on the bottom of his advertisements he puts 'Proprietor Lt. Cdr A. Jones R.N.R. (Retd)'. It might not sound important but to serving people or those who have retired it reassures them that it is run by someone who understands their needs and enjoys a chat over a pint. Simple but effective.

I chose two Guest Houses in Athenaeum Street, which runs off Citadel Road down towards the City Centre. This street has many Guest Houses and they all help one another. **The Brittany Guest House** is owned and run by Linda and Mike Rust, both from Cornwall. It is second nature to Linda because from being quite small she has always helped her parents with the guest house they owned. She says she does not know how to do anything else, which is strictly untrue because she is a very capable, caring lady.

With her parent's financial help, she and Mike bought the then closed down Brittany Guest House five years ago. Dad was next door running his Caledonia Guest House, so they were not too far distant if a cry for help was needed. These two capable people then turned too and stripped the house from top to bottom, decorated, refurbished, re-wired and achieved eight well furnished, comfortable, modern letting rooms. The house now welcomes visitors for short stays but more often than not acquires its clientele from representatives and people working in the area who come back to them regularly. Mike and Linda do everything themselves from the cooking to the cleaning. They like it this way because they know that everything for the comfort of their guests is as they would have it.

Interesting couple this because of their varied interests. They are both keep fit fanatics and work out each day although not together because one of them needs to be at Brittany to see to customers and potential guests. They first met when Linda went to hear a band in which Mike was singing. Now she has become part of the band and helps with backing vocals. There are six of them who play under the name 'Red, Hot and Blue'. Whilst they do not see it as a profession they do give a very professional performance which is appreciated in Pubs and for the many charitable functions for which they play. They are great supporters of Mike Turner and his Cavitron Fund, one of Plymouth's most successfully run charities.

Recently parking meters have been installed in Athenaeum Street but that is not a worry to guests at Brittany House which has a Car Park at the rear.

My reason for choosing **The Adanac Guest House** was because it is owned and run by Joyce Rumble one of the most caring women you are ever likely to meet and someone who has suffered quite a lot of trauma in her own life.

In 1988 Joyce's husband David, who has since died, was made redundant from the Evening Herald where he worked as an engraver. He had been there 32 years and with their children they lived a quietly comfortable life in a three bedroomed bungalow in Plymstock. The last thought in their minds was running a guest house but with children to bring up they knew that another source of income had to be found. Buying The Adanac was a major step. It used all David's redundancy money, it up-rooted them from the home and all the family found it quite difficult to adapt but this is where Joyce's caring attitude came into play. Looking after people, especially those away from home enabled her to look forward instead of regretting the loss of the past.

There are seven letting rooms in The Adanac and before they could start taking guests there was a lot of work to be done. This helped and the rebirth of this Victorian house made her feel they had achieved something. It was almost eighteen months before they had a holiday of any sort. The guests they acquired have become friends and the trade comes now by word of mouth or from people coming back again and again. They are usually business people, salespeople, Navy personnel on courses or Theatre Royal visitors. Joyce finds them interesting and challenging although some of them have become almost part of her family; she has one person who has been with her for over two years continuously and another for the same length of time almost continuously. I heard about her from a young man who has lived there for over a year and treats it like home.

The trade remains much the same all the year round except for a quiet time in January and February at weekends. Joyce needs these weekends to recover because once Spring arrives it's non-stop, seven days a week until Christmas.

Just to give you an insight into this remarkable lady I would like to tell you about her younger son, Jim, who is adopted. His parents were her friends in Plymouth and when they died this small boy was left in the care of an aunt and uncle who just could not cope with him. He was made a Ward of Court and placed in a home belonging to the City Council. Joyce was horrified and requested permission to adopt him. This was refused for no apparent reason but after much discussion she and her husband were permitted to become Jim's custodians. As Jim's father had been a Naval Officer and Jim was feeling so unwanted and confused she suggested, and in the end insisted, that he be allowed to go to a Naval boarding school in Suffolk. After endless meetings, one of them with thirteen people including heaven alone knows how many social workers, no decision was reached. It was referred back to Court and the Judge gave his approval. Jim has now settled down and for the first time this last summer, Joyce saw evidence that the love she had given him was being reciprocated and he felt truly her son.

No one could stay here without being aware of the warmth of this courageous lady and her family.

Plymouth at one time had many gates into the town. Gascoigne Gate - where Gascoyne Place is now. Queens Gate by Freedom Fields, Frankfort Gate now a shopping precinct, and Hoe Gate, the town exit to the Citadel and the Hoe, amongst others. **The Hoe Gate House** owned all the land around the latter but over the years it was sold off in little parcels and just the house was left. Marcia Prowse's parents, Mr and Mrs Williams from a well known Barbican family, bought the house in the 1930s and it has been a Guest House ever since 1957.

Generations of Barbican folk seldom move far away and Marcia will tell you that her grandparents had a boarding house and restaurant on the Barbican many years ago. She is following in their footsteps with this immaculate and very well run establishment. It has five well appointed rooms that are very attractive and spacious, and caters for just the right number to enable Marcia to attend to her guests personally. It is more than comfortable and every morning you come down to a breakfast with fresh eggs and local produce.

In such close proximity to the sea, I know of people who make the effort to get up sufficiently early whilst staying here, to take a walk across Plymouth Hoe, blow away the cobwebs, whip up an appetite and return to do justice to the excellent breakfast.

I was entertained by Marcia's stories of the war years when many nights were spent in air-raid shelters. She told me that the most comfortable shelter in Plymouth was just down the road from Hoe Gate House in New Street, H Dunn & Son, which was a Pilchard Factory!

One of Marcia's dreams is that Hoe Gate Street will be returned to its former glory when the Barbican is pedestrianised. She knows that beneath the tarmac in the road are the original cobblestones of earlier times. This is an interesting lady with a great love of, and a feel for, this most treasured part of Plymouth. Marcia hopes too that modern technology may be able to restore the old deeds of her property, parts of which were destroyed by fire during World War II when the family's solicitors' office was bombed. She has some damaged bits, all charred and stuck together in a rectangular block and understands that research going on at the moment in Manchester University Chemistry Department may well come up with a successful way to decipher the whole document. It would make fascinating reading.

Looking right over the Bowling Green on the Hoe is a delightful hotel of that name. **The Bowling Green Hotel** is a tall, elegant building, kept immaculately by David and Paddy Dawkins. It is light and airy, prettily furnished and very comfortable. You can only get Bed and Breakfast here but with the wealth of eating houses in walking distance this does not constitute any problem.

The house is very much alive and yet has that restfulness that is so important after a busy day. Equally it provides a stimulus for the day to come when you arrive downstairs after a good night's sleep to sit in the attractive dining room awaiting one of the best breakfast's in Plymouth.

Many visitors have made The Bowling Green their second home whenever they come to the city. People appearing in the Theatre Royal for example find it ideal. Nobody fusses them or remonstrates if they get up late. The Dawkins are a friendly couple and you will find them easy to get on with.

There are two Guest Houses down in West Hoe, close to the seafront, that I am happy to recommend. **The Fairmont** in Pier Street is owned by Bob and Carole Temme, both Plymothians who came into the business, seven years ago when Carole wanted something of her own. Bob has a successful carpet cleaning business which flourishes, despite the recession but Carole, believes in safety first and looked for a business which would sustain them both should Bob not be able to carry on his demanding, physical work because of an accident or illness. A guest house seemed the ideal solution and they have certainly made a success of it.

The Temmes are unpretentious people who make no fuss over anything. Their guests feel at liberty here with very few rules and regulations to harry them. Mainly it is for bed and breakfast only that people come to the Fairmont, but if you want Carole to produce an evening meal, she will. You will never leave the table hungry! There are eight letting rooms and Carole finds that they are filled mostly by people who come to Plymouth to work rather than for a holiday. Gone are the days when she would have bookings for whole weeks or even two weeks from holidaymakers. This tends to be a one or two night stay now and the people who arrive are usually touring Devon and Cornwall.

Parking has become a problem in West Hoe. Double yellow lines have been put along the back lanes and parking meters at the front. The Temmes are overcoming this by bringing forward their plans to create a garage and parking space at the rear of the property.

I have always enjoyed going to Pier Street because on the other side of the road from the Fairmont is what my grandchildren call 'The Steering Wheel Park'. It is a splendid place with swings, climbing frames and a variety of other pieces of equipment, all of them free to the users. Alongside it is what is best described as a Childrens Paradise! There are cars and scooters to drive, boats to drive round the pond, crazy golf, a remote control racing car arena, trampolines and several other exciting things. This section costs a penny or two and before we set out for the Steering Wheel Park, my two grandsons have their ration of money given to them with which they can get the appropriate tokens on arrival. They usually get more because the owner Mr Hammett and I have enjoyed many chats whilst the children play. He is a fascinating man, an enthusiastic golfer, part time lecturer at the University and a guest house owner - his hotel is literally across the road from the park. He sees the need to take Plymouth firmly by the scruff of the neck and make it wake up to the vast natural resources it has and which should be displayed to the world. Like the Temmes he is aware that the type of visitor to Plymouth is changing. Sea and sand are no longer the criteria for holidays.

Walk to the other side of this park and you come to the Bouncy Castle and the trains which zoom round the small track, bells clanging all day long throughout the summer. The park is a pleasant place to be with its trees and huge rockface making a powerful backdrop. Ahead of you is the magnificence of Plymouth Sound.

Redundancy can do one or two things to people. Some turn their faces to the wall but others have a fighting spirit and enough 'get up and go' enthusiasm to tackle something new. This is what happened to Chris Davis. He was made redundant from the Dockyard at the age of 40. Job hunting proved fruitless. He took a computer course at the College of Further Education but found the qualification level too low to be of any benefit in getting a job.

Whilst he and Sandra, his wife, lived in Peverell they had taken in foreign students from the Susan Sparrow Language School. When Sandra accepted an invitation to go to Switzerland to visit some of their former student guests she was pleasantly surprised at everyone saying how much they had appreciated the hospitality of the Davis's. When she came back she suggested to Chris that it might be an idea to look for a guest house and make this their business. This was in 1988 at the height of the property boom. Prices were high and even with the sale of their own home they could not afford the cost of an existing guest house.

The property they settled on is now the **Cassandra Guest House** in Crescent Avenue, a quiet cul de sac just off the sea front. It was a fairly run down property when they acquired it and in use as bed sitters. Chris fortunately was more than capable of tackling the refurbishment. They started on the guest quarters and rapidly acquired more people from the Susan Sparrow Language School, mostly people they knew already who had come back for a further course. At this point Chris snapped his Achilles tendon and spent three months in plaster which nearly put the cat amongst the pigeons but with the courage and resourcefulness that this couple had shown they finally reached the point of no return, applied for a Fire Certificate, joined the Plymouth Marketing Bureau and the Cassandra Guest House was born. They have not looked back since.

Their criteria for success is to provide a standard which they themselves would find acceptable elsewhere, try to be friendly and flexible, give value for money and make the house accessible at all times. You have only to read the letters from former guests to know that the criteria work. They have invitations to visit people all over the world, which sadly they are too busy to accept but who knows.......

The only down side they see in their new career is that it does mean that they get far too little time to spend with their small son.

With so much emphasis in this chapter on hotels and guest houses close to the sea, one must not forget the many good small hotels on the other side of the City Centre. When people travelled by train more than by road, the hotels and guest houses within walking distance of the station flourished. As this traffic dwindled so did the establishments until in recent years they have been given a new lease of life and have become as important, as comfortable and attractive as their comparable establishments on the Hoe.

North Road East running from North Hill down to the station has many hotels and guest houses. I have chosen two that I like very much. The first is the **Victoria Court Hotel** on the junction of North Road East and Houndiscombe Road. Elaine and Nick Robinson are the owners and they deserve high praise for the work they have carried out in this nice establishment. They have the English Tourist Board Commended Three Crowns and the AA one star which speaks of a certain standard but really tells you nothing of the personal service, the warmth and individual welcome that you will find here. The hotel can accommodate over 30 guests in the extremely well appointed bedrooms most of which are en suite.

Every room has a colour TV, complimentary beverage trays, direct dial telephones, radios and clock alarms. The lounge is a pleasant place in which to sit and meet friends and the Victorian cocktail bar is much admired.

It is the willingness to cope with the wishes of guests that makes the Victoria Court special. For example if you have the need to be up and about early, you can always have breakfast before the normal starting time of 7.30am. All you have to do is to ask. Normally breakfast is served from 7.30am - 9.00am and you can indulge in a full English breakfast, or for the more health and figure conscious, perhaps just a yoghurt and black coffee. I regret that I can never resists a good breakfast when I am away in an hotel - I reserve the yogurt and black coffee for when I am at home! In the evenings this light and airy dining room is a relaxing place in which to enjoy dinner. The menu offers a selection of three course meals, with emphasis on old fashioned home-styled cooking. At any time of the day you can order tea, coffee, biscuits or sandwiches right up to 10pm. Marvellous for the late arrival.

Sometimes the dining room is used for business meetings. Ideal really because the hotel has easy access from the main A38 which is within 300 yards of the hotel. It is also within minutes of the city centre, the coach and railway stations. Private parking is available at the rear of the building.

The Grosvenor Park Hotel, also in North Road East, is a hotel with a difference. Roy and Mary Wallis are the resident proprietors. They both come from Solihull in Birmingham and found themselves in Plymouth basically because Mary fell in love with the city when she was working with Carvella shoes and setting up departments for the company within the House of Fraser stores. When she was doing this task in Dingles she heard that Roy was being made redundant. This made them decide to stay in Plymouth and for seven years, Mary managed Carvela shoes in Dingles. But they both wanted to set up a business of their own.

During her years on the road for Carvella, Mary had stayed in some pretty dreadful places and knew that she could make a better job of it herself. This is what took them into the hotel business. They bought the Grosvenor Park, spent a lot of time, money and thought on the decor and refurbishments. Many of the fine features of what was two houses, have been retained, including a wonderful black lead fireplace in the sitting room.

The central staircase which has grown from the division of the two houses serves a definite purpose here and is why the hotel is different. One side of the hotel is kept entirely for students from the University. They all have their own rooms, which are the same standard as everywhere else in the hotel, a common room and a kitchen, so they are self-contained.

The reason for this unit is that many parents came to stay with their offspring whilst they were looking for digs. With such close proximity to the University the Grosvenor Park is ideally situated. Parents were particularly anxious to ensure that their children, during their first year, had some sort of non - interfering people in loco parentis, who would keep a watching brief. This is the role that has fallen to Roy and Mary. One they and the students enjoy. The added bonus is that the parents come to stay when they come to Plymouth for the various University events throughout the year. Many parents have reason to be grateful to Roy and Mary Wallis.

Spanish visitors to Plymouth also make a beeline for the Grosvenor Park because both Roy and Mary speak fluent Spanish - just one of their many talents.

One of the other roles the hotel plays is that of a venue for wedding receptions, evening parties or celebration dinners. The attention to detail makes these occasions a resounding success, and the price is right! Special reduced rates on overnight accommodation and breakfast are available for guests at these functions.

The Wallis's two sons used to run the **Wallis Diving Services** from the hotel. Many would - be divers came to stay and attend the full instruction course. More of that later.

In Sutherland Road, just off North Road East, is another comfortable hotel which has quite a reputation for its food. **Oliver's**, so called because the owner's, Mike and Joy Purser thought it would be an easy name for people of any nationality to say.

This is a small, luxurious hotel with every room fully en suite and designed for business people who want comfort but do not enjoy either the cost or the formality of a larger establishment.

Between them Mike and Joy have many talents. He is an accountant who worked at one time with the City Council. Nowadays he looks after the affairs of various companies and lectures in the University where he is well respected for his knowledge and his ability to work through knotty problems. Joy was a teacher but she always dreamt of having an hotel in which she could use her culinary expertise - she is a very good cook and her meals are memorable.

I remember the **Rosaland Hotel**, at 32 Houndiscombe Road, with a great deal of affection. Many years ago it was run by two men who had strong connections with the theatre and television. Many are the evenings that we spent there enjoying their hospitality, the impromptu music and the fun. The guests in residence always joined in but the downside was the morning after when owners and residents were so hung over that breakfast was not served or required!

Those days have long gone, the hotel runs smoothly and efficiently but it has never lost its sense of wellbeing and happiness. Peter and Heather Shaw are the owners and maintain the connection with the theatre in Plymouth.

Peter and Heather have worked very hard to modernise Rosaland. When we talked to them they were in the process of making all the bedrooms ensuite. Children are very welcome and so are well behaved dogs. A baby-sitting service can be provided.

Situated as it is within walking distance of the city centre, the railway station, the Barbican and the Hoe, it is ideal for people on business, on holiday or indeed, working in the theatre.

You will not be able to see it, but Drakes Leat, which Sir Francis had built to bring water to the city, runs along the bottom of the garden. The waterboard charge an extra 5p a year for this privilege! Another strange by-law says that if there is a Gypsy Fair in Plymouth, the gypsies have the right to dance on the front garden!

Rosaland is welcoming and charming.

So much for suggested places to stay. Something for every taste and pocket I hope.

Now for restaurants and places to eat that again show my catholic taste and cover all sorts of venues. I have already written about some of my favourite spots on the Barbican, Piermasters, Bella Napoli, the Pasta and Pizza Restaurant, the Tudor Tearooms and Green Lanterns.

I am returning to the **Green Lanterns** because I did not do them justice in the earlier chapter. It is thirty years since Kenneth Pappin and his sister-in-law Sally Russell opened the doors of this fine restaurant which has remained one of the best in Plymouth ever since. In those days it was just a Coffee House serving fresh ground coffee and eventually added snacks such as scrambled eggs. It was quite a while before it became a restaurant. Kenneth Pappin will tell you that in those days they could not have imagined themselves running the kind of operation they do now. It would have frightened them to death. It was quite a step when they started serving grills and got a licence.

Green Lanterns

Both Kenneth and Sally are fiercely British and proudly fly the British flag outside the door. This is the place where 'Ye Bill of

Fayre' might offer you a starter of Huntingdon stuffed pears - pear halves with little balls of Stilton mixed with cream, butter and chopped walnuts, to follow with a delicious and delicately flavoured wild duck and then finish with that most British of all dishes, Spotted Dick, a traditional steamed pudding full of currants, sultanas and raisins, served with a hot golden syrup. Quite wonderful.

Because the restaurant is so close to the Barbican Fish Market, the chef can be seen there selecting the best of the day's catch for his 'Special Dish of the Day' which is always interesting and frequently very different. I love the mussels and crab pancakes.

I am always amazed that more Plymothians and business people do not take advantage of the excellent budget lunches that are available. You can enjoy a three course lunch or hot snacks and freshly cut sandwiches in surroundings so rich in history. Perhaps it is because it is a bit off the beaten track for people working in the City Centre but it takes no more than five minutes to stroll down from St Andrews Cross to enter this enchanted place. Make the effort and you will return to work refreshed and relaxed.

Spend an evening here and you will step back in time to when that great Plymothian, Sir John Hawkins was treasurer of the Navy. The building has changed little. It has beamed ceilings, alcoves, panelling, tiny doors, narrow stairways and quiet corners. Situated in New Street, believed to be the oldest street in Plymouth, the Green Lanterns is next door to the Elizabethan Merchant's House.

Over the years the Green Lanterns has attracted many famous people to its tables to dine on traditional English fare. To drop a few names, let us mention Danny la Rue, Rolf Harris and Dave Allen. It is not so many years since the top American television presenter, Walter Cronkite, lunched there. The Green Lanterns appears in most of the leading good food guides, including one in the United States. They all had good taste and I urge you to follow their example and beat a path to The Green Lanterns.

A different level of catering but nonetheless an asset to Plymouth is the arrival of **McDonald's**. Plymouth has long wanted to welcome Big Mac and they wanted to be here, but it was difficult to find a suitable site. The demise of Rumbelows brought the opening McDonalds were looking for and the City Fathers were happy to give planning permission in spite of the fact that the site was away from an 'allocated restaurant area' according to the Abercrombie Plan for Plymouth. The design has been well thought out with everything from the ability to watch TV to a separate children's play area complete with climbing frame, tubes, toys and Cartoon TV. Private birthday parties can also be held here.

It opened with a great flourish and much excited anticipation on the 14th December, in time to catch the Christmas shoppers. From the moment the first customers walked in it was a success. It produced the third record opening in the United Kingdom. Sparkling with cleanliness with a lively staff of ninety, McDonalds can cater for anything up to one thousand people an hour.

The McDonald empire is quite extraordinary. It started in the States in 1955 and there are now 11,000 stores worldwide in over 160 countries. In fact somewhere in the world a new McDonalds opens every fourteen hours. There are four hundred and sixty stores in the United Kingdom as I write, but who knows in twenty four hours time there could be more! Some forty of these are franchised but in the case of Plymouth, one of McDonald's flagships, it is a company store operating under the official name of McDonald's Restaurant (U.K.) Limited.

There is a great deal the general public does not know about the Big Mac. Firstly they are environmentally conscious. For example there is no CFC in any packaging. At regular times every day a litter patrol is sent out to make sure that no McDonalds boxes are left lying about - they remove other litter too.

It is the policy of every store to get involved in the local community so one can expect to see this sort of activity in Plymouth before long. An example of the sort of things that are done is to be seen in Weston-Super-Mare where the store liaised with senior citizens on litter picking. For this McDonald's got an award from Age Resource, for their caring attitude and active involvement. I know of many such instances and particularly of the homes they build in the grounds, or nearby big hospitals, so that families of very sick patients can be housed in accommodation as near to their home surroundings as possible. There is actually a McDonald's store in Guy's hospital which caters for staff, patients and visitors. McDonald's sets a standard which many more companies would do well to follow.

Incidentally McDonald's anticipates opening more stores in Plymouth in the not too distant future. I wonder where and whether the city can cope with it. However they have just opened their 5th store in Leicester so if they can do it there, anything is possible here. McDonald's consider Plymouth to be the gateway to Cornwall, a territory which they are exploring.

McDonalds

Fast service is also one of the benefits of visiting **The Gorge** in Royal Parade. A busy cafe with a very unusual decor that matches its name, this lively place has become almost club - like in some respects: a meeting place at all sorts of times of the day for people working in and around the city centre. You can get an excellent breakfast here from 7am, the price is fantastically cheap and the food plentiful. Throughout the day all manner of food is available from sandwiches to steaks. It is a place shoppers use for coffee and a cream cake or a light lunch. Open seven days a week it offers friendliness and fun accompanied by value for money food and drink.

In a different league is **Les Jardins de Bagatelle** at 11, Old Town Street owned and run by Vasili Nikolu who hails from

Cannes in the South of France. When I heard about his arrival and what he proposed to do I wondered how successful he would be. This small patisserie and coffee shop was an instant success.

Vasili had no intention of opening a business in Plymouth until he came here to play golf and fell in love with the city. From the time he made the decision to open in Plymouth to the day of opening was just four months. The speed was down to his own hard work - all of the interior of the shop was created by his staff and himself. He also gives high praise to Plymouth City Council who could not have been more helpful in ensuring that everything was made as easy as possible and nothing was held up because of red tape.

Everything served here has the taste of France. The bread is wonderful, and the French tarts very special. All through the morning there is a constant stream of people beating a path through his door to purchase the super Baguettes, filled with French ham or chicken and a variety of mayonnaises and Fallot mustards.

The small, elegant coffee shop serves aromatic coffee and Vasili's pastries, the strawberry one is the best I have ever tasted. I have never passed the door without noticing that the place is full. It is great to see such a place succeeding in Plymouth.

Even if you did not enjoy Michael Wong's super food in **Mike's Noodle House** on North Hill, you would go there simply for the man's warmth, friendliness and super sense of humour. However, he specialises in Chinese Noodles and if you were not aware of the many differences you should come here and find out. Once you have, you will come back again and again to sample the huge variety of ways there are to cook the different dishes. The most important ingredient is the freshness. Frequently regulars will leave the choice to Michael to make something for them. He will create something very special for whatever number is required.

Michael is in charge of the kitchen with a staff of three. He loves cooking and says that it is the only thing he does well. 'I was rubbish at school' he admits. He is modest, his cooking is superb and his quick thinking mind does not need educational qualifications to make you realise how intelligent he is.

Born in Hong Kong, Michael Wong moved to England when he was ten years old and although his parents lived in Plymouth he was mainly brought up in Liverpool - you can still here the Liverpool twang which seems at odds from someone who is Chinese. After leaving school he travelled widely and learnt all sorts of attitudes and methods of cooking. He married whilst he was working in Scotland and then returned to Plymouth to set up a Chinese Take Away in Saltash and with a partner, a Chinese restaurant in Torpoint.

In 1991/92 he sold both these businesses and in spite of the recession set up Mike's Noodle House on North Hill. This was an empty shop. The plans are now framed and hanging in the Noodle House. Mike will tell you it is the most expensive picture he has ever owned!

When he first opened he had a true noodle bar in the front window. Here he used to hang raw food and prepare it and cook it in full view of the public. Plymouth people could not cope with this and he found that it turned customers away so it is not used at all at the moment until a minor conversion can be done when he will adapt it to become a take away bar.

It is a fun place to be with excellent food, beautifully presented - Michael believes that is all important. Michael will tell you that there are no millionaires in his business, you just have to love it. He obviously does and so do his growing band of regular customers.

Mayflower Street is the home of several ethnic restaurants, each with its own virtue. Facing each other are the **Megnha Tandoori House** and the Positano. An eating experience whichever one you choose. The Megnha has gradually expanded since it opened in May 1992. Proprietor Syed Abdul Wahid has made sure it is decorative, exotic and romantic. Fine quality pink table clothes adorn the candlelit tables. Around the walls are delightful paintings of ladies picking cotton on a plantation, and boat racing. You could easily imagine that you have been transported 4,000 miles to Bombay or any other city in the Indian sub-continent. Soothing Indian music plays in the background and as you arrive you will be greeted by Shama dressed in a colourful sari, with the dignified grace that is so much part of women from this part of the world.

The Meghna Tandoori

Many Plymothians will remember Mr Wahid for his continental food delicatessen that he opened in Cornwall Street in 1969 at a time when Plymouth had no such luxury anywhere else. It was welcomed with open arms. The Megnha is Mr Wahid's fourth business in the city and to the running of the restaurant he has brought a wealth of experience.

The sad death of the owner of the well known Khyber Restaurant meant the closing down of that business but all is not lost. The wonderful meals that I enjoyed there were cooked by Serazul Islam who has now, with his son, moved to the Megnha so one is able to continue enjoying many of his delicious specialities.

Restaurants in Mr Wahid's native Bangladesh do not sell alcoholic drinks, nor did the Megnha originally, but now it has a licence. The wines are interesting and a new range of special Megnha wines has just been introduced. Indian beers - Tiger, Kingfisher and Cobra as well as Japanese Sake are on offer.

This is somewhere in which to enjoy a traditional, leisurely, Indian meal at its best but with great wisdom, Mr Wahid has added a take away for those in a hurry. The prices in the restaurant and take away are very competitive - no risk of offending your Bank Manager.

The Megnha is open from Monday to Thursday and on Sunday from 12-2.30pm and 5.30pm-11.30pm. Friday and Saturday 12-2.30pm and 5.30pm-midnight.

Two Italians from Positano, a holiday resort on the Amalfi coast, near Sorrento, came to Plymouth for six months to perfect their English. The six months has extended itself to twenty years and now Luciano Costantin and Sabato Cinque have married here, raised families and opened **The Positano**. They have never forgotten their origins and try to visit their home each year.

For years they worked in an Italian restaurant on the Barbican which sadly suffered the effects of the recession and these two men needed to carve a slightly different future for themselves. The site of the Positano was originally a takeaway pizza and pasta place. It still continues this tradition but a restaurant has been added to look after the business fraternity in the city - and anyone else who wants to try the true flavour of Italian food at its best. The dishes are from every region of Italy and these two, charming and likeable men, specialise in veal dishes and fish, fresh from the Barbican. Accompanied by a wine from the large selection from Italy or the Italian beer Peroni, you have a feast.

The desserts are unmistakably Italian. Luciano told me that the most popular of the luscious concoctions is Tiramisu which consists of cheese, coffee and coffee liquor layered on sponge fingers.

There is an enormous difference in American style pizzas and those that are produced at the Positano. They are as close to anything you can find in Italy, cooked on stone in the traditional way. You can choose from every imaginable mixture for the topping. Mouthwatering, delicious and extremely filling is the verdict.

I hope the Positano succeeds. You will not find better or more willing service in Plymouth. The atmosphere is right and so, too, is the price.

Talking to the number of people needed to compile this book, I have discovered all sorts of facts that I did not know before. For

Positano Restaurant

example did you know that a Dim Sum chef has to have at least ten years experience otherwise those in the know will tell you that it is not the real McCoy? I learnt also that if one part of a kitchen cooks Dim Sum and another does other dishes, the two cannot mix, they must be kept totally separate. **Yang Cheng**, a discreet Chinese restaurant at 30a Western Approach, has a chef who prepares Dim Sum only and certainly meets the criteria. The nearest Dim Sum of equal authenticity, I am informed reliably, is in Bristol.

Yang Cheng is a name the Chinese revere. It is the capital city of Southern China - a city known for the excellence of its food. It was cooked better, better ingredients were procured generic to this part of the country and more herbs because of the climate. This, obviously, is why so many Chinese people use the restaurant. A recommendation indeed. The Good Food Guide of 1991 and 1992 also wrote about Yang Cheng - one of the very few restaurants in the South West that it did write about. Yang Cheng also draws its customers from the Theatre Royal and other celebrities who visit the city. Yachtsmen seek it out when they arrive here for big races and the business fraternity know it well. If you have not been here, do please rectify the omission.

What is written on the menu is only the beginning of what you can have. The chefs will cook all manner of things specially for you - you have only to ask or consult. The restaurant frequently caters for Chinese parties who want things that do not appear on the menu.

The aim is for authentic cuisine, excellent service, elegant and comfortable surroundings and high quality in everything that Yang Cheng does. They reach all their standards and surpass them with flying colours.

In this section I have left three of my particularly favourite restaurants until last. They are all totally different and run by restaurateurs of different nationalities. The first is **Trattoria Pescatore** in Admiralty Street, Stonehouse, tucked away in a backwater which needs seeking out if you are a stranger to the city.

Piero and Rita Caligari have a wealth of experience between them but oddly enough it is not always experience that makes a good restaurant. It is a list of ingredients that marry well that produces a charming venue such as the Trattoria Pescatore. It says much for them that in a time of deep recession it is one of the few restaurants where it is essential to book a table on a Saturday night.

Inside this old and charismatic building, the soft, yet rich decor does much for the ambience. It is intimate, warm and filled with the outgoing personalities of the Caligaris. Rita is English and is a perfect foil for the talented and sometimes temperamental Piero. Here is a man committed to his profession who almost blows a fuse if he does not get the correct service from his suppliers when he wants it. He is right, of course, and the resultant standard of excellence shows in the dishes he lovingly creates.

Their clientele comes from discerning local people who have discovered them and are prepared to share their find with their friends. There is plenty of parking space and it is quite safe to leave your car overnight if you are tempted to enjoy more wine than the limit allows! One of the delights of coming here on a summer's day is the opportunity to sit outside in what is no more than a flower - filled passageway, but a place of tranquillity. I love it and am not alone in my admiration. It won a Plymouth in Bloom award.

A discreet sign on the wall in Frankfurt Gate tells you that you have arrived at **Chez Nous**, surely one of the finest restaurants in Southern England. It is, in le Patron's own words, 'not necessarily the place to be seen, but it is the place to be.' People from all over the world would agree with this. Here the famous can remain anonymous whilst feasting on Jacques' style of cooking - cuisine spontanee.It is not so long ago that Jacque's unbelieving staff were

Trattoria Pescatore

told that Mick Jagger would be dining with them that night. They thought he was teasing them but lo and behold during the course of the evening there was the most famous of the Rolling Stones, complete with his Father. They were on a walking tour of Devon and Cornwall. The Baron de Rothschild and his coach party were also guests in this typically French, informal, elegant and friendly establishment, whilst they were in Plymouth staying at the Copthorne. There are few famous names who have visited Plymouth who have not dined or lunched here over the years that Jacques and Suzanne Marchal have been in situ. For all of them, as for the rest of us less famous, it is a rare treat to be enjoyed and remembered for a very long time.

Jacques and Suzanne came to Plymouth in the seventies by which time he had been trained in his own country, had various culinary experiences elsewhere under his hat, including the Cafe Royal in London. He was ready for Plymouth but at the time it was a brave thing to do to open a restaurant of this calibre in a city, not renowned for its gastronomic juices. In point of fact the timing was good. Plymouth was opening up and seeing a different sort of resident and visitor.

Chez Nous has never displayed a leather bound, flamboyant menu to illustrate the selection available - rather a simple blackboard menu at the back of the restaurant. This is because cuisine spontanee is based on fresh, local produce according to season and availability.

Jacques Marchal is a pleasant contradiction, typically Gallic, with an arrogant charm and dry humour, yet without the' snobbish' prejudices one might expect. He appreciates a personal regard for style but no one is condemned or judged by their manner or dress - only their appreciation of the meal once tried. He does not, however, take affront if someone is put off by the decor and menu. He admits that the home counties have a more sophisticated palate more naturally suited to his style of restaurant and cuisine than the local populace. In his opinion it is simply a case of those outside the South East having been bred to different habits - we are all products of our environment. Chez Nous provides the opportunity to try something different, to gently break local habits.

What would he want to go on and do now that he has so successfully run his own establishment? Chez Nous is featured in all of the leading food guides and is the only venue in Devon to hold a Michelin star. Without hesitation, Jacques replied, to travel to Japan and study there in a monastery for a year, to learn the Japanese culinary art and the philosophy which is an integral part. Would Jacques Marchal then return to open his own Japanese restaurant? No, Plymouth is not big enough to support that or other minority cuisines. For example, really good American style fast food places can be excellent, but they would not have worked here.

The 28 cover restaurant relies upon the business world for a large part of its trade. Jacques looks to them for approximately 10 covers at lunchtime and of an evening the theatre crowd is a popular market.

He encourages his customers to eat as they please, possibly to enjoy a pre-theatre starter and to return at the end of the evening for their entree. His approach obviously works as the majority of his customers, approximately 70% from outside the city, are repeat business who come again and again, introducing on occasions new converts. Indeed this has resulted in many a famous face from very far and wide, sitting in discreet corners of the room, sampling and delighting in the food. No fuss is made, no publicity sought - word of mouth is sufficient for the Marchals.

Jacques Marchal has a good friend in the ebullient Stephen Barrett, who owns and runs **Barretts of Princess Street.** This is a totally different establishment from Chez Nous but it too has its devotees who frequent this cafe-restaurant. What is so different about this place? Yes it is light, airy, stylish and colourful but so too are many places. The whole ambience is hard to define but one cannot deny that it has an air of its own, quite unique and certainly out of the ordinary in Plymouth.

I think I like Barretts because it is the place where you meet old friends, chat over a glass of wine, frequently joined by Stephen. You can treat it as a short stopping place during the course of the day; just a quick glass of wine to recharge your batteries before getting on with the work of the day, drop in for lunch where the menu is full of exciting dishes of the day, cooked by le patron himself. He has set these lunches at a sensible price which includes a glass of wine or a soft drink. It fits the budget of many middle management people. Of course you can spend a great deal more money, sample some wonderful food and glorious wine. I was there the other night when a party of eight who had an unforgettable evening ran up a bill of just short of £500! They were thrilled, felt they had a meal they would remember for years, service that was everything they could have wished for and could not wait for the opportunity to repeat the exercise. There is no doubt about it that it also has another ingredient - its fun. That is because Stephen makes it so.

This fascinating man has studied his market place very astutely and thoroughly. He sees the need to serve healthy food, free from additives. What is the good of getting meat from a super butcher if you do not know what happens at the abattoir? He does not only restrict his progressive thinking to food. He addresses his interest in wine with the same passion. He is now a recognised authority on wine. He writes for many magazines, is the Food Correspondent in Wine Magazine in which he deals with special offer wines to match foods. He is a wine judge for the English Vineyard Association - I had no idea that there are four hundred Wineries in the United Kingdom. He finds time to produce a weekly column for our local evening paper, the Evening Herald, and is a judge at the International Wine Challenge. This takes him all over the world and gives him the opportunity to taste many more wines than he would otherwise be able to do. He was telling me the other day about his experience in the States where he was introduced to a Jewish Vineyard. He found the experience exhilarating - the wine awful!

In his newspaper column last week he wrote about the difficulty of getting some of the wines that are advertised in the papers, magazines and television. We read, get interested and then no one in this part of the country stocks the particular wine. It is almost as if they think that Plymothians are without discernment. I know many wine lovers in the city, me for one, and I love trying something new. I must confess that once I do find something I like I then tend to be resistant to anything else for a while! Perhaps the advent of the new Safeways Superstore will answer the call and in so doing stir the other supermarkets because that is where most of us buy our wine.

In addition to running a Wine Club for anyone who cares to join, in which you gain knowledge and get the benefit of his knowledge about what to buy, he also has some splendid evenings with a theme. If you are on his mailing list - and you should be - just ring and ask to be added - you will receive invitations to a Californian Evening which will include a suitable meal to go with the wines of one of the Californian Vineyards - and there will be plenty of it. Sometimes it is an evening of poetry, it might be one devoted to the Spanish, both food and wine or Italian. Whatever it is, you will find it fun, entertaining, sometimes educational and enormously good value. He charges a set price for the evening. I try not to miss these occasions which happen about six times a year.

Going back to wine, Stephen is currently carrying out research on the allergy factor in wine. People frequently say they are allergic to red wine. It is a sweeping statement and probably untrue. What they are allergic to is the additives in the wine so, hey presto, Barretts has organic wine.

Barretts does a lot for promising artists. Exhibitions of local artists are held several times a year. They usually last for a week and you are invited to call in on the first Saturday to meet the artist, have a glass of wine and perhaps be tempted to buy a painting or two. Sometimes they are priced within anyone's budget, on others you might need to dig more deeply. It is wonderful though to see artists get this great opportunity.

I am sure I will have caused offence at leaving many restaurants out, hopefully I will get the opportunity to do another of these books in two years time and in the meantime I will have the pleasure of doing the rounds and seeking out new gastronomic experiences.

Sometimes cities have some pretty boring pubs and you have to go quite a way outside to find a good watering hole. This is not the case in Plymouth. Yes, of course, we do have our share of run-of-the-mill establishments, though in fairness to those, they are usually much loved by their regular customers. I set myself the task of finding pubs or wine bars that were different in some way or another. I hope you approve of my choice.

Before I start though I will tell you the story of a small brewery, one of the few in the South West, that operates within Furguson's headquarters in Valley Road, Plympton. This three - man brewery nearly became a thing of the past. However it survived and has gone on to become the first in the South West to win a prestigious national beer award.

Dartmoor Best , one of the two beers produced by them, beat 82 other beers from all over Britain in a blind tasting to win the brewing industry's international award for best - in - the - class for draught cask - conditioned beers. The other beer is Dartmoor Strong with an original gravity and, at Christmas, the powerful Cockleroaster. The first barrels of this specially produced real ale were brewed ahead of time to enter a Beaujolais nouveau-style race. I understand the **Boringdon Arms** at Turnchapel got the first delivery to coincide with the pub's Winter Warmers beer festival - an annual event at which the Cockleroaster was much appreciated!

Ian Ward, the brewer, brews three times a week, increasing to four times from Easter, and five during the summer. It is exciting to see a business like this triumphing in spite of the recession.

The story could have been quite different because at one time Halls' Oxford and West Brewery then owned Furgusons as part of the West Country regional trading arm of Allied Breweries, which owned a number of pubs in the Plymouth area. They wanted to close the brewery down to concentrate their efforts on expanding their retail estate. However, thankfully, they changed their minds and agreed to transfer the brewery to the free trade company Furgusons, which operated its drinks wholesale company within the same building.

Under the control of Ian Ward, the brewery has grown from strength to strength and now supplies many free trade customers throughout Devon and Cornwall, as well as the Ansells tied pub estate - the people I came to see at Furgusons.

I am going to start with a group of Ansells Breweries establishments. I knew most of them but my enthusiasm was increased after I had visited the Area Manager, Lionel Smith, at the Furguson building in Valley Road, Plympton. This man lives and breathes pubs. If you had no interest in pubs before you visited him you certainly would by the time you left. I have no doubt that it is his dedication that spurs on the excellent tenants and licensees he has in the pubs I am going to tell you about.

My intention was to write a piece about **The Woodside** in Gasking Street, just off Ebrington Street but when I went there, the landlords, Angie and Tony Luxton handed me a poem which says it all.

HAPPY CUSTOMER, THE WOODSIDE, PLYMOUTH

Ernie Morrison

I have lived many years amongst strangers,
I've known life to be harder than hell,
And I've known what it is to be cold and alone,
In the midst of a hot summer spell.

Experience has taught me survival,
To be strong when the going is bad,
To never despair; persevere and forbear
And smile when you're sadder than sad.

It has had me so low, life seemed hopeless,
I have struggled to hold up my head,
But I don't give a damn for the judgement of man.
There'll be judgement enough when I'm dead.

There are moments I find worth the living.
There are people I'm BLESSED with as friends.
When this life seems determined to crush you
Human warmth saves your soul in the end.

And that's what I find at 'The Woodside'.
There's a warmth and a welcome for all,
And when one of their number has trouble or pain
I have seen how they answer the call.

There are friends who are friends of 'convenience'.
There are those who use friendship for gain,
But I've never felt cold at 'The Woodside'
Never sought out their friendship in vain.

So have all your hotels and discos
All the places you choose to frequent,
Just leave me at peace down 'The Woodside'
Where long happy hours I have spent.

So here's to you Angie and Tony,
And here's to your bonny blonde kids
And here's to success at 'The Woodside',
And a pint in the pot for a 'quid'.

Long may you reign at 'The Woodside',
And long may your warmth spread around,
And long may rewards come abounding your way.
You're the best bloody pub in the town!

I am indebted to Ernie Morrison for this poem. I could not have written about the sense of well being that you experience here, half as eloquently. Not so long ago the Woodside became the toast of Ansells when they came top in a 'mystery customer survey'. Anonymous independent assessors made an undercover visit to the pub in Gaskell Street, and judged it the best Ansells watering hole in the South West.

The Luxtons were obviously thrilled but say they always try to do their best. Ansells will say that the pub and the staff had to be at their very best to reach the high percentage rating that they achieved. A thoroughly nice establishment to visit both for the Luxtons, their staff and the regular customers.

Not far away from the Woodside is **The Unity** in Eastlake Walk, a very popular meeting place for the younger members of the working fraternity in the city. It is pleasant, well furnished, has good food and is run by one of the liveliest and most efficient landladies in the business, Hilary Cowles. Ansells seem to have cornered the market in finding first rate female licensees as you will find out in this chapter.

One of the great things about the Unity is that it is a place the female sex feel happy to go into when they are on their own. There are not too many pubs like that.

In a totally different vein is **James Street Vaults**, just off North Road East and tucked in behind the University car park. It stays open all day and is probably the most popular of all the pubs in Plymouth for students. They are well fed here at reasonable prices. Their high spirits are not discouraged but kept under control and it is a pub of which Ansells can be proud.

Two more of this brewery's pubs in the heart of the city are without doubt my favourites. **The China House** at Marrowbone Slip, Sutton Harbour, has graced the waterfront of Sutton Pool in various guises since the 17th century. It is a curious building which from the other side of Sutton Pool looks like an old wooden ship that has somehow found its hull stripped of its wood, leaving only the ribs to hold back the water. It is surrounded by water on three sides and if you wonder at its odd name it is because it was built on the site where William Cookworthy set up his china factory. In its restoration it lost all the evils of the intervening centuries - concrete floors and a tin roof and brought back were the old wooden floors and an interior that would not have been too unlike the days of William Cookworthy. There are flagstones from the North of England, panelling and old pews from a church in Bristol and everything has a sense of age and history. Not so long ago a first floor restaurant was added which has a wonderful open verandah with views over the harbour towards the Citadel. For anyone with an interest in old Plymouth, a vast collection of old Plymouth photographs, maps and prints decorates the walls. I understand that they belong to Crispin Gill who writes a regular column for the Western Evening Herald and is the powerhouse behind the revitalised 'Old Plymouth Society'. It is worth going to the China House for this alone. You will see views of Barbican regattas, the fish market, Tamar barges and pictures of William Cookworthy himself, Joshua Reynolds, Captain Cook and Smeaton. David Cheyne was the architect and it is an achievement of which he should be justly proud.

So much for the building itself but that alone does not constitute a good hostelry. Mo Law - another of Ansells brilliant female managers - runs this vibrant establishment with grace and flair. Bistro - style food is extremely reasonable and in summer barbecues are held frequently. Recently a small Jazz Festival proved enormously successful and will be repeated in 1993.

If you haven't yet been do try and arrange a visit. The sense of spaciousness is terrific and yet the tables and chairs are arranged in singles and doubles in their own little intimate area.

One of the bonuses here is the large car park, a rarity in city pubs.

The China House

The Bank at Derry's Cross was once exactly that. In fact, it was the main branch in Plymouth of Lloyds Bank. I remember it as such when it faced the Plymouth branch of the Bank of England, where once I worked. Not many people even remember that such a building existed. Today The Bank is one of the most comfortable pubs in Plymouth. Stylish in its decor and adventurous in its food, it attracts a clientele from all over the city and many from outside who come in to shop or visit its next door neighbour the Theatre Royal. The facade of the old building is still there and so are some of the old features which remind us of its former occupation. Added on now is a spacious and attractive conservatory which is a popular meeting place.

Stuart and Tracy James who run the Bank have just been crowned the top Ansells licensees in Britain. They are delighted and plan to hang the 'sword of excellence' in the bar. The title is theirs for a year. To gain this accolade they beat off challenges from more than 600 other Ansells licensees including those in the brewery's traditional Midlands heartland.

One other Ansells hostelry I want to mention is **The Unicorn**, slightly outside the town centre on the way to Plympton. Easy to find, you just go to the Marsh Mills roundabout, follow the sign for Plympton and about a mile along the road the pub stands back from the road in its own large car park. It has always been a popular venue ever since it opened, but not until the advent of Liz Elliott did it become as successful as it is today. This lady is the manageress in her own right but she does have the added benefit of having a very supportive husband who although he has another job in civil engineering, turns to in the evenings and weekends and does all the cellar work.

The Unicorn is a far cry from Woburn Abbey and the Duke and Duchess of Bedford, but that is where she first acquired an interest in catering. Her mother was the cook at Woburn and Liz was pot washing there for pocket money, by the time she was nine years old. By the time she was twelve she was doing starters and desserts for proper wages and at thirteen was in the main restaurant, starting with two tables. Many Americans visited Woburn. They expected and got good service. The accolade came when Liz was the first ever waitress 'in the house' for the Duke and Duchess. Liz's mother was mentioned in later years in a book produced by the Bedfords. Woburn, of course, was used for many films and 'The Persuaders' series was filmed there so Liz got her share of excitement in meeting Roger Moore and Tony Curtis.

In those days, working in Plymouth was not in her mind although her grandparents and greatgrandparents came from the city. It was not until her husband was head-hunted and found the new job was in Plymouth that she came here. That was in 1984. Being idle has never appealed to Liz, and so she became a waitress at Piermasters, then a stockroom assistant at British Home Stores, which she hated because she missed dealing with the public. After a while she returned to Piermasters as deputy manager. It was the advent of The Copthorne in Plymouth that took her into the hotel business, first as a senior waitress - a job that lasted three weeks before the hotel recognised her ability and she was promoted to supervisor of the hotel's coffee house, Bentleys. Before long she found herself coping with breakfast in the restaurant and finally taking over the Burlington Restaurant dealing with breakfast and the a la carte menu. That was not the end of her meteoric rise. Looking after staff in the restaurant and coffee house showed her to be a caring and understanding person. Youngsters in the hotel came to her with their problems and so she was invited to become a personnel officer. It took just three months for her to be made personnel manager and within six months she had passed all the requisite exams. This attribute still comes in useful now. In spite of her busy life, Liz finds time to lecture on Personnel, Hotel, Catering and Licensed Management at the College of Further Education.

All this tells the story of one of the most able, and interesting pub managers in Plymouth. However, as Jiminy Cricket would say ' and there's more'. It was Nicole Quinn of the Unity who introduced Lionel Smith to Liz and Barry. He persuaded them to come for an interview with a view to taking over an Ansells pub although he did not expect one to become available for 6-9 months. They accepted and in less than a week they were offered the Unicorn. At the same time Barry was head-hunted again and so after 4 weeks away training and carrying out the requisite S.R.I. tests, they sold their house, changed their jobs and moved into the Unicorn.

One of the first things Liz did was to write to Dave Lee Travis to ask if the pub could take part in Treble Top. Within three weeks they were on air and won! Because of a misunderstanding with their opponents, an Irish team, the contest was splashed all over the Sun and the Mirror. Great publicity for the Unicorn.

In her innocence, when Lionel Smith asked Liz to apply for the British Innkeeper, she did so thinking it was to become a member. She had no idea it was a competition for an award. On Christmas Eve, 1992, she was a regional finalist. On the 13th January, 1993, the judges interviewed her and she is now waiting to hear if she is through to the final. The finalists will be announced at the end of March, just after this book has gone to print so you will have to look in the newspaper for the result. Liz is thrilled to have got so far. She says it is only because she has had such tremendous support and encouragement from everyone. With such a competitive lady there can only be one place - the winner's rostrum. There never has been a manager who has won the award so this would also be a first.

The Unicorn is a renowned pub for its food and is also known as a Big Steak House. There are only 120-130 of these in the United Kingdom and the Unicorn is in the top ten. So there is no doubt that you will enjoy a meal or a drink here and certainly the management will ensure you are warmly welcomed.

Coming back into the centre of Plymouth, the **Pen and Parchment** in St Andrews Street, just behind the Magistrates Court, is a regular watering hole for people from the Law Courts, the press, solicitors, accountants and many more of the business community at lunchtimes and has a pretty good evening trade with a mixture of age groups from students to senior citizens drawn from all over the City.

Alan and Irene Bragg, the landlords, have not always been in the business. In fact, Alan was a tanker driver for Esso for twenty years and Irene worked at Arrow Hart for a number of years. Irene's family have had pubs for years and for a long time Irene and Alan took over for them at holiday times and when there was sickness. They caught the bug and started looking for their own pub. The Clarence in King Street was their first venture. They took over the Pen & Parchment in July 1991 and have never looked back.

Once upon a time this pub was called The Swan, but was renamed in 1986. Extensive renovations were carried out at the Pen & Parchment by Alan & Irene in October 1991. Food is served Monday to Friday 12.00 noon until 2.15pm.

Just up the road from the Pen and Parchment by the Magistrates Court, is **Rackhams**, a wine bar that has opened quite recently, but has become one of the most successful venues in the city. Not large, it has a comfortable bar and a cellar restaurant which is intimate and serves some of the most delicious and ridiculously cheap food in the city. It has become the haunt of the press, television, lawyers, accountants and so on who find it entertaining, relaxing and a place where they are certain to meet friends or rapidly find themselves included in the conversations going on. I was told by one habitue that he goes there to enjoy the wine certainly, but as much to get a game of chess or on a Saturday morning to read the newspapers and drink coffee.

It has taken very little time for this to become an established venue, much of it due to the likeable and slightly unusual owner, Arend van der Marel, a Dutchman who has made his home in Plymouth.

I am hopscotching about the city a bit but one Swan Inn you should not miss is **The Swan** at Devonport. The address is Cornwall Beach, Devonport, and you will find it right down by the edge of the Tamar. The earliest licensee recorded on a wall in the pub dates back to 1791: the latest are David and Kitty Cooke and their son, Terry.

You might consider it is not a particularly salubrious area with the dockyard enclosing it to left and right and council maisonettes behind, but the river in front, with all its activity, makes it very attractive. There is quite a large square to the right of the pub bounded on the far side by the Piermaster's house, a two storey orange and red building in the Dutch style with a false roof frontage and steeply pitched tiled roof. The whole corner is a preservation area. This means that although the Piermaster's house is currently used as a store it cannot be demolished or dramatically altered, which is good because it is a fine example of its type, and is in a good state of repair structurally.

Violent storms two years ago damaged The Swan extensively on the top floor and the roof. This has all been repaired and renovated. At the same time the huge waves and winds sank the floating pontoon just off the square. The whole area was so badly damaged that the council had to put in a new floating pontoon and bridge and recobble the square and surrounds. It looks splendid now.

This floating pontoon and the adjacent slipway are the only free moorings this side of the river: something that David Owen has been bothered about for a long time and the Groundwork Trust have tried to rectify with their pamphlet 'Landfalls - The Yachtsman's Guide to Landings and Slipways' in the Plymouth area. During the season, private hire boats tie up for a couple of hours before they continue on their way, great for the passengers and a chance to enjoy the exceptional hospitality of this excellent pub.

Terry Cooke is a connoisseur of Real Ale and he makes sure that the eight Real Ales on at any one time are in tip top condition.

As this is a Free House it is not tied to any range of beers. There is an extensive home-cooked bar menu. Finger buffet parties are quite frequently held in one of the three rooms, there is a music licence, and on Thursday, Friday and Saturday nights live music with a mixture of style and sound produces good entertainment.

You will find your fellow drinkers at The Swan to be a cross section of the community which makes for an interesting visit.

The pub was named after a sloop called 'The Swan' ordered by the Admiralty in May, 1766, and launched in November 1767. For anyone who does not know what a sloop is, it is the one with a single main mast and two big triangle sails - the sort we drew as children. In practice they also had extra sails rigged forward to a bowsprit.

If anyone knows of one of Her Majesty's ships of the past called H.M.S. Avondale then Arthur Squire, the landlord of **The Avondale** in Keyham Road, just outside the Dockyard Gates, would like to know. He and his wife, Betty, have been in this fascinating pub - as much fascinating because of the landlord as for anything else - since the tenth of December 1950. For all of those years Arthur has searched for a picture or the crest of this ship. Arthur is a Plymothian and was born in a pub, The Valiant Soldier, in Notte Street, no longer in existence. Betty came from Birmingham, with a background of the law and the church. She could not find work there so she moved to Plymouth, a city with a flattened centre, no signs to help her find her way around and little else. She has watched the re-incarnation of the city with great interest and at last feels that she has been accepted!

Right next to H.M. Dockyard, Arthur carries not only 100% proof rum but 125% proof. It was at the end of July in 1970 that the Navy decreed the tot should be no more. At that time Arthur had cheap spirits for half an hour in the morning and half an hour in the evening. Just after the Navy stopped tot time, he sold fifteen bottles of 100% proof rum in half an hour! He had to put the price up from two shillings to two shillings and sixpence because he could not spare the staff to serve only cheap rum and no beer. It was a day of mourning, everyone wore black armbands. Arthur still holds an anniversary wake every year to commemorate this black day, and still has tot-time twice a day! You will find a poem in the bar entitled 'A Matelot's farewell to his Tot'.

Breakfast at the Avondale is renowned. You can eat this gigantic feast anytime from 7am. The Dockyard opens at 7.30am and the nightshift come off at the same time. Arthur has no doubt about the importance of good food. You have only to look at his girth to know he enjoys his victuals and that he married a good cook who still does about ninety per cent of the cooking here.

The Squires love pub life. On Navy Days the Avondale is open all day, Sunday included - the magistrates made a mistake one year and granted an all day licence for the Sunday of Navy Days. This is an occasion when Arthur dresses up as a pirate - and for that matter any special occasion will do as an excuse to don the costume. He used to hire it but the firm went out of business recently and so he bought it. Navy people traditionally like strong drinks and Arthur makes some truly potent cocktails although he will not use additives or substitutes. If the recipe says pineapple juice that is what you get, nothing else.

The Frog and Frigate at West Hoe, overlooking the ferryport and Mount Edgecumbe, is truly the 'Village Pub in the City'. Comfortable, providing a wide range of bar snacks complimented with good beer, wine and spirits, the friendly atmosphere provided by Babs and Nick Nicholls makes it a popular pub for visitors and locals. It also has a room for families or functions available. It even caters for pub sports, with an excellent pool area and darts throw.

There is another pub which is good fun, probably because the landlord, Yorkie, served many years as a chef in the Navy and is used to making sure that customers are happy. If you mention the name **The Two Trees,** which is the correct name for this establishment in Union Street just by Toys R Us, most naval people would not know where you meant. They call it ' The Twigs '! Whatever name it is called is immaterial. It is a good spot, and a lively place.

Yorkie and his partner, Rachael, are keen fund raisers for local charities. The Life Boat is their favourite but they also support Plymouth Self Help for which Yorkie keeps a 'Swear Box' in the pub. It fills rapidly at 10p a time!

On the road to Kingsbridge, but only a little way out of town, you will see a signpost to your right marked Hooe and Turnchapel. Both villages have special pubs. In Lake Road is the Royal Oak. For eleven years this delightful pub has been in the competent hands of Sheila and Jeff Walker. Sheila has been in the trade for thirty years, her grandparents were publicans and her mother was born in a pub. This is a lady who can never envisage retiring and her husband Jeff, who was a builder, but moved into the business when they took over the **Royal Oak** in 1984, has also caught the bug!

It is no wonder really because this is a beautiful village pub literally on the edge of Hooe Lake. The area might be considered to be part of the city of Plymouth but it is nonetheless regarded as a village by the locals. Very different from some of the pubs that Sheila has had in her many years in the business. She was at one time the only female manager Plymouth Breweries had when she ran The Queen and Constitution in Devonport - nicknamed 'Hell's Kitchen'. She moved from there to the Penguin for Courage - this is now The Tap and Barrel. Then in 1976 she took on the tenancy of the Wellington, just off North Hill, a hectic hostelry with a split personality. The pub was frequented by doctors and nurses from the two hospitals close by and the then School of Maritime students.

The years have taught this intrepid lady quite a lot about her profession and it is this expertise that has taken her to the Ladies Central Council of the Licensed Victuallers National Homes, who look after licensees who have fallen on hard times - there have been a lot of those lately. She has been voted Vice Chairman for this year and has been to London to take office. This was a postal vote so it is a considerable honour. It also means that she will be Chairman for the following year. A great honour, but it does mean that the Royal Oak will find itself without its popular landlady for the year. I have no doubt that Jeff will cope admirably.

Like the Two Trees, or should I say Mrs Miggins Pie Shop, the Royal Oak is a keen supporter of local charity. In this case it is St Luke's Hospice which is just up the road from them. £10,000 has been raised by the customers and a bathroom in the Hospice has been named the Royal Oak. It was bought, and is maintained, by these caring customers.

I have talked about Sheila and Jeff but told you little about the pub itself which is over three hundred years old and was once a farmhouse with cowsheds and a dairy. Much has been done in the way of restoration even to putting in timber and units of the period which they diligently sought out at auction. An original fireplace in one corner of the lounge has an open bookcase above it full of books and you will frequently find customers dipping into this library corner while enjoying a drink.

The huge blackboard tells of the day's menu, specials and snacks and on Sundays this must be one of the very few pubs left in the Plymouth area where you will find the traditional cheese and biscuits on the bar. You will also be very welcome if you want to stay a night or two in the comfortable letting bedrooms. You can be sure of a good night's sleep and a super breakfast.

The Boringdon Arms at Turnchapel was built originally as the Quarrymaster's residence in the early 18th century. It is now a popular Freehouse with a beer garden where the quarry entrance once was. With a landlord who has a passion for good ale you can rest assured that every sip of every pint is sheer nectar. The Pub keeps cask conditioned Addlestones Cider and traditional ales from several breweries including Summerskills and Butcombe, drawn from the stone cellar through traditional hand pumps.

There is an extensive bar menu which includes delicious home-made chilli, cottage pies and a speciality known as 'Bori Burners' which have gained a certain notoriety. These are seriously hot curries, available at lunchtime and evenings about an hour after the bar opens to about an hour before closing time. Fish suppers, summer barbecues, Folk evenings, traditional skittles and other events are organised according to demand and season.

It is undoubtedly a great pub and has the added benefit of being able to offer comfortable Bed and Breakfast accommodation at very reasonable prices. Most of the rooms have sea views and all have wash basins with hot and cold water. Children under two are not charged providing they share a room with their parents and children from 2-8 years old are only half price, again if they are sharing with parents.

Apart from being so well situated for a detailed tour of Plymouth and the many places of interest roundabout, Brewery visits, Sea fishing trips, Diving courses, Sailing and the hire of boats can be arranged through the Pub.

If you were to continue up the Kingsbridge Road just a little bit farther you would come to **The Elburton**, an imposing pub that sits on a crossroads. Elaine and Richard Worth are mine hosts whose task it is to cater mainly for their local trade. This increases in size during the summer months when holidaymakers pull into the large car park after they have been to the beach - there are several nearby. It is a comfortable place built in 1904 to offer refreshments to travellers. Elburton was still a village then, and Elaine, who was born here, says her grandfather can remember the pub being built.

The Elburton is quite a sporting pub. It has the usual darts, euchre and pool teams and the quiz team plays in a local league. The pub sponsors a local football team, Elburton Villa Football Club, now in the new Devon County Premier League. On Boxing Day the pub has its own football match - Bar versus the Lounge - an occasion of much mirth and a good excuse for a drink and some of Elaine's excellent food. The proceeds all go to charity.

Finally to what is believed to be the oldest inn in Plymouth, dating back to Medieval times, **The Seven Stars** in Tamerton. While it has retained much of its character, Michael Hamlyn, mine host, has extended the back of the pub with a huge conservatory in the Victorian style which blends in remarkably well. It is full of greenery, mainly in hanging baskets, but also has two graceful weeping fig trees and an enormous rubber plant.

Typical of an olde worlde village pub but larger than most, it can cope admirably with the busy lunchtime trade when people come from quite a distance to savour the excellence of the food. The menu is extensive and every day sees innovative and interesting dishes on a blackboard. Food is also available in the evening but it tends to be more of a drinker's pub then.

You would think that with three pubs in this small village it would be difficult for them all to survive but they do and the secret is that they are all different and cater for entirely different tastes.

Plymouth can no longer be said to be lacking in good places to lunch, dine, or stay, can it?

CHAPTER 4

The City Centre

To say that the Germans did the City a favour by destroying its
Centre will probably bring the wrath of Plymouthians on my grey
head. Nostalgically, of course, I look to the past and remember the
various streets with warmth and pleasure. Even today over fifty
years later I sometimes sit trying to recall all the shops that made
up George Street, Bedford Street and Old Town Street. Drake
Circus is not quite so difficult because that did not disappear in its
entirety until much later. Memories are wonderful and without
them as you get older, life would not hold much. I remember when
the young used to congregate in the cafe which was part of Boots
the Chemist in George Street. It was a great place for Saturday
morning coffee and it had a good lending library. Just across the
street was W.H. Smiths which competed for library customers with
its own form of subscription lending. At the top was the old
Prudential building and at the bottom, Derry's Clock and Lloyds
Bank - now the Bank pub. From there the road wandered around to

Derry's Clock today next to the Bank pub

the right where it joined the less fashionable Union Street.
However I still revert to my opening remark: the destruction of all
those streets has meant that we have one of the best laid out
shopping areas in the country. The traffic of 1993 could not contend
with the narrow streets nor would we have been able to have such
splendid stores. One of the best vistas anywhere is the sweep that

takes the eye from the top of Armada Way in Mayflower Street right through to the War Memorial on Plymouth Hoe. Planners no doubt would have found a way to make room for developments but every suggestion would have run the gauntlet of displeasure from everyone. With the total devastation at the end of the war, the City had no choice: a new beginning was the only solution.

Because of the damage Plymouth was the first city to get permits for building materials - then in desperately short supply - and so the rebuilding began. Ghostly remains were bulldozed and the new street plans laid down. The centre is clearly marked now whereas before, from about the 1870's it had two distinctive centres. Guildhall Square was flanked by St Andrew's Tower, the Guildhall, the General Post Office and the municipal offices and the other started with Derry's Clock at the junction of Union Street. It took years for the new centre to come to fruition and is still going on today but the achievement has been something worth waiting for. Today, pedestrianized, we have every major store surrounded by independents offering the customer almost everything they could wish for - providing they have the money of course.

Derry's Clock at the junction of Union Street

The lay out is simple, almost like a square with long, straight streets running from end to end and crossed at the top, middle and bottom by intersections. Everywhere is within easy walking distance. If the planners made any mistakes it was in not adding the occasional bend here and there which might have stopped the onslaught of the wind when it blows unrestrained from the sea, making walking hard and the use of umbrellas impossible, not to mention the cold that eats into your very soul if you are waiting at one of the many bus stops which line the shopping side of Royal Parade.

The premier street is Royal Parade dominated by the mother church of St Andrews, the Guildhall, the Civic Centre and the Theatre Royal with a vast roundabout at each end keeping the traffic moving effectively. At the St Andrew's end the roundabout has some charming cherry trees which blossom in profusion for a short time every spring and are chivvied by the dancing fountains which toss streams of water into the sky. A pleasant welcome for anyone entering the heart of the city. Later in the year the trees twinkle with white fairy lights and golden angels sit atop, adding enchantment to the pre - Christmas scene. At that end too is the General Post Office and the tall impressive NatWest building.

On the opposite side of the road from the theatre, the church and the civic buildings, stand the imposing department stores. On an imaginary walk from St Andrew's Cross at the top of Royal Parade I could pop into a good newsagent to collect a paper, take a look at some camping equipment next door, then into Lloyds Bank to get some money to go on a spending spree. Argos is next door - an efficient way of shopping, I suppose, but you feel a bit like a battery hen! Choose the items you require from a catalogue, hand over the order, stand on one leg and then the other waiting for the golden egg to arrive at the other end. Good value but not much fun.

Debenhams would be the first store I would reach, right next door to Argos. It reached out its long arms and gathered under its umbrella, two pre-war stores, Spooners and Yeos. Before the bombing Spooners used to grace the corner at the top of Bedford Street encompassing the bend and ending just inside Old Town Street. Yeos was further down towards the old George Street. Both were popular establishments especially with the many people who came from outside the city. Middle of the road in fashion and in price. Debenhams has taken on that mantle today throughout the country in its various stores, it has the widest range of goods from cosmetics to cookware, dresses to divans. It straddles a walk - through between its two buildings appropriately named Spooners and Yeos. Spooners and Yeos had come a long way from the little draper's shop opened by Joseph Spooner in 1858 in competition with his friend John Yeo, who twice became mayor of Plymouth. Spooners specialised in pioneering motorized deliveries and created a reputation for complete house furnishing whilst Yeos was a 'cash only' venture.

What I discovered about Debenhams interested me far more than what they actually sell because we all know about that, and what a successful group Debenhams is. Paul Tregellas, the Store Manager, is one of the senior managers in the group and responsible for the Plymouth branch. Running a big store is an enormous undertaking and only a competent person with the additional ingredient of flair can hope to be really successful. Paul certainly comes in to this category and has both the well - being of the store and its employees always in the forefront of his mind.

It is the methods that are employed to produce proficiency that intrigued me. I suggested to him that stocktaking must be a nightmare but I was quickly corrected. Gone are the days of individual stocktaking as we all know it and in has come the centralised computer which records in the central warehouses everything that is sold from a pin to a three piece suite. It takes a stock check at the same time and automatically programmes replacements for the various stores without anyone having to order. The only down side is that it makes it more difficult to be individualistic. Special orders take longer to acquire. What is automatically re-ordered is promptly loaded on the enormous containers that leave the depot for the stores, arriving on certain days of the week. What it does show is lines that are selling fast and should be continued and those that are dragging their feet and will need to be taken off. It is even clever enough to recognise trends in different parts of the country. There is no doubt that we in the West Country have very determined likes and dislikes which differ from our sisters and brothers in the North.

Just before Christmas, during the late night shopping, Debenhams became almost paralysed because of the business they were doing. Surely they must have been cheering at the upturn in these times of recession. Of course Paul and his staff were thrilled but it was the modern tills that were causing the paralysis: they could not take money fast enough and customers were restless. Put more tills on, the call would have been in the past, or just take the money, but modern technology has killed that. Every till is connected to the main warehouse and the system would be totally disrupted if the rules were not followed. It must have been frustrating for the staff as well knowing that they could have done even more business. This has since been rectified, and the transaction times have been halved.

I hate shopping at the best of times and according to my friends who are ardent shoppers, I am a spoilsport. I will not spend endless and frequently fruitless time looking around on the off chance that somewhere there might be something I would like better than the article upon which I have decided! Debenhams has always been a happy hunting ground for me. I found that the Eastex section which is a shop within a shop, has exactly what I like in suits and staff who are courteous, full of common sense and deal with my needs admirably. This is only one of the many departments and shops within a shop in which you will find the same sort of service and goods at prices which are acceptable.

Next door virtually to Debenhams is **Dingles**, part of the House of Fraser Group, who have every reason to be grateful to their neighbours for the generous help they received after the nonsensical fire on the evening of December 19th, 1988, started by a mindless, militant rights group because they objected to Dingles selling furs. For Peter Fairweather and his staff that night must have filled them with anger and the shattering thought that the House of Fraser might decide not to rebuild.

It happened almost forty years on from September 1st, 1951, when the resurgent Dingles opened its doors in Plymouth, after the Blitz - the first major store to emerge. Indeed it was the first new department store to open in Great Britain since 1938. It was, and is a prime site, and on the opening day nearly 40,000 people came through the doors of the store. Nylons, groceries and tinned fruits were in great demand - still hard to buy after the deprivation of the war years. Some people came simply to ride on the escalators, a novelty in Plymouth and the first to be installed in a West Country shop.

Peter Fairweather will tell you that the morning after the fire, having helped the police with their enquiries, he returned to the building at mid-day. Uppermost in his mind was the welfare of his staff who had turned up for work to find desolation and possibly no jobs. His practical mind was telling him that with the looming recession, the main board in London might well decide that the high market value of this prestigious site, together with the insurance would be a better option than rebuilding. It was with a heavy heart that he waited for the board to arrive. His anxiety was needless. Almost the first words spoken to him were ' How soon can we re - open? '

From that moment it was all systems go. Peter and his staff rolled up their sleeves, started clearing away the debris and, just like the war years, found a way to carry on. After the bombing raids of 1941 Dingles' building was totally destroyed and various departments were housed in large private houses around the city. Ingleside on Mutley Plain housed the haberdashery and millinery, and the shoe department found a home in a shop close to Gateways. John Yeos, incidentally, occupied what is now Gateways; they too were homeless. Charlton House on Mannamead Road housed Dingles' children's clothes and babywear if my memory serves me correctly.

This time it was slightly different. On January 19th 1989, 5,000 people queued up for Dingles' fire clearance sale, in temporary premises secured at Estover. The old Habitat premises in Campbell Court were purchased as an outlet for furnishings and electrical goods whilst the staff and contractors worked all out to get the ground and first floors at Royal Parade opened by the end of March.

There is no question in Peter Fairweather's mind that without the intense loyalty of his staff this would never have come about. He is a modest man who would not blow his own trumpet but I can promise you that whereas he is absolutely right about his staff, many of whom have been with Dingles for years - whole families of them - it is his ability to lead from the front that was the catalyst. It is this same ability that makes him such an excellent Chairman of the Retail Committee of the Chamber of Commerce. He constantly puts pressure on the Council and the Marketing Bureau for the things that Plymouth needs and must achieve to be strong.

It was not until September, 1990, that the store was fully re-opened. It has style, elegance and just that something extra and yet the prices are little or no different from other stores. It is a wonderful and therapeutic place in which to shop. The entrance from New George Street leads you directly to the cosmetic counters, always staffed by immaculately turned out, attractive women offering every leading brand, and each has its own alluring scent. Makes you feel cosseted even to be there. At the other end leading on to Royal Parade the more dignified men's department is quietly ready to dress any man in whatever 'Sir' might require. There is still the sense of service to the customer being of major importance in Dingles.

Gathering material with which to write this book, I was given a free rein to wander wherever I would in the store. This I did and was able to observe the caring attitude towards customers and the obvious pride the staff took in their store - yes, they do feel it belongs to them which is why it is such a pleasant place to shop, even for someone like me who has an aversion to the task.

At the end of a day's shopping anywhere it is worth taking the lift to the top floor restaurant which looks right over Plymouth. It is a restful, spacious place and the coffee is good. This is the venue for many charity events which Dingles' staff support throughout the year. Sometimes very adventurous with people abseiling down the outer walls to the street which seems a long way below. Dingles itself is always willing to give a helping hand to any worthwhile cause and just before Christmas an opportunity came up to help a chronically sick youngster who has a brain tumour. He wanted above all things to have a TV satellite system. The idea came from the Starlight Foundation which tries to grant the wishes of terminally and chronically sick children.

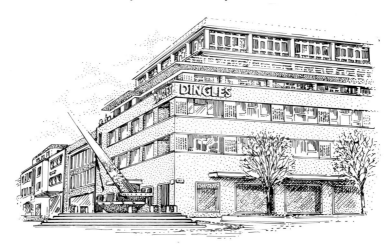

Dingles

Dingles became the fairy godmother and one happy boy had the system fitted well before Christmas.

I wonder how many people know that Dingles only came into being because in 1880 a 39 - year - old Cornishman, Edward Dingle, became dissatisfied with his job as manager of Spooners, then a drapery store in Bedford Street and now part of Debenhams. He left the store and started business for himself. Within a year he was employing thirteen shop assistants, twelve dressmakers and two boys. It would not surprise me to find that Dingles' staff records probably show that relations of the original assistants still work for the store.

Further down Royal Parade and occupying an imposing corner site which covers the whole of Raleigh Street and then turns into New George Street, is the **Plymouth and South Devon Cooperative Society's** Department store. This is a unique operation. The store is vast and covers everything you need to buy from newspapers to electrical goods, food to furnishings. The Society is one of the largest employers in Plymouth, second only to the Dockyard. What makes it so different is that apart from dividends to its shareholders it is bound under co-operative rules to plough money back into the business and more especially to provide all sorts of extraneous functions for the good of the people of Plymouth, not only its 108,000 members. For example it has a first class Educational Centre in Western College Road, Mannamead, which is open to everyone for a wide choice of educational and leisure activities for every member of the family. In addition, the Society has a superb, permanent caravan site at Stoke Beach, Newton Ferrers.

The first shop was opened in 1860 on the Barbican and the constant improvements to all the stores have given the Society an enviable reputation. Co-operative House today is bright and modern and very much alive. It offers the largest range of products and services in town, including banking, hair and beauty salons , opticians and even a chiropodist. From this central building it controls the many and varied services including the famous Devon Dairy range of butter, creams and yoghurts which are produced in its dairy at Radnor Place which is one of the busiest in the country, working round the clock supplying milk for doorstep delivery and retail outlets in Devon and Cornwall. All around the City there are Plymco Superstores, Supermarkets and Late Shops as part of this vast network providing top quality food and drinks. Plymco Shopping Centre at Transit Way, Honicknowle is a large complex which even has an outside play area for children and an indoor 'Playden' for toddlers - ideal for making shopping more relaxing or whilst enjoying a pleasant snack. There's also a petrol station and many specialist shops. The most satisfying thing for Plymouth is that the Society profits are invested in South Devon to provide the best facilities for South Devon shoppers and do not go to enhance the riches of a parent company elsewhere.

As you turn from The Co-op into New George Street you are almost opposite one of the entrances to the **Pannier Market**. A recent survey by the National Federation of Consumer Groups found that Plymouth came out in the top ten of markets in the whole of the country. The survey took a long and hard look at what shoppers across the country wanted to find in their local market. The survey was marked on a scale on one to five, with Plymouth scoring four or five in many areas that shoppers felt were important, like the wide choice of goods and cleanliness of stalls. The survey also found that Plymouth was the cheapest as well.

The market traders are represented by the Plymouth Market Traders' Association whose chairman is Ray Robins of Express Goldsmith whose busy shop within the market is stocked superbly. The Secretary is another hardworking man, Jon Pope of J & J Hardware from whom you can buy almost anything in this line. The Association has a 10-strong committee who work alongside the City Council always with the aim to improve facilities. It is a world of its own but not isolated; every trader is very much part of the community and eager to keep their customers. They are well aware that over the years the out of town supermarkets have lured many people away.

The history of Plymouth Retail Markets is interesting. Henry III first granted a market charter to the Prior and Convent of Plympton in 1245 and gave them the right to hold a market in what is now the Barbican area of the City. After the Incorporation of Plymouth as a municipality by Act of Parliament in 1439 the newly formed Corporation acted quickly to obtain the following year, a Royal Charter from Henry VI to hold open markets, on Mondays and Thursdays.

A covered market was provided in 1565 when a new Guildhall was built on what is believed to have been the site of the original open markets, close to the present day Bretonside Bus Station. The building was raised on granite piers with the space beneath being used for the market. The entire building was taken down and rebuilt on the same site between July and September 1606 and thereafter it remained in use until 1800.

From the 17th century onwards and probably earlier, the Corporation kept the market clean and in repair but leased the profits to a private person. A Mr Battersbye took 'The Markett Standinges' for 99 years on the lifes of his wife, son and daughter. He paid a premium of £100 and an annual rent of £5. This system of renting the profits of the market continued until 1892 when the Corporation took the profits and ran the market itself.

The demolition of the Jacobean Guildhall in 1800 heralded a new beginning for the market and four years later property was purchased on which a new market hall was erected, on a site between where British Home Stores and Marks and Spencers now stand. The market traded very profitably and was rebuilt in stages between 1885 and 1896 and remained in use as a market until 1959.

Before the war the Pannier Market was used almost entirely for the sale of farm produce; fruit being sold mostly by street traders from barrows. In addition there was a separate covered meat market, wholesale meat market, corn exchange and some 40 shops, together with an open air fish market in an adjacent street. The Pannier Market was little used during the week but on Saturdays was packed with about 200 farmers and growers.

The Market was a place of magic for me as a youngster. The wide lanes in the market thronged with people, the sizzling sound of the oil lamps lighting the stalls, the plucked poultry hanging from steel bars. The smell of fresh saffron cake and the tubs of thick clotted cream, Stallholders calling to each other across the way. High up, the glass covering was interlaced with green painted wrought iron which threw strange shadows across the stalls. Sometimes it looked like dragons and my imagination would run riot. It was wonderful.

Miraculously the market buildings withstood the onslaught of German Bombers in 1941. Bombed out shopkeepers including Woolworths, Marks and Spencers and many other multiples were given sites in the market hall where concrete stalls were built for them. The ordinary market traders were moved outside to a succession of corrugated iron stalls arranged each side of one of the adjacent streets which became known as Tinpan Alley. It was not the same. The magic had gone but as the City Centre was rebuilt retail traders moved into new shops and the market traders drifted back into the market. The fruit traders lost their pitches when the old streets in the City Centre disappeared and many of them came into the market where they rented the stalls built for the shopkeepers. The premises were demolished in 1959 on the completion of the existing Plymouth market complex by which time the character of the old market had completely changed from the pre-war days.

It did not take long for a new market spirit to grow and in the 1960's The Market Trader's Association was formed to protect their interest and to fight increased rents. That fight still continues, but today's battles are waged energetically in an effort to ensure that more of the profits generated by the market complex are ploughed back into providing better facilities for both the public and the traders. For example electronic doors at the entrance, canopies over the open stalls. At present the groundswell of opinion is that there should be a non-slip floor. To do this properly the market would have to close its doors for a few days, something that has not happened since it first moved to its present site in 1958. About 90% of the traders belong to the Association so they have a strong lobby. Meetings are held every six to eight weeks with the council to keep things moving.

The social activities of the Market Traders Association are useful occasions for them all to meet and have some fun. Not the easiest occasions to arrange but they do try to do something to celebrate Christmas and perhaps a boat trip up to Calstock in the summer. It helps their relationship with one another and the friendly attitude that comes across when you shop in the market shows this. I cannot quite conjure up the magic that the market generated in my youth but I am quite sure youngsters love coming to shop here.

A typical member of the market fraternity is Marg Finch who with her husband, Henry, has run a meat, poultry and game business for over thirty years. They started keeping chickens after they were married and thought it would be a good idea to get a stall. They were not wrong in their assumption; you have only to see what a large number of regular customers they have. It is Marg who is always 'front of house' so to speak; she keeps Henry and their son busy with the preparation of orders in the workroom behind the market.

Times and customs have forced many market traders to deal in fresh, pre-packed goods that busy shoppers can pick up quickly. It does not mean though that the cheery welcome you get from stallholders has diminished. That is certainly not the case. I love the cheerful banter that goes on between all of the stallholders. Other things have changed, too. It would not have been possible for my parents to purchase some of the exotic fruit and vegetables that are now part of every day life. Green peppers are now as commonplace as apples. Marrows are probably less usual than mange tout. Fruit of all kind is available all the year round and so are the enormous range of salad ingredients. I enquired from Allen Burt, whose stall has an abundance of the freshest and crispest vegetables and fruit available, what changes he has seen.

Allen told me that he can remember when his father used to push a fruit and veg barrow up past the old Western Morning News building, with his mother pushing him in a pram behind. In fact he has a photograph of this on the front of his stall. Over the years he has developed a big connection with the city's hotels and restaurants to whom he delivers daily. Whilst I was there he had a telephone call from one hotel desperate to get hold of some fancy lettuce like lollo rosso and raddichio. This did not bother him; he sells these exotic members of the lettuce family every day as well as cherry tomatoes, yellow courgettes and Indian coriander. In today's market they are commonplace.

One thing he did point out to me is that many people think these more unusual things, such as coriander, are too expensive. They are not in general and once having bought some coriander for example, it will keep for weeks stored in the fridge. It certainly adds an authentic flavour to curries and many other spicy dishes. He suggested a recipe to me that I have tried and found delicious:

To serve 4 people you need:

3 tablespoons butter	1 small onion, chopped
½ teaspoon peeled & grated	1 small tomato
fresh ginger	6 eggs beaten

½ chopped green chilli   salt & pepper to taste
1 tbs finely chopped   ⅛ teaspoon ground
     fresh coriander   turmeric

Melt the butter in a non stick frying pan and saute onions until soft. Add the ginger, chilli, coriander, turmeric, cumin and tomato. Stir and cook for 3-4 minutes. Add the beaten eggs with the salt and pepper. Continue to stir gently until they form soft, thick curds. Serve with toast.

All the ingredients can be purchased from Allen, of course.

It is not only produce that is sold in the market. The stalls are brilliantly varied in colour and contents. You can find good picture frames, buy a comfortable or stylish pair of shoes, acquire excellent fabrics for dressmaking or furnishing. There are pots and pans, bric a brac, herbal remedies, jewellers, florists and a whole host more. Nor should one forget the fishmongers who have shrunk in number over the years but from whom you will not get better fish anywhere in the city nor at such competitive prices. From prawns and lobster to whiting and pollock you will be alright here. Filleting and gutting is all part of the service.

For all the Pannier Market's fishmongers, rising time is about 4am in order to get down to the fish auctions on the Barbican to get the best fish at the best prices, so that the benefits can be passed on to their customers. It's a hard life but they seem to thrive on it and are never averse to chatting to their regulars about new ways to cook the wide variety of fish on offer.

It is probably the atmosphere which strikes you most as you walk in to this different, cheerful world, away from the traffic. It is never quiet but always buzzing with an underlying excitement. Colourful new awnings decorate the 'daily benches' which traditionally offer local growers the opportunity to sell their home grown produce at the market. These days many of the daily benches are used regularly by the same traders but there was a time when farmers would queue from early in the mornings to make sure they secured a bench. They were allocated on a first come, first-served basis. Once in possession of a bench, produce was sold throughout the day but the rules said stock had to be cleared by 5pm It was a practical and affordable way for locally grown produce to be sold - and still is for that matter. Permanent stalls are much more expensive and are operated on a weekly licence scheme. It is not unknown for stalls and their goodwill to be sold for as much as £15,000 when someone leaves.

If you just want a grandstand view then perched on the balcony overlooking the activity of the market are six cafeterias each offering its own specialities. A great place and Plymouth is lucky to have it.

Two totally different shops in Market Avenue please me. They are totally disparate and show what a variety the city centre has to offer. At 4 Market Avenue, **Medland's Pet Stores** is a business that started pre-war in Flora Street, but was bombed and later relocated in its present site in 1958. The owner is Bill Hitchins who has other stores at Crownhill, Roborough and Tavistock. He is a nutritionalist who qualified at Seal Hayne Agricultural College near Newton Abbot and is very knowledgeable when it comes to dealing with the pet food market which has become very sophisticated. Medlands sells everything for domestic pets and Bill and his staff are more than willing to answer questions, or to delve a little where necessary to solve a problem. Knowing the rights and wrongs of foodstuffs enables him to buy the right type of bulk and split it down for customers. He frequently sees himself giving advice on diets to anxious pet owners.

One of Bill Hitchin's concerns about Plymouth is the growth of the suburban supermarkets which could cause a backlash on trade in the City Centre. He has great faith in himself in being able to compete as a specialist in his own market, but if the public go to buy their overall goods elsewhere, who would be left for him to serve in his shop? This is not a lone voice speaking. I have heard the same cry many times in my travels round the city talking to people for this book.

It was Bill's family background that really interested me. He comes from an agricultural family firm which was started in 1829, mainly connected with horses. His family had the contract to supply the Dockyard with horses for transport and working power machines. In 1919 they were supplying 250 horses. Stonehouse based, they had stables in Octagon Street. Every morning the string of horses was trekked to the Dockyard. They were worked five days a week and were entitled to a fortnight's holiday each year, just like any employee. Their holiday though was fourteen days grazing at Tamerton.

The firm had a warrant dated 1890 which authorised them to supply horses to the Duke of Edinburgh's household when he was in the area. This Duke would have been one of Queen Victoria's sons not our present Duke. They also supplied garrison horses and up to ten years ago regularly supplied forage to the Royal Marines.

With all these horses to feed, Bill's predecessors used to send their own hay cutters onto the farms, and with a special compacter, the hay was bundled ready for stringing. Special hay waggon barns were built, mainly in East Cornwall to enable the hay to be collected from staging posts for the final journey into Plymouth.

The decline of horse power within the Dockyard made Bill's father look for another complimentary business and so he acquired Medlands. By 1958 the contract with the Dockyard was down to eight horses. No longer viable, Bill's father terminated the contract and in 1981 wound up his agricultural business taking the best of what remained into the present business.

Although my own family stabled horses in the Octagon until it was bombed in 1941, I had no idea that such contracts existed. I wonder how many Plymouth people do remember?

If you have pets do go to Medlands. You will find everything you need and probably get a few additions to the story I have just told you.

Now for **The Hungry Palate** on the other side of Market Avenue. I let out a cheer when Jacques Marchal of Chez Nous told me about the opening of this wonderful shop. Roger Cashman is the owner, a Plymothian who has had the guts to up sticks from London, where he ran a successful cheese shop and open in Plymouth, not renowned for successful delicatessens or specialist shops of this nature.

Every imaginable cheese is available inside The Hungry Palate. If there is one you would like to try, Roger will happily provide you with a taster. He is good about suggesting cheeses for a dinner party or just explaining the origin of an unfamiliar type. In addition to the cheese he also has probably the best pork pies and Cornish pasties to be found in the City. There are quiches, home-cooked hams and other cold meats. You can buy sandwiches and rolls filled with a variety of goodies or find jars of pickled walnuts on the shelves together with Gentleman's Relish which I can never find in a supermarket.

From time to time he sets up cheese and wine parties and tastings, helped by Sally Wetherbee of Devon Herbs at Brentor. Go into the shop, try the cheese and talk to this well-informed, rather shy man who really does know all about the cheeses of the world.

Much has been done to make the pedestrianzed area attractive and pleasant for shoppers. The massive sun dial is the focal point but everywhere there are trees and flower beds: wooden benches tempt one to linger in the sun and enjoy the busy populace going about its business. Christmas late night shopping has become a feature in the city. It is a time for the Salvation Army and other bands to play carols, for street entertainers to weave their magic. A time for the spirit of Christmas to develop. To add to the fairy lights the Council put up, the stores erect their own magical touches especially Dingles and the Co-op. Children think it is fairyland - aren't we all children at heart when we see this sort of thing?

Just above the Co-operative in New George Street is **W.H. Smith**, as well known by name as any other business in the world. We have been lucky in Plymouth to have a brand new, purpose built store for our use. It is light, airy, spacious and well laid out. Perhaps it is the writer in me that makes a visit to a store of this kind exciting. I love looking round the stationary, the pens, the pencils, crayons and all the bits and pieces. The vast range of greetings cards is a Godsend to someone like me who likes to buy a number of cards at one time and then hoard them for a suitable occasion. I like the busy air at the front tills where a fast moving queue of people wait to pay for their newspapers and magazines but best of all I like browsing upstairs amongst the books, always having a look to see if any of mine are on display. Sometimes I am lucky and even after all these years of writing and being published I still get the same thrill when I see them on the shelves.

W.H. Smith has been in business for over two hundred years and during that time it has grown from the small newsvendors in Little Grosvenor Street, London opened by Henry Walton Smith and his wife Anna in 1792, a few months before he died. When Anna died in 1816 'H & W Smith', trading now as newsagents and stationers passed to her two sons. By 1828 William Henry had proved himself to be the more capable businessman and so the business emerged as W.H. Smith.

It has never looked back, opening its first bookstall at Euston Station on November 1st 1848 followed by others as 'railway mania' hit England. These bookstalls became outlets for cheap editions of fiction evolved for railway travellers - including the popular 'yellowbacks'. Then in 1860 William Henry saw an opening for another venture, the lending library, which became part of W.H. Smith's bookstalls and shops throughout England and Wales, with nearly one thousand branches by the time changing social habits made them no longer viable. I remember the branch in old George Street before the war where I had a subscription. In fact I still have one or two copies of the brown covered, hardback, lending books which were sold to the readers for a song, after the library had finished with them.

By 1850 W.H. Smith & Son were recognised as the principal newspaper distribution house in the country, and so this giant progressed acquiring its own printing works en route. William Henry Smith retired and his son William Henry II took on a partner, barrister William Lethbridge, so he could devote more time to his political ambitions. By 1868 he was an MP and in 1874 he retired from active partnership to become a full time politician. The Gilbert and Sullivan song with the famous line 'Now I am the Ruler of the Queen's Nav-ee' from H.M.S Pinafore was aimed at his appointment as First Lord of the Admiralty.

When this great man died in 1891, his widow was created Viscountess Hambleden and his son, who became the second Viscount in 1913, became the head of the business.

In the ensuing years the expansion continued, a branch was opened in Paris in 1903 and in Brussels in 1920. In 1928 the death of the second Viscount Hambleden resulted in heavy death duties and it necessitated the formation of a private limited company in 1929 in which all the partners became directors. More than 5,000 men and women employees of W.H. Smith went into the forces in World War II. The blitz caused the loss of shops and bookstalls. Never lost for ideas the company immediately started mobile bookstalls, to serve the public while bombed structures were under repair.

One can go on for ever about this much loved English institution which since 1949 has been a public company. It has never stopped being innovative taking on board cable services, later to become the Television Services Division which committed the company to the growing cable and satellite television industry. Screensport was launched in 1984 and Lifestyle was first transmitted in 1985. These have since been sold in 1992. With interests in music and videos, W.H. Smith's has gone a long way since those early newsvending days.

Something that is really not relevant to this book is the fact that 620,000 titles are currently in print and 60,000 new titles are added to this list every year. It allows W.H. Smith's to be very choosy about the books they will stock. Whilst virtually all paperback fiction gets a showing - each book is allowed a window of two to three months to prove itself - a far smaller proportion of other books never reaches its shelves. Only one in ten hardback novels published is chosen and only 40% of these make a profit

Swindon for a long time has been the centre of W.H. Smith's retail organisation and perhaps the most salutary moment for an author is a visit to the shredder. If my books are returned unsold from shops, they are fed along a conveyor belt by two women who punch in instructions, a magic eye reads the bar code and the condemned books disappear down a big black hole to become part of a waste bale loaded on to lorries for recycling. It can only be described as a book abattoir - very depressing.

Between W.H. Smith and the old Western Morning News building is the only independent store left in Plymouth, **Lawsons**. Known and beloved by its many fans, it sells an amazing range of goods from tools and machinery, to cake decorating equipment, model kits and every size of nail and screw. It is modern, well laid out and very up to date in its marketing but underlying all this the present owners and the staff never forget its beginnings.

John Lawson, with his wife Jennifer, now represent the family, helped by their efficient and courteous manager, Roger Hodgkiss. From them I learnt that it all started in 1904 when F.T.B. Lawson became a tool merchant and rented a shop from a Mr Winnacott at 13, Frankfort Street. From day one he set out to give service to his customers and the letter of his, that I have been privileged to see, and which I have copied here, illustrates the point. That desire to give service and sell only quality goods still applies today.

Dear Sir,

I have pleasure in submitting to you my latest illustrated Catalogue of Engineers' and Joiners' Tools and Machines.

The tools herein listed are made by manufacturers having the highest reputation.

With very few exceptions (specially mentioned) every tool in this list is fully warranted to be of the best material, workmanship, and finish, and any faulty article will be readily exchanged if returned within one month from the date of purchase.

My object all through has been to supply best quality at as low a price for ready money as is possible; as I am satisfied that best tools are the cheapest in the end.

The variety of tools is so great that I cannot include everything in a catalogue of this description. I shall be pleased to quote prices of any other articles required on receipt of specification.

The list is arranged alphabetically, and an index is also given.

This list cancels all previous prices of the goods mentioned herein.

Prices are subject to change without notice.

Earnestly soliciting your orders and enquiries, which shall at all times have my best attention.

I am,
Yours respectfully,
F.T.B. LAWSON

In this time of recession we should all 'earnestly solicit' orders. The 1993 Lawsons do and that is why they are successful and expanding. Plymouth is not their only store. In 1979 they opened in Totnes and in April 1992 they took on a big store in Okehampton Road, Tavistock.

To return to the history of Lawsons which intrigues me. F.T.B. Lawson was the son of a Methodist minister who travelled to the West Indies and he had a brother who also became a minister but did not go quite so far afield to find his flock. He settled in Guernsey. Whilst visiting his brother, F.T.B fell in love and married a Guernsey girl, daughter of a tool merchant on the island. One side of her family was involved in horticulture and had a large business growing tomatoes, many of which were exported via Plymouth.

F.T.B. became very interested and decided to try and grow tomatoes in Plymouth. One must remember this was before the days of scientific soil analysis. They did the next best thing. A whole cartload of Elburton soil was sent to Guernsey to see if the tomato plants would grow. This was a success and Guernsey staff came over to start growing in the greenhouses of what is now the Elburton Vinery. This was hugely successful and 1910 was the date. The name over the door of the business in Elburton was 'Dorey and Lawson' recognising the interest of the Guernsey connection.

This started the Lawson interest in horticulture which is carried on today.

During the 'Blitz' of Plymouth, Lawsons was gutted. They moved temporarily to three shops in Pound Street and Saltash Street. When the city centre was rebuilt in 1952, the City had taken over all the land and no freeholds were available. The Council offered beneficial terms to businesses who were prepared to move back into the centre. The now defunct business of Underhills was going to take the spot where Lawsons are. At the last minute they changed their minds and Lawsons found themselves in exactly the same site as their original shop but now renamed New George Street. A happy coincidence.

F.T.B. Lawson died in 1952 and was succeeded by his son who was far more interested in politics. He became an Alderman, a magistrate and a member of the National Parks Commission. He was a man of great social conscience and founded the Lawson House for youngsters on probation. John Lawson came into the business in 1961 and learnt the trade but it was not until 1971, after a big family meeting, when a firm-minded brother- in-law made decisions for them, that Francis Lawson retired. John took over running the shop and his brother-in-law ran the horticultural business. It was the best thing that ever happened and they have grown in size and stature ever since.

Talking to John you get an insight into the past. He told me that in the early 1930's the great Mr Hornby himself came to the shop and sold his famous train sets and Meccano to Lawsons. Since that time Lawsons have always had an account with Meccano or their successors. He showed me some Meccano magazines dated for various months in 1932 carrying small box adverts for Lawsons. For any small boy or girl Lawsons today is still paradise and even for the adult children amongst us!

John Lawson can remember his father remarking that John's grandfather had not done too badly in his first year in 1904. He made £389. John looked at the books and corrected his father. 'No, he made 3 pounds 8 shillings and 9 pence'!

I think that it is the Lawson family's ability to keep the past alive and treasure its artefacts and at the same time be so positive about the present and the future, that ensures their success.

British Home Stores in Armada Way is one of the liveliest and pleasantest places to shop. Under the direction of a quiet unassuming man, David Tinkler, whose untimely death was a great loss to British Home Stores and Plymouth retailers, it has weathered the storm of losing its identity when the Conran touch was imposed on all B.H.S stores. At that time it lost most of its traditional customers who did not like the new image. Now it has shed that and become a store of the 1990's, sparkling in its cleanliness and lay out, colourful in its goods and realistic in price. The staff are happy to work there. When I visited I had coffee in the staff room which was comfortably furnished with a TV, magazines and papers. A place in which to forget about the stresses and strains of the busy life in the store outside.

At Christmas my daughter bought some fairy lights for the Christmas Tree from B.H.S but when she got them home they would not work. She rang and was put through to Customer Services who could not have been more helpful. I returned them for her next day and when I got to the desk they had the replacement box there ready and waiting. I was treated courteously and received an apology for the trouble it had caused us. The new box had been tested before it was given to me to make sure that the lights worked. Oddly enough it is this sort of thing that one remembers. For years you can shop and be satisfied and probably not think about recommending the establishment but when something is wrong and you get treated so well, it is never forgotten. I have told several people since how good B.H.S is.

With Peter Fairweather of Dingles and Paul Tregellas of Debenhams, David Tinkler used to be a member of the pressure group who fight for the well - being of the retailers in the City Centre. He was one of the first who fought for the area to be pedestrianized. His presence will be missed but British Home Stores are renowned for their staff training and I am quite sure the new incumbent will follow in David Tinkler's footsteps.

Also in Armada Way, opposite Dingles, is **Priors**, owned and run by the indomitable Mrs Prior, who has been in a wheelchair since 1962. This is a business like no other to be found in England. Basically it sells clothes and underwear for women and children. That is putting it very simply. Mrs Prior's range of stock suits so many Plymothians and those who come in from the country. It is the only shop that still sells what we would call old fashioned 'knickers' in pure wool. Much in demand I hasten to add and purchased by people who ring in from all over the place. Whilst I was with her she was taking orders from a lady in Kent and another in Cornwall.

Mrs Prior will not be offended, nor will her staff who are quite wonderful, if I say that it is an old-fashioned shop in every sense of the word. The service is pre-war, chairs are still provided for customers to sit on. Children seem to behave when they are brought here to be fitted out with school uniform.

When you see her wheeling herself around her shop, it is hard to envisage this gallant lady as the owner of a Dancing School but this is so and I expect there are many people of my age who remember her insistence on deportment and grace as well as the correctness of the steps. For six years she was a Wren, something she thoroughly enjoyed but when the war was over she and her husband opened Priors. Stock was difficult to get but they fought to get what was available and frequently had goods that people like Dingles would have given their eye teeth for. Even now Dingles refer customers to Priors. The shop is if anything over-stocked today with an unbelievable selection, with even the old fashioned liberty bodice of my young days. Her customers are regulars and happy to be there. Prices are sensible and the quality excellent.

Ill health has dogged Mrs Prior but she never complains. She will be 76 years old in July 1993 and has no intention of giving up. I believe it is the interest she has in her fabulous shop, her staff and her customers that keeps her going. It is certainly not modern medicine!

There cannot be many people in Plymouth who have Ken Towle's love and knowledge of tropical and freshwater fish. He does not remember a time when he did not keep fish and when he grew up, his one desire was to have a shop where he could breed and sell fish to other people, passing on advice and knowledge at the same time. His first shop was in Union Street and then he moved to his present establishment on North Hill, **Devon Tropicals**, which has become the mecca for all tropical fish enthusiasts.

For many years this site has been associated with fish or ponds or something of that nature but never as attractive as it is now. Ken told me that when he was making one lot of improvements he uncovered old ponds linked to the main drains since Victorian times. You will find him an enthusiastic and interesting man to talk to.

In addition to the fish, he sells all the required equipment and feeding stuffs and for some years now he has specialised in breeding endangered species, supplying them throughout the country and all around the world. It is a fascinating business and one can understand how Ken Towle has made it not only his lifetime work but his enduring hobby as well.

Just below Plymouth Library and the Museum is a small row of shops which seem to change hands with a fair amount of regularity; but one that has been there for years is the well-established and highly regarded **Maison Terry**. This Unisex hair dressing establishment was founded in 1932 and bought by grandmother of the present owner, Jonathan Terry in 1935.

If you were to ask most of the salons in the city today where their staff were trained you would probably find that in almost every case at least one member trained at Maison Terry. Some left after their apprenticeship to go elsewhere, some stayed on and then left to start their own businesses, but whatever the circumstances it points to the service this establishment has given to Plymouth over more than sixty years.

Times have changed and so have fashions. Maison Terry has always been innovative; in the late 50's a coffee bar was installed and used the first Expresso coffee machine in Plymouth. It became quite the thing to meet one's friends here. In 1972 Maison Terry became the first unisex salon in Plymouth. More mundanely, although I think very interesting, there was a time when the young apprentices were sent off down to Nazareth House, the orphanage run by dedicated nuns. Here they would cut the hair of all the children. It was not a visit the children enjoyed, they used to hide but eventually they would be rounded up and the cutting would start. Half an hour later, every child had a totally similar haircut a la Maison Terry! I am not sure who paid who!

The building in Drake Circus has recently had a face - lift and is now back to its former glory. The upper part is available for offices whilst downstairs this busy, successful establishment offers every conceivable hairdressing and styling service to its clientele and attracts people of all ages. It has become an institution in the city but never sits on its laurels. Jonathan Terry constantly looks for what is good and what is new so that he can pass it on to his customers.

Incidentally if you are wanting a good take - away sandwich then the recently arrived **'Doorstep'** sandwich shop almost next door to Maison Terry sells super, fresh and well filled sandwiches with a tremendous variety of fillings. They also have a delivery service for offices. Go in there in the mornings and it is a hive of activity with orders being prepared and customers constantly streaming in and out to collect their lunch. Sensible prices too.

Another interesting hair studio is **Apex** at 22, North Road East, owned by New Zealander Paul Goldsmith and his Plymouth - born wife Melanie. Paul had four salons in New Zealand but when he and Melanie moved to Plymouth to live they spotted this site for sale. Melanie was homesick and so the chance of working in her home city in familiar surroundings was the deciding factor: they bought Apex.

Like Maison Terry, Apex, in a roundabout way, has had a long association with Plymouth. It can be traced back to 1932 when salons were opened by Samuel Stouts in Spooners and Pophams. These were days of gentility and graciousness. Mr Stout was a perfectionist both in hairstyling and manners. He employed a man to open the door for his female customers! The bombing of 1941 put paid to all this. Pophams and Spooners were both destroyed but the redoubtable Samuel Stouts was not deterred. he found Apex's present site and opened within a week or so of the bombing. The building has traded as a hairdressing salon ever since.

Ideas and styles, hair care and grooming may have changed over the years but Paul and Melanie Goldsmith still maintain high standards of service and good manners. Not that they or anyone else can afford to employ a doorman anymore. Every client has a consultation on their first visit and the notes are carefully recorded on their personal card. The surroundings are relaxing and spotlessly clean. Melanie is particularly good with long hair - not always the case in hairdressers as I know to my cost. Anyone would be happy to have their hair styled here. Paul Goldsmith also runs a professional hair salon management service and hopes to have a men's salon before long.

Only a short way down North Road East going towards the railway station you will find **Vanity Fayre** in Cameo House. This is the most relaxing place to be. It is a Health and Beauty Salon, charmingly furnished and decorated and run by two charming ladies. Turid Langfjord hails from Norway where she trained as a beautician covering all aspects of the beauty scene. She married an Englishman and met her partner Jane Wright in Plymouth five years ago through their mutual interests in beauty treatments. They became firm friends and decided to put their skills together and venture into a business of their own.

When they found Cameo House they were so thrilled that they were busy ripping off the old wallpaper in the rooms while the man who sold it to them was moving out. Their enthusiasm has not waned and they give great pleasure to all their clients in the skilful and professional manner in which they give treatments. They are both easy to talk to and one need have no fears about entrusting even the most delicate of skins to their ministration.

In addition to facials for all skin types they will tint your eyelashes and shape your eyebrows, carry out wedding make-up, give make up lessons, cope with recalcitrant nails whilst they manicure, show you how to handle nail extensions, waxing, electrolysis and many other treatments. Aromatherapy is available using only the purest, finest oils. This gives you an experience of total relaxation of body and mind. If you really want to pamper yourself the full day of beauty is five hours of sheer bliss with a light lunch included.

Vanity Fayre is a find.

Ebrington Street has changed considerably in the last year or two. From being slightly run down it has had an influx of new businesses which have given the street a new look. I love Goulds which seems to sell any form of clothing and equipment. This is a splendid Edwardian building with the wrought iron work above the shop still intact. Every day the staff busy themselves hanging articles for sale outside the front door. It has an old fashioned look which I hope it never loses.

Across the road is **Stephen Loye Drums and Percussion**: what an incredible establishment. Something that Plymouth has never had before. Stephen Loye is a professional drummer and not so long ago he decided it was time for Plymouth's drumming enthusiasts to have a place to see and try drums and percussion. By no means are they all professionals! Stephen caters for the beginner with a suitable kit and no one need be shy or feel embarrassed about asking naive questions. This is a man who lives and breathes drums and is happy to share his knowledge with anyone who is interested. Of course he does get the more experienced and the professionals. For them he carries top brand equipment and is in tune with those wishing to part - exchange for higher grade kit. He also offers a good after sales service and firmly believes that to be successful he must keep his customers happy at all times.

Also available at these well stocked premises are many educational instruments including glockenspiels, percussion tubular bells, congas and xylophones. There are drums for marching, brass and military bands and cymbals too.

A top professional in his field, he took up his first drum sticks at Burleigh School: alas, now no more. He played for pop bands gaining experience and then went on to 'Plymouth Sounds', 'Clockwork Orange' and 'Time and Motion'.

He told me that he wanted to explore other aspects of drumming so he went into jazz playing with the Rod Mason jazz band and with Acker Bilk. His wide experience has been gained with cabaret work, and backing various stars including Freddie Starr, Dick Emery, Bruce Forsyth, Tommy Steele and Bernie Clifton. This has taken him all over the country and whilst he is not too enthusiastic about studio work he has enjoyed sessions with 'Cupid's Inspiration' and 'Thunderclap Newman'.

Now he is the resident drummer with 'Street Life Show Band', although he does not go to all their gigs. He teaches drums and percussion in Southway Comprehensive School and is more than willing to visit other schools to offer professional advice on percussion.

If you are in need of tuition or advice contact him at 60 Ebrington Street or telephone 0752 255040.

Further along Ebrington Street is a shop that calls itself **Totally Crackers!** The owners, Sue Groves and her daughter, Samantha, are two highly intelligent, interesting women who have built this business and the very successful **Upstairs, Downstairs** in Camden Street from virtually nothing.

It all started when Sue began selling antiques on a stall in Wood's Market above Burton's old shop. When Woods closed down she looked for another opening and found the shop in Camden Street, very much a backwater, but it made no difference. Before very long her collection of original Victorian garments, and right up to those of the 1960's, was attracting customers from all over the world. If you go in to 'Upstairs Downstairs' you will think you have stepped back in time; you will be surrounded by everything from genuine antiques to what Sue cheerfully calls grot! It is the sort of place which attracts the BBC wardrobe department when they are looking for period clothes. Not so long ago they arrived early one morning by train, selected what they wanted and returned on the train complete with clothes baskets full of costumes.

A German designer is another regular visitor. He buys old clothes and uses the materials as a basis for re-designing outfits.

Whilst Upstairs, Downstairs was growing steadily, Sue's daughter, Samantha, a teacher by profession, came to join her using the upstairs rooms in Camden Street doing costume hire. The business, entitled Totally Crackers, grew rapidly and outgrew Camden Street and so in 1989 the move was made to Ebrington Street where it has grown yet again. In this business they hire any sort of costume for any occasion. They have over 3,000 costumes in stock but will also make a costume if necessary. You can literally be Madame Pompadour one minute and a chimney sweep the next. Talking of chimney sweeps, Totally Crackers also provides a full bridal service, even down to dyeing wedding shoes to match, and producing a chimney sweep for good luck. Currently they are supplying 300 costumes for a medieval banquet, organising Murder Mystery weekends - in costume naturally, doing costumes for a performance of the Wizard of Wobbling Rock. They provide jugglers, fireeaters and Face-painters - I met one of the latter at the National Shire Horse Centre last summer when he painted the faces of my grandchildren. Professional make-up workshops are part of their scenario and they also sell theatrical make-up. There seems to be no end to their talents and their amazing energy. I found it absolutely fascinating.

In Exeter Street, I have grown fond of **Bottoms Up** a wine shop with a difference. The staff are totally interested in the wines they sell, and all of them have passed at least one of the trade's exams before they join the company. It is a pleasure to wander in there and be able to ask as many questions as you wish, and frequently be invited to taste a wine or two as an introduction to a new vineyard or a new country perhaps. I suppose one of the nicest things about Bottoms Up is that you are never pressurised into purchasing a wine out of your price range. I have found that if I say to one of them that I want wines for a dinner party, both red and white and my budget only allows for a certain amount, they will go out of their way to find suitable wines. This sort of friendly service would be a boon to anyone who is not too sure about wines. There is no pretension and you would never feel that you were being patronised.

Quite frequently it is a meeting place for a lot of people. One evening I spotted two or three bank managers nattering whilst they chose their wines, quite obviously used to gathering there. It is that sort of place, and for people with a love of wines it is most definitely preferable to the supermarkets. Another of its virtues is that you can park right outside.

Bottoms up

Now for a success story. On the other side of Exeter Street is the **Shower Shop** owned and run by John Langman who was made redundant by the Dockyard a few years ago. It sells showers, needless to say, but does much more than that. Here is a man who knows every make of shower inside out, and who discovered a niche in the market place for someone who could repair instant heat showers and provide the parts for people who wanted to do it for themselves. You have probably seen one of his vans around the city with the name 'The Shower Doctor' written on it in bold letters. There are many residents in Plymouth who have heaved a sigh of relief when they have seen it pull up at their door. For those buying their first shower, the Shower Shop stocks almost every make and every kilowatt.

In addition the business has many more facets. You can go downstairs in his shop and see a whole range of bathrooms plumbed in. It makes choosing so much easier especially when he can also offer you tiles that will complete the picture. In fact you can buy everything for your bathroom here from bath mats to soap dishes, shower curtains to towel rails. He has an enormous range from which to choose and if he does not stock it he will get it for you.

One of his great successes in this new career was the contract he obtained to install showers and baths for disabled people in the city. It took some years to achieve this but once done his work has benefited so many people.

This fine showroom did not happen overnight. It took him quite a number of years to have sufficient confidence to open his first shop. This he did in Hyde Park whilst he was still working in the dockyard. His experience there encouraged him and before one year was out he made a move to a much larger shop in Stoke village. Finally he came to Exeter Street, persuaded Kevin Waterman, of Lloyds Bank, who was then the Manager in Devonport Road, Stoke, to lend him sufficient money and the move was made.

John Langman is probably one of the hardest grafters I know. He has never been afraid to role up his sleeves and do the dirty work. When I see him today sitting in his well furnished office complete with computers and security cameras, I see what can be done when a man's lifetime career comes to an end and in order to provide for his family, something has to take its place. He is one of many dockyard employees who have taken the step to run their own business. It has not always been as successful as this one but the old tenet that 'Success is achieved by those who try and then try harder' is apt.

Visit the shop, if only to see what is available: - sooner or later you will need his services or those of the Shower Doctor.

Mayflower Street has developed in the last thirty years and become a thriving community. If you wander down it from the Drake Circus end, in the space of six or seven premises you will find a super Indian Restaurant, the Meghna, the Positano with its excellent Italian food, the well established Croquembouche, famed for its delectable cakes and gateaux, and then tucked in amongst them are two stylish clothes shops. One for men and the other for women.

Jon Saberton is a man of Plymouth but not a Plymothian. He comes originally from the Isle of Ely in Cambridgeshire, a place I discovered and fell in love with when I was writing my book on East Anglia two years ago. With a background in retail management, he worked both for Austin Reed in the West End of London and for Dingles here in Plymouth. It was the latter's failure to recognise his worth that made him decide to open a business of his own. This step he took in 1963 and acquired the site he still has for his first shop.

It was a time when Carnaby Street was all the rage and in order to make sure that Plymouth fashion for men was not behind the times, he used to set out on the sleeper train to London, arrive at 7am and wander round the metropolis to see what was being displayed in the windows, bringing those fashions to Plymouth. Not an easy task because finding the manufacturers was difficult, their names and whereabouts were closely guarded. He was persistent and eventually found the contacts he needed to supply him with what his fashion conscious customers demanded. He was certainly unique in Plymouth at that time and many of those early customers still go to him. Times have changed, fashions have altered totally but Jon Saberton has never failed to keep abreast of current trends.

It was not only stock that was difficult for him. Mayflower Street was almost barren. His was the only shop open on one side and even that did not have a pavement outside at first. A tactful but firm word with the council put this right in 24hours, but only outside his shop. It still meant he was beset by dirt and grit. Another phone call, another firm word and back the men came to complete the job. Jon Saberton was underway.

In the succeeding years Jon's philosophy has never changed. He is a man who believes that style and workmanship are more important than designer labels. He looks for the cut, the workmanship and the materials. His service to his customers is second to none and deservedly he has created a regular following both in the Mayflower Street shop, and the branch in Salcombe which opened in 1965 and Torquay in 1970.

He has not always been in Mayflower Street. An increase in business in the 1970's when flared trousers were all the rage, sent sales rocketing and he moved to a larger unit in Drakes Circus. He stayed for eight years by which time Burton's Top Men shops started eating into his market place and he upped sticks and returned to his original site.

There is more to being a successful retailer than coping with one's own business. The life of the community is very important and Jon Saberton has never shirked making his presence felt. In 1984 he was Chairman of the Chamber of Commerce and Industry, a role that enabled him to fight for Plymouth to be more alive to tourism. His efforts certainly helped towards the formation of

Plymouth Marketing Bureau which works so hard today for the promotion of the city. He is a man who has travelled widely in America and become an admirer of their shopping malls: something we could do with here. He would even go so far as to advocate covering in the whole of the city centre. I am not too sure about that.

Jon Saberton's other dream which has yet to be fulfilled is the proposed North Cross Tower. A change of heart in the council has put back this project but I can see what he means when he describes the view from the 600ft tower. The whole of our superb coastline would be on view. Maybe it will come to fruition in the future. In the meantime this man of vision will ensure that the men of Plymouth can have the most stylish clothes available.

Francesca on the opposite side of Mayflower Street is equally elegant. Twenty years ago Dorothy Vosper started this business in a shop in Drake's Circus because she wanted to sell quality clothes. Plymouth, for all its big stores, has always had a dearth of individual dress shops for women. Her principle has always been to find interesting, unusual clothes that will delight the eye but must be wearable. She has achieved this over the years and now is classified as a shop that deals in International designer wear.

The move from Drake Circus to Mayflower Street has proved very successful. It is easier to park and there are lots of different sorts of shops in the street which produces a good passing trade. Looking in the window at Francesca is always a pleasure and very tempting! Time to lock away the credit cards.

Francesca is run not only by Dorothy but her accomplished daughter, Francine whose eye for colour and meticulous attention to detail frequently makes it possible for her to buy an outfit on spec but with a customer in mind. That customer is almost guaranteed to buy it. Francine told me that more and more they buy from the smaller designers who give them better value and frequently more interesting materials. Buying is a difficult business and fraught with uncertainty.

The problem is that they have to buy 6-8 months in advance so in February they will be buying for the following winter. Not only is it hard to judge the trends it is equally difficult to gauge the cashflow. The two large annual clothes shows are being attended by less and less buyers as the recession has taken its toll. Even thriving businesses are tending to stay away and wait for the representatives to call later on.

Francine has firm opinions on what should be done. She believes that in order to cut down this long lead in time, manufacturers will have to produce smaller ranges more often. In the States they have four seasons compared to our three. There is less choice in each but it is more practical and is the way that we will probably go as well.

At the moment Germany seems to take about 75% of the market with the Americans rising steadily. The French English and Italians have about 5%. This is likely to get worse because the French and Italians have priced themselves out of the English market place.

Francesca has proved, like Jon Saberton, that customers will remain faithful to a favoured source. Customers who have been coming here for years know that they will be offered the right clothes, they know there is no pressure on them to buy and are very welcome to come in just for a chat when they are in Mayflower Street. Francescas will always gain more customers because of these two competent, pleasant ladies. They would give even the most timid woman confidence and get her to trust in their judgment.

The Armada Centre has become a major part of life in the City Centre. I know it is full of interesting shops and that Sainsburys is an integral part but I had never really thought about the actual operation of running such a centre. It is an eye-opener. John Brady is the Manager for Mabey Developments who own the site and Maxwell House and Iceland on the other side of Mayflower Street. He has been there since the centre was just a lump of concrete in October 1985. By February 17th 1986 it was up and running but with **Sainsburys** the sole store or shop. Later in the same month Laura Ashley opened as the first tenant of a smaller unit.

That tells us nothing really. What fascinated me was all the intricate and detailed planning there has to be to make this vast complex tick. Originally designed and built for 20 shops and 2 kiosks with an open entrance closed by means of a roller shutter door for night-time security. Since these early days the shops have become thirty by internal redesigning and the two kiosks remain. More importantly a giant porch has been added in the front area which keeps out the winds using the automatic doors as the shield.

The entire centre is computer controlled and so it takes only ten people to care for the whole building. Cleaners work all day long so that they are visible and ready with the mop or dustpan for spillages by the public. It is very efficient and at the same time the staff are friendly: something that John Brady is insistent upon. He wants the centre to have a good atmosphere. I was surprised how little vandalism there is even in odd corners and the loos. John Brady tells me this is because of the efficiency of cameras and the use of mirrors - not in the loos I hasten to add! The visible presence of the staff also helps.

Everything is done 'in house' in the Armada Centre, even design and advertising work. Having been given a guided tour I realised that what one sees is only a part of what the building consists of. Behind the scenes there is as much space again as that which is visible: fire alleyways, delivery walkways for example. Underneath and still accessible from Mayflower Street is a huge delivery area, able to take several large lorries and a dozen cars all at once. Alongside this is the electrical room with all the SWEB connections, fuse boxes, meters, computer controls, with the primary control back in John's office. Yet another room has two large industrial gas heaters to provide warmth to the centre. All these controls are duplicated at the other end of the delivery area for Sainsbury's independent systems.

Above the general shopping area, as well as alongside Sainsbury's are car parking areas. These are administered by Sainsburys during the day but become John's responsibility overnight.

Up on the roof are two banks of 4 huge extractor fans. These were put in to enable any smoke, from a fire perhaps, to be cleared from the whole centre in two minutes. Should a fire ever occur the public are safe because the installation of the automatic front doors, whilst limiting the smoke clearance, has meant that a smoke curtain has been installed where the old roller shutter door was. This creates a smoke-free area low down so that people can still see and escape in the event of a major fire. All this is quite a

responsibility for John Brady and his staff but it is a challenge
which they rise to admirably.

The Armada Centre

I am addicted to Sainsburys and resist being lured away to the
supermarkets further afield. I have nothing against them but I have
grown accustomed to the familiar surroundings of Sainsbury and I
know where to find everything. Monthly shopping is eased by the
thought that the Copthorne is close at hand if I need a drink and
just down the escalator from the store is a very good coffee house.

My loyalty is also to Sainsburys because they were the first to
venture into Plymouth and gave us easy access to some of the
products that were missing from other shops. I also have to tell you
that I am addicted to Sainsburys 'Choir of the Year' contest on the
television and whenever I see Lord Sainsbury present the winners
with their trophies, I am glad that my few pennies have gone into
the Sainsbury coffers!!

To any stranger coming to Plymouth, the Armada Centre
should be high on the list of things to see. It is a collection of shops
of all kinds, some large, some small, some obviously successful and
some feeling the current economic pinch, but it is always nice to be
there.

Coffee Plus is a busy cafe with the self service queue seldom
empty but the service behind the counter is fast and willing. I have
to confess to having never eaten a meal there but I am told that the

food is good, plentiful and not too expensive. I can certainly vouch for their coffee and their sticky buns and scones. It is an ideal place to rest your weary legs if you have been shopping in the Centre or even further afield in Mayflower Street. The banquette seating creates an air of intimacy even in such a busy place.

Sport Kiting has become a professional sport and was on show at the Barcelona Olympics. **Highflyers** who have a retail site in the Armada Centre as well as at Trebetheric in North Cornwall and Roche Victoria Business Park, just outside Bodmin, are the largest manufacturers of Sport Kites in Europe. They export 85% of their production all over the world.

Because theirs is a fun product, the shop is a very happy place to be. Kite buying seems to be almost recession proof whether it is for the serious competitor who is looking for the best design and quality or for the massive numbers of the public who have taken to kite flying to relax. Highflyers not only sells its own products in the Armada Centre but scale size rockets as well, which need no wind at all to set them going. Having said that, the modern kite will fly when the wind is at its least strength.

Nick Finnemore, the Managing Director of the company tells me that much of their work is liaising with schools because both kites, for their aerodynamics, and rockets come within the school National Curriculum: - we were never allowed to study kite flying in my day!

As a leisure activity Highflyers finds its customers come as families rather than individuals. It is a sport for all ages and something one can do all the year round which has the added benefit of not damaging the environment. All the retail staff employed by Highflyers, Nick's father, Bill, in the case of the Armada Centre, spend two to three months in the factory helping to manufacture the kites and also to learn administration, before going into a shop. They certainly are knowledgeable and fascinating to listen to.

In the U.S.A sport kiting has overtaken surfing in popularity and there are competitions currently worth 30,000 dollars for the first prize. Highflyers was recently appointed by the R.A.F to manufacture Red Arrow Kites, under that name and also produce kites for the Red Arrows.

The unique selling point for Highflyers, apart from their innovative designs and latest technology application - like carbon fibre struts - is that every kite, whatever the price, £5-£300, is fully assembled and adjusted in the factory before being dismantled and packed for sale. This means that even novices can put kites together and they do fly first time.

Bill Finnemore quite frequently hears people say, ' I always had trouble before getting kites to fly but I managed alright when it was up in the air.' A few days later they are back with such comments 'Have you got anything bigger or more complicated - it is so easy to fly these.'

Corporate work comes to them as well. MFI advertisements use kites and so do Benneton and Coates. A Cornish farmer asked for a Friesian cow windsock. This was produced and within days Highflyers was swamped with copycat orders from other farmers. The current best-seller is the black spider windsock.

Plymouth University have formed their own Kite Club and named it after one of Highflyers most popular lines 'Wild Thang'. Nick Finnemore was flattered, naturally.

You cannot miss this bright, colourful shop by the escalators. It is fantastic: the weird shapes stop you in your tracks at first but they become logical when you study them.

I visited the **Tie Rack** with a friend of mine who wanted a tie and a matching handkerchief for her son-in-law. Instead of being left to wade through the hundreds of ties to find what we wanted, a polite assistant asked if she could help. We were grateful. This is where the Tie Rack showed its paces. First of all the girl asked what colour suit the tie was to be worn with. Grey, was the answer. Next question: is it a plain grey, dark or light? Dark. Fine, with a stripe or without? Plain. Having established these basic factors, the girl whose name we discovered was Karen Dale and is the Manageress, produced a swatch of materials and then asked about shirts. This whittled it down a bit because the shirt was a striped blue and white. From then on she brought us ties and handkerchiefs which would go with the garments. It sounds a lengthy process but it was not. Karen was quick, thoughtful, and efficient. We left with a tie and handkerchief that was received by the recipient with enormous pleasure. Something he would wear and not consign to the dark recesses of a cupboard. never to see the light of day again. I wonder how many sons-in-law or sons for that matter have done that to gifts they hate?

I felt this was wonderful service, something which would bring me back to the Tie Rack whenever I wanted to buy this sort of present. More shops could do with this sort of sales training which was competent, ensured the sale, but was never aggressive.

The Tie Rack must have one of the best ranges of ties and matching handkerchiefs in the city. Every colour, spots, stripes, floral and plain conservative. They are to be congratulated.

The name **Chesters** above a shop next door to the Tie Rack, is significant only because it is the name of the owners' dog! Rosemary and Neville Webb came to Plymouth from Hertfordshire in 1987 and opened Chesters on the 6th December 1989. It was their first venture into a business of their own. Their basic premise was the desire to sell luxury high class chocolates and associated gifts and somewhere that people would be happy to shop in. They have trained their staff to put the customer first, second and last!

If you have ever wondered what to give someone, do go here because apart from the wonderful, top quality, hand-made Belgian chocolates, the presentation is superb. You can have anything gift-wrapped in creative ways so that the simplest gift looks stunning. This eager and dedicated couple constantly think about different ways of presentation.

Rosemary, who is running the business at the moment whilst Neville is in Saudi Arabia, believes in asking questions of her customers to discover what is going to answer their needs. For example, using the right coloured ribbon when wrapping a gift.

What to put the choice from the 72 different chocolates in, is the secret ingredient. You will find attractive pieces of Dartington Glass for example which, when the chocolates have been eaten, will be a permanent reminder of the giver.

Rosemary will deliver chocolates anywhere in Plymouth. She regularly delivers to the hotels for special occasions and to the services as well for Ladies' nights. Every item will be individually wrapped.

In a separate little bay in the shop is a range of farmhouse preserves, honey, pickles and mixed spices. They are all preservative and artificial additive free and make nice gifts in their own right. For ice cream lovers, Langage Farm ice cream is sold during the summer.

Rosemary and Neville have a concession in her parents shop in Hemel Hempstead. Chesters of Plymouth ties in beautifully with Shirley Hall Florists. Perhaps we may find the same sort of concession happening near Plymouth.

I enjoyed my visit but for someone who puts on weight as easily as I do, the temptation to make a pig of myself is too great to make it a regular happening.

One of the reasons why the Armada Centre is successful and will become more so is because the majority of businesses who are part of it, are individually run or have a desire to create something different in Plymouth. Anthony Horwich of **Healthy Pulses**, is just such a man.

For most of his working life he has been involved with food marketing and mainly healthy foods. He headed the launch for 'Shape Yoghurts' when he was head of marketing for St Ivel and was also the Product Development Manager for Farleys. When they were taken over he was offered the opportunity of staying with the company and moving to Nottingham or being made redundant. Like so many others he had settled in Plymouth, loved it and doubted if he would find anywhere else better. He looked around for an opportunity and hit upon a health food shop. Now Healthy Pulses is one of the few health food shops in the city and one of the biggest in the country; most are 600 square feet but this one boasts 1200 square feet.

Trading in the Armada Centre is not always easy. Anthony finds that it is often difficult to persuade people to walk from the main shopping streets unless they have a specific purpose. I believe that not enough people know about all the fascinating and very different shops there are for them to explore. It is a pleasure to come here and one should not need encouragement.

It has taken some years for health foods to become recognised as part of one's diet and not regarded as quirky. We are all being made aware by the media and the press of the benefits of healthy eating and so more and more people are turning to health food shops for the products they read about and for advice on how to use them.

Anthony Horwich has purposely tried to create an upmarket superstore offering a different and more specific range of products, presented by a staff who like himself are knowledgeable. He himself is a fountain of knowledge and is happy that people come to the shop and ask for him specifically. This happened whilst I was there: some customers wanted his objective advice on certain products.

This underlines my earlier remarks about service and what will bring people to the Armada Centre. Certainly the shops that do well here all have this ingredient in common.

Anthony Horwich's marketing experience has proved invaluable. Shortly after he opened, he organised an informal get - together of medical practitioners who dealt with alternative medicine. This was a great public relations exercise leading to many long term links with people like the Natural Health and Healing Centre in Lipson Road and Unity House in Outland Road. They now recommend each other whenever possible. When time allows, Anthony Horwich gives talks, sharing his knowledge and understanding of health foods. The fees for this he donates to the Natural Healing Centre which is about to open another centre for the self help treatment of cancer using the 'Bristol' method.

Healthy Pulse provides everything you need in the way of healthy living whether it is evening primrose oil, garlic or the help that is available from Anthony Horwich and his well informed staff.

The Baggage Centre has been in the Armada Centre for the last six years but had a presence in the city long before that when it had a concession in Plymouth Co-operative at Derry's Cross. The first Baggage Centre was in Cardiff and it quickly expanded to its present 83 outlets all over the country.

The central buying system for the group means that the very latest in this field is available almost as soon as it comes on the market bringing the latest fashions and technological developments quickly to Plymouth.

The Manageress, Doris Hayter was born and bred in Plymouth but moved away to Surrey where she and her husband had a retail food store but like most Plymothians she felt the pull of the city and returned about eight years ago. She runs the shop with three part-time staff whom she cheerfully describes as middle-aged. The reason for this is that they give better service and are more understanding of the customers needs. Whatever reason, they are courteous and well informed. Her choice and instinct was right.

It is an extraordinary shop. You can buy anything remotely connected with travel from a giant trunk to an electrical multi-adaptor for world-wide use or an electronic mosquito killer. There are trunks, suitcases, flight bags, backpacks for children, handbags, purses, briefcases and a myriad collection of gifts. One of the latest lines is a childrens toy box which is halfway between a trunk and a tuck box.

There will always be a need for cases and bags to carry and protect our possessions whatever the fashion or the technological changes. The Baggage Centre is just another reason why you should regularly use the Armada Centre.

A barometer of healthy trading for government statistics is whether the shoe-repair business is doing well. If it is the government is in trouble: people are having shoes repaired rather than buying new ones. It always seems to me that no matter what the financial climate is, there is always room for a good shoe-repairer especially when he can cut keys and do engraving as well.

I found **Feet First** in the Armada Centre owned and operated by Garry Pardew, a young man with a purpose and a dream: he would like to have a chain of Feet First right across the country. He is young enough and sufficiently committed to make this dream come true even if this is his first venture.

Feet First copes with every sort of shoe repair as well as leather clothes. In fact he will do anything. When I was there he was repairing some aluminium step ladders for a client. He is quick, sensibly priced and willing to give a good service.

His story is interesting. He was trained by Timpsons in shoe repairs and key cutting. This exercise they were turning into a franchise operation. Garry wanted to take up a franchise but the man, another Timpson manager, who was to partner him, pulled out at the last minute. On his own he could not afford it. A sympathetic and astute cousin put up the money as a silent partner for Garry to start on his own. It was then that lady luck played a hand. Garry was able to buy first class equipment from an independent shoe repairer who was retiring because of ill health. He ended up with quality equipment at an affordable price making him able to provide a full range of services for his customers.

Garry Pardew is another fine example of someone who faced adversity but was determined to succeed. He is a nice man, knows his trade, works very hard and I believe he could fulfil his dream. We many well see 'Feet First' all over the country.

Situated in busy Cornwall street is **Bambini** owned by Carole Hodges, who is half Italian, hence the name Bambini. Carole's grandfather ran the Admiral McBride on the Barbican for many years, so Carole is well versed in the life of Plymouth.

The name Bambini obviously suggests children to you and this is a shop full of the most beautiful clothes for youngsters. It is a place of specialist babywear and toys not available in the big multiples and offers Continental fashions. Carole says she would buy British if they were available. The outfits are all co-ordinated in colours and themes to cover socks, skirts, trousers, blouses, tops, mittens, scarfs, coats etc.

The same desire for co-ordination is now apparent for people who are seeking bedroom accessories like mobiles, wooden bookends and pictures. There are toys there in solid wood shapes that are beautifully made. It is a shop for all seasons for the young and one where mothers - or grandmothers - will find help in dressing their young. Carole is acquiring a range of fabrics and themes for different age groups so that a family with several children might have all the children in co-ordinated outfits for a special occasion. In summer for example the nautical look is a perennial favourite with both boys and girls.

Carole Hodges just oozes enthusiasm for her business and Bambini is certainly a very happy place to visit.

I had not realised until I was talking to Carole that she is married to Kevin Hodges, who plays for Torquay United Football Club.

At the junction of Western Approach and Union Street is **Grevan Cars Limited**, they are the BMW dealers for Plymouth and much more besides but I am going to tell you about them in chapter twelve.

San Sebastian Square

CHAPTER 5
The Media, The Theatre, The Press

The seeds of an adventure which was to play an enormous part in the life of Plymouth and the West Country, were germinated in that most sober and elegant of buildings, the Proprietary Library. Built by Foulston it graced the old Cornwall Street until the German bombs laid it to waste in 1941. Today, equally staid and sober, the library has its home in Alton Terrace, facing on to North Hill.

The seeds grew in 1860 in the capable hands of the four planters, William Hunt, Alfred Rooker, William Saunders and Edward Spender, to bear fruit and become the Western Morning News, a paper which with the Western Evening Herald has become renowned for the highest standard of journalism and strict political independence. They were an interesting quartet: Hunt had always had a leaning towards journalism. He lost considerable sums of money when a local paper, the Western Courier failed. He retired from local journalism but continued as Plymouth correspondent for the London Daily News, an appointment made by Charles Dickens as editor. Alfred Rooker was a respected Tavistock solicitor who was held in such high regard in Plymouth that he was elected to the Council and made an alderman without ever having to fight an election. He later became Mayor of Plymouth. William Saunders and Edward Spender were brothers-in-law and successful entrepreneurs who came to Plymouth from Bath seeking new businesses. Instead of going into newspapers these two men could well have invested their money in China Clay or Cornish tin and copper mines but thankfully they turned all their considerable energies into a truly speculative investment, the Western Morning News.

It is a far cry from the modest offices that the **Western Morning News** first inhabited in Bedford Street, opposite the old Globe Theatre, to the magnificent and imposing 'Ship of State' at Derriford to which they have moved this year. For those of us old enough to remember, the original building eventually became Vickerys, an outfitters which was taken over by Dingles just before World War II whilst the Globe Theatre became the old Prudential building.

The dreams and aspirations of the four men who met under the dome of the Proprietary Library fade into insignificance in what has been achieved today with modern technology. The first issue was a little four page paper with six column's to each page. The front page was devoted to advertising and the cost just one penny. Yet how much we should be grateful to them.

It so happened that this new phenomenon, a daily paper in the West, appeared just two days after Plymouth altered its clocks to conform with Greenwich Mean Time. Like most provincial areas, Plymouth used true solar time, which is about sixteen minutes later than London. It was the arrival of the train and the telegraph that made it happen. Compiling timetables otherwise would have become impossible!

In 1860, however, the times were sufficiently exciting for the public to clamour for news, and a real paper bringing news in the morning, some twelve hours before such national newspapers as The Times appeared was nothing short of a miracle. What an achievement for Hunt who supervised the 'lay-out' and Spender who was the Editor. National news was morse-coded along the new telegraph lines and the Westcountry was almost the first to know what was happening. The times were extraordinary. Napoleon, like Hitler, had been defeated, and Plymouth Sound had become a safe anchorage thanks to the building of the Breakwater by John Rennie, aided by Napoleonic Prisoners. Isambard Kingdom Brunel had spanned the River Tamar with an enormous bridge that opened Cornwall to the whole country and started tourism on a grand scale. Victoria was on the throne encouraging her dear Lord Palmerston to create the coastal defences now known as Palmerston 'follies'.

These 'follies' were the subject of Edward Spender's first attack on the Government just ten days after the paper was launched. His editorial read ' If Plymouth is to maintain her position as capital of the West, if we are to avail ourselves of the advantages offered by the opening of the railways and docks which are now giving us new life and energy, we must keep our town unfettered by these military works that have usually been fatal to every place surrounded by them'.

If the vehemence of that statement rings a bell then it is probably because of the equal ferocity with which Colin Davison, the present Editor of the Western Morning News, and Alan Cooper, of the Evening Herald, fight for the future of the Dockyard and other local and West Country issues today. Alan Cooper urges Plymothians, too, to 'Wake Up' and grasp the opportunity to get this great City moving into the 21st Century. The result of the attack on Palmerston's 'Follies' led to a Royal Commission which, for once, produced improvements. The message to these two editors who follow the great example of their predecessors is keep fighting! You are doing a great job without fear or favour.

Plymouth also had the Plymouth Journal, owned and edited weekly by an ambitious Londoner and friend of Charles Dickens, Isaac Latimer. The growing success of the Western Morning News drove him to set up in opposition and just five months after the birth of this paper, he launched the Western Daily Mercury, strictly adhering to Liberal principals. The two papers were to battle for circulation for many years to come.

It was not many years before William Saunders withdrew from his newspaper venture, and a company, headed by Spender, was formed to take over the business. Sadly in 1878 Spender was drowned while bathing with two of his sons at Whitsand. A granite cross still stands at Tregonhawke cliffs above the point where they drowned.

Whilst Spender was Chairman of the company he had recruited a young reporter, Albert Groser, from the Mercury and he became Editor and showed his great gift for organisation and an outstanding knowledge of railway time-tables!! As new railway lines came into being he put this knowledge to good use in using a train from one place to catch a train on a rival line to another to speed delivery.

His son-in-law, Albert Hurd, writing about him said he would have made a great manager for any railway company. Albert Hurd learnt his skill as a naval reporter whilst he was with the Morning News, an expertise for which he was eventually awarded a knighthood. If the name sounds familiar you are right - his great-nephew, Douglas Hurd, is the present Foreign Secretary and also a writer of some distinction.

The two papers have never lost the spirit of enterprise, nor fearless reporting. Albert Groser added to the paper's laurels continuously. He managed to get dispatches back from various minor wars being fought in Africa long before the London newspapers and sometimes even the Government had got wind of them. With the interest of the armed services close to their hearts, West Country people followed keenly every item of news. The Ashanti War of 1873 and the Zulu War of 1878-9, when the Plymouth man, Major Chard won the V.C at Rorke's Drift, were notable instances. He now lies beneath a memorial window in the wonderful 450 year old church at Hatch Beauchamp in Somerset. Plymouth breeds brave men. Major Chard won his V.C for his leadership which had given the willpower to 100 men of the South Wales Borderers to withstand the onslaught of 3000 Zulus for 12 hours, suffering fewer than 30 casualties.

Groser made full use of the fact that the mail steamers from Africa and many parts of the world made their first call at Plymouth - rumour has it that he paid the porters at the Duke of Cornwall Hotel to keep a lookout for these great vessels as they steamed in; the Duke has a wonderful Crow's Nest perched right on top of the building which certainly was used for keeping an eye on the liners and making sure that the Duke of Cornwall's porters were at Millbay as soon as the tenders brought the passengers ashore, touting for business for the hotel. Groser's scoops were frequently the subject of Parliamentary questions - 'Will the Secretary of State tell us if this report in today's Western Morning News is correct?' This brilliant editor kept the paper ahead right up to the last successful march to Khartoum, and when Stanley emerged from Africa after years of silence it was not only Livingstone who was there - Groser sent a special commissioner to meet him.

Albert Groser's reign as Editor from 1878-1895 coincided with revolutionary changes in printing processes which have been going on ever since; how would he have reacted to the computer controlled printing of today, I wonder.

In 1895 the Mercury started an evening paper, the Western Evening Herald, which was a great success from its first issue. Thomas Owen, Member of Parliament for Launceston, bought the Mercury in 1897, and founded a new company, the Western Newspaper Co. Ltd. In 1920 the company was acquired by Sir Leicester Harmsworth, M.P. for Caithness and Sutherland, who had been closely associated with his elder brothers, Alfred, Harold and Cecil, the future Lords Northcliffe, Rothermere and Harmsworth, in their newspaper and periodical enterprises, which had transformed the face of journalism.

In 1921, after sixty years of intense rivalry, the Western Morning News and the Western Daily Mercury merged and so the Western Evening Herald also came under the control of The Western Morning News Co. Ltd. using the premises of the Mercury in Frankfort Street as their headquarters.

Another era began on December 1st, 1938, when the building so familiar to us for years, Leicester Harmsworth House in New George Street, was opened as the home of the company and its many interests, including the two prestigious newspapers, the Western Morning News and the Western Evening Herald. It had been built on the same site as the old Mercury offices which had hardly changed since they were built in 1860, 75 years before. It was an astonishing performance because whilst the premises were being rebuilt there was no loss of production. New machinery was installed, more modern equipment, and the editorial staff emerged from their Dickensian cubby holes into a great open plan floor office with everyone in one room, editors and all. Only the editor-in-chief, James Palmer, had his separate office. They thought the space palatial but when I went there at the invitation of Colin Davison to sit in on a daily editorial meeting my immediate reaction was how cramped the working space was. The new spacious offices at Derriford have given them liberation yet again. The traditionalists amongst us will be delighted to know that Plymouth has been promised that the famous facade of the Evening Herald and Western Morning News building in New George Street will be preserved for the future.

The premises will be redeveloped to create new retail units. The Evening Herald and Western Morning News now have a city centre shop in Armada Way for the convenience of their city centre customers. The present alleyway between the Western Morning News Company office, and the SWEB store in New George Street will be filled in and replaced by an attractive mall running through the centre of the new scheme. The car park for the disabled at the rear of the old building will be retained and improved.

No sooner had the new offices, in what is now New George Street, been opened than war broke out in 1939. Paper rationing made the printing of newspapers difficult. James Palmer was removed to Bristol as Chief Regional Information Office at the Ministry of Information and W. Owen Mills, the editor of the Evening Herald, took over from him, running both papers. It must be one of their proudest records that in spite of the blitz which devastated everything around Leicester Harmsworth House, and cut off electricity, water and gas, nonetheless there was never a day that went past without a paper being produced.

It was only the presence of staff in the building that saved it from certain destruction by fire during the night of March 21st 1941. They threw firebombs off the roof, literally, and put out what fires did start. When the All Clear sounded every building around them was either flattened or on fire. The staff collected what copy was in hand and the type that had been set, and piled into the private cars of the staff. Led by Fred Crisp, a sub-editor, who was also a dispatch rider for the Civil Defence services, they weaved their way out of Plymouth around great craters in the road, trying to avoid debris falling around them from burning buildings, and managed to get to the company's Exeter offices where, with the help of local staff called in, they produced a four page tabloid Morning News which must have looked much like the very first edition in 1860.

Private cars brought the papers back to Plymouth, seeking out remaining newsagents as they went and delivering them with their supply of papers. Wonderful stuff and representative of the way that Plymouth withstood this dreadful time.

When power was restored the Herald moved back to Plymouth but it was to be some years before the Western Morning News returned in 1944. That great editor, Noel Vinson, took over as editor in 1948. He had been assistant editor for the previous year and before that news editor of the Herald for a short time. A Plymothian, with a true love for the city and a great feel for journalism, he was the right man for the job. Always fair he nonetheless demanded a very high standard from his staff, which he got. The Western Morning News immediately took on a new face. Out went the advertising on the front page to be replaced by headline news. His first front page carried the story of the death of Tommy Handley, an all time favourite comedian who became famous for the radio show ITMA - It's That Man Again.

Noel Vinson did not have an easy time in those first few years. Industrial disputes disrupted both papers sometimes just 'working to rule' but finally in the summer of 1959 a strike stopped printing for five weeks. Rumour has it that Noel Vinson taught his journalists how to play bridge during that time! He certainly was a great player himself, captaining the Devon Bridge team for some years and becoming a founder member of The Plymouth Bridge Club which is still going strong today in Moor View House, just off Mutley Plain by the Fortescue. He partnered my mother on many occasions and I still use the silver tankards she won as a winner of the Western Morning News Bridge Cup.

Both the Western Morning News and the Evening Herald have always had editors of stature and this tradition continues. Colin Davison runs a tight ship with his staff and contributors covering a wide variety of subjects in what is surely one of the most successful morning provincial papers. It is fair, non-political, and tackles life from the Mendips to the Isles of Scilly with different editions for different parts of the territory. It is truly the voice of the West of England.

Alan Cooper with the Evening Herald is very much the voice of Plymouth. The Herald fearlessly tackles every social and commercial problem. The paper is sharp on its news content, friendly, encourages local comment, and does not hesitate to print controversial letters that are frequently neither flattering to the City or the Council, the Church or the Media. It is a paper eagerly awaited by its devotees and a successful medium for anyone wanting to advertise, as is witnessed by the endless columns night after night offering everything from a cockatoo to a computer.

In March, 1992, the Evening Herald was named as Britain's Community Newspaper of the Year at a glittering award ceremony in London. It won this prestigious award for its Wake up Plymouth campaign. Alan Cooper must have felt very proud and delighted when he received the trophy from the hands of the then Dr David Owen who was still the MP for Devonport and not Lord Owen as we now know him. It must have been a moment, too, of gratification for the editor as he stood before more than 800 senior newspaper executives from all over Europe. The judges praised the Herald for a campaign that brought pride to the city with the aim of ensuring continued prosperity.

The Herald fought off challenges from the Leicester Mercury and the weekly Southampton Advertiser to clinch the award at the Grosvenor House Hotel in London's Park Lane. The three papers were short listed from entries which came in in their hundreds, from all over Britain.

There is no doubt that this lively campaign rattled a few cages in Whitehall and had quite a lot to do with the Ministry of Defence bringing forward the release date of land that could be used for new investment, as well as the Royal William Yard which has been released back to Plymouth. An Urban Development Corporation has been created.

With the new building at Derriford comes the latest machinery. I understand that the cost of the building and the machinery was in the region of £33 million with the new press costing £10 million. When I was printing out some of the pages of this book on my Amstrad word processor which takes over a minute to print a page, I could not help comparing it with the new machinery's capability of producing 60,000 copies of the Evening Herald in just one hour. Staggering, isn't it? It can also print two publications at the same time at each end of the press.

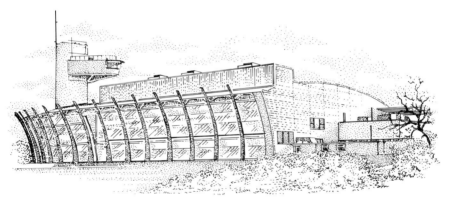

The new building of the Western Morning News Company

The £10 million Goss HT60 is one of only four in the country and has been specially developed for provincial newspapers. Another feather in Plymouth's cap. It will also print the free newspapers, the Plymouth Extra and Homeseeker. It will also contract print other weekly newspapers and the Daily Mail and Mail on Sunday copies for the South West of England. It will represent the largest and most influential news gathering, publishing and printing organisation in the South West. Plymouth can be proud of its two leading daily papers and if the original quartet, Hunt, Rooker, Saunders and Spender are watching from on high their heads must be too big for their haloes - swollen with justifiable pride.

For years **The Sunday Independent** has enlivened reading on the Sabbath. It has seen a whole host of different owners come and go and been the nursery of many a budding journalist who has gone on to do greater things especially in the days when it belonged to Mirror Group Newspapers. In those days, as I remember, it was used to train young journalists for Fleet Street. One of the City's Lord Mayors, Reg Scott was Managing Director of the local company. He has been retired for a number of years but still works unceasingly for the city and county. He is a Devon County Councillor.

John Theobald, once the paper's editor, for many years, has become a Plymothian by the length of his stay rather than birth. He is regularly to be seen in and around Plymouth and still writes pithy articles for both the Western Morning News and the Evening Herald. Whilst his interests have never been political he has always taken great interest in what has happened in Plymouth. His hard work for the Cavitron Fund has given Mike Turner, the chairman, the support needed to exceed the £100,000 target they set for 1992. It is a charity which is devoted to raising money for the neurological department at Derriford. He has been known to enjoy a glass of wine or two and you meet him in all the most interesting watering holes such as Barretts in Princess Street, Rackhams in St Andrews Street and several others. It is the smell of printer's ink and the journalist in him that keeps him on top of interesting titbits about which he writes with the same skill and thoroughness that he applied in making the Sunday Independent in his day one of the most popular weekly papers in the West Country.

It has had rough days since those times and changed ownership three times but every Sunday, the present lively, experienced editor, John Noble, puts out a newspaper that still pleases its loyal readership. Talking to him you realise the difficulty of putting together a newsworthy Regional Sunday paper. You and I read stories and do not always think about the work and the frustration that goes into finding them. Imagine for one minute that you are a reporter or the editor of such a tabloid. You have unearthed a good, interesting story which will please your readers. The written word has been edited ready for the presses, the photographer has brought back some brilliant and totally applicable pictures, and then on Saturday evening, just as you are about to put the paper to bed, you open the Evening Herald only to find they have got there before you. Maddening and particularly irritating when, had you been part of a daily paper you would have been ahead of any of the other dailies, having nurtured the story since the early part of the week. This, John Noble tells me, is one of the hardest pills to swallow.

Plymouth has always been strangely resistant to things theatrical and even today when we have the **Theatre Royal**, probably the finest provincial theatre in the country with certainly the finest director in Roger Redfarn, it is not Plymothians who form the giant part of the audience but people from as far away as Bristol who travel by coach, train and car to enjoy the super shows that are mounted.

Historically it has never really been any different although before the war the city supported two major theatres, the old Theatre Royal and the Palace in Union Street as well as some smaller ones including the Repertory Theatre in Princess Street. There is something resistant within the local populace against supporting anything theatrical unless it is the very excellent amateur companies which have always flourished here. It took a very long time to reach the decision to build the new theatre. Friends of the Palace Theatre felt that should have been refurbished, and councillors resented the idea of investing vast sums in a theatre of any kind. However one looks at it the Palace would not have been any good today. It just hasn't got the facilities, the modern equipment and is woefully lacking in parking space.

Even so every time I drive past this wonderful old music hall built in 1898 I can conjure up visions of the many stars the theatre helped to launch. The long, winding corridor that used to lead one to the stalls, had walls covered with old bills, Carrol Levis and his Plymouth and B.B.C. Discoveries, Eddie Gray and Arthur English, Cardew Robinson, Morton Fraser and his Harmonicas, Morecombe and Wise, Dick Emery, Frankie Howerd. One poster gave equal billing to Benny Hill and Cherry Lind. There will be few who do not remember the great Benny Hill, but I wonder how many remember Cherry Lind and the fact that she was a Plymothian, daughter of George East who used to conduct his Palm Court Orchestra in Pophams restaurant. Pophams was a department store in which Lloyds Bank and Argos are now housed. The famous Lillie Langtry, Max Miller and Gracie Fields also graced the Palace stage. Gracie used to come regularly and stay with Fred Eteson in the Ship Inn in Cawsand. I saw the great Richard Tauber in 'Old Chelsea' in this theatre and over the years many more famous musicals including South Pacific, Oklahoma and Paint Your Wagon. I have no doubt the decision to build the new Theatre Royal was the right one, but oh, the memories, and the smell of the greasepaint as you pass by!

The new Theatre Royal has just celebrated its tenth anniversary, and has proved without a shadow of doubt that with the right auditorium, the right backstage equipment, good management and above all an adventurous, brilliant Artistic Director which it has in Roger Redfarn, it is a bonus for the city. It can cock a snoot at all those sceptics who condemned it as a white elephant whilst it was being built.

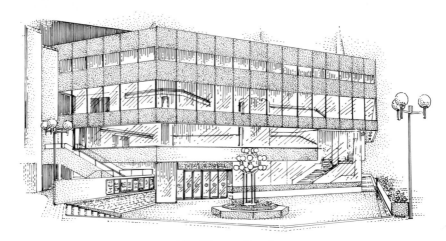

The Theatre Royal

In 1992 some 400,000 people saw a variety of productions, some of which were Plymouth born and went on to become hits in the West End. It is not only the theatre which gains from these attendance figures. Studies show that for every pound spent in the theatre £1.67 was spent in the immediate city centre. Restaurants gain custom, people who come by coach for performances from distances, arrive early to give them time to explore and spend money in Plymouth's very good shops. Taxis gain and sometimes people stay overnight in hotels. Even buying an evening newspaper counts. It is reckoned that about 436 jobs in the city are supported by the theatre - a ratio of 2.8 jobs for every one in the theatre. Because of its position in Royal Parade it has also become a rendezvous for people meeting for a drink, a coffee, lunch or supper, who have not the least intention of going to whatever show is playing but simply enjoy the atmosphere the theatre generates.

No one would argue that it was the advent of Roger Redfarn in 1984 which brought the theatre to life. I have never been quite sure how such a consummate professional was persuaded to take on the role of Artistic Director in a theatre which was struggling, to say the least, at that moment. He says that he felt that a council who had the guts to build such a theatre deserved some backing and he had an instinctive feeling that he could do the job. Such modesty is inherent in this talented, internationally acclaimed man. When you first meet him you might be justified in thinking he is a touch flamboyant but underneath that protective exterior is a man of such sensitivity that he grieves over the cares of the world, bites his nails with worry over first nights, the future of the city, the country and the world.

Here is a man who knew when he was seven years old and fell in love with Judy Garland, that the theatre was going to be his career. He will tell you that he met her years later and his idol kissed him; he did not wash his face for a week! Here is a man who has never been out of work since he left Birmingham School of Drama with a degree. He spent some years with regional theatre companies doing various jobs - once being an assistant stage manager with Penelope Keith. As a director he spent five years at the Belgrade in Coventry and his work as a freelance director took him all over the globe from America, Japan, and Australia to Europe.

His contribution to the Theatre Royal is invaluable. Not only for the various productions which have so successfully transferred to the West End but for his passionate commitment to the City. He has directed several of the Royal's community productions on a gigantic scale. The Plymouth Blitz was commemorated with a cast of 400 in 'High Heels in the Rubble'. Music of the Night is his latest extravaganza with a cast involving 1,000 local performers in the open air at the Citadel. It rained, needless to say, but the audiences of more than 4,000 could not have cared less. They loved it and it was an occasion Plymouth will long remember. Who could resist the excitement,the singing, the dancing, the bands of the Royal Marines and the Royal Artillery performing numbers that included a tribute to Andrew Lloyd Webber, music from Oliver, Me and My Girl, Finlandia, Pomp and Circumstance, Les Miserables and many more? The finale was the most spectacular fireworks display Plymouth has ever seen. Quite superb.

It is not only in this country that Roger Redfarn directs. He has taken shows to Gdynia in Poland and brought their production of Fiddler on the Roof over here. The theatre is involved heavily every August in the dynamic workshops in drama and opera for 10-18 year olds. The three week summer school which has young people from Spain, Poland, France and Germany as well as from here, is an intensive cross-media festival aimed at breaking the barriers of language, culture and the media. It is not only the Theatre Royal which takes part but the Barbican Theatre, Plymouth Arts Centre and Plymouth City Museum and Art Gallery. Funding is not easy to come by but it is helped by the European Arts Festival and Business Partners in the Arts.

Throughout the year there are all sorts of activities connected with the Theatre which has rehearsal rooms, storage and other spaces in Devonport. TRAC is the supporters club of the Theatre and offers excellent discounts on theatre seats for anyone joining them. They also have responsibility for a lot of costumes which are available for hire for Fancy Dress occasions and for amateur productions.

Plymouth has been the birthplace of several famous theatrical stars whose appreciation of the Theatre Royal runs high. In this last year or so I have spoken to two of them in their dressing rooms. The first, Donald Sinden, whose early years were spent in the city. He was appearing with Michael Williams and Sandra Dickinson in the Ray Cooney Farce 'Out of Order'. A demanding role if ever there was one. We chatted awhile about his past recollections of Plymouth and playing in the old Palace Theatre. Not a comfortable place, as he recalled it. I first met him some forty years ago when he and his wife, Diana, were lunching with Nigel Davenport and his first wife, Helena. It was a day he will never forget. He had almost decided to turn his back on the theatre because he was fed up at only being offered understudy roles. In the middle of lunch the telephone range and it was Donald's agent. He rang to tell him that he had got a part in the film 'The Cruel Sea'. It was that role that turned the tide for him and his career has gone from strength to strength.

Barbican - born Jack Tripp is not as well known as Donald Sinden but in the theatre he is one of the greatest Pantomime Dames ever. He appeared with the inimitable Roy Hudd and June Whitfield in the 1991 Pantomime 'Babes in the Woods'. This was probably the best pantomime I have ever seen and I have been going annually for sixty years or more. Much of it came down to direction and the great insight and love of pantomime that Roy Hudd has. It was true pantomime, relying on the time honoured jokes and hisses, 'Yes he will' or 'No he won't'. Slick routines which relied on perfect timing made it a pleasure to watch and had the audience eating out of their hands. Jack Tripp has this magic at his finger tips. Seventy years young he knows how to play an audience with the artistry and skill of a violinist on the strings of his violin. He tells me that you behave totally differently at matinees in the school holidays than you do after the children have gone back, and you have the out - of - town Senior Citizens in the audience. A different gesture here and a different intonation will produce laughs in the right places. There is no need for smut - how right he is. I saw Les Dawson this year as Dame in Dick Whittington, a colourful pantomime made outstanding by the brilliance of Patrick Mower as King Rat, Michelle Dotrice as the fairy and Peter Goodwright as the Baron. Les Dawson relied on the gestures and facial expressions we are so used to on the television and laced them with some unnecessary innuendos. I was disappointed. Let us hope that Jack Tripp will come back again soon before he decides to retire.

Jack told me about the weekly visits he used to make to the Palace Theatre in his childhood with his father who was a baker on the Barbican. His father never missed a Monday night and had his regular seat, and if the young Tripps were well behaved one would be allowed to go with Father. Jack saw all the greats of the day including Harry Lauder, Wilson, Keppel and Betty, Gracie Fields and 'Burlington Bertie' sung by Ella Sheilds. Wonderful days that he will always remember.

Brighton is Jack Tripp's home now, near his good neighbour Dora Bryan. He was telling me that he really only does the

Pantomime season now. There was a time when he toured in Summer Season with the great Folderols but those days have gone and so has that type of theatre.

The advent of **Plymouth Pavilions** has given the City a new dimension. In this modern building you are able to catch a concert, visit an exhibition, relax in a pool or even ice skate where you could once catch a train.

On the site of the former Millbay Railway Station, Plymouth, which once saw such illustrious travellers as Anna Pavlova and Maurice Chevalier catching a fast train to London, is now Plymouth Pavilions; a £30 million multi-purpose leisure, conference and entertainment complex.

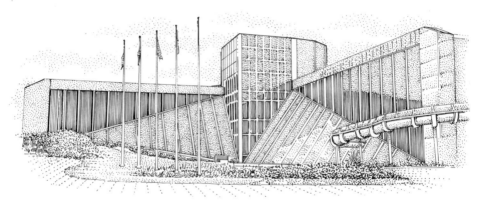

Plymouth Pavilions

Open all year round, except Christmas Day, the venue boasts an Arena which is able to cope with such technical diversities as a heavy metal concert, or an antiques fair to a World Class Sporting event.

This multi-purpose Arena has already played host to some of the top names in the industry including Tom Jones, Shirley Bassey, Wet Wet Wet and Gary Glitter no-less!

The Pavilions also boasts some of the best leisure facilities for miles.

Swimming will never be the same again after a visit to the aptly named Atlantis Pool. A gently shelving beach area transports you to a tropical dream island with a shipwrecked galleon, wave machine, waterfalls, jacuzzi and two special flumes, one which snakes outside the building before returning to a plunge pool inside!

From the tropical to a positively bracing atmosphere and you will be in the Alpine Village themed Swiss Lake Ice Rink, a must for all the family of any ability.

Refreshments are amply provided for all visitors to the Pavilions, whatever their taste, in four separate areas. A 33 metre Europa Bar provides refreshment for all thirsty concert goers. Cafe Calvados with its sunken seating area is the ideal rendezvous for anything from a coffee to a light lunch.

Waves Cafe is a uniquely situated fast food outlet right next to the pool! Last, but not least, Cook's Bar is an intimate bistro bar, ideally situated at the top of the complex giving you a superb 'birds-eye' view of Plymouth City Centre.

All in all, Plymouth Pavilions is a venue which really does have something for everyone.

Commented Chairman of Plymouth Pavilions Board of Directors, John Ingham.

"Since its opening in September '91, Plymouth Pavilions has proved itself to be an asset not only to the residents of Plymouth and the South West, but also visitors to the area.

I am confident that the future of our prime entertainment, conference and leisure complex will be a bright one".

The amateur operatic and dramatic companies have given the city much pleasure over many years and they all have their devoted followers. The loss of the Palace was quite a body blow especially to the Carmenians and the Plymouth Operatic Society. Together with the Gilbert and Sullivan Fellowship they all now use the Theatre Royal for their annual productions and the smaller stage of the Athenaeum Theatre for some other productions. This theatre is home to the Western College Players, The Tamaritans

The Athenaeum Theatre post war

and the local Music Festival. It's main purpose is to provide a base for the members of the Athenaeum Society who frequently host some fine lectures and the occasional film. The Athenaeum is one of the many buildings designed by the Roborough based architects, **Pearn and Proctor**, since World War II. They, incidentally, have their offices in what was the Old Court House at Roborough which still has the cells intact. Mr Proctor tells me it is for people who do not pay their bills!

The Athenaeum today

Apart from the Arts Centre in Looe Street, which provides so much that is good in the world of film for those who like the unusual, the only remaining buildings showing the silver screen in Plymouth are the **Drake Odeon** and the MGM both at Derry's Cross and each with several small film theatres within. I wondered who decided what films were to be shown and how the two enterprises worked in concert, if at all.

Apparently each cinema shows films by certain companies, for example Disney, and can at a later date show films that have already been run in the other cinema if they wish. However, if Plymouth only had one cinema, then the agreement would be for that cinema to take a mixture of the films on offer by MGM or Odeon. Sounds complicated, but I am assured that both the Drake-Odeon and MGM work professionally, and amicably.

It does not make up for the time when Plymouth had several cinemas. If you missed a film in those days in the big theatres, you could be sure, in time, that you would be able to see it in the Belgrave on Mutley Plain, now a Snooker Hall, or the Plaza in the centre, which is now a restaurant and health club, the State Cinema in St Budeaux or the Palladium at Ford. Those have disappeared in the last twenty or thirty years but there were many more before World War II in Union Street.

The name of the **Drake Odeon** is special, the only one in the country. It was originally called the Drake, but the name Odeon was added recently. I must say the Drake's Galleon on the front of the building does look very attractive when it is lit up at night.

The foyer of the Drake Odeon is a busy place. Apart from selling seats to the various screens there is also a licensed food outlet and a shop selling all kinds of gifts, from cuddly toys to post cards. You are more than welcome to visit all or any of these activities.

One of the questions I asked was about staffing a cinema like the Drake Odeon. Few people probably realise the sort of hours that cinema staff work - day times as well as evenings. It takes a good Manager to run a happy ship under these conditions and from what Mr Rosser, the general manager, told me, he is the man for the job. His staff from the cleaners to the chief technician, Mr Wilson, who has been there since the cinema opened in 1958, seem to be contented and work in harmony. This atmosphere comes over when you visit the Drake. It is a happy place.

Mr Rosser, although not a Plymothian, is a great ambassador for the city and will not have a bad word said about his adopted home, which he and his family love. His only mild criticism is that perhaps something could be done to bring more life into the centre of Plymouth at night.

Since before the war the **B.B.C** has broadcast from Seymour Road. Television became part of the output in the fifties. It has quietly gone about its business producing local radio and television for the region without ever getting involved in the complications that have become second nature to Independent Television. Today this lively, friendly establishment has a great output and links at different times of the day with other B.B.C regional broadcasting as far away as Gloucester.

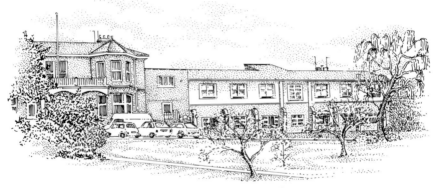

B.B.C. Seymour Road

Radio Devon's programme presenters have almost as big a following as their television counterparts. People like Craig Rich, for example, combine dual roles of broadcasting on air during the day, and presenting the television weather on the Spotlight programme. His likeable, warmhearted presence is requested with regularity to open fetes, bazaars, shops and endless charity gatherings which he does with willingness, grace and a great lack of pretension.

Exeter based Douglas Mounce has his own fan club. He travels daily from his home in Exeter to present the morning programme. I meet him from time to time when he is judging talent contests or something of that ilk and I am changing my hat and becoming a reporter for Stage and Television Today. He is great as a Dame in Pantomime, as many people will know, having had the fun of seeing him. One of his idols is Jack Tripp, a Plymothian, who must be the greatest of all Pantomime Dames. I asked him what makes a good broadcaster. His reply was that he is intensely interested in people and when he is on air he feels as if he is talking to people he knows. That certainly is what comes over and why he has so many fans.

David Bassett is one of the great pros of radio. His daily programme attracts a large following and he is an astute and unrelenting interviewer. I was asked to join him one afternoon about three or four years ago to talk, for what I thought was a brief time - ten minutes at longest, about a book I had just written. Forty minutes later I left the studio having discussed everything from my love of football, and Liverpool in particular, to my time in Malta as a naval wife. I was shattered but he was unperturbed, stopping every now and again to play some music, unscrew his battered thermos and refresh himself with a cup of tea. He is to be seen riding his bicycle about the City no matter what the weather, one of the familiar and invincible figures of City life..

The senior producer at Radio Devon is Ian Phillips who, apart from being a dedicated broadcaster is a firm believer in the advantages of good local radio. What he and the team are trying to do is to make the general public in Plymouth aware of them and to get them to realise that they are welcome to call in at anytime to air their views and raise questions which Craig Rich, Douglas Mounce, David Bassett and the team will bend over backwards to answer.

New technology has given the Radio Devon staff, with the flick of a key on their desktop computers, the ability to garner news quickly, be sure that they are not repeating stories that have already gone out elsewhere in the region and, equally to be able to connect up with other stations in the Westcountry region which extends to Bristol and Gloucester.

One studio is devoted to links with Broadcasting House in London so that MPs and other guests can speak from Plymouth or vice versa.

I was interested to see how the region has been divided up. For example County programmes go out from Plymouth and

Exacter, local programmes from Plymouth and a sub-region has been created to include Radio Devon and Radio Cornwall. The Saturday night regional programmes cover Somerset, Bristol and Gloucester as well as Devon and Cornwall.

Ian Phillips tells me that they tend to cater for the 35 -plus listener rather than the younger ones whose interest lies far more with Radio One. I come well into the latter bracket, and found Radio Devon a friendly place with a contented and dedicated staff.

Watching the way in which programmes are put together and put out took me back to my days in the B.B.C at Broadcasting House in London when we recorded everything on records. Tapes and cassettes were still things of the future. It was quite a difficult business. Imagine having to edit a programme; you could not erase a bit or even splice it together. The height of sophistication was a yellow pencil which used to mark the places where cuts needed to be made or applause taken out if the programme was running too long. I had responsibility for 'In Town Tonight' which always overran, and also for 'Take it From Here' with Jimmy Edwards and June Whitfield, a great favourite, which was recorded weekly. The daily soap, 'Mrs Dale's Diary' also came into my care until the dreadful day when I was bringing the disc back from the studios in Oxford Street to Broadcasting House for the afternoon programme which went out at 4.15pm. On the way I stopped for a drink in the B.B.C Club and ran into friends. Mrs Dale was left down beside my chair completely forgotten. I returned to Broadcasting House oblivious of the fact and it was not until the engineers were screaming for the disc that I realised what I had done. Too late, the programme did not go out and next day the papers carried front page headlines 'B.B.C loses Mrs Dale'. I expected the sack but all I got was a polite if somewhat terse memorandum requesting that anything in transit from Oxford Street or Aeolian Hall in Bond Street or indeed from any studio should be directly returned and not the subject of a detour - the gin and tonics were not mentioned!

Those, too, were the days when the announcers, the great John Snagge, and Alvar Lidell, amongst others were expected to wear a dinner jacket when they read the news at night on Saturdays - they were never seen and frequently only bowed to the rules by wearing the jacket with ordinary trousers. Crazy rules.

Plymouth's other radio station is the well loved **Plymouth Sound**, quite a different cup of tea from Radio Devon. You will find it tucked away off Alma Road. It is a place of great crusades, tackling all sorts of social problems and opening up the airways to listeners who ring in with all kinds of problems.

When you walk in through its front door you sometimes would believe that you had taken a trip through the looking glass or into an Aladdin's Cave. I went to see the boss lady, Louise Churchill, who greeted me in the most informal manner. She had removed her shoes; it had been a long day and her feet were tired. Ushered into her office we had to find somewhere for me to sit because everywhere was full of goods that had been donated by listeners for the charity that was receiving support at that moment.

Plymouth Sound certainly has its serious side and does influence quite a lot of what goes on in the City. It has listeners of all ages who expect Louise and her colleagues to do anything from finding a lost cat to getting the Council to change its mind about certain traffic lights. It is a voice that is appreciated and its fans have total faith in the successful outcome of whatever channel is being pursued at that moment and the sincerity of the broadcasters.

The B.B.C. carried the onus of providing the Westcountry with television for some years, until with a fanfare of trumpets Westward Television, with Peter Cadbury at the helm, burst upon the scene in its new building at Derry's Cross in 1961. Television was exciting in those days. Programmes broke down quite regularly, the skill of the continuity announcer and the versatility of the 'Anchormen' such as Barry Westward, Reggie Bosanquet and Kenneth Macleod, were called into play almost daily. There was an air of expectancy, too, with local people who suddenly found themselves with 'Television Personalities' doing their shopping in the market, or standing at the bar of a local hostelry enjoying a pint. Plymouth was lucky in that respect; it attracted a number of well known people to its Independent Television Station and spotting the face became a local pastime.

On a more serious note good programmes were made 'in house' on subjects dear to the heart of the Westcountry. Ted Tuckerman became a feature with his fishing spot. His call sign 'Tight Lines' was well known. The gardening programme, the programmes for women, all had a following. Many people would never miss the easy going humour and knowledge of Clive Gunnell as he took us walking around the Westcountry.

In the course of time internal and boardroom politics caused Westward to lose its franchise to Television South West. A change that the general public hardly noticed except for the Golden Hind that was missing on the screen at the beginning and end of programmes, to be replaced with the new T.S.W. Palm Tree logo. The same faces were on the screen every day, the building was still in use. What we did miss was the friendliness of the early days as more and more journalists took over in programmes, and there was less of the entrepreneurial abilities of performers. Autocues were used. Scripts, which had to be learned before Westward Diary went out every day, were discarded for the Idiot Board that rolled away in front of the speaker but out of sight of the audience. Spontaneity was discouraged. Television was beginning to become part of the furniture and no longer exciting.

Oddly the excitement only returned towards the end of T.S.W's time in office! People were going to pastures new or retiring. An air of sadness prevailed, but on that final programme on New Year's Eve, 1992, it was one big party. A party of nostalgia, more than a few tears, with almost all the famous and familiar names we had grown used to seeing over the years. Sue King fronted the programme with that doyen of Anchormen, Kenneth Macleod. The construction of the programme was a director's nightmare, but they sailed through the hour - long screening with a professionalism that one expected. When the programme finished over five hundred people drank, ate and danced the night away as they waited for midnight to strike. As the chimes of Big Ben sounded the hour, there was almost an uncanny silence. The engineer switched off, the lights went out, T.S.W was no more, and Westcountry Television sprang into life. For many it also heralded retirement, an unchartered future or for the lucky ones new opportunity.

Ian Stirling, a favourite at T.S.W and an expert on the 'Soaps' - it was almost as enjoyable hearing his lead in to Coronation Street, as it was to watch the programme - joined the company with a spot all his own, talking about every Soap, from Brookside to Emmerdale, Coronation Street to Take the High Road. Ruth Langsford too has gone to the new company, and I am sure we will see some of the other familiar faces as time goes by.

John Bartlett was there on that final night having spent years with both companies. This talented director has won many awards over the years for his work and he has a fund of fascinating trivia about the past. He remembers going out one morning at 5am to board the great French liner the Iles de France as it lay just inside the Breakwater; his quarry Bob Hope who was preparing to come ashore before going on to London. John says that even at the ungodly hour of the morning Bob Hope was alert, surrounded by his gag men and highly entertaining.

What a wealth of talent these two now defunct companies nurtured for Television. David Vine was once the Sports Reporter for Westward and how revered a name he has become amongst Sports Commentators. A young Sports writer for the company was Colin Malam whose columns I still enjoy in the Sunday papers. Then there was Jeremy Hands, a cub reporter who left Westward to become a household name at the time of the Falkland Conflict. Clive Gunnell must rate high on the list for the excellence of his walks around the region. His love of the country and a genius for winkling out interesting and sometimes offbeat places and people, made his slot in the programme one not to be missed.

Angela Rippon is one of Plymouth's own and this able lady endeared herself to us, first of all on the local newspaper before she went to the B.B.C and then to Westward. Her career has soared since those days but she will be the first to admit that Westward did her proud. Who will forget her dignity and immaculate enunciation when she read the News for the B.B.C - the first woman to do so. I will probably always remember her for that wonderful appearance with Morecombe and Wise.

Jan Leeming followed in Angela's footsteps having first spent some time at Westward as a reporter and announcer. There is another lady of great charm and poise. The other female who graces our screens regularly today is the irrepressible Judy Spiers, another Plymouth girl whose family own the Michael Spiers Jewellery shop in the City. She was always game for anything and didn't mind taking quite considerable personal risks to present a good feature. I wondered how her bubbling enthusiasm would cope with the more confined restraints of the B.B.C when she went to Pebble Mill but within a few months she had made her mark and the same sizzling personality leaps out of the screen whenever you watch her today.

Stuart Hutchison was a much loved announcer for many years and when he left the front of house to become a script writer, his friendly face was sadly missed. He is now a member of the Royal Shakespeare Company and it is not so long ago that he trod the boards of the Theatre Royal. More recently a friend of mine rang me from Bristol to say he was appearing there. Of course he and his co-announcers parented the inimitable rabbit, Gus Honeybun, whose daily presence on the screen dealing with childrens birthdays is something that is badly missed. Gus, for anyone who has not heard, has returned to Dartmoor and to his family but I am told he will be making guest appearances at Flambards in Helston.

Good programmes in their thousands have come from Westward and T.S.W over the last three decades and there have been some total disasters, the most major of them, and one that will go down in Television history, was 'Simply Wonderful' which opened the franchise for TSW. So awful is it that it is destined to be shown time and again in the sort of 'It will be alright on the Night' programmes. Meanwhile it resides in the National Film Archives.

How many people remember the early days when people like Cliff Richard would walk into Studio 1 to mime his latest record. It was used for chat shows, and at one time hired out for the Henson Organisation to record a series of Mother Goose Stories which eventually won an Emmy award. We know this organisation more for The Muppets. Then there were programmes like Landmark and Treasure Hunt with Kenneth Horne, Keith Fordyce, Kenneth Macleod and David Rogers as the Quizzmasters.

Few people will know that a tunnel exists connecting the Athenaeum Theatre to the Studios so that equipment could be moved in and out when the theatre was used for programmes, as it was in the early days. This very same tunnel provided an escape route for The Beatles one night when they were appearing at what is now the MGM cinema.

They were the great days of television which will never quite be repeated because today's television stations require less staff, have more sophisticated equipment and it is far easier to go on location than it was thirty years ago. Plymouth and the West Country should always be grateful for this band of people, professionals everyone of them, who brought Independent

Television to us so many years ago and for the next thirty years did a sterling job.

Hopefully a great deal of the film and video footage used by Westward and TSW together with BBC footage of the same period will become part of a charity in July, which will provide a library of film and video covering the South West for historians, students and the general public.

All sorts of film has turned up in odd places. Recently a Marconi engineer who fitted the Westward studios out thirty years ago, found some archive material in the attic of his house in Winchester. Chris Hunt contacted Peter Rodgers, former head of engineering at TSW and the technical advisor to the proposed charitable trust. Peter was delighted to be given the film which showed the launch of Westward Television. It shows the special train hired by Westward before it started broadcasting in April 1961. It was used as part of a publicity drive and travelled all around Devon, Cornwall and Somerset. It shows the train in London, speeches by the Lord Mayor of London and Peter Cadbury who was the boss of Westward.

TSW's reputation can never have been higher than in their last few months. They remained professional, competent and cheerful right to the end.

This professionalism and the sadness felt by their viewers has not made it an easy task for the new operators **Westcountry Television** to take over their mantle, but judging from the beginnings they will carry on this tradition of high standards. They are certainly innovative both in their presentation and in the content of the programmes I have seen so far. It will be interesting to watch their development over the next year or so when they have got all their small studios around the Region in action, and the building in Langage has become accustomed to its new role.

Tackling an hour long programme between six and seven o'clock five days a week is brave. People outside the Television world probably find it hard to visualise the amount of material that has to be gathered to make such a programme possible. It has to be topical, it has to be interesting, it has to give every part of the region its fair share of viewing time. The Presenters have to be not only decorative and personable as indeed our new ones are, they

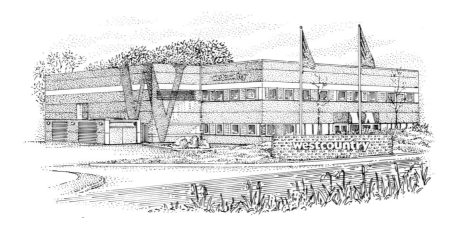

Westcountry Television

must also be skilled enough to hold the hour together. Westcountry has found the answer in Katy Haswell and David Foster.

I have read the avalanche of letters in the Evening Herald, most of which have not been complimentary to the new company. At this stage that is unfair. They are brand new even to having a totally new building at Langage. It all needs fine tuning and I am quite sure some programmes will disappear without trace but I wish them well. It is an exciting building to visit. Everything is buzzing there. Every day is a new challenge. It is almost as though Television is re-incarnated at Westcountry Television.

What is different in today's world of Television is the advent of various studios and people who accept commissions to produce programmes both for the B.B.C and Westcountry Television. It is becoming increasingly accepted in the credits at the end of a programme to read that a company that is not a Television Station has made whatever one has just viewed. One such operation is **Denham Productions** at Breakwater Road, Oreston. Owned by Chris Denham and Colin Rowe both emigres from local B.B.C, they produce a whole range of interesting pieces. They know their business, Colin Rowe is a gifted cameraman and Chris is used to fronting a programme. It is a good blend of talent. You can go to them to get a Video made for your business, to promote whatever you will. They are creative and full of commonsense. It need not frighten the living daylights out of you when you think of the cost of doing something of this nature. Give them a ring about your business or your idea, the number is 0752 404840. They are always willing to chat, ply you with coffee or something stronger if needs be.

The reasons for putting out so many commissioned programmes is no more than one simple word, 'Cost'. 'In House' Directors,, cameramen, researchers and all the many people who are involved in programme making have become expensive luxuries. To do it effectively requires a far greater number of permanent staff than any company wishes to carry. Commission an Independent Production Company to make a programme and there is only a one off payment for each subject covered. The commissioning company agrees a fixed price for a certain length programme or series. Apart from quality, it is no longer involved in any other expense than writing the cheque when the job is finished and accepted. It can pour with rain and hold up filming for days. The Producer can run off with the Director's wife, the cast can go sick, and any other of a million interruptions doesn't cost the TV company a penny. The company's only concern is that they will have the programme on time for viewing, and I am quite sure if the finished programme is late, a penalty clause built into the contract will be severe.

It all makes economic sense but I cannot help wondering if the general public is going to be the loser. We are liable to find ourselves limited in the type of programme on offer. I doubt if ever again we will see real blockbusters. For example would an Independent company be able to produce the brilliant 'Survival' type programme without hefty financial support? For anyone old enough to remember the mighty epics, 'The Forsyth Saga' and 'The Pallisers' which cost a fortune to make, must be a thing of the past.

The one thing that does please me enormously is the entrepreneurial spirit of those who knew that their days at TSW were numbered and that it was unlikely Westcountry Television would offer them anything. Many of them have struck out and started their own businesses doing something on the periphery of Television. It is the right spirit and I am sure that it is the right way to go.

CHAPTER 6

Money makes the City go round

Like any other city or town Plymouth has great need of its financial services whether it be the Clearing Banks, namely **Lloyds, National Westminster, Barclays, Midland** and **T.S.B.,** well known worldwide, or the more personal and specialist services required for all kinds of different reasons. It is a hard world out there and recent years have made it imperative to have a greater understanding and depth of knowledge than in years gone by. Almost everyone has a bank account of some kind and usually cheque cards and probably a Visa, Access, Switch, Amex, Connect or Diners card.

No longer wet about the ears and having known what it is to have money at one end of the scale and being completely broke at the other, I thought I knew a little about the workings of the financial world but my knowledge is sadly out of date, and I was soon re-educated in my travels as I searched for information and talked to anyone in this field who was willing to enlighten me. We are fortunate in this city in the number of willing experts there are to ease one's way through.

It is a morass, a spider's web, a great big black hole into which one can fall all too easily, even if you do read that the National Westminster has helped more small businesses than any other bank, Lloyds is the caring bank, Midland listens and T.S.B likes to say 'Yes'! I have forgotten how Barclays promote themselves - perhaps they should get a new advertising agency!

It is disturbing when we read that banks are shedding staff. There was a time when once personnel joined a bank there they stayed for their working life. Now no one's job is safe. I met the manager of one of the biggest Midland branches in the City, at the Plymouth Breakfast Club, held once a quarter in the Moat House. A gathering in which the guest list reads like a Who's Who of professional business in the City. Started some time ago by an enterprising, attractive woman, Ros James, who runs her own Insurance Brokerage from an office at Queen Anne's Battery. More of her business later. She linked up with Peat Marwick, McLintock and the club was born. It meets at 8am for a glass or two of Bucks Fizz, followed by an excellent breakfast, a short speech from the guest of honour who can be almost anyone with something interesting to tell us about Plymouth's needs and happenings. The meeting before last was addressed by the Chairman of the Groundwork Trust, the one I went to this week by Commander Lloyd Foster, the Commodore of the Royal Western Yacht Club, who apart from being extremely amusing, enlightened most of us on the need for the disabled and visually impaired to have facilities for sailing. He was looking for funding for this very worthwhile cause and received a cheque for £360 from the Breakfast Club to help this excellent scheme.

Looking round the room in which we were eating I saw and felt the power of the men and women there who one way or another control quite a lot of what happens in our lives. There were members from the banks, the building societies, the accountants, the insurance world, solicitors and many more influential people.

Going back to the Midland manager, he really underlined for me what I was discovering from every bank, that he felt himself to be far more a general manager running a business than a banker. His job was to organise, motivate and keep control. With more than 12,000 accounts at his branch he hadn't a hope of getting to know more than a few of his customers. Very different from the tenets of banking when he first joined. We talked briefly about the use of automated services which are gradually taking over. The use and abuse of cash cards and credit cards came into the equation as well. Of all the cards that are available Switch is the one that provides thieves with the easiest means of getting money illegally. He quoted some millions of pounds that are lost this way every year.

A Midland Branch

Years of experience within the banking industry does not seem to be any protection against redundancy. I learnt that it is becoming quite common practice for managers to be offered a redundancy package which they are entitled to refuse but should they have the temerity to do so they may only remain providing they are prepared to take demotion. There is worse to come. The following year they would be offered another redundancy package, nowhere as good as the first because the amount reflected the less senior role.

This is no reflection on any one bank because wherever I went I found this indifferent treatment to be standard. It amazes me that the banks have such loyal staff even if morale is low. From my own personal experience with **Nat West** over twenty years, I have always been treated with courtesy, patience and tolerance - and no, I am not trying to protect my overdraft!

The role of bank managers has changed too. There is no such animal as an entrepreneurial Bank Manager. Such activity is frowned upon. Gut instinct as to whether a business or a person is worth backing is overridden by the soulless computer. This monster only relates hard facts. You can be successful and have satisfactory trading figures, yet in the past there is a black mark somewhere on your credit rating so the unrelenting computer says 'no' to almost any request. This can be disastrous for some businesses. The reality of this was brought home to me by the **T.S.B.** who are busy replacing their senior branch managers with juniors who are only given authority to lend within the band of £500 - £1,000 to anyone. After that it has to be the computer's decision.

For the individual customer, too, times have changed. The personal touch has disappeared and been replaced by specialists - your 'Personal Banker' as Barclays call them. The trouble is that they change so often you never get to know them or they you and even less do they understand your needs. This means that you rarely get to see 'The Manager' and even if you do he is not empowered to give you financial advice in case he offends the Lautro or Fimbra rulings. I have been lucky in as much as I bank at **National Westminster** on Mutley Plain and in the twenty years I have banked there each manager has believed in the open door policy which has meant that I have always been able to talk about problems and successes. Each incumbent has not always been able to solve the problem or obligingly say 'yes' but I have always found them comforting and understanding. I, like many people, live in daily dread that this reassuring shoulder may be removed.

I remember well the time when one of my twin daughters got married and I ran up a gigantic personal and unsecured overdraft which after the event needed tackling; I was still Persona Grata. I called in at the branch with the unmarried twin and a piece of wedding cake just after the wedding. The manager looked at her slightly strangely, enquired how the wedding went and one or two other niceties. The accompanying twin cottoned on to the fact that he was muddling her with the bride. She put him right and in so doing the man turned a paler shade of grey. 'My God,' he said, his voice trembling, "There cannot be two of you! You are not thinking of getting married are you?" Today I doubt such a facility would be available as readily. It was permitted because the manager knew me and he had the right of making the decision knowing that if I undertook to repay the money I would do so. Such decisions today are taken at Head Office level, to whom I am just a number.

Whether it is because Mutley Plain has the advantage of being a long, wide, straight street leading from the residential area of the city into the centre or simply because it has always been a useful shopping area, it has managed to retain a curious air of prosperity and dignity about it. Most of its buildings are old even if they have had modern facades installed. It is the home of two supermarkets, Gateway and Plymouth Co-op. It has building societies, solicitors, chemists and takeaways but more and more it has become a place of professional business.

Nat West, Mutley Plain, still manages to retain something of the old-fashioned look about it which is reassuring. Customers are people who need greeting with a cheery smile, which they get in abundance from the counter staff. Sometimes this is not a two-way response. A pity, smiling is a great tonic and costs nothing. A beautician will tell you that indeed it uses less muscles - 17 to be precise, instead of the 42 if you frown! One young man at the branch even remembers my account number when I ring up for a balance - probably it tells you how often I need reassurance but nonetheless it keeps the personal touch and is much appreciated.

None of the banks seem to make any special provision for blind or disabled people. I wonder if they have ever given it consideration at the highest level. It was brought home to me when I watched a blind lady arrive in my branch where there is a system of collecting a number from a roll which when it corresponds with a flashing light above the counter means it is your turn. This lady had no idea what her number was nor could she see when her number was flashing. My son noticed her and exchanged his earlier number with hers, guiding her to the right counter. Here she was greeted by a welcoming girl who obviously knew her, dealt with her needs, sorting out brand new notes so that by touch, the lady could recognise whether she was handling a fiver or tenner, and placing coins in appropriately marked bags. The girl could do no more because such is the need for security that she was locked securely behind her counter and unassailable. The lady was reliant on the general public rather than the bank. Had she been in a wheelchair access would have been impossible because of the steps that lead into the bank.

I noticed a letter in our local evening paper which endorses what I have just written about - the humanity of bank employees, Nat West in particular. It was from the Public Relations Officer of St Luke's Hospice League of Friends and he was high in praise of a lady, Val Dunn, of the Nat West, who by her tireless efforts, and the willingness on the part of the staff to dig deep into their pockets had presented a cheque for £2,200 to the cause.

Reading the Daily Telegraph the other day I was amused to see that Nat West are making a little money for themselves by selling off 82,000 of their Piggy Banks for 45p each. Apparently children are no longer attracted to the little pink porkers. If you wanted to buy one yourself it would cost you between £3.50 and £7.50 to acquire what is supposedly a collector's item. Somebody has got a good deal out of the bank.

Whilst I am talking about the National Westminster it is quite interesting to look back at some of the old branches which were almost always privately owned banks before they came under the bigger financial umbrella. One has to remember in doing so that before it became National Westminster it was the National Provincial. One of the first businesses it acquired in Devonport was in Fore Street in which I worked for 6 months in 1941. Previously owned by Husband & Co, the owner, Thomas Husband was forced to sell the bank in 1839 due to the extravagant spending of his sons! I wonder how many customers he rapped over the knuckles for over-spending whilst he was trying to tackle the problems within his own business?

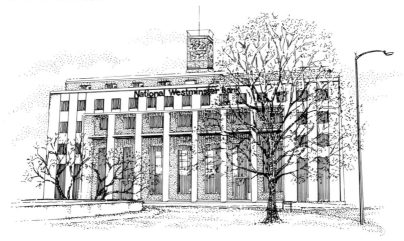

National Westminster at St. Andrews Cross

There is no doubt that much of the general public, especially the small businessman, is not happy with the policy of the big banks, particularly in relationship to charges. There are always two sides to any story and it was to **Lloyds'** Kevin Waterman, that I went to talk about the role of regional banking today. In 1992 he was the manager of Lloyds Bank Area Director's office, Tamar, which covers the Plymouth branches and surrounding branches in both East Cornwall and parts of the South Hams but for some years he was the branch manager in the Devonport Road, Stoke, branch and before that at various other branches. A man of wide experience and a liking for people.

It was he who painted the bank's side of the story. The layman forgets the enormous cost the banks incur operating people's personal accounts and this was particularly brought home to him when the Dockyard started paying their employees by cheque rather than the traditional cash. Not a popular move but on the face of it great for the banks in the Devonport area. Banks found themselves opening literally thousands of accounts. Good business? Promotion for the Manager? Not a bit of it, mainly a large headache, because for many customers the account was credited with the salary or wage, and the full amount was drawn out the same day. The bank made little, found itself with the cost of administration, printing cheque books, paying in books, providing statements, the staff put under pressure on pay days and all for little gain to the bank. Someone has to cover this sort of cost, so obviously it becomes reflected in the charges to every customer. It was an angle I had not considered before. Basically we should look on bank charges much in the same way we do for service charges for water, electricity, gas etc. Yes, I know we groan about those too.

Talking to Kevin Waterman was fascinating. He comes from a banking family who had all worked for merchant bankers Barings, or C. Hoare and Co. in London - very upmarket, and in the past private banks. Hoare's still is, I believe.

The pace of life in these banks is totally different from the general run of the mill. Until recently frock coated staff served their respected and highly valued clientele. If you go into the bank you will find it panelled and gracious, a far cry from the modernistic Lloyds building across the road. Coutts, of course, is where the Queen banks. When in 1969 Kevin realised that at Hoare's he had little hope of promotion other than stepping into dead men's shoes, he made the move to Lloyds. It was quite a traumatic change for him and took him some time to get used to. The transition has obviously been successful. His senior role in Lloyds headquarters at Crownhill is proof of that. Incidentally, he is to be congratulated on the major honour of being elected a Fellow of the Chartered Institute of Bankers. It is the highest grade of membership, awarded in recognition of his status in the banking profession and for his contribution towards banking education.

From him I also learnt that it is almost as difficult to get a job in a bank today as it is to get work as an actor! Gone are the days when school leavers could look to the banks for their first - and frequently lifetime job. Or guarantees that graduates can look for entry into the banks at a higher level. At the present time there is almost no intake. One wonders what sort of skilled people will be lost to other professions in a few years to come. The machine in the hole in the wall will have to do instead, I suppose.

Lloyds are to be congratulated in funding a project that over the next three years will put small businesses in the South West, some of them from Plymouth, under the spotlight. The objective is to target the successes of small businesses in a bid to boost the bank's services to South West firms.

The bank will look at the most successful aspects of small companies which will then be used to shape the operations of the bank's small business unit in order to offer greater advice and support. In the bank's opinion the recession offers a prime opportunity to focus on the difficulties being experienced by small firms and to see how some of them have managed to find their way through this minefield. The information garnered will be used to tailor the bank's services to small businesses so that they can improve their support, helping to generate those success factors in other businesses. The quarterly reports which are to be published should make interesting reading especially when you consider that Plymouth has an enormous number of small businesses which have come into being, in many cases, from the men being no longer required in the Dockyard. They have invested their redundancy money in all manner of outlets. I have visited several of them and look forward to writing about them in another chapter.

In general discussion with several of Plymouth's bank managers I found a consensus of opinion that it was becoming more and more patently obvious that financial management should become part of the educational curriculum. Fewer young people would get into monetary difficulties if they were taught simple budgeting from an early age and slightly more complex matters as they grew older. With increasing numbers of people buying their own homes, using credit cards and all the ancillary services, it is a subject that needs to be grasped at an early age. Many of these managers were prepared to give some of their time to visiting schools to give talks. Modern Plymouthians need to know about handling money at an early age if we are to become a force in this country and in Europe with which Plymouth has close links. Perhaps something that the educational hierarchy should consider.

Talking about private banks and handling money reminds me of my seven years with the Bank of England. I wonder how many people remember, or even know, that Plymouth had a branch of the Old Lady of Threadneedle Street, which survived the bombing and stood virtually where the China Garden restaurant is today. You did not apply for a job there - you were introduced by someone who knew your family!

The young ladies who worked there, from these carefully selected families, used to report at the branch at 9am and could expect to leave by 4pm. We had to wear either grey, navy or black suits or dresses, hats, gloves and no coloured nail varnish. A string of pearls and pearl earrings were the only jewellery permitted other than wedding and engagement rings. Stockings were the other requirement. Sounds daft but in wartime that was not always easy. The more adventurous of us painted our legs with a repulsive sort of tan coloured paint and then attempted to draw a straight line up the back of the leg. Frowned upon of course, but there was a war on! The Bank of England, not nationalised in those days, does not have managers. It has Agents. The customers, too, were different. The Bank of England was where the other banks banked, as well as the Post Office, the armed services and the Dockyard. Apart from that there were no more than a hundred private customers.

As members of staff we were also given the privilege of using its banking facilities. It was quite something to have a Bank of England cheque book something I missed when I left to become the first English woman cashier in Barclays, Dominion, Colonial and Overseas - as it was then: Barclays International today - in Valletta, Malta. That is another story which will come into my memoirs 'Sixty Eight Misspent Years' to be published after my death - a promise I have made to my children!!

We were incredibly well cared for - lunch was provided and for that we used to go over to the Duke of Cornwall Hotel where a special room was set aside for us. On marriage we were given dowries, the amount varying according to the years of service. I very nearly did not qualify for mine - I eloped one afternoon at the end of working hours, got married in the Registry Office which was then in Thorn Park and promptly returned to the Bank the next day. It took the Mandarins sitting in Threadneedle Street some time to decide whether this was quite cricket!

One of my tasks was to check notes for forgeries, something that seems to be coming to the fore again. I have read that pub managers in Plymouth are refusing to take £50 notes because of the number of forgeries in circulation. My role was not exactly demanding but carried the benefit of an additional half day's leave if one was detected. All this changed in 1941 when Hitler bombarded England not only with bombs but with a deluge of forged five pound notes; they were the large white variety then, not these awful notes we have now when ageing eyes have difficulty in deciding whether you are taking a five or ten pound note out of your purse. As for the silver coins - well! The hope was to disrupt the economy. Finding forged notes became a daily happening. At one time I had clocked up a year's leave in half days. That benefit came to a rapid end!

When I left the Bank of England to join my husband in Malta in 1947, I was seconded to Barclays D.C.& O but I will always remember the Agent, a Mr Hopkins, presenting me with a leaving gift and adding to it a little speech, summed up with the words that they would miss me although he was not too sure that I had a banking temperament!

It was quite interesting the other day watching one of the bright young ladies on Nat West's staff discover a £50 forgery and then report it. She had no idea I knew what she was doing - it took me back in time. At least they haven't found a machine that will automatically do that task yet - or have they? We used to count these notes in their thousands and detection was not difficult because the slightest variation on the note jumped out at you. I am told that a machine is in use in the banks, as it is in commercial businesses, but the tellers still prefer the old fashioned way of detection by touch - it's quicker!

From the Bank of England you could see Lloyds Bank across the road. This building is now the successful 'Bank' pub. I wonder how many people who drink there would believe that two of Lloyds staff would stack about half a million in used notes, packed in brown parcels containing £5,000, onto a rickety trolley and just push it over the road to the Bank of England. No one thought about armed robbers in those days. Bank counters were unprotected by bullet proof screens, which reminds me of a splendid print I have with the caption: Bank Clerk to Customer, 'I am sorry, madam, I cannot cash this cheque across the counter'. Reply from customer, 'Never mind, I'll just come round the other side'! All that sort of freedom has gone as we protect ourselves against attacking thugs.

It was not until the American forces arrived in Plymouth and used the Bank of England as their paymaster that the bank's staff realised people, other than themselves, were not quite so sanguine or so trusting. The Americans arrived with an armoured truck escorted by at least two other vehicles from which troops leapt and surrounded the building, rifles at the ready.

One of our jobs was to escort money and bullion from Plymouth to London or to one of the other Bank of England branches in Liverpool, Southampton or Bristol. This we would do with no other protection for the consignment than two members of staff sitting in a reserved compartment next to the wagon in which the money was stacked. We were paid £5 'Danger Money' for this exercise. So laid back was it that I can remember sitting on a tea chest which housed thousands of pounds, on Platform 7 of North Road Station waiting for the arrival of the train and being asked by a fellow traveller what time the train was due to leave!

Those were the days of banking when we did not have machines; we had to count every column of figures in our heads and at the end of the day we had to balance to the penny. If we did not we stayed in the Bank until we did. I can remember several tortuous times when I had a date and was not allowed to leave because we were 2 shillings out! Now I am told that the Banks would rather make mistakes and pay for them than have sufficient staff or pay overtime to ensure an accurate balance is made. It is an eye opener and makes one realise how carefully statements should be checked.

What is the future of banking? Will we really be deprived of our own branches and be reduced to punching machines for the service we require? Will home computing have its place in the controlling of one's housekeeping? What happens though if you are a small trader and need change? What happens if your cash card wears out and gets jammed? For someone like me who can remember the days when grocers used to produce a chair at the counter for the customer to sit on whilst giving an order, an order which would then be delivered by a boy on a bike, I realise that I have survived the loss of all that and got used to self service supermarkets, so I suppose one would adapt eventually. I would prefer to back the opinion of University of Plymouth lecturer, Dr Ian Chaston, who is convinced that High Street banks should go back to the good old days and provide the right services and backing for local firms.

This was music to my ears. Dr Chaston, who is the principal lecturer of the University's Plymouth Business School, has just completed a five-year study of the relationship between South West firms and their banks. His findings are alarming, demonstrating a worrying breakdown between local businesses and their banks. He believes there is an urgent need to rekindle the old feeling that you should be able to rely on your bank to be helpful instead of ever demanding.

Old fashioned values, he believes, are important and require re-emphasis to rebuild business confidence. He calls for a fundamental shift in the way UK banks work with their business clients. He is not suggesting a new breed of banker, thank God, but quite the opposite, going back to the old ways of doing things. To the fifties and sixties, in fact, when the branch manager had an in-depth knowledge of local businesses, and was seen as an important external source of advice and assistance in managing the financial aspects of the business.

Dr Chaston proposes that the lending authority should be moved away from the regional headquarters and placed back with the branch manager who is nearest to the customer which would encourage bankers at all levels to be more pro-active in seeking ways of helping business clients who have the potential to develop successful enterprises.

How right he is, especially if this city of ours is to find a way of rebuilding confidence and working relationships between business and the banks, particularly in the small business sector. Without this initiative economic recovery is going to remain more of a hope than a fact.

Most people still regard the clearing banks as their means of getting help for expansion or to provide the bridging at awkward moments. Plymouth now has another source of assistance from **Trevint** who operate from Trevint House, Strangways Villas Truro, but nonetheless have been in a position to assist several local companies. They work with the support of the Devon and Cornwall Training and Enterprise Council. Their business is bringing investors and companies together through its **'Business Angels' Programme**. As a result of this they are playing a leading role in opening up new areas of finance, impartially, efficiently and confidentially.

Having recognised that Devon and Cornwall as a region is rich in enterprising companies with great potential, they have aligned that potential with a sizeable community of experienced individuals - some still active, others retired - including directors and professionals who are looking for suitable investments. Many of these people wish to play a 'Hands-On' role whereby they can play an active part in getting the most from their investment by helping a business really expand.

For many companies just providing the finance is simply not enough. Perhaps even more vital to the success of the company are the management skills and business acumen of the experienced investor which helped generate his wealth in the first place. In short by investing enthusiasm and enterprise as well as finance, a Business Angel helps overcome not only the equity gap but the all-important experience gap, too.

It is quite a new world for many small or medium size businesses. Not unlike a dating agency which works towards a marriage. In the first instance potential investors complete a simple questionnaire. This helps identify the type and size of investment as well as the market sector in which the Angel might be interested. At the same time, companies requiring finance are screened and those with potential are entered into a database. This is matched in a three stage process against investors to arrange a suitable 'marriage'. If the match shows spark the investor is sent a summary of the business plan.

One of the most important aspects of any 'Marriage' is compatability. As with any relationship, it is vital that both parties can work together for mutual benefit. If the chemistry isn't right the match should not even be considered.

Trevint is perhaps unique in successfully combining strict commercial disciplines with an overall regard for the prosperity of the region.

Devon and Cornwall have a higher proportion of small and medium sized businesses than anywhere in the U.K. However this wealth of opportunity has not, until the advent of Trevint, been matched by a corresponding availability of financial infrastructure.

You may ask what is in it for the Business Angel? Well, it allows the investor the opportunity to shape his or her own financial return by virtue of their own efforts.

The participating companies are usually on a growth curve possibly wanting to open into an unexplored niche. This can be a relatively high-risk area where the financial reward may be unpredictable. The point is that the satisfaction derived from being an angel is only partly measured in terms of return on capital employed. It is more about 'hot buttons'... the thrill and excitement of being there. The sheer fun of being at the sharp end of a dynamic new enterprise. The knowledge that but for the courage in becoming an Angel, it might never have happened. It also requires a long term view and the vision to see potential turn into profit, even if it takes a little time.

Investment funds are available from £5,000 to £500,000 so it appeals to a vast number of people whether they be Angels or those looking for Angelic assistance.

It appeals to the Angel who has retired from a senior position with a large company and can see the immediacy of the venture. The short chain of command and the ability to modify course and attack new markets quickly and directly. It is the thrill of driving a highly manoeuvrable power boat after leaving the bridge of a huge tanker - a simile highly applicable to Plymouth.

Having dealt with large businesses and decisions that may take months, a deciding factor here may be the utter simplicity. Convinced of the feasibility of the venture and satisfied that a working relationship can be established, the marriage can proceed remarkably quickly.

How does the business of looking for an Angel find help in this way? It may be referred from banks, accountants, solicitors or financial advisors. Others can go directly to Trevint's offices in Devon and Cornwall. John Berry is the Managing Director and his telephone number is 0872 223883 or 0392 435666.

It should also be remembered that Trevint offer a complete range of services that few can match. They have a management consultancy team who have had direct experience in running businesses for themselves and others. Grant advice helps make Trevint a 'one-stop' resource centre where all your business problems can be resolved. Training is available across a broad spectrum of disciplines by a team who work within a 'quality standard' and benefit from an on going development programme.

The DTI Enterprise Initiative Consultancy allows one to take advantage of government subsidies and ensures value for money.

The Management Service enables you to take an experienced Trevint Director into your business to advise and support in key strategic areas such as Finance and Marketing.

They are capable of dealing with investment management, corporate finance, business plans, mergers and acquisitions, the preparation of prospectuses and willingly introduce businesses to City finance, where investment capital is required. No one at Trevint has overlooked the need for European initiatives and their expertise is invaluable in matching companies with financial institutions, grant authorities and professionals throughout Europe.

Many of us do not know what the unobtrusive **Nykredit** do in their building in what was the old Plymouth Telephone Exchange. The entrance to their offices is subdued and there is an air about the place as if nothing is urgent but under that quiet exterior is a hive of intense activity financing and supporting businesses of every shape and size throughout the country. Most of their clients hardly even know where Plymouth is but this does not take away from the value of such a prestigious business in the heart of the city.

Nykredit, a Danish company, acquired a Plymouth based bank some years ago and despite pressure to move, the company has remained in Plymouth. Like many others, the Danish parent company did not really believe that any financial organisation could run successfully outside the City of London and certainly not in somewhere so deep in the South West. It was almost as if they thought England stopped at Bristol. However, the efforts of the locally based staff, reflecting so well the qualities of tenacity and strength of character of west country people, have ensured a continuing presence for Nykredit in Plymouth. The more successful that companies like Nykredit become in the City of Plymouth the more readily will it be recognised that this great city is a place of influence.

For centuries men of business have been used to organise and regulate the finances of people both in the private sector and in business. I suppose the modern equivalent is the accountant. How powerful they have become. With a plethora of good national and international companies in Plymouth it was not easy to choose one of the major firms to write about. Most of us recognise the names of the big companies today because the recession has brought so many businesses to their knees and in need of help from Receivers who almost always are accountants. We read daily about Peat Marwick McClintock, Touche Ross, Ernst & Young, Grant Thornton, Cork Gully, an arm of Coopers & Lybrand being appointed as receivers or liquidators.

It was to **Coopers & Lybrand** that I went to seek out one of the partners, firstly because he was kind enough to spare time for me and secondly because I could not resist the fact that he was called Francis Drake. This Francis Drake has not been in Plymouth for many years and was quite astounded at the furore his arrival caused in the City. Coopers & Lybrand's Public Relations department worked overtime sorting out photocalls alongside Sir Francis Drake's statue on Plymouth Hoe and the present Francis Drake was interviewed endlessly. The excitement has, of course, died down but it was especially interesting to me to discover that he was a direct descendant of Drake and had lost sight of where there were other members of the Drake family.

I found myself talking to him about **Buckland Abbey** on the outskirts of Plymouth, and how it came to belong to the City. Although Sir Francis died childless, his brother inherited the 13th-century Cistercian monastery with the vast estates that Drake had acquired in his life time. He was no financial lightweight. He was very aware of the value of money and looked for every means by which he might acquire greater wealth. I wonder who was his accountant? Buckland Abbey was held in the family until 1946 by which time it belonged to the Drakes of Ash at Yarcombe and it was Captain Meyrick of that family who ordered the sale of Buckland Abbey. Fortunately just five days before it was to be auctioned it was bought by Captain Arthur Rudd, a Yelverton landowner, who later gave the Abbey to the National Trust on the understanding that it would be carefully restored and, on completion, the City of Plymouth should take over the responsibility and open the Abbey to the public as a Drake Naval and West Country Folk Museum. This was done and now all Plymouth and people from around the world can enjoy the beauty that it has to offer. I was also able to tell today's Francis Drake that the manor at Sampford Spiney, once belonging to Sir Francis. is now occupied by Andrew Spedding and his family, another of Drake's descendants, who incidentally writes for the other series of books that I do, 'An Invitation to Lunch, Dine, Stay and Visit'.

We eventually got back to the purpose of my visit. One of the greatest pleasures I have had in compiling this book is the garnering of interesting stories and links which I would never have known about otherwise. Why did this Francis Drake choose to come to Plymouth? The answer came without hesitation. The quality of life here is so much better for bringing up a family. Plymouth and the surrounding area offer just about everything that one could need.

Coopers & Lybrand have a respected name throughout the world. They are the largest firm of accountants and management consultants in the United Kingdom. In addition to being able to handle the most complex of tasks they continue to provide advice and deliver their services through personal contact with their clients.

I first knew about them when I married, and acquired one of their senior partners, Henry Benson, as a cousin by marriage. In those days, as I remember, they had not ventured all over the country and the world. The questions I wanted answered were really fairly simple. What were the differences between the smaller local accountancy firms and the giants? Why should an individual or a company choose the latter which inevitably must cost more? I have to admit the answers I got were nowhere near as simple as the question but the fact, basically, is that the bigger firms have more resources from which to provide expert advice and assistance in every possible way that a client might conceivably require. This is particularly important today with so many changing regulations, so many opportunities for companies to look in Europe for new openings. The smaller companies are expert in their own right but possibly have neither the experience nor a partner specialising in the many and varied aspects of financial controls.

You have only to look at the wide range of booklets arrayed in the reception area of any large chartered accountants, bank or solicitors to recognise that skill, time and a great deal of money has been invested in what they do. Coopers & Lybrand are no exception. Summing up what I heard, saw and subsequently read, their mission is to be the leading business advisors. This is reflected in the fact that no longer do they just employ accountants. Their professionals include economists, engineers, I.T. and telecommunications specialists, strategists, marketing professionals, lawyers, actuaries, human resource and recruitment specialists, insolvency practitioners, educationalists, public sector advisors, corporate finance and acquisition specialists. Slightly overwhelming isn't it?

In the last year or so they have acted on over 100 deals worth over £900 million for companies such as Pilkington and Hanson. They act for both public and private companies.

Insolvency Practitioners tend to be part of these bigger accountancy companies. Sadly this has become quite a large and lucrative part of so many of the bigger firms. Yet on the bright side because of the expertise of the appointed receivers many companies have been rescued and have been able to continue because the receiver has known where to pinpoint the good areas of an ailing business and find a buyer or an investor willing to take on the challenge. It is an expensive business and one that no firm of chartered accountants would touch unless the company could upfront sufficient money to make the work entailed viable. The lack of these funds is frequently why a company goes to the wall even though it might well be salvageable. The advice for anyone in this situation or teetering towards the brink is to ask for a meeting, which is free of charge, and then take the advice given. Most small businesses tend to struggle along until it is too late when perhaps approaching Coopers & Lybrand or a similar company at an earlier date might save the day. Even in these hard times we have already seen from the activities of Trevint that there are people out there interested and willing to invest time and finance in good businesses.

For some people going to see one's accountant is almost as dire as visiting the dentist. The reception area of these firms is all important. If the receptionist is welcoming then the first ordeal is over. A comfortable chair, magazines and a cup of coffee whilst I waited to see Francis Drake allowed me to put myself in the position of a client. Yes, I would feel reassured here. There are many offices I have visited which have been soulless and depressing. That must affect staff as much as the client. Familiarity breeds contempt and I suppose those who own offices of that kind must have grown used to it but I wish they would open their eyes and see if they themselves would really like to be the visitor.

How do accountants keep up with the constantly changing goal posts of regulations concerning tax, VAT etc? With great difficulty I suspect. Recently I had a visit from the VAT man - something else we all dread. In this instance, the Inspector, Mr Wallace, could not have been nicer nor more helpful. He used to be with what he calls the 'rummage department'. In other words active Customs duty which he thoroughly enjoyed. That is very much a 'hands on' occupation which includes haring about Plymouth Sound in inflatable rubber boats in order to board suspicious yachts or other marine craft trying to get in unnoticed. He was a circumspect man and did not reveal the secrets of his trade but from my office we see quite a lot of activity especially as the Customs and Excise have a vast warehouse directly below us in which they have all manner of merchandise - a bit like an Aladdin's Cave. Because of the easy access from France and Spain, Plymouth is a centre of the drug traffic and it is only the vigilance of the Customs men that prevents it being more serious than it is.

My purpose in mentioning Mr Wallace was because he was quite honest about the difficulty in keeping up with all the VAT regulations. Of course, one can get advice from accountants on how to proceed but even they have similar difficulties, so fast do things change. The advice Mr Wallace would give to any young business with questions to ask, is to ring or go and see the VAT enquiry office who are delighted to help and are completely on the ball when it comes to the changing rules.

Mr Wallace also told us of seminars that he and some of his colleagues run in conjunction with Enterprise Plymouth, in which they unravel the mysteries of the complex laws and help new businesses to start on the right lines. These are fairly informal occasions and discussions take place over tea and biscuits. How many of us know the advantages of Cash Accounting for example? I did not even know what it meant let alone that it was advantageous to young companies with a turnover of less than £300,000.

Another assumption on my part was that a visitation from the VAT man was a regular occurrence but this is not so unless there is any major misdemeanour. It can be anything from two to six years from the start of a business before someone comes to see you. Their work load is so heavy that more frequent visits are just about impossible which is why businesses are asked to keep their records for a minimum of six years.

One way and another most of us have dealings with building societies during the course of our lives. In the present climate paying the mortgage has become a number one priority and a frequent heartache to many people. Plymouth is no different from anywhere else. What concerns me is that there seems to be no standard policy operating. The reaction of the various societies to people in trouble with their mortgages varies tremendously. People who know how to fight their battles fare better than most because they will not take the local branch's dictum as the only one, and go directly to Head Offices who have more scope to co-operate with mortgagees if the going is getting tough. Some societies seem to have an abundance of common sense. For example the Chelsea Building Society took the view with one situation that although the arrears were enormous it was better to keep the family in their home rather than repossess. For two years they have allowed that family to pay only half the required monthly payment with the proviso that at the end of that time the mortgage payment will revert to its rightful amount. A generous and sensible solution for which the family are extremely grateful. This underlines what can be done if both parties are willing. In this case the family went directly to the Head Office in Cheltenham, told their story in quite a short space of time to the man handling their case. He was sympathetic, understanding and when the proposal came from the branch on his say so, the terms were clearly laid down and have had to be adhered to. It was worth going to the top. The moral of the story is that building societies want to help but do not always know how, so if you cannot get assistance from the local branch, go higher. You have nothing to lose and everything to gain.

One building society manager, to whom I talked told me that the greatest problem they have is that people in trouble through redundancy, loss of job or the failure of a business, tend not to pay the mortgage and the arrears just mount. He said to me that if only people would pay even a third of the sum due each month and at the same time start a dialogue, half the re-possessions would probably not happen. I suppose pride, perhaps optimism that things will get better, gets in the way and suddenly it is too late to do anything. Ignoring letters and telephone calls is something else that does not help when there are problems. Facing up to it is the only answer. It will not go away of its own accord.

Like the Clearing Banks the various building societies in the city take an active part in community life. **The Halifax** is no exception. Undoubtedly the biggest of them all, the Halifax in Plymouth has a Business Development Officer, part of whose job is to support worthwhile causes. He told me that the Halifax is committed to the local community and countrywide, not just locally. I talked to him just after he had presented a cheque for £1,000 to Andrew Ashley, Managing Director of **Enterprise Plymouth Limited**. The donation was towards a Youth Enterprise Centre to help 16-25 years old start up in business.

The business advice centre at Enterprise Plymouth Limited was formed in 1984 with the direct involvement of P.C.C. to answer the needs of people who, threatened with redundancy, are contemplating self-employment. Andrew Ashley finds that Enterprise Agencies are busier than they have ever been and more and more people are coming to them for advice before starting their own business. Enterprise Plymouth is part of 'Business in the Community' and provides assistance and guidance to new and existing small businesses. Within its wide range of activities it gives practical assistance to innovators who have ideas but lack funds or marketing experience to get their product to the people. That is simplifying their role. When you walk into the building in Somerset Place, Stoke, you can just feel the 'get up and go' attitude. Experts in all sorts of fields are there to offer guidance not just in starting a business but on - going. It is somewhere where you can call in for a chat to air views, talk out problems or whatever is needed. Donations from the bigger companies like the one from the Halifax, are always gratefully received and you will see from the board in the entrance hall that many Plymouth businesses including National Westminster, the Midland, Lloyds Bank and Peat Marwick McLintock are regular supporters.

Enterprise Plymouth is not the only place from which young people wanting to start their own businesses, can get help. **The Prince's Youth Business Trust** is a charity which helps young people set up in business by offering advice and finance. Their aim is to help you if your circumstances make it especially difficult to get started. It is specifically for people aged between 18 and 25, up to 30 if you are disabled. There are loans of up to £5,000 with very reasonable repayments and a bursary of up to £1,500 per person in a business. There is also a grant of £250 which can be used for market research. All you need is a good project, determination and the will to succeed. One of the nicest things about it is that it does not look unfavourably on young offenders who have been daft enough to get into trouble and are looking for a second chance in life.

Andrew Smy is the Regional Manager, a man of great talent and enthusiasm who thought that after he retired from the Devon Property Department he would relax and pursue his favourite pastimes, sailing and photography. His retirement present was a set of charts on the Irish Sea and Outer Hebrides to help him navigate his boat around the British Isles - something he had always wanted to do. He found himself caught up in this very worthwhile trust and abandoned the idea of sailing any further once he reached Fowey! Supposedly he only works two days a week but once you become interested in the Prince's Youth Business Trust it tends to winkle its way into your life almost every day in some form or another.

To find out about the Trust you can write to The Prince's Youth Business Trust at 6th floor, Inter-City House, Plymouth Station, Plymouth PL4 6AA or telephone 0752 251051. It seems to me that the only stipulation, other than a good idea is that you must have tried elsewhere to raise the money. Presumably if your bank has said No, that suffices.

What they will want from you is your ideas plus a business plan. Sounds a bit daunting if you have not done anything like this before but this is where Enterprise Plymouth comes into it. You can go there and they will help you sort the business plan, the market place and many other things before you are in a position to present your case to the board of the Trust. What is so encouraging about the work of the Trust is that the rate of survival of people it has supported is over sixty six per cent after 3 years - a much better success rate than the banks'. This is really because of the dedication of the people working for the trust. They are skilled and wise. Their Business Adviser, Bill Bates, is a retired bank manager and with him on the board are a senior accountant, a director of one of the Clearing Banks, a well versed solicitor and the manager of a big Building firm. It is this board that determines the awards. They try to work fairly swiftly so that an applicant is not left in uncertainty any longer than necessary.

You would be amazed at the breadth of enterprises in which the Trust has invested money. A Graduate set up as a clown, a co-operative graphic and design studio, a maker of children's furniture to name but a few. Everyone who receives financial help from the Trust is allocated a volunteer business adviser who will give free business advice.

The Trust also provides valuable marketing opportunities. It stages an annual trade show and arranges space in other exhibitions to enable young people to display their wares to large audiences. Advantageous start up insurance , free legal advice, the opportunity to buy low-cost well maintained vans, free membership of a breakdown service, publicity, video training packages on accountancy and computers as well as competition prizes for money, fax and answering machines, are all part of what is on offer. It is a scheme that has been admirably thought out. To cap it all, almost always National Westminster will match the grant from the Trust with a £1,500 loan.

I had not realised that **The Prince's Business Youth Trust and The Prince's Trust** were not one and the same thing. Whilst they are complimentary to one another they act independently and answer different needs. I was lucky enough to meet a super lady, Jeanie Moore, who currently chairs the West Devon Committee for the Prince's Trust. Her bubbling personality, deep commitment, sense of humour and her 'people handling' ability make her the ideal person for this demanding role. Her committee makes grants of up to £800 to individual applicants and £2,500 to local organisations, with one of her committee visiting every single applicant. Her main job is to ensure that her committee acts swiftly when young people contact them. She told me that she knows of no other grant-giving organisation where those responsible for giving grants meet and talk with potential recipients. If the word 'committee' makes you think of stuffy grey - suited ageing gentlemen who have no notion of the needs of the young, you would be totally out of order in this context. Jeanie's band are made up of alive, alert people from all walks of life, most of them in the eighteen to sixty bracket.

They are active men and women who keenly relish the task of helping a young person or persons who may have quite unusual requests, perhaps holding on to a dream which seems to have no hope of becoming reality until they talk with a member of the committee. The Prince's Trust can give them a lifeline which may well lead to confidence in themselves, growth and personal freedom. Taking risks in grant-giving is one of the greatest strengths of the Prince's Trust.

One of the most rewarding moments in Jeanie's chairmanship has been the formation of the Integrated Dance Company, mainly people with learning difficulties, who received £900 from the Devon Committee which really gave the company an enormous boost and got people to take them more seriously. What they have achieved is more than the ability to dance and put on shows which are always well received. They are very special people whom the Trust has been able to help stand proudly and say 'Look what we have achieved'. Not so long ago they danced for the Trust's founder, the Prince of Wales, in the Pavilions.

All the pomp and circumstance that surrounds a Royal visit is tossed aside when Prince Charles walks into a room. He does not only come to meet officials and local worthies but the young people the Trust is designed to help. He is inspirational to them.

Individuals, too, know the joy of receiving a grant. Mark Wilde, for example, is blind. He was given £500 to purchase a very sick horse which he nursed back to health. He is now training the horse to enable him to enter shows and cross country events. Mark and his horse, like the Integrated Dance Company, are recipients of a Mercury Communications Award. Stewart Rae suffers from dyslexia and was a self-confessed disaster at school. He says he found the Trust amazing. They really cared, unlike most people who do not give youngsters with his problem much encouragement or recognition. He was given £500 and encouraged to attend a City and Guilds Master Cabinet Makers course. All the time he was doing the course he was urged on by the Trust. He has since started producing magnificent clock cabinets, and hopes to start up his own business. He was another top Mercury Communications Awards winner.

It does not matter how outlandish or seemingly impossible your request for help might be, The Prince's Trust will look at it sensibly and sympathetically.

The Royal Jubilee Trusts are managed by the Prince's Trust and offer financial help to all sorts of projects. I found it quite hard to grasp how many and varied, were the aspects of the work of the Prince's Trust. There were tens of thousands of individuals who contributed to the King George's Jubilee Appeal in 1935 and the Queen's Silver Jubilee Appeal in 1977 and it is their generosity that continues to pay dividends today.

The endowments created at that time are invested by the the the Prince's Trust and underpin much of the Trust's local and national work, enabling them to launch new ventures or assist in funding existing ones. For example, a grant of £50,000 over three years helped to set up Saneline, a national service which provides telephone counselling in the field of mental illness, giving advice and information during evenings and weekends.

A grant of £35,000 over two years was awarded to help the core costs of Fairbridge, a leading charity working with the most disadvantaged inner city groups. It has a programme involving challenging outdoor activities, with job skills and counselling. The grant has helped Fairbridge to expand from twelve to sixteen centres across the UK.

One project is Volunteers. The idea behind Volunteers is not a new one, but Volunteers is. A great deal is done, and has always been done by voluntary organisations throughout the country. Community service already exists. People between 16 and 24 years of age are already involved to a greater or lesser degree including Plymothians. But until Volunteers, a large number were just not included. Let's face it, most people get little opportunity to do anything other than their chosen career or their unchosen unemployment. That's what makes Volunteers so interesting and necessary. It is an opportunity to spend some time doing voluntary work. It is not for no-hopers. It is not another source of free or cheap labour. It is not for do-gooders. It is not for ethnic minorities, or ethnic majorities. It is not for the unemployed, the handicapped, or young offenders or indeed anyone in particular. It is for everyone in general.

Volunteers aims to enable young people to develop their own personal qualities by working in the community as part of a team drawn from widely differing backgrounds. The programme has developed from that pioneered by the Community Venture during the 1980s.

It comprises:

A team of 15 young people (from work, unemployment and education).

A complete programme lasting 60 days (either block or day release)

A five day residential team-building experience and 40 days on practical projects and placements of a social care and environmental/conservation nature in the community.

Another fantastic opportunity which the Prince's Trust provides is the intensive seven day camp 'Work, Sport & Leisure' for 400 young people held at Caister-on-Sea, Norfolk. It is no easy option. Helpers and delegates work hard from the time they get up in the morning to the time they fall into bed at night. The participants get so much out of it. They will tell you that they return home feeling like real people again. They realise their abilities, find a new faith in the human race and realise that the world is not a dead end but a place of opportunity open to them all. What is so especially good is the fact that three months after the 1992 'Work, Sport and Leisure' course 64% of the participants are in full time work or education.

All this takes a tremendous amount of funding. From 1991-1996 the Trust's five year development plan needs to raise £20 million. Spectacular events have raised, and go on raising, vast sums. The support and sponsorship of businesses, even in these hard times, has been unstinting. Mercury Communications and Severn Trent Plc. are major sponsors, but if you read the annual report of the Prince's Trust you will see some 250 other familiar names who all lend their support in various ways. A charity of this dynamism working closely with others can really achieve a positive difference to a young person's life. We may not always know or hear about the work of The Prince's Trust or be aware of certain individuals in Plymouth benefiting from it but rest assured it is happening every day of every week, thanks to The Prince of Wales' vision and the tremendous team of people who work to fulfil it.

Different sections of Plymouth's Business Community still within the world of money, are insurance brokers. To survive in today's market place you have to be different and I found myself talking to a man who proves this almost every day. Derek Spargo is the principal of **Spargo & Co**, Registered Insurance Brokers and Independent Financial Advisers, working from an office at 164 Armada Way, Plymouth. He is a man in his mid forties with a wealth of experience who does not bat an eye when he receives a request to arrange public liability for a pet llama or to insure a machine valued at over a third of a million, which has the sole job of smashing test tubes at a predetermined rate! He does do some more mundane insurance as well such as for the company who do the assembly and linings for the brakes of every Formula One racing car or for the keel of 'Drum', the boat belonging to Duran Duran which sank!

Derek Spargo is a Devonian who has been in the insurance business since he left college in 1963. The company he joined sent him off to Birmingham to learn liability underwriting, a skill he has perfected over the years. He started Spargo and Co in 1984, specialising in commercial and business insurance. You do not go to him to get cover for the contents of your house or to insure your car. Many of his present clients are people from the Dockyard who started businesses with their redundancy money.

His secret of success, in my humble opinion, is that he speaks in a language that his clients can understand, not the jargon that so many insurance men use which bewilders the listener or bores them to death. He keeps everything as simple as possible and the advice he gives is based on long experience. Derek uses solvency experts to check on insurance companies before he places any sizable business. This shrewd move avoided any of his clients suffering as a result of the recent collapse of the Municipal Idemnity Corporation. This was the ninth largest U.K. insurance company and had a Grade A listing as recently as 1991. Incredible actually to think that in 1990 it had a premium income of £572 million and nett assets exceeding £1 billion. It fell because the company was carrying too much open - ended liability: for example public liability and product liability which in this case brought upon them the horrendous costs of defending civil actions against councils in courts.

What does Derek Spargo see for the future of the insurance world in Plymouth? He sees insurance companies already pulling out of small branches and utilising good, computerised brokers instead. This is a trend that will increase. Plymouth is close to the end of the computer line and therefore it is very important to have top class computerisation, the latest development of which is electronic data information where computer and screen plug directly into the insurance companies' computer systems. He sees European Insurance companies coming into the U.K. and insurance companies pulling out of various markets. He quoted one example in which a major insurance company has been providing plumbing cover since 1924 to a company which has never had a claim. The premium is worth thousands but renewal has been refused.

Spargo and Co is a prime example of a determined business increasing its share of the market place during the recession.

Across the road from the Elizabethan House and close to the Magistrates Court, or more congenially, two splendid pubs, **The Abbey** and the **Pen & Parchment**, is **Mandrake Associates**, specialists in the insurance and financial services field. The business which was set up in 1974, soon comprised offices in Plymouth, Wisbech and Abingdon caring for the insurance needs of the Royal Navy, the R.A.F. and Army respectively. Unless you are a member of the armed services you will probably not appreciate their particular and diverse needs in this field which are frequently not pertinent at all to civilians. The success of the company led to it being taken over by Hambro Countrywide in 1986, and by this time the scope of business had broadened to encompass in addition to service personnel, civilian and corporate clients.

Alan Bridgeman joined Mandrake in 1988 and became the local director in 1989. A Londoner, he thought he was coming to a backwater, and I am not sure that he thought he would enjoy living so far from the metropolis. Now, he returns to London for business reasons and enjoys the faster pace of life whilst he is there but he is always relieved when he gets back to Plymouth. Alan is a firm believer in the necessity to attract and keep people within this complex industry by means of better training and greater support from their companies. When he recruits - and in spite of the recession he could do with two more experienced consultants - he looks for people who have wide experience across the spectrum of financial services. His standards are high and he is not in the least interested in anyone who has not the ability to generate business from recommendations by existing clients and centres of influence such as solicitors, accountants and other professional groups.

One begins to appreciate the complexity of the financial services world today, when you talk to this dedicated man. He explained to me concisely the differences between a company which only deals with its own products and the 'independents', usually members of Fimbra, of which Mandrake is one. Here it is a question of offering several different companies' products and finding the most appropriate ones for the individual concerned.

I discovered that it is not so easy to successfully operate as an Independent today and several smaller companies are joining together - not merging - but with the purpose of co-ordinating research administration and compliance - called networking - which enables them to keep their independence.

Alan Bridgeman sees a smaller number of 'independents' in the future, but those that remain will be stronger and provide a wider, deeper service becoming more specialised. They will have to be seen to be offering something different by providing a much more comprehensive financial planning service for both personal and corporate clients. He also believes that the banks and building societies will suck up volume, and standard business and larger institutions will be created by mergers throughout Europe.

This busy man is responsible for the company's Birmingham office as well as Plymouth. I have no doubt that it is his wide experience - he spent some years as a manager of the Bristol and West Building Society in Liskeard and Plymouth - that makes Mandrake successful.

One unexpected and almost total change in the way of life in Plymouth is the arrival of the property management services. A few years ago it was almost impossible to rent an unfurnished property and quite difficult to obtain anything furnished that was worthwhile. The value of a good service of this kind was not even recognised here. Strange really when you consider that Plymouth has one of the most transient populations outside London.

A man of vision, Charles Knapper, recognised that there was a niche in this market place and formed **I.P.C. Management Agency**. Before I go more deeply into that I must tell you about this most colourful of characters. It is worth a visit to the County Courts to see him in action! No, he is not a lawyer but he soon will be. This is a swashbuckling entrepreneur of the 20th century who finds out what is necessary to do a job well and then sets about learning every facet of the craft. A one time naval engineer, he found himself becoming unpopular with the establishment because he had outside interests - he bought and then let properties. It was not long before his income from the property letting outstripped his service pay. The time had come for stepping ashore and taking the risk of being able to turn his part time occupation into a full scale professional business.

With a partner, who also left the Navy, they opened shop and found themselves in a foreign world. It was one thing to work a small operation cushioned by the Navy - something so many service people have discovered - another to face the stringency of the business world. Charles, a dapper man, openly admits he was naive and can almost feel himself blushing with embarrassment when he thinks back on how green he was. This did not last long; this is a man who quickly grasps the essence of anything he needs to learn.

Today some seven years later his various property businesses flourish with perhaps less emphasis, in the economic climate of 1993, on his estate agency. The main thrust is the management of property for people.

What does Charles Knapper's I.P.C. Management Agency do? For every property it handles, he undertakes, with his disciplined and quite tough staff, to manage a property for you from thoroughly vetting the ingoing tenants, inspecting the property at regular intervals during the term of the let and where necessary taking court action to ensure the rent is paid and the agreement upheld.

The property owner has no worries from the moment the agreement is signed with I.P.C. Charles Knapper has no qualms about taking people to court if need be. This is a man who has learnt so much about the law relating to property that he does not need to use solicitors for his cases. His regular and successfully fought appearances in court caused so much uproar amongst the legal fraternity that he was eventually banned from the courts by the judge. Nothing defeats Charles. He immediately appealed to the Lord Chancellor and got the ban reversed. It says much for English justice that the judge, having accepted the decision, has since treated Charles Knapper with the utmost courtesy and fairness, and I suspect a mutual respect has arisen. Charles, in return, is taking a law degree to prevent a similar situation arising and also, more importantly, to add to the strength of the excellent service his company gives to people wanting to let their properties furnished or unfurnished.

An interesting tip to would - be clients is that an unfurnished house will always be taken care of with more consideration than a furnished one by the tenants, which is why the rent charged for both types are usually equal sums, if not marginally more for unfurnished.

For anyone interested, the average rents in Plymouth are about £350pcm, whereas up-market rural and country homes can be as much as £800pcm in the South Hams and £600 in East Cornwall, and you could expect to pay up to £650pcm for a two-bedroomed flat overlooking The Sound on Grand Parade.

Over the last twelve months there has been an increase in the transient population in Plymouth. That, coupled with the present lack of confidence in the property market, has meant that more people than ever are looking to rent. We seem to be developing a very American attitude to property. Yes, people are still buying and keeping property, but when they move or are moved, they do not sell their houses but simply let them, and rent themselves in other locations. Ultimately they keep their own property in a part of the world to which they can return to retire or simply come back to pursue their employment.

The basis of the business has always been residential properties but commercial properties can be taken care of equally efficiently. I.P.C currently handles some 700 property worth about £35 million. They have recently opened an office in Exeter and themselves are moving to larger premises from their current base on North Hill to Mutley Plain.

A new development of the company is the handling of freeholds, a side of the business that Charles Knapper sees increasing with the advent of the new legislation. This is not something of which he approves because of the inherent problems. His reasons are spelt out quite clearly. The new legislation demands that where more than two leases are involved in one property and they exercise their option to purchase the freehold, a limited company must be set up to administer the maintenance etc. Most people are not aware of the responsibilities involved in running a limited company and consequently they are almost bound to make mistakes. The most common is likely to be the non-return of information annually to Company's House - as required by law. If such mal-administration of the limited company occurs, the legislation permits the property to revert to the Crown. As the Crown will not be actually administering the company on a practical, day - to - day basis, the ensuing mess could be horrific. If the leaseholder wanted to sell the property in such circumstances who would want to buy it? A well run and fair maintenance company such as I.P.C can actually help to sell a lease but Charles Knapper sees a lot of misery for people in this situation.

What should you and I look for from the services of a management agency? In a fair world we would not need one but that is Utopia and people do break their contracts with others. So a competent management agency is required. Apart from the straightforward every day matters it handles, it should have copies of all statutes in force from the Law of Property Act 1925 to the present day that relate to landlord and tenant matters.

They should also have a standard consumer credit licence that includes debt counselling and debt collection, be registered under the Data Protection Act if the agency is computerised, and be licensed to carry out credit checks using one of the credit checking systems.

A professional and competent management agency should also have separate clients' accounts that are bonded under one of the bonding schemes - so they cannot run off with your money - be capable of dealing with the legal affairs of the clients in respect of the letting of their property and have a rapid link to their clients' account bank in order to confirm that cheques and standing orders have cleared into the bank.

In short the agency must base its service on the needs of the client whilst also considering all the legal ramifications of letting. Quite a tall order. I.P.C has all the ingredients.

When they move to Mutley Plain they are going to be almost outside that abomination, the Mutley Plain Public Loo! I have not been told if they will get a rates reduction because of it but they most certainly should. I understand that the City Engineer needed no planning permission to erect it. Quite incredible. For any stranger who has not yet seen this horrendous edifice, I have to tell you that it is a public loo plonked down on the pavement right outside shops and offices. There were many other places on Mutley Plain that would have been infinitely more suitable but it mattered not how many people protested, how many petitions were signed, it remains in situ and I also have to report that it is equally horrific inside. I went to investigate the other day and hope that no visitor to Plymouth would ever need to use it - their opinion of Plymouth would reach rock bottom.

At the Breakfast Club I found myself sitting next to Ian Adams, a large, friendly man, with a passionate love of football, who is a legal executive working with the firm of Curtis Solicitors on Mutley Plain. He tells me that his office is literally behind the dreaded public lavatory, hated by every Plymothian. His only consolation is that he believes that Curtis's who were until recently situated in the great Barton building on the other side of the Plain, got change of use for their offices quite easily because the Council did not dare to say 'No' in view of the charming view he has to put up with. Many Plymothians will remember that Wheelers, the old family firm of drapers, and Page, Keen and Page, jewellers, occupied these premises before the advent of Curtis and before Wheelers were driven out of business by the arrival of this unforgiving monstrosity.

Curtis's are an active firm of solicitors who have built themselves a considerable client list in recent years. Ian Adams told me that underneath his sober, professional appearance, is the soul of a frustrated sport's journalist who would have loved to take that role as a full time employment. He gets a taste of what might have been when he reports on Plymouth Argyle away games for the Western Morning News. His other hobby is horse racing and until recently he had a share in several horses but in order to help his son to follow in his footsteps as a lawyer this exciting pastime, which is a trifle expensive to say the least, has had to be put to one side. I enjoyed talking to him for his sense of fun and wit and also to be re-assured that solicitors are human!

Probably the most human of all solicitors in this City is Tony Holland, the senior partner of **Foot and Bowden**. He brought honour to Plymouth when he became President of The Law Society, an onerous role carrying great weight which he carried out splendidly. This is a man, and a firm, from which no one need ever be frightened to ask for help. It is based in a gracious building on North Hill and all its offices - at least those that one sees - are places of warmth. You walk into reception and find it not unlike going into someone's sitting room. The chairs are comfortable, the carpet rich and the smiling, welcoming, receptionist sits at an elegant desk.

The Foot family have been part of Plymouth's history for some years now. I remember Isaac Foot, who was a friend of my grandfather's. As a child I remember the ferocity of the political debates across the dining table. The next generation of Foots have been equally vociferous in their various fields. Michael Foot is probably one of the finest orators of our time. Another brother, Lord Foot, with Tony Holland heads Foot and Bowden. The practice provides a vast range of specialist services for individuals and companies and yet has managed to retain the air of a family business. Not an easy task today when the bigger firms have heaven alone knows how many partners, and the client as an individual feels a bit like a parcel passed from one office to another, never really knowing the person who is answering their current need.

I talked to Tony Holland in his office which he shares with Lord Foot. Apart from his enormous energy which he puts into anything that can be done to bring Plymouth into the 21st century, he is also a great Wagnerian fan and will travel anywhere to hear these great operas. He told me that he considered it his duty to pass on this love of Wagner to his three sons. Whenever Covent Garden had a Wagnerian performance he would take whichever son was available to hear it. If it interfered with school then they would go up returning on the night train in time for school the following day. On one occasion, it was a performance of The Ring, I think. Through a technical fault the performance started late and they had to leave the theatre before the curtain came down. Son number three was the recipient of this treat and always held it against his father that he had been deprived because of not hearing the end. Many years later the Hollands travelled once more to Covent Garden for The Ring and Tony felt the debt had been repaid. Imagine his chagrin when he found that he had taken the wrong son! He is still teased unmercifully by his family about this omission.

Tony Holland's other great love is Horatio Hornblower, indeed all the Forester stories. When I saw him he had just discovered that the B.B.C. were thinking of filming a new series of the intrepid sailor's voyages and had the temerity to consider using Milford Haven as the port in which to film. Plymouth, as we all know, is the rightful place. Totally unhappy about this he immediately tackled the Council and the B.B.C. and would not stay quiet until he got a commitment from the city's Chief Executive, to fight our corner. It was not just authenticity that would have been lacking but Plymouth would have missed out on the enormous publicity such a series would produce. What the outcome will be is still in the balance. Having over - spent on their budget by £60 million, I rather suspect the B.B.C. will quietly shelve what would undoubtedly be a lavish and expensive series to make.

This is a man who would give any client a sense of well being and the same spirit is carried out throughout the practice. I have reason to know because one of the partners, Gary Streeter, is now the M.P. for the constituency in which I live. Here is another man who has always fought for the underdog or for anyone in trouble, even as a Councillor before he was elected to succeed Alan Clark. I have personal experience of his kindness and caring for an elderly couple who were my neighbours. That caring is carried on now by Sally Meen, a lady who has won my admiration for her careful handling recently as an executor of a will.

Carrying on the Foot tradition is the firm of solicitors **Nash**, whose founder, David Foot Nash, was related to the Foots and like them a lifelong Methodist. In fact at one time I believe that only Methodists were ever employed in the firm. Both David Foot Nash and his partner, Cecil Howett, attended chapel regularly. Cecil played the organ in the Embankment Methodist Chapel which is now the Christian Centre. It was not just any organ either but a vast Wurlitzer which once graced a cinema. There will not be all that many people who will remember this part of cinema life. Before the show began, there would be the sound of organ music and slowly from the bowels of the building the organ would rise majestically, and be seen in its full glory. Played by the resident organist who usually had almost as great a following as television people do today. Dudley Savage was the man in charge of this mighty machine in what was the Royal Cinema in Derry's Cross.

When the Embankment Church closed, Cecil and his Wurlitzer found a new home in Salisbury Road Methodist Chapel.

Nash have recently moved into the elegant and gracious Beaumont House in Ebrington Street, a building that they rescued from almost certain destruction and restored wonderfully, adding on a wing that looks as though it has always been part of the main building. It was quite a brave move on the company's part. Their old headquarters in Sussex Street was almost Dickensian in character and inconveniently spread. The contrast in working conditions can do nothing but improve the morale of the staff and make visiting one's solicitor far more pleasurable. David Searle, the senior partner, is not a Plymothian and I forgot to ask him if he is a Methodist! This compact, well organised firm of some ten partners, provides a comprehensive service which lives up to the traditions and standards set for them by David Foot Nash and his partners.

Nash Solicitors

When I asked David Searle what brought him specifically to Plymouth, he had no hesitation in answering 'Sailing'. He and his wife spend every possible minute they can aboard their boat. His comment merely confirms what so many people have told me: Plymouth is a good place in which to live and work. As you will see from what I have written in this chapter it also offers a comprehensive range of services to its citizens.

It would have been impossible to write about all the excellent firms offering legal advice, financial services and opportunities there are available in Plymouth, and so my selection has been taken from odd angles, from which I have been able to illustrate stories about people within this area of life in the City. In the index at the back you will find other firms listed with their addresses and telephone numbers.

St. Andrew's Church

CHAPTER 7

Plymouth and the Church

Christianity is alive and well in Plymouth. Possibly not in the number of churchgoers, which like everywhere else, has taken a nose dive in the last decade, but in the activity of the various denominations and the spin - offs from them. Some people will tell you they are not conscious Christians but they do work for which the Lord would applaud them.

I have taken the liberty of introducing you to a poem by Pam Weaver which rang a chord with me and is so pertinent today.

'What a wonderful surprise Lord!'
I flung the door wide open. 'Do come
in'. As he walked past the
telephone, I remembered my frequent
gossipy phone calls. The colour in my
face rose. He didn't say anything, but
I saw a wounded look in His eye.

'Come into the sitting room.' I said
but the TV was on and I didn't want
him to see the movie I was watching
so I added 'On second thoughts, come
into the kitchen while I make us some
coffee.' He didn't say anything but I
knew He was hurt.

While he sat at the kitchen table I
realised how few people I have
invited home. I always meant to ask
them over, but... He didn't say
anything, and I avoided His eye.

He looked at the car parked outside
'I call it the Lord's car' I told him
proudly 'It's only insured for me to
drive but if I've got time (which isn't
very often) I'll take anybody
anywhere.' He smiled and I realised
how silly that sounds.

I changed the subject. 'While you're
here,' I said 'I'll take you upstairs. 'I
didn't want Him to see my expensive
pills, potions and lotions in the
bathroom. He didn't say anything
but I closed the door.

We stopped outside my favourite
room, the place where I relax by
myself. As usual, I didn't invite Him
in. He didn't say anything but I hung
my head in shame.

'Everything is so cluttered, Lord', I
mumbled. 'I'm not ready for you yet.
Can you come back when I've tidied
up?' He put his hands gently on my shoulder and smiled.

'Shall we do it together, Child?'

My religious upbringing would have confused anyone. My
father came from Methodist stock but was Church of England, my
mother's family were firm Wesleyans yet I was sent, at the age of
3½ to the Anglo-Catholic convent, St Dunstans Abbey, in North
Road West. So when I came to look at the various denominations in
order to write about them in this book, I was not unnerved by the
differences; after all the purpose behind them all is to do the work
of God.

The mother church of **St Andrew** was my first choice; a
church I know well and in which my son was married to a
beautiful girl upon whom the sun shone, through the wonderful
Piper windows, even though it was a December afternoon. There
was time before the service began to look about me and conjure up
thoughts of the past. Sir Francis Drake would have knelt in prayer
here asking for blessing before he sailed and in thanksgiving when
he returned from one of his successful voyages.

History tells us that in the middle of the sermon one Sunday
morning in 1573, the vicar was in full flight only realising at the
end of the dissertation he was alone in his church. The
congregation had tiptoed out, not from boredom, but because the
news had filtered into the church that Drake was in harbour having

been away for a year on one of his most successful voyages to the West Indies.

To my left in the north transept, and cut off from the body of the church by a glass screen, adorned with the crest of the Royal Air Force, was the chapel of St Philip and above the chapel altar a memorial to the men of St Andrews who died in the two World Wars. On either side of the altar are memorials to Plymouth policemen and firemen killed in 1939-45.

On the north wall are two modern tablets telling us of the 'hearts' of two great men, Martin Frobisher, commander of one of Drake's divisions in the Armada battles, and Robert Blake, Cromwell's admiral who died as his ship entered Plymouth Sound in 1675. The latter was returning from a successful mission destroying the Spanish treasure fleet in the Canaries.

A lady has lain sleeping in an ancient tomb for some 750 years. She is probably Joan Valletort, whose family were the Norman lords of Plymouth and lived to the west of the church. She was mistress to Richard, Earl of Cornwall, the brother of King Henry III. It was from that line that the Earls of Mount Edgcumbe are descended.

Behind me the Piper window at the base of the tower pays glorious tribute to the memory of William Waldorf, the second Viscount Astor who was MP for Sutton from 1910-1919 and Lord Mayor for all the years of the Second World War. He died in 1952.

The window represents the instruments of the passion, with the ladder, the reed and the spear representing a St Andrews cross. Every symbol in the design depicts an event in the Crucifixion, from the thirty pieces of silver to the crowing cock.

The big central monument on the west wall, with a carving of a woman kneeling and her children around her is to Elizabeth Calmady, wife of Edward Calmady, who died in 1645. The Calmadys used much of their wealth gained from the Newfoundland fishing business, which flourished for centuries, for the benefit of the people of Plymouth.

My mind then wandered slightly again to the past and a thought for Catherine of Aragon who landed in Plymouth before journeying to London to meet her bridegroom, Prince Arthur, brother of Henry, later to become Henry VIII and the subsequent husband of Catherine. She came to this church to worship and to pray. The vicar then was the extraordinary Adrian de Castello, secretary to the Borgia Pope who arranged the marriage of Catherine. He acquired many high church offices in England and was made a cardinal, yet never set foot on English soil. This valiant lady would have had no idea at that time that her eventual divorce from Henry VIII would lead to the break with Rome and the formation of the Church of England.

Beautiful flowers adorned the church as they do every day and magnificently at the time of the Flower Festival. The church has a sense of well being that comes from loving care and more importantly a large congregation, swollen at Christmas and Easter. At Midnight Mass on Christmas Eve there is never a seat to be had well before the service starts.

The wonderful atmosphere of the church is particularly poignant when you know that in the Blitz of 1941 only the walls were left standing. It says much for the spirit of its people that the next morning a board was nailed up over the door and on it was 'Resurgam' - I will rise again. That message went through every part of Plymouth reeling under the constant attention of the Nazi bombers. Plymouth did not flinch. The shell of St Andrews became a symbol of the determination of Plymothians not to be defeated by the miseries of the nightly bombing.

St Andrews did rise again and in 1957, rebuilt, redesigned internally, it was reconsecrated. Yet it was still essentially the church created 500 years earlier.

Listen to the peal of ten bells from the tower. The oldest recorded bell is 1594, the youngest 1874. A carillon plays popular tunes and hymns at 4pm and 8pm. At the top of the tower you get a wonderful panoramic view of the city and as far out to sea as the horizon permits. One unexplained oddity is the name of Francis Chichester carved into the lead of the tower. As far as anyone knows this remarkable solo circumnavigator who sailed triumphantly into Plymouth at the end of his epic voyage, never set foot in the tower, let alone climbed it.

In its history St Andrews has had many vicars, many of whom have become bishops. The present incumbent, Prebendary John

Watson, on the face of it appears to be a mild, gentle man yet he never flinches in his outspokenness if he takes issue on a gritty subject and he fights like a tiger for his beliefs and for the well being of his clergy and his parishioners. He is a much loved man and deservedly so. St Andrews has flourished under his care. He has always generated a team spirit and it is this that makes the many associations within the church so successful. It starts with the very young and continues with the youth, the young marrieds and so on. Every night there is some activity and a newcomer to the city or to the church is made very welcome. I have attended churches where for years you can still feel an outsider. Not so here, there is always a smiling welcome.

Walking through the side door of the **Methodist Central Hall** on a Tuesday morning brought home to me that a place of worship is not just for Sundays! This was like walking into a business - the business of the Lord. It was buzzing with activity. In addition to the full time staff led by the Minister, there is a willing rota of members who man the coffee lounge, look after the flowers, organise the various groups that meet each week and orchestrate the many outside activities. The Day Centre has regular meetings for elderly members and provides an opportunity for those who may be almost housebound to come to the Hall and enjoy the company of others. Transport is always readily available for anyone who needs it. Everyone enjoys a lunch prepared and served by the ever willing kitchen ladies. Church members entertain afterwards with music, songs, monologues and a gentle exercise to music!

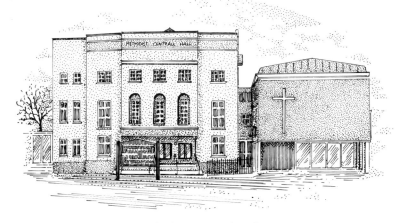

Methodist Central Hall

The Ladies Circle extends a warm welcome to any lady of whatever age to come and join them for their meetings and outings. They were off to play skittles at the Fursdon Leisure Centre when I met them and only the night before I had been to the pantomime in the Theatre Royal where a whole block of seats was occupied by an enthusiastic party from the church. They were not averse to shouting 'Oh no he's not' at the top of their voices!

I noticed that the Editor of the 'Messenger' the monthly magazine produced by Central Hall, was blessed with the surname George. The name brought back memories of my childhood and my grandfather George who was a leading member of the Wesleyan chapel in Stuart Road, Stoke, a chapel destroyed in the Blitz. He ruled the roost there in much the same way as he did his family.

Every Sunday the entire household went to morning service. It was in short walking distance from his home and it was a sort of crocodile that wended its way to the stark chapel. In order of seniority we were seated in the three front pews with the servants sitting behind us. Grandfather George having got us settled, produced silver coins for us to give to the collection. My child's tithe was sixpence, the servants one shilling, the ladies a florin, and the men a half a crown. This was followed by a ceremonial removal from his black and white striped waistcoat of a gold pocket knife and a stick of black liquorice. A piece for each of us was cut off to keep us quiet during the sermon.

The moment the preacher reached the pulpit to begin his oration, out would come grandfather's gold Hunter watch. It would be placed on the ledge in front of him, he would nod his head as a signal for us to suck the liquorice and then he would sit back with his eyes closed. I never knew whether he had a quick forty winks but I did know that if the unfortunate preacher spoke for one second longer than the allotted twenty minutes he would be abruptly stopped by a piercing glare from grandfather George and what can only be described as a 'humphing' noise emanating from his mouth which caused his walrus moustache to lift up and down rhythmically. Worse would follow. Sunday lunch was always attended by the resident Minister and his wife or a visiting preacher who was invariably a young man and terrified by this awesome tyrant. The entire conversation during the meal would be dominated by grandfather who spoke at length about people who liked the sound of their own voices!

I always viewed Methodism as a cold and forbidding religion, perhaps because it lacked the colour and drama of the High Church St Peter's in Wyndham Square which used to be the parish church for the pupils of St Dunstans and where I attended mass with regularity all my schooldays. It is only in more recent years that I have discovered the warmth and humanity that is so much a part of today's Methodist approach. The services are full of a different sort of colour, the richness of the choirs and a true sense of evangelism. John Wesley would be proud of them.

The difference between the work of the Central Hall and the other Plymouth Methodist churches was explained to me by Jeffrey Sharp. The Hall, which withstood the Blitz and doubled as a Concert Hall for many years, is the power house bringing together all the mainstream activities and sending members out in the world as missionaries. The other Methodist churches are part of a circuit of their own with their own Superintendent Minister. Rather like parish churches being responsible to a Diocese I suppose.

I understand planning has resumed on the redevelopment of the Drake Circus area, which would bring about the demise of the Central Hall as we know it now. It will be replaced in the new structure but replacements are never quite the same. There will still be many Plymothians who remember the building being used for wartime concerts - the only place they could be held virtually. It has stood in this prime position since 1939 when it was built on the same ground that had been the Ebenezer Methodist Church since 1817. I suppose commonsense has to prevail when you think how valuable the site is in such an expensive part of the city centre.

The lively **Baptist Church** on Mutley Plain is another hive of activity. Every Sunday it has large congregations and during the week spreads the ministry throughout Plymouth. I was lucky enough to spend time with a lifelong Baptist, Hedley Miller, whose love of his church is shown in a book 'The first 100 years' from 1869-1969 in which he co-operated in writing, when the centenary of the Church was commemorated. His grandfather used to recall how exciting it had been to look down from the crowded gallery on the opening day. He vividly remembered how as a boy he watched collection plates being carried down the aisles below him piled high with golden sovereigns.

Externally with its fine style of Palladian architecture, the church has not changed much. Internally, a valuable foyer has been incorporated and in 1990, although the solid granite pillars supporting the arch above the organ chamber remain, considerable revamping occurred in order to facilitate modern worship. The pulpit was enlarged to form a rostrum, the platform enlarged to accommodate a music group and the organ replaced with a magnificent three manual Ahlborn Computing Organ with seventy stops and combinations.

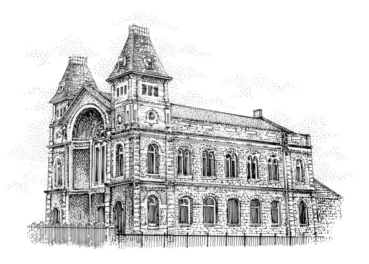

Mutley Baptist Church

In the joyful singing of songs and hymns in Mutley Baptist there is an exuberance which sends the sound flying to the lofty ceiling. What is it about non-conformist services that makes the singing so cheerful and enjoyable? The hymns are not so different to the Church of England but unless you are in a major church there the similarity ends. Could it be that the Church of England is not willing to adopt modern sound and new approaches to services? .

The letter that is given to you if you are a stranger really says it all.

Dear Friend,

We are delighted that you joined us in worship today and hope that you found the service both challenging and uplifting.

If you live locally we trust you will feel able to join us again. We would like to give you a more personal welcome and hope that you will let us have your name and address on the enclosed card, so that someone can call on you fairly soon and try to help you settle among us.

We would be glad to offer friendship and to assist in any way possible. Please do not hesitate to contact any of us. The best way to make contact is through our Church Reception, and office telephone number. You will see that a large range of activities are offered for all age groups and you and your family would be welcome to join any of these as appropriate. We can also provide you with fuller information if you wish.'

I have personal experience of their welcoming arms. A few years back I had students living in my house to help cope with the mortgage and one of them was a Baptist from Bristol. During the time of her stay here she was visited regularly by members of the congregation and asked out on several occasions for Sunday lunch. For a youngster on her first adventure away from home this was especially good and one that I hope would be extended to children of mine were they in the same situation.

There is nothing stuffy about the Baptists. You just have to look at some of their notices to know that. One especially amused me. It said:

> You don't need LUCOZADE to get you going
> on Saturday mornings, you need the

MUTLEY MAULERS

It did not refer to people suffering from the morning after the night before, nor to a gang of thugs but to the very active and competitive church football team for those aged between 10-15 years who meet in the Hurrell Room of the church on Saturday mornings. This is only one of the many group activities.

On another tack altogether is the Ladies Prayer Chain. There are three chains each day, the first starting at 8am then 1pm and 6pm, so requests are passed on to about 30 people during the day.

Each member of the chain is committed to pass the message on to the next person who then prays about it. All requests for prayer are treated as strictly confidential.

If you would like more information or if you have a matter for prayer, please telephone Una Gowing (266838), who will pass it on at the appropriate times.

Sometimes I watch 'This is the Day' on BBC One on Sunday mornings at 9.30am and I often wondered what happened when at some time during the programme the presenter says, ' This church will pray for all your requests during the week.' Somehow I envisaged a constant vigil by the congregation throughout a week but if Mutley Baptist's system is used then it does become practical.

Single parents are in need of as much help as they can get and the national organisation, **Christian Link Association of Single Parents**, or **CLASP** for short, has a branch at Mutley to provide fellowship, friendship and mutual support to those who find themselves bringing up children alone.

The Mutley branch meets fortnightly, generally on Friday evenings, and the meetings vary considerably in format. Included are regular Bible studies, guest speakers and outings to both secular and Christian events. There are also times for sharing and praying together. Babysitters can be arranged if necessary. For full details see the CLASP programme on the notice board in the reception area. New members are warmly welcomed.

Various other groups are of equal or possibly more importance to the Church and members. Every member of the congregation for example is encouraged to join a House Group, usually in their neighbourhood. These serve not only as prayer and study groups but as natural caring groups too. A place where problems can be shared and practical help found.

There is also a team of people committed to caring for the sick, regularly visiting the housebound and helping others with special needs. If ever you feel in need of comfort, or help, or a visit, no matter what your age, circumstances or religion, please just let them know. Ring the Church on Plymouth 663784 and a message to the Pastoral Team will be passed on.

I read in the Evening Herald the other day that the homeless are being cared for by volunteers from the church during the winter months. They have been given the use of the former police station at Longfield House, Greenbank which is open to people facing a night on the streets. Up to twenty homeless men and women can be accommodated at the Night Light shelter. Four members of Mutley Baptist stay overnight to help them settle in. British Telecom has provided a phone free of charge and Devon Health Authority, which owns the building, gave the green light for the project to go ahead.

The Junior Church is strong and very well organised with various departments starting at creche level with children up to 1è years and ending with a bible class for teenagers of fifteen.

Like the Methodists in Central Hall there is a regular luncheon club called Lunch Break which meets every Wednesday in the Coffee Lounge at 12.15pm where a hot two course meal with a cup of tea costs only £1.40. Bookings are accepted up to 12 noon on Mondays. Ring Plymouth 663784.

Throughout its history, Mutley Baptist has been true to the gospel and remained a united church through times of change and outlook generally. Its nine ministers have been men of differing gifts but with one theological outlook.

I am always interested in origins and from Hedley Miller I learnt how the Baptists came to Plymouth and carved out a place in the life of the city. The first minister, Abraham Cheare, was called in 1648 by 150 members to look after their church in How Street which had been founded in 1637. Abraham was a rebel and refused to conform to the religious laws of Charles II and spent many of the succeeding years imprisoned, culminating in the harshest of conditions on Drakes Island in Plymouth Sound where he died in 1668 at the young age of 42. Undaunted the members still met in various locations and over the years established new churches. The Blitz destroyed the main venue built in 1845 in George Street and if you want to take a look at the Civic Flag Staff in Royal Parade that is where the church stood. Today there are several churches in and on the outskirts of the city.

The Roundabout Day Nursery gave me my first introduction to the work of the **Christian Centre** based in the old Embankment Road Methodist Church at Cattedown Roundabout. My daughter was off to Hong Kong for a short time with her naval husband and my grandson was to be left with us. I am not a domestic creature and have never been particularly good with small children so I looked for a Day Nursery and was lucky enough to be introduced to the one here and to the Christian and very caring head of the Nursery, Mrs Smyth. Hamish loved his time at The Roundabout. He spent all day there and came home tired but happy and well fed. He learnt a lot, too, and even took part in a Nativity play which they put on in the church. This is one of the best, if not the best nursery in the city and never lacks for children.

The Christian Centre

It is strange that once you get talking to people about some aspect of a place you learn something else. I found out that my very elderly next door neighbours lunched in the building every day on a plentiful three course meal at a very low cost. Not only were they fed but they were fetched and brought home every day by the Centre's minibus. If the weather in the afternoon was nice enough the driver would take them on a tour of Dartmoor or over to Torbay for tea. It was Christian caring at its very best and I have been even more impressed in recent weeks when approaching the end of his life, Bill, my neighbour, because of a heart problem was unable to climb the stairs in the Centre to reach the Luncheon Club, so his meals were brought up to the house for him.

It was in this church that Bill's funeral service was held. It was the happiest one I have ever attended. No one was in mourning, in fact we were asked to wear red, Bill's favourite colour. The sense of love, the work of God and the certainty of life ever after came over so strongly. I left the church enriched.

The history of the work of **Elim** in Plymouth is worth recording. Sixty five years ago it all began following a series of revival and healing campaigns conducted by the Welsh evangelists, George and Stephen Jefferies. In the early 1920's revival meetings were held in the Army Drill Hall and the records show that throughout the campaign meeting the evangelists preached before capacity crowds of some 2,600 at each meeting. The religious enthusiasm did not limit itself to the Elims but rubbed off also on churches of all denominations in the city and established the Elim Fellowship in 1925.

For many years the Church did not have a proper home; the congregation made do with an old iron foundry in Rendle Street, a dis-used and very run down church in Emma Place and for some 27 years between 1955 and 1982 the old Foot Built Mission in Notte Street which the congregation acquired from Isaac Foot's family. Nothing prevented them worshipping together, even the fact that during the years of World War II they had no home at all and were compelled to worship in the foyer of an old cinema in Union Street which was bombed on two occasions, a cafe on Mutley Plain and in the old Stonehouse Town Hall. Talking to older members of the Church you will discover that those days are remembered with affection and not distress.

I wonder how many people remember the immediate post-war, successful tent campaign that was held on a bombed site at the lower end of what is now Royal Parade. All the evangelical activity produced an ever large congregation and it was quite obvious that the Notte Street premises were too small and they sought new premises. A difficult task which was finally resolved when they purchased the dilapidated premises vacated by the Embankment Road Methodist Church at Cattedown Roundabout.

It needed courage and vision to tackle the project. Both were there in abundance and all the time improvements have been and are being made. The community programme now consists of the Day Nursery, a Luncheon Club for senior citizens, a Residential and Nursing Home at Stoke, a Training School for Church Works and most recently Kings School, a Day School.

Kings School was conceived because parents of children in the Day Nursery wanted a school to which they could send their offspring which would be run on the same Christian lines as the Nursery.It started with the first year and then the second year being housed in rooms at the Christian Centre but it too has grown, acquired what was Warrens School and is now full fledged and in its own premises.

To meet the needs of a growing congregation it has become necessary to hold multiple morning services and on Sunday evenings the Church disperses to six area presences around the city. During the week 24 care groups look after the spiritual needs of the congregation which are now served by a pastoral team of three led by a Pastor and his staff.

I talked with Mr Nicholls who runs the Centre. It was from him that I learnt that the Elim Fellowship believes that discipleship includes a commitment to each other and goes beyond sharing beliefs and religious practices. In the same way Church membership means much more than just attending a Church service, giving the offerings and keeping certain rules and regulations. Their concern is for the quality of individual and corporate lives.

The Elim joyous worship is no doubt why the church is always full.

Going beyond sharing beliefs and religious practices is something that is happening between the **Roman Catholic Cathedral** in Wyndham Street and the vast **St Peter's Anglican Church** in Wyndham Square. They frequently share services and always work together for the benefit of the young, the elderly and the homeless. They are responsible too for 'Cloisters' a club they founded jointly as a centre for people to meet. The ecumenical approach goes way beyond what one normally finds.

St Peter's which was badly bombed during the Plymouth Blitz also acts as a place of worship for the Greek Orthodox Church which cares for the many Greeks who live in the city. I went to the wedding of an English girl to a Greek here. A strange experience. The traditional English wedding service came first to which none of the invited Greek guests arrived except for the Bridegroom's immediate family. They turned up in force though for the Greek

Orthodox part and for the splendid reception in the New Continental Hotel. That was a truly Greek occasion and quite delightful.

150 years ago, Father George Prynne and the Sisters of Mercy of the Community of St Mary the Virgin at Wantage gave themselves unstintingly to the parish of St Peter's. During their time they had to face two outbreaks of cholera as well as the various diseases which afflicted the poor people around them. Following in that tradition Father Sam Philpott, a cheerful, warmhearted character, found himself needing to be equally unstinting in his running of his sprawling inner city parish.

Sam Philpott has been here for fourteen years now and whilst there can be no doubt that he prays for everyone, he is far more a 'hands on' priest who tackles almost impossible tasks, certain of only one thing and that is GOD's wish for him to do the work. Over the fourteen years he has produced outstanding results. The derelict, bleak St Peter's Hostel in King Street was his first project. Having transformed that, most of the work being done by himself and his parishioners on a shoestring, he realised that to really get things done he needed to be part of a partnership in action rather than an isolated force competing, possibly unwittingly, against other units. He gathered round him the Stoneham Housing Association, the Probation and Social Services, and from then onwards it has been all go.

It might be said to have been divine intervention when a mighty storm on Boxing Day in 1979 blew off the roof of the redundant All Saints Church in Harwell Street. The church was demolished and became Annwyl Close, 22 purpose built flats providing temporary accommodation for deprived people who were then helped to cope with an alien world. They were encouraged to polish up whatever skills they had and strike out for independence. The church hall next door, a pathetic, almost derelict eyesore, was transformed into the headquarters of the go - ahead development team under the guiding hand of the Probation Service. It also provides room for a creche run by the city council.

By now the efforts of Father Sam were being recognised everywhere. Grants became available and this human dynamo was joined by other people with a social conscience on other projects. **Devonport Guildhall** opened its doors to the very successful

Rainbow Project which provides a playschool and support for mothers. You may remember it was one of the projects in which Anneka Rice became involved and with publicity from her programme more and more volunteers came forward to do the never ending tasks required to make the project succeed. The Ship Hostel and the hugely popular Green Bike Scheme, all started from the enthusiasm of the good Father.

Almost two years ago a one-to-one counselling service for offenders on probation was started. It is designed to help them cope with this period and to make good use of their time whether it is at work or leisure or in community service. In the domestic field, the upstairs vestry of St Peters has become a haven for couples having marital difficulties. Trained volunteers act as mediators and I understand the success rate is quite high.

Other churches look to Father Sam and St Peter's to help them with their projects and one of the most remarkable schemes is one in North Prospect which teaches youngsters how to repair cars - not for joyriding I hasten to add - but they do get offered the chance of taking part in some stock car racing if they make the grade.

This man's work and his encouragement to others is surely what Christianity is all about.

Presbyterians have their own church out at Hartley and Sherwell Congregational church stands firm as it has done all my life just by the former Polytechnic. All that has changed is the overall name. They are known now as the United Reform Church. There are Pentecostal Churches, an active Mormon Tabernacle, and of course, the Synagogue.

One I have not mentioned however is the wonderful **Salvation Army** who have served Plymouth so well for so long and who are active wherever there is a need. Christmas would not be the same without the Salvation Army playing carols in the City Centre and parading through the streets on Sundays with the drums banging out their message. Nor would the homeless find food and warmth without the help of this brave band of men and women assisted by the other denominations throughout Plymouth.

The Devonport House hostel run by the Salvation Army is for single, homeless men and its services are more in demand today than ever. The 69 beds available are full every night and many more could be filled if they were there. In the worst of the winter weather extra bed space is made available by putting mattresses on the floor of the recreation room.

Major Huggins, the Army's social services sectional officer will tell you that the largest number of residents on average are in the 55 to 65 age bracket, with most staying for between six months and a year but with a significant number remaining up to five years. Many of these men were institutionalised before they arrived at Devonport House and cannot now function in any other setting.

Money is needed for this great work and not the least of it to refurbish and repair the hostel. It will cost about £400,000, a sum I have no doubt the Army will raise. How grateful we should be to them and their colleagues throughout the world.

Homeless people are on the conscience of everyone of us and Plymouth, whilst not as affected as many places, still has its share. Much is done for them especially by the churches and particularly **Plymouth's Ship Hostel** in George Place just up the road from my office. They expected a surge of homeless people seeking shelter over Christmas but for some extraordinary reason it failed to materialise. Just thirty people turned up to spend the festive season at the hostel which was geared to accommodate the estimated 100 people sleeping rough in and around the city.

I was told that the response from the public for volunteers, food and clothing vital to the hostel's needs, was tremendous and will undoubtedly come into play in the cold months of January and February when the problems for the homeless are at their worst.

Caring for the homeless is not just that. The Ship takes it a lot further, working with the Social Services to get their regular inmates housed in accommodation of their own. I know of someone quite recently who was at rock bottom when he was taken in by The Ship. He was counselled, helped and some weeks later, far fitter and more able to cope, they found him a flat and the wherewithal to furnish it. The man's self respect and dignity was restored. It is work that frequently goes unsung and not even known to exist by many Plymothians.

The work of many charitable organisations in the city raises thousands of pounds for various causes every year and it would be impossible to name every one. The hard core of organisers who generously give their time and spur on those of us who lag behind deserve our thanks and approbation. Plymouth people are warm-hearted, Christian spirited, and generous but not everyone is prepared nor able to give up all their spare time to their espoused causes. Each and everyone of us at some time in our lives will have need of either for ourselves or families, of these great services. Who does not know of someone who has been cared for in **St Luke's Hospice**, received treatment with machinery provided by the Cavitron Fund, found MIND a comfort or given thanks for the help of The League of Friends. Wonderful, caring people in each charity and they are purely representative of the hundreds of different causes supported in the City. Thank you.

Sherwell Church

CHAPTER 8.

The Importance of Education

If Plymouth had nothing else to boast about it could certainly hold its head up high in the education sector. From the newly acquired status of its university to nursery schools,play groups it has an excellence that places it high in the league. To use a football term I would place it at the top of the Premier Division with the elite.

I can only attempt to give you some idea of the scope and range of the educational facilities open to Plymothians or to those who would adopt the city. For anyone wanting to relocate and has the welfare of their children's education in the foreground of their minds, Plymouth could not be better. You do not have to be wealthy to provide a first class grounding for the future of your offspring. I do not pretend that there is not still much to be done to bring some of the older schools into line but that is being done at a steady pace. For example a new comprehensive school will open in September 1993. Birmingham deputy head teacher, Val Jones, has been appointed head. This school, Parkside Comprehensive, is one of the last pieces in the programme to convert all of Plymouth's secondary modern schools into comprehensives. Devonport and St Peter's Church of England schools are the last of their kind in the region to be converted in a twelve year plan, under the banner of this new school.

The benefits of good pre-school nursery care and education are firm foundations for life so perhaps that is where my educational journey should start. It is recognised that children of this generation need educational stimulus much earlier than in the past. The two and three year old is no longer happy to play at home all day; more demanding activities are required. Having said that I went to St Dunstans in 1928 when I was just over three years of age, so maybe not much has changed. I spent the next fourteen years there. More of that later.

One of the first people I went to see when I started the research for this book was Mary Smyth at the **Roundabout Nursery** in the Christian Centre at Cattedown roundabout. This is one of the most welcoming pre-school nurseries I encountered. Children love it and find the mixture of play and learning wonderful. This dedicated Christian lady is also in charge of Les Enfants in the annexe of Kings School in Hartley Road, Mannamead. Here this small, part-time class for 2-3 year olds has an emphasis on preparing your child for pre-school education. There are also some part and full-time places available for children of 0-2 years in the small nursery. The great thing about this nursery and the Roundabout is that it is open all the year round and caters for working parents needs.

Suzi Beaman, who is still only 22, won the Live Wire Competition for the most outstanding business in the South West in 1991 with her imaginative **Holding the Reins** Nanny Agency and for the running of a day nursery unit at **Widewell School**, Lulworth Drive, Roborough. The day nursery is licensed for 18 children with full and part-time places available 51 weeks in the year from Monday-Friday between 7.45am and 5.30pm

The nursery is a spacious classroom, equipped with toilet and washbasin facilities. It is a paradise for a small child allowing them to pursue messy activities and constructive play, quiet time with books and games, or physical activities like bike riding, and there is also a grassed play area.

In September 1992, Suzi started another nursery in **St Andrews School** opposite the Pavilions, run on exactly the same successful lines and she hopes to start a third in 1993. As a help to the Pavilions she does operate a creche within that building for special events.

I wanted to find out what started this lively, intelligent young woman in this demanding business. She told me that she left school with no qualifications but always with a desire to be a nanny. To further this ambition she studied for the National Nursery Examination Board's certificate and having qualified and spent a while in Newcastle nannying, she came back to Plymouth. Starting the business at 19 was almost a spur of the moment idea. Her family have many members who all run their own businesses so she got a lot of encouragement. Sensibly she went to Enterprise Plymouth and obtained tremendous help from them; she cannot speak highly enough of them. They helped her when things went wrong, including when the ceiling fell down in her office!

The first business was the Nanny Agency, the purpose of which was to put nannies and clients in direct contact with each other. Suzi now has over 500 girls on her books, all of whom have been thoroughly vetted and interviewed. She knows the history and the desires of the girls so well that she can almost produce a nanny who is tailor-made for the client.

On top of running the three businesses, Suzi still finds time to give talks at colleges and schools and to take on girls for work experience. A dedicated and determined young lady whose youth is refreshing and in whose care I would not hesitate to leave a child.

Treetops Day Nursery has provided top quality pre-school education for over 25 years. It now takes the children of some of its former pupils! It used to be in Greenbank if my memory serves me correctly but now it has its being at 111, Church Road Plymstock. The same friendly welcoming atmosphere still provides a happy place for children to play and learn together.

The spacious tree-filled garden is wonderful for small things to go adventuring and let their imaginations run riot.

On the other side of the city at Eggbuckland is the Frogmore **Montessori Nursery School** for children from 18 months to 8 years. Maureen Taylor runs this efficient and unique establishment where the curriculum and teaching materials are carefully selected allowing children both the freedom and structure to progress physically, socially, emotionally and intellectually,

French and swimming are part of the Montessori environment which has proved wonderful for thousands of children over the years.

Plympton has its own **Beechstowe Day Nursery** in which nursery care and education is given by a qualified staff in small groups. Children come here as early as 18 months and stay until they are five. The seven purpose designed activity rooms are full of light, friendly and provide a wonderful environment for a structured day with formal teaching of rising fives. The happy, caring atmosphere is another strong point. Children love the garden which has all the things they love most, sandpits, climbing frames, slides and swings. Music is part of the curriculum and the children are taken on frequent excursions.

Kiddicare Day Nursery in North Street, Plymouth, ideally situated close to the Town Centre, is run by the Children and Lone Parents Charity.

It offers a cheap and cheerful service for parents with young children aged 2-5 years.

The nursery facilities consist of three large rooms and a garden, ample space in which the children are encouraged to have fun, make new friendships and learn through play with the various activities provided.

I must mention at this moment an excellent book 'Parents' Guide to Plymouth' by Geraldine Lane who covers so many diverse things that parents need to know. It is primarily aimed at parents of under 5's although many items will also be of interest to parents of older children.

The big step for the five year old is their first real school. A time of excitement and sometimes trauma. For parents it is frequently a moment when tears well, and there is a sense of loss. Ridiculous really but I bet there are very few mums who have not experienced it. The first time the little darlings try on their uniforms pulls at the heart strings and as you see them disappear into school, into the hands of another a part of your life has gone. Having got over the emotion most of us will heave a sigh of relief!

At this age Plymouth has many different schools to offer. An example of one of the best state primary and junior schools one could wish for is **Hyde Park Infants and Juniors**. This slightly uncompromising building has warmth inside, classrooms that have been brought to life by the dedicated staff and pupils who respond to the desire to learn with an enthusiasm that is infectious.

I had the honour of being asked to speak to two classes about publishing and how you get a book ready to go to print. They had carried out a project themselves and groups of four children had written and designed their own book. The subject matter was their own choice and the results creative and fascinating. There were pop up books, stories of trips to the seaside, a voyage to the moon; a wonderful range of vivid and imaginative work. To judge which was best was almost impossible.

When I had finished talking I asked them about Plymouth and how they thought it should be. The environment was one of the main things; they wanted more trees in the parks, less litter and they wanted it to be safer. I had forgotten how perceptive the very young could be. It says much for the quality of their teachers that these young minds were being given the opportunity to learn quickly about caring for their home city.

One poignant memory I have of Hyde Park is during the intense bombing of Plymouth. I lived with my parents just up the road from the school and one night while my father and I were doing our bit patrolling in case incendiary bombs came hurtling down and needed extinguishing, we looked up towards the sky and there was a new phenomenon floating down on a parachute - a land mine. It was coming directly towards us and in the stupid way one behaves at times of high tension, my father and I shook hands and wished each other goodbye! I am still here and my father lived for many more years. The land mine landed on the roof of the school.

In Seymour Road, Mannamead is the **Western College Preparatory School**, - known affectionately as Busy Bees, a school where many Plymouth children have been well taught before going on to senior schools. They were well established when I was a child over sixty years ago, and are still flourishing. They were based in a smaller building in those days in Western College Road, from which they get their name. Now in Seymour Road they have more room including a garden. Educationally they have reason to be proud. I read in the Western Evening Herald quite recently that three pupils were awarded scholarships to senior schools, at Badminton School, Bristol, Stover School, Newton Abbot and at my old school, St Dunstans Abbey in Plymouth.

Children I have met from Busy Bees over the years have always been happy, well adjusted and well mannered.

One of Plymouth's remarkable schools is **King's School**. Remarkable because it opened its doors as a direct request of the parents of the children at the Roundabout Nursery. When children left the Nursery School parents were looking for suitable schools in which to place their children. They approached Mrs Smyth to provide such a school.

After discussions with the leadership of the Christian Centre it was decided to open a reception class for rising fives in one spare room, near to the nursery complex. The venture soon showed every indication that it would be a success and a search for a new building commenced. After a time the Hartley Road building became available. It was purchased and now King's School caters for 3-11 year olds and is co-educational. There is a nursery unit for those aged 0-3 on site.

Educationally it offers a broad challenge in a Christian-based, co-educational environment teaching the National Curriculum. There are small classes, an emphasis on developing confidence, self-discipline and social skills.

The building is gracious, with a large playground and hard sports pitch. Parental involvement is encouraged. It also offers holiday and aftercare for working parents. King's School is a remarkable establishment offering an excellent education at moderate fees.

One needs to say a bit more about this school because if ever you have doubted the power of prayer this is a story which underlines how much we are all dependent on the Supreme Power.

When King's School was about to commence it did not have a qualified teacher. Pressure was put on Mary Smyth to advertise for a suitably trained person. This she resisted because she wanted a committed Christian. She remembers sitting in her office and banging her desk in sheer frustration saying ' Lord, you started all this! You must know who my teacher is - now I need to know'.

Later that day a face came into her mind. A girl she had met about two years previously. She knew her parents but did not even know if the girl was a teacher. Mary rang up the parents to be told that yes, the daughter was a teacher but was only working in a part time capacity. Teresa was the girl's name and she was married. neither she nor her husband were too keen on what Mary was offering but once Mary's vision had been explained they prayed together and Teresa joined the school. She is still there.

The following year the church spent £12,000 on another classroom and equipment and now had a total of 32 children. New premises were becoming an essential. Everything they looked at that was suitable they could not afford. Everything they could afford was refused planning consent without prohibitive conversion costs.

Suddenly out of the blue, after a lot of prayer, someone appeared at the Christian Centre saying that they had a school which had now closed and would the premises be of interest to them? They moved in at Easter, 1991, and now have 136 children. the staff are all committed Christians. Their salaries are a little low at the moment but they feel they are fulfilling their role as teachers.

The school had a normal visit from H.M. Inspector of Schools this summer who said the calibre of the staff was amazing and wanted to know Mary Smyth's recruiting methods. He was more than a little startled to be told ' By prayer'. His reply 'Keep doing it, it works.'

King's School

I have already written about Les Enfants which also flourishes.

The Ridgeway School in Plympton was opened in 1983 and is a mixed comprehensive catering for 880 pupils aged 11-18. The headmaster, Jon Lawson, is intensely proud of the record that the school has achieved in ten years. The GCSE pass rate is one of the highest in West Devon and with the A level results it improves significantly each year. Last year's sixth formers chalked up an 81% pass rate.

Coombe Dean School at Plymstock is another fine educational establishment with a visionary headteacher, Peter Reid. His school is a fine example of the comprehensive system which looks beyond the conventional curriculum to see what can be done to prepare its pupils for the outside world.

Several schools in the Plymouth area have Governors who are part of the commerce and industry sector. One, Victor Parson, is a Governor of the **John Kitto Community College** in Honicknowle and also on the governing board of the university. In the case of **Coombe Dean**, interest in the school has been taken by one of the earliest American companies to come to Plymouth, **Gleason**. The Director and General Manager, Robert Ball who is Plymouth born and bred believed the Coombe Dean project would greatly benefit future education in the locality and asked Peter Reid how Gleason could help.

Peter Reid explained his vision and concept of a business centre within the school with state-of-the-art equipment, running courses in finance, business management and secretarial skills. The centre was to be open for members of the community and available throughout the day, in the evenings and at weekends. Quite a vision.

Peter Reid had asked for £20,000 for the building and £25-27,000 for the equipment. After studying the proposals and costings, the Gleason Memorial Fund presented the school with a cheque for £47,000.

The new, well - equipped building allows 16-17 year old students to follow vocational courses without leaving the school site. The facilities are also available to pupils from other years and to adults, and courses are run in the evenings and in holidays.

The Director and General Manager of Gleason's Plymouth plant is delighted. He says 'Our company needs highly trained young people and many of our best apprentices have come from Coombe Dean.'

For me I was thrilled about the co-operation there is in Plymouth between industry and education.

To have chosen just one or two comprehensives in the city may seem inexcusable to the others but please believe that everyone of them has a standard of excellence and offers great opportunities to the children who go there.

Plymouth and Birmingham, I believe, are the only cities who still have grammar schools. Plymouth has excellent examples. I have chosen to write about **Devonport High School** for Boys as an example of the ability of these schools to produce outstanding results.

The headmaster, Mr Peck, has been at the school for a long time as have many of his staff. This grammar school was founded in 1896 originally in Devonport, but it moved in 1945 to the premises of the Stoke Military Hospital where it is housed in buildings dating from 1797. These ancient walls lend a great character to the school and overlook extensive playing fields. It draws its pupils not only from the whole of Plymouth but also from a wide area of West Devon and from South East Cornwall. Admission is at ll years but pupils are admitted at any age, with a significant number joining the sixth form for 'A' Level courses.

There are some 780 pupils in the school: small enough to maintain a strong sense of identity, division of the school into three parts for both academic and pastoral purposes ensures that every pupil is well known and well looked after.

Strong links are kept with parents, both through individual meetings and in formal consultation evenings, and these precede the taking of all-important decisions about a boy's curriculum or career. Experience has shown that it is perfectly possible for any boy gaining entry to the school to go on to university if that is his wish. Some, of course, enter employment at sixteen or after 'A' Level, and the school has maintained its traditional capacity for preparing young men for entry into the Royal Navy. Academic and industrial awards help many pupils to support their courses in higher education.

It is not all study at Devonport High School. Physical development and participation in sport is an important element in school life. Rugby, soccer and basketball are the main winter sports, with strong interest in badminton, squash, hockey and cross-country running; in summer the main emphasis is on athletics and cricket. That the school is as successful in sport as it is in academic studies is undoubted. In recent years they have won county or area titles in 11 different sports, representing the county in 19, and competing in no fewer than 11 different sports at schools' national level.

A strong musical tradition is sustained by many boys learning one of a range of fourteen instruments, which coupled with the enthusiasm for drama, enables the school to mount major musical or dramatic productions every year. The more accomplished musicians play for the county orchestras, while a large number forming the school's 'Big Band' undertake annual visits to international musical events abroad.

Links have been established with industry, especially with British Aerospace through the Sainsbury Trust's engineering scheme and through a number of practising engineers directly supporting the work of various subject departments. The school also makes good use of industry and the City's institutions of higher education for assistance with technological and design project work.

One of the most exciting projects of the last few years has been the acquisition of a house in Uzel in Brittany which gives pupils a regular opportunity of staying and studying in France. By living in a small community, using the resources of the area, and through associating with local schools, pupils are gaining an invaluable insight into the French way of life and so are better prepared for playing a full part in Europe.

Mr Peck will tell you that the Parent Teacher Association to which all parents and members of staff automatically belong, has been invaluable in bringing about improvements in the school's facilities. Guided by a large committee drawn from parents with children at every stage in the school, parents have become increasingly involved in raising funds for practical projects and in developing social activities to bring parents closer together, and in serving as governors of the School.

What I have said about Devonport High School for Boys is equally true about **Devonport High School for Girls** and

Devonport High School for Boys

Plymouth High School for Girls. The standard is high and girls go on to many high-powered careers.

Plymouth's two major independent schools are **Plymouth College** founded in 1877 and amalgamated with Mannamead School in 1896 and **St Dunstan's Abbey for Girls** founded at the eastern end of the Royal Naval Burial Ground in 1848.

When I went to call upon the Surgeon Captain at the Royal Naval Hospital he gave me a book on the history of the hospital and in it I found a poignant reminder of its past connection with St Dunstans. It came from the reminiscences of my first headmistress at the school, Sister Margaret Teresa, the Mother Superior.

'I may mention another memory that does not fade - that of the many funerals which passed the School from the R.N. Hospital. The band and muffled drums, the tramp of feet outside, the girls inside standing silent till the band had passed, then a short prayer for the dead, and work resumed. I wonder how many souls have been speeded by St Dunstan's children's prayers'.

Reading this sad little piece brought back the memory to me as well. I can remember standing by my desk, bobbed blonde head suitably lowered, black tunic, white shirt, red sash, denoting that I belonged to Downton House, my black woollen stockings trying to slip down my little legs in their buttoned shoes. The music was always the Dead March from Saul and I never hear it now without vividly remembering those days, regrettably regular occurrences.

Throughout my schooldays and for many who came after me, St Dunstans was synonymous with the Sisters of St Marys, Wantage, the Anglican Order whose work included not only teaching but via the Mother House in Wyndham Square, care of people in the parish of St Peters. This is the church in which Father Sam Philpott now does such sterling work. In those days the Sisters outnumbered the lay teachers and regular attendance in the school chapel and at St Peters was a required part of one's education, no matter what your creed. St Dunstans will always remain in my mind as a place of happiness, fun, dedication, chocolate cake on Fridays and Saints Days for tea, the annual Ascensiontide picnic for the whole school, myrtle in a bride's bouquet from a bush in the Sisters' Garden - my sister had her sprig although I escaped that pleasure, I eloped!

When I went to see Robin Bye, the headmaster, I had a superbly nostalgic time wandering through the school corridors, looking in through the doors of long-remembered classrooms, seeking out the odd corners in the grounds which were sacrosanct to sixth formers. He and I talked of the past and the present and were each able to help the other with our research: he into the past and me, the present. The Sisters have long gone, St Peters is no longer part of the school's religious upbringing but the atmosphere was still there. The girls were well mannered, their pride in the school was as great as mine and I only wish that my granddaughter lived near enough for her to get her education here.

The scholastic achievements of the school have never been higher and under Mr Bye's leadership it will continue to improve. He is a man who has adapted his career to become a specialist in the running of girls' schools. This interested me. I had never considered that one might have to take this sort of decision but apparently if a man opts for the distaff side then he is unlikely ever to become headmaster of a boys' school. I can understand that there are innumerable differences and I think it has to be a brave man to take on girls!

St Dunstans has not always had good facilities for sport or for non-academic activities. This is an area in which Robin Bye started his plans for the improvement of the school. The accommodation for pupils and boarders was obviously the priority. It is hoped that a house opposite the school gate may be used for senior boarding, with two large dormitories being turned into classrooms.

An all-purpose hockey pitch on the school campus is a must and hopefully with the help of the very strong Parent Teachers Association there will be a new sports hall.

The school is environmentally conscious, an area of rain forest was named after the school as a result of a fashion show organised by Utopia, an evolvement group in the school. You could tell the Sisters of Wantage were no longer there - male students from St Boniface and Devonport High School for boys joined St Dunstan's sixth formers and staff at the fashion show. In my time, apart from the visits of Father Hardy and Father Howard from St Peters, males were strictly non persona grata.

Boys too are welcome in the school from the age of 4-7 these days. It is a good education for them and the mixture at this age of the very young of both sexes has a civilising effect.

St. Dunstan's in 1993 felt as morally sound as it was in the nineteen twenties and thirties. A school to be proud of.

Plymouth College is beloved by Plymothians and known throughout the world with respect and affection by the many ex-patriates who passed through its portals in the early and most formative days of their lives. I read a book on the history of the school by Charles Robert Serpell, who died in 1949 and had had a longer intimate connection with the school than any other man, and so I have drawn on his knowledge, his comments and experiences to add my tribute to this great school.

By profession a lawyer, Charles Serpell was prominent in many directions in the life of Plymouth; but it is safe to say that of all his public work that which he undertook for the school lay nearest to his heart. His opening paragraph which I have taken the liberty of copying verbatim says so much.

'Seventy years in the life of a school is long enough to cover many generations of boys. By the time one of these boys reaches that age he has at most only another decade or so before him. But the school to which he was for a few years contributing for good or ill, consciously or unconsciously, the influence of his personality may well go on making history for centuries. If the school has survived it has anyhow probably got itself well established. It will have created records and acquired traditions such as to justify hopes of still greater achievement. But how did the school which has reached this so respectable age begin at all?'

Plymouth College began in 1877 in the building that is illustrated here. A school that had almagamated with Mannamead School, its senior by a few years. The classrooms, the well worn floors, the carvings of initials on some of the wood still speaks of generations past. This building is still the heart of the school but over the years it has grown tentacles, not in most cases attached so perhaps satellites would be a better word. There is a Sports Hall, a Science Block, new Common rooms, a theatre. Almost the whole of a gracious row of houses alongside the school has been purchased over the years making comfortable quarters for those who board. Whenever another property comes up there is always the hope that funds will be there for the school to acquire it. There may be everything that a school of the 1990's requires but no matter what is added it will never lose its original character. Its staff list speaks of Oxbridge graduates and men of letters from other universities but none the less qualified. They in their turn teach the young men who come here to a sufficiently high standard to emulate themselves in the ability to obtain university places and to enter professions and industry all over the world.

Famous names have started their days here, the services have always been able to rely on entries from Plymouth College. The law, accountancy and the Theatre have all claimed their number. One common bond always holds them altogether - the School. They meet in London for reunions, they gather in Plymouth for social occasions and it is always with pride that they talk of the past, the present and what they hope will be the future. Many have sons or grandsons currently in school.

The familiar playing fields which stretch out before the school to the borders of Devon Terrace and Ford Park Road are constantly in use. The old Cricket Pavilion of Charles Serpell's time has gone and been replaced by a solid stone affair. On summer afternoons the gentle click of a cricket ball as it hits the cricket bat and soars through the air to the boundary brings forth the oohs and aahs according to which eleven you support. It is a sight that pleases every Plymothian who passes by.

For the very young from 4½-11 years, Plymouth College has its Preparatory School just a mile or so away in Munday House,

Plymouth College

Hartley. The classes are small, there are a wide range of extra-curricular activities and specialist subject teaching. Full or weekly boarders are looked after splendidly and throughout all that time contact is maintained with the senior school to prepare these youngsters for their next step.

The University of Plymouth has a fine reputation, even though it is not yet one year old. From the days when it was a Technical School at Drake Circus it has always worked to a very high standard. After the war new buildings were added and have continued to be added bringing it first Polytechnic status and the final accolade that of a University.

A place here is highly regarded and whether it is for full time students or for those taking degrees or courses, perhaps released by their companies to do so, the range of subjects is vast. The motto 'The Quest to be Best' was applicable in the 1989/90 annual review of the Polytechnic and the purpose has not changed. The University also runs courses at partner colleges in Plymouth and across the region while always looking to Industry for substantial help which is willingly given.

It is far more than a place of education, it is also a place of research much of which ranks high in national and international league tables. In the last week I have been approached as a recent victim of a burglary and asked if I would be prepared to help with a survey the University has been commissioned to do in conjunction with Devon and Cornwall Police. The objective is to find out what can be done to improve security and the support that victims of such traumatic happenings need.

Marine Biologists work closely with the National Marine Aquarium and the Marine Biological Association about which I have written earlier in this book. A computerised system that could lead to a more effective use of foetal monitoring, saving patient stress and Health service money through a reduction in unnecessary caesarean births, is being developed in the faculty of Technology's School of Electronic, Communication and Electrical Engineering. The Analytical Chemistry Unit of the Department of Environmental Sciences, using its fast and incredibly accurate, inductively coupled plasma mass-spectrometer has been used to monitor contaminated milk, confirm that arsenic in fish is not harmful to humans and investigate trace element levels in supplements eaten by vegetarians and vegans. There are scientists testing gases that could help win the ozone layer war.

Perhaps more on the level of understanding of simpler minds like mine, is The Business School which is of enormous help to small businesses. They will tell you that 'In love there is said to be the seven-year ITCH. For small business the hazard is the three-year HITCH. But Plymouth Business School expertise is there to help!' Small to medium sized enterprises represent a major component of the economy of the South West which is why the Business School has been heavily involved in research, consultancy and training initiatives to assist the growth of smaller firms in Devon and Cornwall.

Whatever their subject, students of the University of Plymouth find that the life is fulfilling, the work quite tough but the sports, the social life, the accommodation available in the city, and above all the surroundings are some of the best in the country.

Subjects which adults can study at times that suit them and in small classes, have for years been the purpose of the education policy at **Swarthmore Adult Education Centre** on Mutley Plain. Here you can opt for anything from Spanish for Beginners to the Dynamics of Art Therapy. There are several language classes at different levels, Keep Fit, 'So you think you can't sing', Drawing and Painting, Life Classes, Archaeology. There must be well over 100 different classes available in the morning, afternoon and evening. It is a remarkable place with an interesting background.

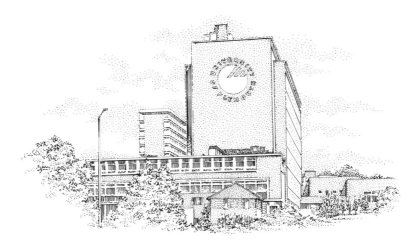

University of Plymouth

It was founded in 1920 by the Society of Friends (Quakers) but it is now run democratically by representatives of all groups involved in the centre. Courses are organised under the auspices of Devon County Council and Exeter University and are available to all those over school age who wish to take advantage of them at whatever stage of their lives that suits them best.

Richard Allman is the Warden and holds all the various activities together. When I saw him he was deeply concerned about the possible cuts in government funding. One hopes that this will never happen. It is so important and there is a groundswell of people who are becoming more and more desirous of expanding their knowledge even in later life.

I remember the Swarthmore from my young days when I was taught First Aid by St John Ambulance. I remember the friendly coffee bar and I also remember when various small theatre companies used the stage and auditorium for productions. The great actress, Joan Plowright, widow of Lord Olivier, trod the boards here on more than one occasion. We went there for the sheer pleasure of seeing live theatre, the seats were hard and the auditorium frequently cold, but nothing would have kept us away.

Something educational but totally different is **West Devon Outdoor Education Centre** at Martinsgate, Bretonside. The Director is Martin Northcott who has held this onerous post for 15 years. It is a Devon County Council facility for providing outdoor activity for West Devon - football, rugby and cricket are not included. It is largely self-financing but it is subsidised by Devon. The basis of the activities is 50% teaching the skill itself and 50% developing the persons themselves. For example, teaching sailing to workers in industry does not just teach them the skill of sailing but also develops judgemental abilities to cope with varying conditions and options.

The range of activities covers sailing, caving, climbing, canoeing, kyaking, cycling and a series of task-based activities for encouraging problem-solving and personal development. I wondered who the end users would be and I rapidly discovered that companies send managers, supervisors and employment trainees. There are children still at school and Social Services referrals.

One of Martin Northcott's desires is to see more of a partnership develop between companies and schools. Much as Gleason has done for Coombe Dean with a Business School so perhaps a company could adopt a school with a view to help fund outdoor activities. This would help provide a continuity from primary education right through to industrial training and management development where appropriate. It could also continue as a service to the community.

This is a busy place with a secretary and a staff of six full time people as well as Martin. This number is added to in the summer when it almost doubles. There are more activities as well then, of course.

One area of future development is with people needing special help, and perhaps volunteers could be found to provide the higher staff/trainee ratio this would require.

West Devon Outdoor Education centre was totally new to me and I wonder how many more Plymothians did not know it existed. It is tremendous work and I hope it will get the support that Martin Northcott and his dedicated team need.

The biggest private training organisation in Great Britain is the nationwide company, **Astra Training Services Ltd**. It comprises over 40 training centres, a national management training service and the Head Office based in Sheffield. The company was created on 1st May 1990. Here in Plymouth is one of the centres based in Strode Road on the Newnham Industrial Estate in Plympton.

The major service it offers is delivery of training, either in its own centre or employer premises. The company also provides a consultancy service for those employers who need help in identifying their training needs, formulating training plans and implementing training programmes. A recruitment service is included in this consultancy provision. The company develops and sells open learning and other training support material.

Astra currently provides over 250 different programmes in its range of services. These have been designed so as to up- date, extend or develop new skills for both the employed and the unemployed. Current or additional programmes may be customised to suit the ever changing needs of employers and employees.

Companies have come to expect and receive a quality of service which is assured through the development and maintenance of a quality management system. The system is subjected to third party endorsement by independent experts on a regular basis. Plymouth gained the BS5750 Part I Certification for Management Quality and Excellence in 1992.

Like any good training centre much depends on the quality of the men or women at the top. In Plymouth we have three committed men at the helm. John Humphreys, the Centre manager is a Welshman but can claim the West Country because he was brought up in Somerset. His background is in engineering at the top end doing work for BAC/Rolls Royce. He has worked with the Department of Employment and on new Youth Training Programmes. He moved to Plymouth in 1985 to start the first Open T.E.C. High Technology Projects and became the Centre Manager in 1988 before it became Astra Training Services.

John Boulting is also a Welshman but obtained his teaching certificate whilst he was in Australia and is responsible for contracts with Government departments.

The third member of this powerful triumvirate is Dennis Birch, the Contracts Manager who sells the training to industry.

The quality of training demands high standards from these three men which they maintain and pass on to anyone under training.

Someone who has never been daunted by any challenge is Suzanne Sparrow whose **Suzanne Sparrow Plymouth Language School** in North Road East is known throughout Europe and far beyond. This determined lady, who was once a boating WREN in the years of the war, started quite modestly having seen the need for the teaching of languages outside schools and for the adult population.

In 1987 it became apparent that she was running out of space for her classes and if she was to expand and meet the needs of the pupils clamouring at her doors a new building was needed. Nothing was suitable until she found in North Road East an hotel which the owners wanted to sell. For a very short time she became the owner of this hotel, gradually getting rid of her customers and on Boxing Day 1987 she and her right hand man, Peter Clarke with some willing volunteers started tearing the building apart. They re-wired, knocked down walls, tore off endless layers of ugly wall paper, plastered, papered and painted and by the first day of term on January 4th, there was a complete transformation. The Suzanne Sparrow Plymouth Language School opened its doors with more classrooms, more space and more pupils.

There are few languages that are not taught. Certainly those of the Western world with Russian, Chinese and Japanese added to them but it is English that is being taught to foreigners in the main rather than the other way round. It is taken very seriously although the element of fun is always there in anything that Suzanne Sparrow undertakes. Pupils come from foreign parts for a few weeks, a term or maybe a very short time. Part of the school's purpose is to find suitable accommodation for these visitors and preferably in homes where they will be encouraged to speak English and at the same time not feel homesick.

It has taken some years to acquire the number of families prepared to offer this accommodation but now it falls into a fairly regular pattern. The families have become Suzanne's friends and the pupils invariably invite their hosts, and frequently Suzanne and Peter, to visit them in their homes. Suzanne has more invitations in any year than she can possibly accept.

The quality of the work done in the school is recognised by the British Council who carry out spot checks every three years. Their praise is high. Business men send employees for lessons when it is necessary for them to work abroad. This is becoming more and more important as we strengthen our links with Europe.

Suzanne Sparrow was at one time the Chairman of the Chamber of Commerce, quite an accolade. Women do not usually get offered this chair. It is strange how fate plays a part in life. Peter was teaching in France when he met Suzanne Sparrow. He had no intention of coming back to Britain but resisting the persuasion of this charming lady is hard and Peter returned to England and to the Suzanne Sparrow Plymouth Language School. A move he has never regretted.

For me the people I have talked to in this chapter have given me yet another insight into Plymouth. I appreciate I have left much out: the **College of St Mark and St John** or Marjon as it is known, for one. This excellent Teacher Training College has done much for many students. Sadly I was never able to talk to anyone there to get sufficient information to do them justice. This is not their fault and Plymouth is proud to have their presence.

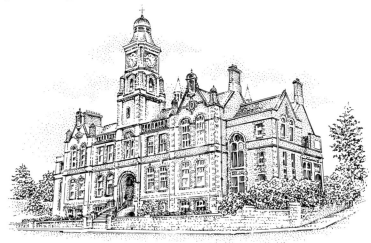

An old building of Devonport Technical College

CHAPTER 9

Sport for All

My family tease me unmercifully because I am the archetypal armchair sportsperson! I am glued to the television every Saturday. I read the sports columns of the daily newspapers avidly and I am prone to long for a golfer to miss a putt if he happens to be playing for the wrong team! I cheerfully hurl abuse at referees, and sigh with frustration if Steve Davis misses a simple black. This does not really qualify me to write in depth about the wide range of sporting activities that Plymouth has to offer. However a book on the city without a chapter on sport would be like an egg without a yolk. Whether you are a participant or a spectator, the enthusiasm for matters sporting is an integral part of life in the city.

Surrounded by the rivers and the sea, **Queen Annes's Battery** seems a natural starting point. This purpose-built marina is the home of many businesses, not all of them associated with yachts and sailing. It is the home of the annual boat show which creates interest and business for many people. It is also a time when inventions are on display. Prince Charles' Business Youth Award was the source from which the inventor of a car trailer that converts to a boat was financed. Trevor Thompson, who is only 24 was made redundant and this enterprise has given him a new zest for life.

The managing director of Queen Anne's Battery is an intrepid yachtsman, Mark Gatehouse, who in 1992 was named as the city's Yachtsman of the Year by the Port of Plymouth Sailing Association and became the first person to receive a new trophy at the association's first prize giving ceremony. He is a regular transatlantic sailor and 1992 saw him claiming victory as the second monohull and first British yacht to cross the finishing line in the Radio Europe I single-handed transatlantic race from Plymouth to Newport, Rhode Island.

It is the ability of Queen Anne's Battery to act as a gathering point for yachts that has enabled Plymouth to attract major sailing events. Since the removal of the **Royal Western Yacht Club** from its old premises, now occupied by the Waterfront, and its occupation of purpose built accommodation at Queen Anne's

Battery, the link between the marina and the Royal Western has made it much easier to attract events and to acquire sponsors.

When yachts are arriving at Queen Anne's Battery for these occasions, it is a colourful and wonderful sight. The boats of all shapes and sizes rock gently alongside, their halyards tinkling. When they put to sea Plymouth Sound is the scene of a flurry of activity with the yachts making for the starting line and followed by a bevy of smaller boats, all anxious to speed them on their way. Most of the crew and passengers on them wish that they were about to take part in a great adventure. They are in need of all sorts of services the city can offer the boats, from chandlery to engineering. The chatter of yachtsmen in many different languages produces a tremendous atmosphere and the bar of the Royal Western Yacht Club is a natural meeting place for the fraternity. Many of these sailors know each other well from other races.

It is not always the big yachts which take pride of place at the marina. Throughout the year local yachtsmen keep their boats berthed here. It is safe, protected and friendly, with every facility a yachtsman could wish for.

Queen Anne's Battery

Plymouth has seen many great moments of triumph and sadness when boats return after memorable voyages. No one will ever forget the arrival of Sir Francis Chichester in Gypsy Moth. That was in the days of the Royal Western's former home but one is always reminded of these great occasions when one looks at the number of stunning photographs in the club.

Founded in 1827, few organising bodies in international sport can claim a bigger role on the world stage than the Royal Western Yacht Club. It is quite difficult to imagine our ancestors visiting a yacht club in the early 19th century but that is what they did. Plymouth for centuries had been inseparable from every kind of maritime venture and so it should not surprise me that it gave birth to one of the first yacht clubs.

It was not originally called the Royal Western but answered to the name of the Port of Plymouth Royal Clarence Regatta Club and its purpose was to organise an annual regatta, to provide an interesting and informative social programme, and through racing to stimulate improvements in naval architecture. If you talk to the Commodore, Commander Lloyd Foster, or to the Secretary, Major John Lewis, you will find the aims are much the same today: certainly the principles are upheld.

In the early days the club showed its strength in long-distance cruising. Members' yachts wearing the blue ensign for which their royal patron, Queen Victoria, had granted a warrant, were received in the farthest corners of the globe from Brazil to Russia, Capetown to Ceylon.

Even at the very beginning the club did more than run an annual regatta. It organised each year a series of races for J-class yachts, which continued right up until 1934.

Yachts competing in such races never ventured too far offshore. With Plymouth as its base, the starting point for the voyages of Anson, Drake and Cook, it was natural that the world's first ocean race should be sailed under the burgee of the Royal Western Yacht Club. The course was round the Fastnet rock, and the year was the year of my birth, 1925. It was at dinner in the club afterwards that the Ocean Racing Club, later to become the Royal Ocean Racing Club,was conceived.

The Fastnet Race remains one of the ocean racing classics for fully-crewed yachts. The Royal Western has been instrumental in organising the finishing arrangements ever since.

Perhaps the unique claim to recognition the Royal Western has in the world of yachting today is for short-handed ocean racing. For the last 30 years, since the inception of the first single-handed ocean race, the club has been at the forefront of short-handed racing. In addition to those which it organises directly, there are others which it has inspired.

Probably the most exciting race and the one that thrills even those who are not nautically minded, is the Single-Handed Transatlantic Race which all began in 1959 when an ex-Royal Marines Cockleshell war hero called Blondie Hasler, who was making a name for himself all over again as an innovator in sailing, wrote to the Royal Western Yacht Club to ask if the club would organise a single-handed race across the Atlantic in which he and Francis Chichester would take part. The Club agreed, and the first race was sailed in 1960 with sponsorship by the Observer newspaper. There were four entries and the race was won by Francis Chichester in 40½ days.

What has marked out the Single-Handed Transatlantic Race as an event of far-reaching importance, is not, as one might expect, simply that competitors are single-handed. Nor that it launched Sir Francis Chichester's remarkable sailing career. Nor even that yachting in France can be directly attributed to it. It was, in fact, the far sighted approach of the Royal Western Yacht Club which ran, and still runs, the race under its own liberal rules, allowing lines of development which would have been strangled at birth in conventional yacht racing. The club allowed multihulls, indeed yachts of all types to race together. It permitted sponsorship, and introduced rules to guide and control its growth. The club encouraged invention and experimentation: self steering systems for example, would not have reached the current state of the art without the incentive provided by the race.

All this development has had a measurable influence on sailing boats today. Compare the time of the first winner (40½ days) with the last (10 days).

Another suggestion of Blondie Hasler's taken up by the club was the Round Britain and Ireland Race - two-handed in recognition of the demands of long distance racing close to land. There are four compulsory stops of 48 hours each. I have a particular interest in this race this year because my colleague, Andrew 'Spud' Spedding, is a competitor.

The club also organises a two-handed transatlantic race which is fitted into the calendar between the four-yearly single handed event. The first two-handed transatlantic race took place in 1981 and is now an established part of the racing calendar.

Other Royal Western events include an autumn and winter series attracting over 100 boats per race, a race from Plymouth to its twinned city in Spain, San Sebastian, and a three-legged race to France and the Channel Islands. The club plays host, too, to international Ton Cup events, to national championships for keelboat classes like the Sigma 33 and J24, and to the new and spectacular Ultra 30s. The club also encourages and supports a strong cadet section, with weekly training sessions during the summer.

It is a long time since the original members in the time of Queen Victoria looked out over the waterfront in Plymouth and planned the first regatta. If they could see what the club has since achieved, what kind of mark it has made on the world of sailing, and how it has lived up to those early ideals, they would probably be astounded. They would certainly be proud.

The members of the Royal Western use the club for many purposes including the splendid social functions which are regular happenings. I was there not so very long ago having tea with David Owen, now Lord Owen, and I learnt how often businesses of the local branch of the CBI use its facilities. In fact David Owen was addressing just such a gathering in the evening that we met. The setting is wonderful and the facilities excellent.

The Sea Chest Nautical Bookshop is one of the many thriving businesses within the marina. You will find it in the Dolphin Building. Owned and run by Robert Dearn, an ex air sea rescue man stationed at R.A.F. Mountbatten, and a Yachtmaster Examiner with the island Sailing Club at Salcombe. He specialises in charts and tide tables as well as a whole library of nautical books from knots, rope and canvaswork to voyages, narratives and biography, radio, radar and electronics and world cruising & passage planning. He is one of about fourteen Admiralty chart agents in the country: charts which have to be corrected daily. He

Established

A.D. 1827.

Royal Western Yacht Club

has pilotage information for all round the world, a secondhand section on maritime affairs, particularly useful for finding an out of print book, and a hundred other interests. Mail order is quite a significant part of his business.

I had no idea that the correction and updating of Admiralty charts was carried out on such a daily basis. Each day the postman delivers a package from the Hydrographics department at Taunton. In the package will be any alterations for example a buoy or a lightship being re-positioned. Bob Dearn then has to alter the appropriate charts in stock. It genuinely is a daily routine for him; I was amazed that there could possibly be so many changes. I love bookshops anyway and the Sea Chest was a new and fascinating experience.

One bright and sparkling lady, **Ros James**, runs her insurance business from an office in Queen Anne's Battery. Her business deals mainly with commercial funding, an area in which she has considerable expertise. If you ever want to explore this avenue she will be delighted to advise you.

Ros James lives in Tavistock but for some years has worked in the insurance industry in Plymouth. At one time she was one of the success stories of the Business Mortgage Co, now Nykredit. Her enthusiasm for commerce is infectious and so is the determination with which she holds together Plymouth Breakfast Club in conjunction with Peat Marwick. This is an informal club that meets for breakfast three times a year in the Moat House, enjoys a first class breakfast, some Bucks Fizz and words of wisdom, fun and interest from a guest speaker.There are normally about a hundred people there from all walks of professional life in the City. We meet at 8am and one can expect to be away from there before 9.15am in time for the day's work. I find it interesting as much to watch all the liveliest minds in Plymouth at work so early in the morning, as I do for anything else. The idea for the Breakfast Club was entirely Ros James's and with her usual finesse she has managed to keep it going very successfully.

The other two marinas in the City are Sutton Harbour which tends to be used by 'sitting tenants' rather more than visitors and the **Mayflower Marina** on the Devonport side of the city tucked away from the hustle and bustle of commercial life in Richmond Walk. It offers a wonderful anchorage for yachtsmen, and more importantly offers them total security. It has marvellous facilities including shower rooms which are designed as individual rather than communal bathing houses. Quite an innovation and one that I would like to see emulated by many more marinas.

There are several smaller yacht clubs in Plymouth including the oldest and very prestigious **Royal Corinthian**, and the lively **Mayflower Sailing Club** with its headquarters just by the Mayflower Steps. This is a club for the small boat enthusiasts and every weekend you will see members boats racing in the Sound. They frequently host regattas and racing weeks for specific designs of boats.

Whilst I am still talking about the water it is the moment to talk about **Fort Bovisand** which has a site of over 30 acres and includes a breakwater fort. There is a diving course to which pupils are compelled to come back in order to take their exams no matter where they have been instructed.

People from all over the world travel to Fort Bovisand for commercial diving training. The Plymouth centre is the only place in the world which operates open water examinations for the certification scheme for welding and inspection personnel organisation.

A mock up of an oil rig structure is situated below the fort and divers taking the exam have to study it for various flaws which were deliberately added during its construction.

During the inspection a diver will have to take photographs and make various notes on the structure.Above water Bovisand instructors can monitor a diver's progress via pictures transmitted from a small video camera attached to commercial diving helmets.

Once the diver has completed his inspection he will tackle a written paper in a room on the fort.

Commercial diving really took off during the exploration for oil and gas in the USA during the 1960's and this continued into the 1970s with the discovery of oil in the North Sea.

A glamorous job? It is a different world where only the tough survive and you certainly do not meet any commercial divers over the age of 45.

Fort Bovisand is not only there for commercial purposes. Commander Alan Bax, the man in charge, with his qualified instructors runs a number of courses for sport diving. For example, you can take a five day diving holiday which is planned to bring all level of divers together for a week of varied and interesting dives from shore, inflatable or one of the diving launches, depending on the prevailing environmental conditions. It also gives visiting divers the opportunity to visit some of the many centres of maritime interest in Plymouth and its surroundings.

All the bother of organising and planning is taken care of by the experienced and knowledgeable marshals and boat skippers, so you really can enjoy yourself. Personal Diving equipment, extra cylinders, compasses and so on are available from Fort Bovisand's hire centre, but all necessary safety equipment - inflatable, resuscitator, radios, etc - is provided.

Every summer a Bovisand Camp is held and whether you have just learned to dive, or have been diving for some time the 'Camp' is designed to provide the opportunity to learn about, and take part in, one or more of the fascinating activities which can be enjoyed after the first thrill of learning to dive. The Camp is divided into six modules each of 5 days, and those who are learning to dive during the summer might think it worthwhile to adjust the timing of their course to fit in with a Summer Camp module.

There are all sorts of leisure activities too including underwater photography. The list is endless, some of it practical and some of it just for fun.

One aspect of the work of Fort Bovisand is its use to medicine. For example, victims of attempted suicide, and cancer patients given an accidental radiation overdose, are just some of the people who have benefited from treatment in the Fort Bovisand recompression chambers. Plymouth's pioneering Diving Diseases Research Centre has become famous for saving the lives of divers suffering from the bends. Now an increasing number of patients who have never been diving in their lives are being treated in the centre's recompression chambers, often with dramatic results. One man who will vouch for this and champions the cause of high oxygen therapy after undergoing a course of treatment in a recompression chamber, is Jeff Harris, the owner of **Just Leather** in Cornwall Street. He had an unsuccessful operation at Greenbank Hospital after doctors diagnosed cancer of the jaw. He was told he would need another operation this time to rebuild the jaw with bone from his hip. But one of the consultants at Greenbank had been to America and knew about hyperbaric oxygen treatment so he suggested that Mr Harris try it.

Before and after the second operation Mr Harris received a series of treatments in a recompression chamber and made a remarkably swift recovery. It was totally successful and Mr Harris has been given the all clear by his doctors who say his jaw is now free of the disease.

The DDRC is desperately in need of funds mainly for a new purpose-built recompression chamber that would allow for frail and disabled patients. This is all very new and the DDRC's two doctors need to carry out more trials. They are convinced that high pressure oxygen is the most effective treatment for victims of severe carbon monoxide poisoning and for certain types of chronic infection.

Returning to Fort Bovisand itself. This very successful operation has developed quickly over the last few years and more and more buildings are being converted into accommodation both for self-catering use and for schools and groups who want to use the facilities and the expertise of the Diving Centre. The accommodation and the classrooms are frequently used by Joint Service personnel.

People from all over the world come to the courses and yet for most of them the only way they discovered the existence of Fort Bovisand was by word of mouth.

One odd thing Commander Bax told me was that it is difficult to get Plymothians to try diving. In order to rectify that it is perfectly in order to telephone and make an appointment to visit Fort Bovisand which will cost you nothing. The object of the visit would be to try the equipment and have a go in the harbour just to see if you like it. A very fair offer - I wish I was younger.

Have you ever tried hot air ballooning? It is incredible, the world seems far away and the sense of peace and beauty is overpowering. **The Apollo Balloon Company Limited**, based at Highland House, Highland Street, Ivybridge, offers us the chance to do what the managing director, John Watkins, describes as 'dance the light fantastic across the rugged wilderness of Dartmoor and the valleys of the South Hams'. He is now in the fourth year of operation and has two hot air balloons Apollo Moonchaser and Apollo Moonduster. Over one thousand balloonists have now experienced the unique sensation of a balloon flight in Devon. Flights are scheduled throughout the year usually early in the morning or early evening when the weather is more stable. The launch is from sites selected with regard to the wind direction so as to provide a flight path of outstanding beauty and a flight time of approximately one hour.

At the end of the flight you receive a flight certificate and enjoy a glass or two of apres-balloon champagne. It is absolutely wonderful.

It all begins to become magical when you meet the pilot and crew and watch with eager anticipation as Apollo Moonchaser is spread and inflated. Acres of coloured nylon are transformed into an aircraft of inspiring beauty: a perfect mix of simplicity combined with modern design.

The moment you climb aboard, the butterflies will start flapping inside you but the traditionally constructed wicker basket is sturdy, your captain calm and professional and as the balloon lifts you gently into the sky your whole world changes. Early morning sunshine makes the countryside glisten, and picks out rivers and streams like diamonds as they snake their path from the high plateaus of Dartmoor, past the ancient hut circles of the Beaker civilisations and on through the swathe of green foothills and valleys for which Devon is famous. Late afternoon and evening flights hold similar enchantments and for the wildlife enthusiasts, you will be surprised at how often the balloon will catch unawares, a fox, a hare or a deer.

You need have no worry about the landing site. From the moment you take off until you land the radio is in contact with the recovery crew who meet you with the company's Land Rover retrieve vehicle and return you to base - after the champagne, of course.

It is a truly fantastic experience. Wonderful for individuals and marvellous for corporate events. For the latter the company are more than happy to arrange launch sites so as to conform with an entertainment itinerary. John Watkins is very used to working closely with Devon's major hotels and conference venues.

A Balloon Flight

The scene of the **Golden Clay Shoot** is a wooded, secluded Devon valley with a fast flowing stream running down from Dartmoor. Ponds reflect the occasional buzzard circling far overhead.

Those who have shot clays before will love this exceptional setting. For beginners it's the perfect place to taste the excitement of this new sport, with friendly advice and encouragement.

For everyone the emphasis is on safety, an element of competition - and enormous fun!

There are a variety of stands in the valley equipped with modern traps capable of throwing clays in hundreds of ways to simulate the different flight characteristics of wildfowl and game birds. They vary the challenge for guests, from the 'driven pheasant' to the more exacting 'springing teal'.

Each guest is issued with one of to-day's most suitable clay-shooting guns, a modern over-and-under twelve bore. Lighter 20 bore guns are supplied for ladies. Guests pass from stand to stand, getting new angles on the excitement of clay shooting.

The Cobbold family own and run these super days, coach their guests, describing the action in advance and showing them the best approach. Everyone wants to do well. But in the end it's the taking part and the enjoyment which make the Golden Clay Shoot a day worth remembering.

A typical day's programme starts at 10am when you are welcomed to Newnham Park and introduced to the guns, their handling, etiquette, and the all important Golden Clay Shoot rules for safety - good shooting is no accident.

At 11 o'clock the shoot starts and it is surprising how quickly those new to the sport gain confidence and quickly become caught up in the excitement.

Everyone stops at 12.30 and returns to an excellent lunch in the elegance of the Georgian dining room. Alternatively for half-day events a barbecue at the shooting grounds is organised.

You are not allowed to linger over lunch for too long. At two o'clock there is more individual shooting, with the climax of the day, a 'Flurry'. Pairs compete against other pairs, seeing who can break the most clays thrown continuously during two minutes of rapid fire.

By four thirty when you are just beginning to feel the exertions of the day, you are given a Devonshire cream tea, followed by prize-giving, with a Golden Clay Shoot memento for every guest as well as individual photographs taken during the day's shooting as a reminder of a day of excitement and achievement.

All this goes on within a few minutes drive from the city centre, airport and A38 for the M5.

It is always the background stories that interest me. Newnham Park Estate was a victim of the European Common Agricultural Policy. Michael Cobbold told me that it was difficult to know what to do with redundant farmland that is no longer viable but is part of an estate which has been in his wife's family for over 900 years and which was entailed to her in 1950 - the third time in 200 years that it passed through the female line. Since that time the Cobbolds have broken the entail and will only pass the house on to their children if they want it. Michael Cobbold describes the house and estate, beautiful as it undoubtedly is, as a 'Millstone in the Making' for future generations. Very sad. The house is so gracious. An early Georgian building '5 window square'.

By 1970 the Cobbolds decided that being absentee landlords was not a good idea and so they moved into the house. Like all big houses today it is expensive to run and the necessity spawned the idea for using the land and the house for private and corporate days out Clay Pigeon shooting. The latter are usually the guests because it is more difficult to get enough individuals together.

Michael Cobbold is always looking for other ways in which the estate can be used. In August of this year Newnham will be the venue for the International Mountain Bike Race as well as for a couple of other national races during the year. They also have 'Off-Road' (Landrover) events and are hoping to have a National event in 1994

As a family the Cobbolds genuinely welcome people to the Golden Clay Shoot and to any other occasion. It is a day out that you will remember for always.

From clay pigeon shooting to skiing is quite a step but each has its own aficionados. At the **Plymouth Ski Centre**, Andrew

Gordon, the General Manager for John Nike Leisuresport, is adding to the number of people who use the centre regularly by ensuring that newcomers understand what the ski-centre is all about. Dri-skiing has been developed as a sport in its own right but Andrew sees it also complimenting snow skiing - using dri-skiing to raise the level of competence for those who cannot get to the snow regularly enough.

The Complex at Alpine Park features the largest floodlit dry ski slopes in the South West incorporating the latest 'state of the art' facilities. The main slope is 160 metres long and 20 metres wide, covered with Ski Tech, a nylon brush matting that is kept slightly moist all the time by a sophisticated mist system. There are also two smaller slopes for beginners and skiers of an intermediate standard. The complex is open every day of the year except Christmas and Boxing Day and the opening hours are extended during December, January and February.

Skiing at Plymouth Ski Centre

Andrew Gordon has done much to make it possible for schools to use the dri-ski slopes. At one time it was far too expensive but the prices have been cut to almost half the original rate and school groups are now returning.

If you are unable to attend group lessons, private tuition is available. Courses can be arranged at any level from beginners to advanced and expert. This is the ideal way to improve technique on a personal basis.

Disabled skiers are very welcome and the complex has a number of instructors qualified to teach the disabled. Andrew Gordon has set up a club for disabled skiers under the auspices of the BSCD for which he will greatly appreciate volunteer helpers. Equipment and money is not needed - that is already available.

The list of different options at the complex is never ending. There is an over 50's morning run each week as an informal taster lesson for senior citizens, followed by coffee in the bar. I am told it is never too late to take up skiing. There is 'Shape up and Ski' for ladies of all abilities which offers an informal two hours of skiing and keep fit exercises with instruction, followed by coffee in the Alpine Lodge.

A limited number of snowboards are available for hire for use by experienced snowboarders, as well as lessons for those beginners who wish to try this exciting new sport that is rapidly gaining popularity throughout Europe.

The Alpine Lodge Restaurant is open to everyone and offers a wide menu with something for everyone from their famous doorstop sandwiches to a 'ski and fondue'. The food is good and the price is right. A good way to end a visit to the complex.

Andrew Gordon comes from Edinburgh and I wondered why he wanted to come so far south. Firstly the job appealed to him and his wife and secondly he finds Plymouth as beautiful as Edinburgh in its own way and each has a variety of beautiful settings. Another family who are quite happy to become Plymothians by adoption!

The trio who are the partners in **Mountain Action** at Faraday Mill, Roger Thomson, Karen Oliver and Ramon Scott set up their business in Plymouth because the area was not served well for their merchandise. Skiing is the major part of the business and the opening of the dry ski slope underlined the need for somewhere Plymothians could buy what they needed for this sport and for many others.

Traditionally skiing is promoted in winter and rock climbing and walking in summer, hence the name Mountain Action.

Clothing has to be practical and protective and preferably not outrageously fashionable. The essential test is that everything they sell passes a simple criteria -' it does the job' for which it is designed. At the moment colours are bright and strong which enhances safety in the snow. Fluorescent colours are no longer the 'in thing'. A young surfer I met the other day informed me that only amateurs appear in this sort of garish gear!

Most of Mountain Action's winter customers are experienced skiers, as novices tend to hire equipment until they have achieved a level of competence or given up! I was instructed that height and weight dictate ski length and purpose dictates construction. It makes commonsense but was not something I had considered before talking to this well informed partnership. I learnt also that at one time ordinary shoes or boots were used in skiing, but the increasing number of ankle injuries as the sport became more generally accessible brought about the development of large, rigid boots to support the ankles safely. Expert advice is needed to ensure you have the right size, fastenings and systems. It is a complex business and this is why Mountain Action is the ideal place to be if you need advice and equipment.

It has taken a while for the walking and climbing side of the business to grow but with the emphasis and growing momentum in adventure and activity holidays, it is necessary for the would be participant to have the right gear. Widespread media coverage of any sport always boosts trade and this is especially noticeable recently.

Mountain Action has a practice climbing wall upstairs and customers can test potential purchases on site. Brilliant idea. No one minds if you make an idiot of yourself: you will find yourself surrounded by helpful and friendly staff!

At the request of their growing number of customers, Mountain Action are setting up a climbing school. This will be aimed at adults who do not know where to start. Lessons on rope techniques will start the training and the first practical run will be on the internal wall where it is safe. Tackling the rugged world outside will come later.

Even if you are not planning a skiing or climbing holiday it will be more than worthwhile taking yourself to Faraday Mill and seeing what these enterprising people have in stock and what they are prepared to teach you.

My children learnt to swim at **Ballards** and it is for this reason that I am including it in this chapter although Archibald Cassanova Ballard was such a character that he should really be featured in the chapter 'The Time, the Place and the People'.

If you read some of the old newspaper cuttings about Mr Ballard you will discover that he was considered to be a man of taciturn nature, one of the cities most mysterious and controversial figures between the wars and reputed to be a millionaire. What he did do was to give devoted but erratic service to the boys in the neighbourhood. He formed clubs for them and it was his habit to give threepenny bits to the boys who came to his clubs, and promise ten shillings in cash or kind to every boy, when the attendance at the Sunday morning service at the Ballard Institute reached 5,000. This did not go down too well with the public. The boys loved him for himself and for his eccentricities. They never knew what to expect. They could turn up at the club and find they were sent to the cinema or local theatre. On one famous occasion, a certain number of boys found themselves in possession of dinner jackets!

The churches objected that Mr Ballard was robbing them of their Sunday School membership, and incalculating the wrong principles, - that of receiving instead of giving. The Ballard boys wanted their ten shillings and got it when one Sunday the attendance reached 5,800. Their benefactor defended himself by saying that he only gave to those who needed his help.

In 1930 Mr Ballard handed over his institute for boys in Millbay Road to the local education authority, insisting however that the name remained intact. He had grown tired of criticism. Today we would recognise what he was trying to do but in the 1920s he was probably the only man in Plymouth to understand the needs of youth and realise that they had problems. Yet here was a man who was not even a Plymothian. When he was asked why he came to the city from London he replied ' I noticed on a visit in 1923 how unruly the youngsters were. Before he took on the lavish Millbay road site - where British Telecom is now - he had two boys clubs in Treville Street and Athenaeum Lane. He was determined that boys from under-privileged families should be well educated but with a typically Victorian attitude to the education of girls - that was unnecessary!

The Ballard institute was overseen by 12 Trustees. The Plymouth Education Authority was given the right to nominate 7 of the trustees. The Chairman of the Plymouth Education Authority was automatically the chair of the trustees and the Director of Education, the Secretary. There are still 12 trustees today but they are all Plymothians who have an interest in Youth work. If you have the time it is still possible to read the minutes of the trustee's meetings from 1928 onwards. For example on the 29th October 1930 the trustees considered 270 applications for the post of organiser of the Institute, from all over the country. A sub-committee brought the number of applicants down to 12 and at a subsequent meeting a Reverend member of the committee was despatched to London to enquire into the background of one of the applicants. After six months deliberation and the expenditure of large sums of money, the trustees decided not to appoint an organiser after all!

Archibald Ballard might have become frustrated with the council but his philanthropy continued. In 1933 he bought the former Stoke Military Hospital and offered it to the University College of the South-West and Plymouth Education Committee, with the idea it should be used to establish an extension of the University College in Plymouth. The offer was not well received and eventually Mr Ballard withdrew his offer and sold the building to the local authority, for use in primary education.

The original Ballard Institute was bombed in 1943 much at the same time as Archibald Cassanova Ballard died in a home in Teignmouth - a lonely old man.

Temporary premises were used for Ballards until in 1963 the present premises were designed and built and gained recognition for being the best Youth Club in Great Britain. It has its own theatre seating 400, a Games Room, Gym, Television Room, Swimming Pool and Coffee Bar.

At the time it was built somewhere between 7-8000 people a week used the facilities. With the growth of TV, clubs, Videos this declined to such an extent than in the 1980's Plymouth nearly lost this excellent facility. The Trustees had to change the emphasis from the original Trust Charter and become self supporting. This has been very successful and it has become more of a Community Centre. It has changed its name as well. Now it is the Ballard Activity Centre. It receives no financial assistance from any authority or any hand-outs. What it has it earns.

The theatre is under contract to the Theatre Royal for rehearsals during the day. It is quite a regular sight to see visiting stars in the Coffee Shop during breaks. In the evening the theatre is used for Keep Fit, Dance to Music, Aerobics, Weight Watchers, serious Martial Art practice. Rooms are used for meetings and demonstrations. Artists are encouraged to display their work. There is French for children and Yoga. A whole range of activities beneficial to the community.

The swimming pool is not open to the public but it does run at a profit with the help of an education contract for teaching swimming to primary schools. There are also classes at other times for learners. The Public have access from 7-8am and from noon until 1.40pm when there is also a luncheon club. Sub-aqua diving clubs use it for training and underwater hockey is played using snorkels and a puck on the floor of the pool! About 3,000 people use the pool every week.

With everyone now more fitness and diet conscious and senior citizens more active, the centre endeavours to cater for everyone from 3-83 years in a socio/leisure way. I think Archibald Cassanova Ballard would be pleased although he would probably find it hard to understand the changes over the years. He certainly would have been more delighted with this endeavour than he was with the gift of a silver tea and coffee service presented to him in 1939 by the City Council in 'deep appreciation' of his work.

Brian Hearn, the dynamic owner of the **Matchroom Snooker Centre** in Plymouth, is a cousin of the boxing and snooker supremo, Barry Hearn. They vie with each other to see who can work the longest day - Brian is winning at the moment with a 16-hour day. When he heard people say that Plymouth had no need of another snooker club he got annoyed. The Matchroom Snooker Centre is much more than that. He knew exactly what he wanted and planned every detail. The building had been gutted by fire when he first took it over but that was a bonus rather than a hindrance. The building, originally used for light industry, has huge parking facilities.

He is a man who will work for any charity, in particular the Lifeboat Appeal and Cancer Research as well as Operation Santa sponsored by Plymouth Sound. What is a must for him is that all the money goes to charity and is not siphoned off for unnecessary expenses.

The snooker club has a bar and a sales area for players to buy cues, cases etc. The Function Suite has a stage, a bar and food facilities. There are two skittle alleys. Finally there is a body building gym.

The main function room, situated in a separate building, has been designed with care ensuring that everyone can see the stage. The seats are built in tiers. He has made the rooms interesting and full of character. For example he went to Warrington in Lancashire to get curtains and a pelmet from an old theatre for the stage. His aim has always been to provide a first class venue in which working- class people can enjoy themselves at prices that are less than restaurants and pubs. He comes from a working-class Plymouth background himself and feels very strongly about it.

It really is a super place and one that is gaining in popularity all the time. Two or three weeks ago I went to a show there set up by Westcountry Television, 'Searching for a Star'. The evening was immaculately run, a credit to the organisers and to the quality of the performers. The packed audience enjoyed every moment .

Membership is an individual thing. There are no family memberships and the security of members is very important. I understand that Brian intends to open a similar venue in Brest; he already exports tables to France so no doubt it is a sensible move.The Matchroom Snooker Centre in Colebrook, Plympton, is certainly an example of everything that is good in the sporting world and a credit to Plymouth.

I think the **Plymouth Sports Club** epitomises all that is good about the city; the spirit of co-operation and the competitiveness. On the site of the old Plymouth Cricket Club in Outlands road a modern and vibrant sports club has become the largest club of its kind in the area. The membership is over 80,000 and whilst concentrating on cricket the emphasis is equally on hockey, American football, 11 and 6 aside football and squash. The owners of this complex, Bob Widdecombe and Keith White, both dedicated sports enthusiasts, have given their all to this enterprise, not only with the investment of considerable sums of their own money but in the time put in to achieve their aims. Both of them have been involved with the Plymouth Sports Club since 1967 when they were instrumental in conjunction with the City Council, in providing the first two public squash courts at the Plymouth Cricket and Sports Club.

Plymouth Sports Club

Having been actively involved with the Plymouth Cricket and Sports Club for over twenty years, they had a genuine concern when offering a life-line to take over the ailing Plymouth Cricket Club in 1986, with its problems and debts of over £100,000. Bear in mind that without their intervention this debt would have been the moral responsibility of Plymouth City Council. With vision, determination and a great deal of hard work the club is now recognised as one of the best sports complexes in the county catering for all members of the community wishing to play any number of sports.

It has been an incredible achievement made even more remarkable by the fact that the work, in the main, has been done outside their normal business hours. They both have full time occupations. Keith White is the managing director of Michael Spiers (Jewellers) with Bowden and Sons and Leath Jewellers of Taunton thrown in for good measure.

Bob Widdecombe, a former chairman and managing director of Furgusons Soft Drinks, sits as a main board director of Vospers Motor House. He also finds time to sit on a whole host of committees including the Olympic Appeals Committee in company with Keith White. He has supported Plymouth Argyle for over 40 years and is a vice president of the club. Then there is the Plymouth Sports Advisory Council, the presidency of the Wednesday Football League and the chairmanship of the Plymouth Sports Club. Whilst he is a lover of all sport his first loves were football and badminton.

Encouraging youngsters to join and take part in their chosen sport, is Plymouth Sports Club's investment in the future. The club has teams for all ages from the under-tens to eighteen. In this pursuit the club gets tremendous support from the schools. Some schoolmasters are coaches: for example, Barry Mason of Devonport High School, a squash champion himself, gives his time.

Bob Widdecombe believes that the benefits to the young are far greater than the ability to play a game. The modern way of life frequently means that children are not as fit as they might be. They need to have sport available to them. It builds character, gives them a competitive edge, keeps them healthy and out of serious trouble. If you study the European crime figures and the investment made in sports facilities, the down turn in these figures is proof positive of the value of the investment. One we should emulate.

For a city such as Plymouth to have good facilities, and encouragement for youngsters, means that we may well produce a champion: a great ambassador for the city. Bringing championship events to Plymouth is equally important for the whole community, the spin-offs from any large gathering means that the hotels are full up, the pubs and restaurants busy, the city centre buzzing and the tourist attractions getting their share as well. You have only to take note of what happens when the Benson and Hedges Open Golf

Championship is held at St Mellion. It is almost impossible to get a bedroom in the city.

If you analyse what Plymouth Sports Club is used for you will find it is for those who want to try new sports, those who just want to play a game of some kind and then socialise and finally for those who want to achieve excellence. The club already has a squash school of excellence and is repeating the formula for hockey.

A man of vision, Bob Widdecombe has long dreamt of uniting Plymouth Argyle, the Mayflower Centre and Plymouth Sports Club to make a super sports complex with an all-seater football stadium. He was behind a scheme to develop Home Park to do just that. Who knows, maybe one day?

Both Bob's wife and son work at the sports club; his son is a former doubles squash champion for the region, and plays regularly in the Devon Squash League 1st Division.

The enthusiasm of Bob Widdecombe, a Plymothian, for his club, the future of youngsters in Plymouth and his belief that Plymouth is going places, is infectious.

With equal dedication and determination the Bond family established the **St Mellion Golf and Country Club**. The internationally famous course, designed by Jack Nicklaus, is regarded as one of the finest in Europe. The second eighteen hole course known as the Old Course, designed by J. Hamilton Stutt, is just under 6000 yards and provides the perfect complement to the Nicklaus Course. It offers both testing and pleasant golf in the midst of some of Cornwall's most beautiful countryside.

The family have farmed in the Tamar Valley for well over 250 years and they remain firmly committed to agriculture. Brothers Martin and Hermon started with their parents on a 40 acre tenanted holding. They now farm some 1,200 acres on which Martin's sons, Jonathan and Christopher, work following in the family's farming tradition. The pattern of the Bond's farming has changed and adapted over the years to meet the challenges of changing agricultural needs and economic pressures. They were known for the skilful and patient development of the noted Trerule Herd of Landrace pigs, which were sold for breeding throughout this country and all over Europe. They are respected as some of the most skilled and progressive farmers in the South West.

Keen environmentalists, they have planted well over 20,000 trees in the last year. Their farming also extends to those parts of their 500 acre St Mellion Estate which are not used for golf. In addition to the golf courses, the club complex includes a hotel and the luxury Holiday Village.

The Bond's golfing interests also include Looe Golf Club and Lanhydrock Golf Club at Bodmin, which they own and which are managed by Hermon's son, Graham.

The development of St Mellion as a golf and country club began in 1972 out of the brothers' interest in the sport and a perceived need to diversify their farming enterprise. Their drive to achieve the very best resulted in their determination to create a premier International Championship Golf facility. Jack Nicklaus' services were secured, following three weeks in America on an intensive itinerary planned for them by him (12 flights in 6 days) during which the brothers inspected many of the major golf courses there. Thus the design for the new St Mellion Course was born.

The Championship Course was built by the brothers to Jack's design. From working together, Jack Nicklaus became a very close and valued personal friend. This friendship with one of the 'Golfing Greats' of all time, whose sportsmanship, integrity and sincerity is outstanding, is one of the factors which, as the brothers put it, 'Have made it all worthwhile'.

From the Jack Nicklaus Course has flowed national and international golf tournaments including the Benson and Hedges International Open. The brothers have an understandable pride in being personally associated with these tournaments, the PGA (European Tour) leading golf personalities and BBC Television.

For the future the intention is to continue in the pursuit of excellence for St Mellion. The Bond brothers are not involved with the day-to-day running of the club, but make a daily visit to get an overview, and keep an eye on things. They leave the day-to-day running in the hands of a management team.

New plans include the development of a third course and, as the present 24 bedroom hotel is proving inadequate, there are proposals for a new hotel. Also in the pipeline is the development of 199 local houses in the village of St. Mellion which will incorporate the provision of a new village green and other associated facilities.

Whilst St Mellion is in Cornwall and outside Plymouth, what goes on here affects the city. The plans the brothers have can only bring benefits to the city.

St Mellion offers more than golf. It is an excellent venue for conferences and for wedding receptions. The facilities are superb and will cope with everything from a small board meeting to a major launch. Landrover chose to launch their 'Discovery' model in style at St Mellion.

The restaurant and the bars are spacious and comfortable and as welcoming to the non-golfer as to the most dedicated aficionado. The Garden Room Restaurant offers the widest variety of fare from early morning to late in the evening in delightful surroundings and a very relaxed atmosphere where jackets and ties are not required. The 'Coffee Bar' produces sweets, pastries and snacks throughout the day.

Sports enthusiasts of all kinds find the facilities at St Mellion first class. Tennis and squash, badminton, snooker and swimming are all there for you to enjoy. If you need to 'top up' the suntan, try the solarium. Laze in the jacuzzi if you prefer and feel the stresses of life ooze out of you.

Having mastered the indoor pursuits maybe you will feel inclined to try your hand at golf and book a lesson with one of the golf-teaching professionals. Strolling round the perimeter of the golf courses is more than pleasurable. The five hundred acre estate with streams, lakes, woods and rolling hills is a place of tranquillity.

The coast is no distance from St Mellion and within a short drive you will come across a variety of pebble and sandy beaches for surfing, sailboarding, fresh-water or deep-sea fishing. There are stables at hand for those who like to ride and theme parks to entertain the children. A wealth of National Trust properties and gardens entice visitors in the summer.

The success of St Mellion has resulted in others asking for help and advice based on the practical experience of developing land to achieve its maximum potential in the context of commercial viability. Nearly all land has the potential to cater in some way for the leisure industry and to benefit from this. The industry will be looking for major expansion into the countryside during the next decade and the political climate is very much in favour of such ventures. In addition, many rural locations have potential for residential and industrial development which can be carefully harmonised with and suited to the particular area and its local needs.

St Mellion have led the way, and they are prepared to share their expertise through their development and consultancy company of St Mellion Leisure Limited. Who can doubt, with the success of St Mellion that the advice would be sound?

One hole at St. Mellion

When dockyard apprentices originated the Albion Club in 1876 they could not have foreseen that their enthusiasm would lead to the club still being in existence one hundred and seventeen years later. Times have been good for the club and times have been hard. The present season is one of the down times but there is a spirit and feeling of togetherness that comes across when you meet members of this highly respected rugby club now called **Plymouth Albion**. They are a credit to the city in their behaviour when they play away and always in their sportsmanship.

I talked to committee members and to the general manager, Trevor Hargreaves, whose job is to look after the running of the club, its buildings, its grounds and to ensure its financial security. A tall order. One of the great difficulties they have is the position of Plymouth geographically. Away games take them many expensive miles from home. Unlike professional football teams the players all have other jobs and this makes getting away on a Friday in order to travel to the north not an easy proposition. Added to this is the factor that many of the players do not even live in Plymouth and have to travel distances to come to the ground for training. Because of Plymouth Albion's lowly position in the league this also causes a headache. Players with star quality move away and join more successful clubs. For years the services have proved to be a good source of recruiting players but with the diminishing size of the armed forces this, too, is drying up. Nonetheless when you watch a match at the ground in Beacon Park you are left in no doubt about the enthusiasm of the spectators, and the gathering in the clubhouse afterwards never loses the true tradition of apres rugby!

Not many people know that at one time Plymouth Albion shared Home Park with **Plymouth Argyle**. The marriage did not last very long. Neither was comfortable in the other's presence.

Plymouth Argyle has carried the city colours for a very long time. It has as many fans in Cornwall who travel to Home Park , as it has in Plymouth. Like Plymouth Albion it, too, has immense travelling costs; so many of the teams in the league are in the north. The arrival of Peter Shilton as player manager excited everyone in the city whether they were football fans or not. He admitted that the task of trying to keep Plymouth Argyle in the second division was a difficult one but he was encouraged by the goodwill of the supporters. With the help of millionaire chairman Dan Macauley and the board, Peter is certain that the fortunes of the club will improve. He is liked by his players and in his assistant, John McGovern, he has a loyal and able colleague.

Few grounds in the country can be situated in such a beautiful setting. Surrounded by the tree filled Central Park it has almost the feel of being in a rural area. Parking facilities are excellent and little crowd violence is seen with the result that Home Park is a football venue for the family.

Nothing much has changed here over the years apart from improvements to the stands and the facilities. I can remember going there as a child with my mother who was a keen supporter. I remember going there with my son when he was small to watch his team, West Ham. I think the blue and crimson West Ham scarf was the only one in the stadium. He wanted to watch his idol Trevor Brooking. Now Plymouth Argyle has its own hero - Peter Shilton. A sign of great times ahead for this well loved and respected club.

Within the Dockyard walls

CHAPTER 10

The Armed Services, the Dockyard, the Garrison City

It is not so long ago that uniforms were a regular sight all over Plymouth. Men and women of all three services, lived, worked and played within our midst. Today we seldom, if ever, see a uniform. There are two reasons: firstly, the diminishing numbers in the armed services which is a sadness in itself and secondly, the need for security against acts of terrorism. This has prompted the powers that be to issue an instruction to anyone leaving ships, establishments, etc. to wear civilian clothes.

The dockyard and the services have always played a prominent part in our lives and in our economy. The anxiety caused by the uncertainty about Devonport Dockyard has repercussions far beyond Plymouth. It affects industry and suppliers of all kinds throughout Somerset, Devon and Cornwall. I heard the owner of a scaffolding company in Somerset talking on television. He was saying that if the refitting of the Trident submarines was not done here, half his business would go. It is this far reaching uncertainty that brings home to all of us how important the Dockyard and the Services are to the well being of Plymouth.

Devonport currently provides the site for the most significant naval base in Western Europe. There is a N.A.T.O and National Maritime Headquarters, a base for a number of warships, including ten nuclear powered submarines, the Royal Navy's Fleet Maintenance Centre, a barracks and a Royal Dockyard with refit facilities for both surface ships and submarines of all types. Associated with the complex are two armaments depots and an oil fuel depot.

The dockyard is privately managed by **Devonport Management Limited**. Most of the other parts of the base come under the authority of Flag Officer, Plymouth. His Chief - of - Staff, normally a Commodore, directs their daily business. The Flag Officer chairs the Plymouth Command Management Board. As well as officers subordinate to Flag Officer, Plymouth, this board comprises the Principal Supply and Transport Officer, (Naval) and

A warship in the Hamoaze

the Superintendent Ships (responsible for overseeing refits), both responsible through the Director Generals to the Chief of Fleet Support in London.

The aim three hundred years ago was to get windward of the French Navy based at Cherbourg and Brest, but Devonport's strategic situation remains optimal today. It provides ready access to the South Western Approaches, a key area for the security of the sea communications of the United Kingdom, Europe and NATO. It also gives ships and submarines based at Plymouth a head start in any movements into the wider world of the Mediterranean, South Atlantic, Indian Ocean and Gulf. Devonport's easy access to deep water is a major advantage for submarine operations, especially in the context of recently publicised accidents with fishing vessels in shallower waters further north.

Devonport's strategic location makes it the natural location for the national sea area command from 8 degrees West to 52 degrees 30' North, i.e. from the South Western Approaches right through the Channel to the southern North Sea.

Politics should not be brought into play because whatever else changes Devonport will remain advantageously placed. It fills every criterion admirably.

Devonport Link, the company newspaper of Devonport Management Limited, makes interesting reading and brings home the point that DML have contracts other than those with the Ministry of Defence. They work for Shell U.K. Exploration and Production, and refit some of the biggest and most expensive yachts and motor cruisers in the world.

DML launched Charisma Cruising Yachts as a direct result of Chay Blyth's British Steel Challenge. Based on Chay's single handed voyage 21 years ago, the British Steel Challenge is a match race between eleven identical 67' steel yachts round the world against the prevailing winds. Each yacht was manned by 12 trained volunteers led by a skipper chosen by Chay Blyth. They set sail in October 1992.

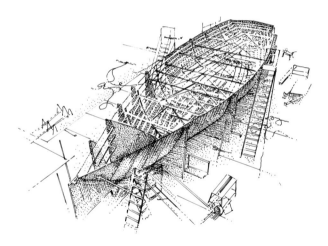

Construction of a British Steel yacht

The Charisma project resulted from the favourable reaction to the steel racing yachts DML built for that race. The elegant softly flowing lines take full advantage of DML's skill in steel fabrication and furnishing to produce yachts which combine the rugged 'go anywhere' strength of steel with superb good looks and excellent sailing qualities: yachts with charisma.

These boats are serious ocean going cruisers, ideal for long crossings to far away places, island hopping in the Indies or cruising the Med. Every aspect has been carefully evaluated to provide a near perfect compromise between performance, comfort and enjoyment. With individual heads and showers ensuite to each two-berth cabin, the yachts are particularly suitable for charter work.

Offering a similar combination of performance, comfort and handling is the 44' cutter. This excellent day-boat has ample overnight accommodation for coastal cruising holidays.

In taking over Devonport Royal Dockyard, DML inherited the marine skills and experience built up over 300 years. Traditional craft skills are allied to modern technology to create an unparalleled breadth of capability. DML entered the 'superyacht' business some time ago and among other projects is proud to have been entrusted with three refits of Royal Yachts, including a major renovation of HMY Britannia.

The company builds GRP motor launches and offers a range of composite moulding and fitting-out services. DML has also worked on a variety of sailing vessels, from maxi racing yachts to the restoration of historic wooden ships. The launching of Charisma yachts fits in with the company's drive to expand the range of products and services it supplies to an ever widening variety of customers.

Building upon the experience gained in the defence sector, DML has successfully expanded its operation into many other diverse businesses in the commercial sector.

A growing DML railway business refurbishes diesel engines and passenger coaches. DML Joinery builds bespoke furniture and shop-fitting equipment for major high street retailers.

DML can also provide a safety related service for the offshore oil and gas industry. It also supplies lightweight fire protection systems based on modern composites, technology which is considerably in advance of anything else available.

All these other activities never detract from its purpose as a Naval Dockyard. In the defence sector its primary function is to support the Royal Navy. The company provides a complete range of design services, including the maintenance and updating of ships' drawings, refit engineering and the integration of new weapon systems into existing ships.

Engineers maintain, refit and modernise the Royal Navy's surface ships, including frigates, aircraft carriers, assault support ships and fleet tankers. Diesel submarines are refitted and nuclear submarines are refitted and refuelled.

DML overhauls virtually every type of weapon system launchers in service in the Royal Navy, with a mechanical and hydraulic engineering workshop, a dedicated electronics workshop, and a specialist roving team who work on board warships, integrating the various sensors and weapons into the ship's central command and control system. Additionally, DML produces an extensive range of spares to support the refits and to provide for the central naval stocks.

One cannot over-stress the importance of DML and the dockyard in the life of the city. I have taken an extract from a document which illustrates how much we depend on DML and the men who work there.

'During 1988/9 DML's total pay bill amounted to £132 million representing a weekly value to the local economy of approximately £2.5 million.

In addition to currently providing more than 5,000 DML jobs with average earnings of more than £300 per week, Devonport Naval Base is home to 13,500 Royal Navy and other MOD Personnel.

It is estimated that the total number of DML, RN and MOD personnel based at Devonport exceeds 21,000. In addition to those direct jobs, the Dockyard provides significant amounts of short-term work for more than 10,000 individual sub-contractors.

This relates exclusively to the local community. Naval Dockyards have a wide network link with major defence contractors which can be described as 'perpetuating a highly independent, non-diversified economy and employment structure'.

In addition to DML's own workforce, many naval personnel and their families also live in Plymouth and the surrounding area, adding to the economic and social consequences of a further reduction in Devonport's work or home-based fleet. Devonport is the central pillar of the Plymouth economy and makes a major contribution to the social and economic life of the southwest region as a whole.'

H.M.S. Drake houses naval personnel ashore. The big complex has a number of new buildings but still retains much of the old that has been there for some hundreds of years. The chapel of St Nicholas within the gates is a popular venue for service weddings. Its quiet beauty is reassuring and its congregation is devoted to its well being.

Across the river, **H.M.S RALEIGH** is the New Entry training establishment for all ratings joining the Royal Navy, Women's Royal Naval Service, RNR, WRNR and the Queen Alexandra Royal Navy Nursing Service. Officers' initial training is not conducted here but at Britannia Royal Naval College in Dartmouth. In addition to basic general training the establishment is also home for the Royal Naval Supply School, Royal Naval Seamanship School and the Command Schools. These are the Firefighting, Nuclear Biological Chemical Defence, Shooting and First Aid training facilities for ships and establishments in the Plymouth Command area.

The present HMS RALEIGH was commissioned on the 9th January 1940, as a shore establishment for naval training of seamen called up under the Military Training Act of 1938. Various minor adjustments occurred during the next 30 years but the first major change began in the summer of 1971 when Marine Engineers Part II training was removed to HMS Sultan and the redevelopment of HMS RALEIGH was put in hand for a complete rebuild and modernisation. It was only then that the establishment took on the role of the Service's New Entry Establishment. Since then it has expanded its task significantly as other naval establishments have shut down and transferred their training to RALEIGH.

The Training tasks are diverse. Initial Part I Training lasts for 7 weeks, each Friday you will see many proud parents crossing the Torpoint Ferry on the way to HMS RALEIGH for the passing out parade. The young sons and daughters who left home to join HMS RALEIGH have suddenly grown up, gained confidence.

All Supply and Secretariat training is carried out in courses of varying length. That for Artificer Apprentices takes 14 weeks.

There is a facility also for youth organisations and Combined Cadet Forces to carry out their training at RALEIGH.

To carry out these tasks RALEIGH has a ship's company of some 750 and, with trainees, there are normally about 2,500 people working in the establishment (a new intake of about 100 ratings joins every week, 43 weeks of the year).

The facilities at RALEIGH are tremendous. The parade ground, where all will finally pass out on completion of their course, still provides one of the most effective ways of instilling teamwork, pride, co-ordination and discipline into those who have recently joined the Service. Jupiter Point, the Sail Training Centre, is on the River Lynher. It has over 91 various craft for water borne training and recreation. The Physical and Recreational Training Centre has excellent sporting facilities, including two gymnasiums, three squash courts, a swimming pool, sauna, solarium and numerous sports pitches. The complex is also used extensively by a wide variety of civilian clubs, organisations and Service personnel generally, as indeed are a number of RALEIGH'S other facilities.

RALEIGH'S firing ranges are contiguous with the establishment at Trevol. All trainees become familiar with the SA80 rifle, firing live rounds and stripping the weapon. The firing range is also used by many external authorities.

RALEIGH is fortunate to have Flag Officer, Plymouth, Royal Marines Band based there. The band is always in demand all over the country but by careful management it is present for the majority of the weekly passing out parades. The band's presence adds depth to the occasions and never fails to delight the 600 or so relatives and friends who visit each week.

One of the most important schools at RALEIGH teaches Firefighting and Damage Control. Events in the Falklands War of 1982 highlighted the need for extensive periods of training in these areas in realistic conditions. Last year the school ran a total of 796 courses for some 21,240 students.

The RN School of Seamanship teaches the basic needs and the terminology used in seamanship. It also teaches Foreign and Commonwealth students: for example, Saudi Arabian Frontier Force, and the Jordanian Coastguard Service.

HMS RALEIGH is a unique and complex establishment with many diverse and important tasks, running almost 100 different courses per year with a throughput of some 44,000 people. The future capability of the Fleet depends to a very large extent upon the results achieved here.

HMS CAMBRIDGE is a name that goes back 321 years, when in 1664 King Charles II named one of the 4 new men-of-war, ordered in view of the expected hostilities with Holland. The King selected the name in honour of the baby Prince James, Duke of Cambridge, second son of the Duke of York, being created a Royal Duke and Knight of the Garter. Cambridge, a 70 gun 3- decker of 860 tons, was launched in the spring of 1666. Since then there have been many ships of the name: the last was a paddle boat hired for use as a minesweeper by the Royal Navy in 1914.

Today's HMS CAMBRIDGE is a shore establishment occupying one of the most beautiful sites in the South Hams at Wembury where it looks out over glorious views of the sea and the coastline. I visited the then Captain, Commander Tighe there one morning when the wind was howling and the seas rolling in, white crested, against the cliffs. I could barely stand up as I was taken by a courteous young sailor from my car to the main building.

I had a particular interest in looking through some of the old records and photographs: my brother-in-law was at one time the Captain. The site was acquired by the Admiralty in 1940 and used as a firing range for training in practical gunnery of the large numbers of men required to man the expanded wartime fleet. It was then known as HM Gunnery Range, Wembury. In 1956 the Gunnery School in HMS DRAKE closed and the Wembury range was commissioned as the seventh HMS CAMBRIDGE exactly one hundred years to the day after the commissioning of the fourth HMS CAMBRIDGE.

The years have gone by but it is still in use as the Royal Navy's gunnery school and firing range, where officers and men receive practical training in gunnery. It is as important to know how to use small arms as it is the bigger weapons.

For the many serving officers, men and their families, Plymouth is home. It is one of the most popular postings in the Royal Navy because of the friendliness of the city and for the facilities that Plymouth offers. No one seeing the faces of wives and girl-friends as they watch the ships sail out can fail to recognise the lonely time ahead for them. It is one of the penalties of marrying into the service. The compensation comes from the knowledge that, on the whole, the ships are not away for too long these days and even if they remain on station in some far distant sea, then their menfolk are flown home when their tour of duty finishes. Gone are the days when a whole ship's company could be away from the home base for years.

There will be many past and present service wives who have stood at Devil's Point watching the ships go and return and, when a commission finishes, seeing the ship sail proudly in with the white pennant streaming from its mast - the longer the ship had been away, the longer the paying off pennant. Those moments of reunion are never forgotten; all the loneliness, the worries, the heartaches, disappear as the ship draws alongside and families are reunited.

We are used to seeing the daily activity in Plymouth Sound as ships come and go but sometimes we forget the floating supermarkets - the ships of the Royal Fleet Auxiliary. These are the ships that carry everything to restock ships at sea. For example if you were to go aboard the 23,000 tonne RFA Fort Austin, the captain might well describe it as an extension of Devonport Dockyard in that they take all the supplies away with them and supply them to other ships when they need them. The Fort Austin can carry 12,800 tonnes of cargo including 2,300 tonnes of refrigerated goods. The ship's motto, is 'Open All Hours'.

Fort Austin can supply the fleet with everything from diesel generators to chocolate bars and carries enough food to supply 15,000 men for a month.

More often than not you will see one of these ships anchored just inside the Breakwater. When you do, just remember this hardworking Fleet Auxiliary without which our ships could not stay at sea.

The Fort Austin is the first of the Royal Fleet Auxiliaries to carry a mixed crew. It will not be strange to the crew members because for years it has been possible for officers to take their wives with them.

The large vessels of the RFA provide cabins with comfortable double beds for married officers. Ratings' accommodation is also more generous than aboard RN warships.

The Royal Naval Engineering College has been part of life in Plymouth since the late 19th century. It was not always housed in its present site. My early remembrances of it are an old, grey-stoned building at Keyham just above the dockyard's St Levan's Gate. It was the war years that started the move to Manadon. Nissen huts were built as classrooms and at night the students returned to their quarters in Hartley Road, now used, I believe, by Plymouth College preparatory school.

The value of RNEC Manadon to the navies of the world has been proven time and time again. With Shrivenham in Wiltshire, which is the Army's equivalent, young officers from all over the world obtain an internationally respected degree and go on to different roles in the services. The student population at Manadon currently is around 450. Well over half these officers are undertaking first or second degrees and the remainder various professional courses.

While the workload at Manadon is demanding it does encourage its officers to take part in the community and social life of the city. I can remember the days when the height of my social ambition was to go to a tea-dance at the college - we could not dance at night because of German bombers. These tea dances were held in the Officers' Mess in Hartley Road and we would dance to the band of the late and much loved Frank Fuge. Today's dances and balls are far more sophisticated but I will take a bet that they have no more fun than we did.

These were the days when the young officers were expected to sign in at night, and before midnight unless they had a late pass. I remember an occasion when one young man asked a colleague to sign in for him. The miscreant's name was Middleditch and when the signature was checked the following morning it read 'Middlediddleditch'! Be sure your sins will find you out.

Those were the days of one of the college's faithful supporters and one time second-in-command, Admiral Louis le Bailly, who I understand lives not too far away in Cornwall. I remember him when he was a Lieutenant Commander and Keyham was still in existence. One of the most interesting things he did in his time at Manadon with the support of his captain, the late Admiral Sir John Walsham, was to plant a number of trees. Not any tree but one from the country of each foreign student. The result today is a fascinating and thriving collection of trees indigenous to àll sorts of places in the world. The white handkerchief tree is probably the most unusual.

Manadon has many happy memories for me, not the least the wedding reception for my daughter who married an officer back from the Falklands.

In March more than 2,000 Royal Marines and Army soldiers from 3 Commando Brigade Royal Marines arrived back in Plymouth having taken part in this year's annual Arctic warfare exercises, code named Battle Griffin 93.

During this exercise these men endured atrocious weather: pouring rain, temperatures which plunged to minus 30 degrees plus heavy snow with avalanche conditions. It claimed the lives of four of their number in separate incidents. Life is tough in this crack force of superbly trained men.

Tours of duty in Northern Ireland's bandit country are part of their brief. For six months at a time they run the gauntlet of possible attack by the Provisional IRA in places like County Fermanagh, which borders the Irish Republic. They live in base camps and border outposts scattered across the unfriendly terrain. There is little social life for them. A visit to the local village pub is out of the question. They are too vulnerable and could by their presence also endanger the lives of other people. The majority of these, a mixed population of Catholics and Protestants, offer friendship. Even those with the desire to see reunification loathe and denounce the violent methods used by the Provisional IRA. It is not a popular posting but accepted phlegmatically.

Plymouth is very proud of the **Royal Marines**. A sense of pride in all their achievements, all over the world, in different theatres and different situations, was underlined for me when they came back from the Falklands conflict. I happened to be travelling on the A38 from Exeter to Plymouth on one of the days when these magnificent men were returning to the city having disembarked at Southampton. The memory of the welcome they received from

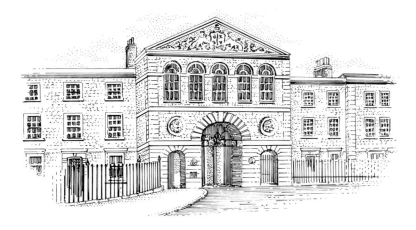

The Barracks at Stonehouse

crowds along the route will remain with me always. Every road that crossed the highway was lined with cheering people. The closer we got to Plymouth the deeper the crowds. Private cars drew in to the inner lane to let the coaches bearing the men go by. Every window of every car was open, the occupants clapping and waving. The Royal Marines were bemused! They had not expected anything like it. Tough men were reduced to tears. I had seen nothing like it since the end of World War II.

The traumatic experience of the Falklands was far greater than that of the Gulf War, but when I talked to one of their officers at the Mount Wise headquarters, I learnt of Operation Haven and discovered this errand of mercy in Kurdistan produced more cases of trauma than any battle, however fierce. The sight of the thousands of helpless people with small children wandering the hillsides, afraid of the vengeance of Saddam Hussein, pierced their hearts. Homeless, almost without food, without shelter and for most of them little hope for the future, they met with the desire from the Royal Marines to help them, to do whatever was humanly possible to ease their pain. In spite of their training, their experiences and their willingness there was little they could do except provide some degree of safety from the Iraqis. It angered them far more than the attack by the Argentinians in the Falklands or the barren wastes of Kuwait.

From what I was told by my friend at Mount Wise and also from other service people, the armed services wish that they could be used for famine relief, disasters of all kinds, epidemics and anything else that could be helped by a trained force of men and women, fully equipped to move supplies, build roads, create camps, irrigate, provide medical care, and set up feeding centres. Wonderful as Oxfam, Save the Children, and all these agencies are, they do not have the expertise to go into difficult territory and logistically run a mission of mercy. It made a lot of sense to me and it would certainly ensure that food, for example, got to the right places and was not left to rot, or be looted on quaysides in strange countries. I have no doubt that for politicians this would not do, but for practical, well trained and experienced service people, it would be fulfilling and more than worthwhile.

The Army presence in the city is provided by 29 Commando Regiment Royal Artillery who work with and support the Royal Marines Commandos. The Regiment has recently moved back into the Royal Citadel on Plymouth Hoe after the buildings received extensive renovation. But the Royal Air Force is a force of the past in Plymouth. R.A.F. Mountbatten, their last bastion is winding down and the men have been posted away.

The Royal Citadel - Main Gateway

The great days when this garrison city had several regiments stationed here, the R.A.F had Mountbatten and Mount Wise with squadrons of Typhoons and Hurricanes based at Harrowbeer, have long gone. Giant battleships no longer steam up the Hamoaze, line astern, towards the Sound followed by a flurry of their escorting destroyers. It is quieter: streamlined, the Ministry of Defence tell us.

For those of us who remember those days, they will never be forgotten. Plymouth achieved greatness then. We have a different future but the essence of Plymouth will always be its pride inthe tradition of the services.

CHAPTER 11

A Spoonful of Medicine

Not many people would necessarily decide where they want to live or work because of the efficiency of a city's medical services, but if they did Plymouth would come high on the list as an option. At all levels the medical profession and the hospitals can hold their heads high. You read of patient neglect, uncaring hospitals, dilatory general practitioners, a National Health Service that cannot cope, but I can quite genuinely say that since I came back to Plymouth in the 60's I have never lacked for first class treatment at whatever level and I do not use anything other than the National Health Service.

It would be stupid of me to suppose that there are not areas which could be immeasurably improved or that more money invested in the Health Service is needed. I look at it in a slightly different way maybe because of my age. When the Health Service first started in 1947 no one could have foreseen the giant steps forward that have been taken in the ensuing decades. There were no transplant operations, no highly expensive treatments, drugs had not advanced much beyond antibiotics and paracetamol. The cost was accounted for in the annual budget. I see that the acute shortage of money available today is because of the great advances. Thank God for them. I think the life saving operations and treatments that are carried out are nothing short of miracles but miracles do not come cheaply. Therefore I am truly thankful that as I get older I can depend on the care and attention I have always received in Plymouth.

That paragraph sounds pious. It is not meant to be. Let me tell you about the instances that I have experienced personally or about which my friends have told me, which underline my statements.

A four year old boy has just had his tonsils and adenoids removed. It could be quite a frightening experience for someone so young but it was made easier for him and his parents by the care that was taken to explain to them what was going to happen. The hospital was **Greenbank**, an old building but with up to date equipment. The children's ward, with its own operating theatre alongside, is a cheerful place where the nurses are friendly and not averse to giving a child a cuddle or two. When Adam arrived to look over the ward on the Friday before the operation he was shown where his bed would be, the huge number of toys available for children, the computer games and, on the more serious side, they did all the preliminary tests that are required before an operation.

Adam was asked to return on the Monday morning with his mum at 7am. He would have his operation in the morning and then be back in the ward by lunchtime. Providing everything was in order he would be allowed to go home the following morning. One of the requirements before he was released would be his ability to eat a piece of toast! In my day when I had my tonsils and adenoids out in Charlton Nursing Home which is now one of the houses belonging to Plymouth College, I spent ten days in the nursing home and was fed on nothing but ice cream and jelly. The reason is the different method of removing the offending organs. In days gone by a guillotine was used to chop out the tonsils, which left the stump raw. Today they are removed with an instrument that just leaves rough edges. It is nowhere near so painful and the purpose of eating the toast is to wear away the ragged edges.

When Adam arrived he was taken with some other children, all having a similar operation, into a small ante room. Here the children were taken step by step through what was going to happen to them. They were shown the small needle which would be inserted in their hand into which the syringe holding the injection would go, they were even shown the plaster that would cover up the tiny little hole afterwards. Absolutely everything was explained simply and without alarming the child. Adam found his name printed out over his bed and, beneath his name, 'Your consultant is Reg'.

For children who were not able to have their parents with them for whatever reason, a nurse stood constantly in loco parentis. The operation was soon over, the family were able to visit, and that night a sleepy Adam snuggled down in his bed knowing that his mum was sleeping in a bed provided by the hospital close by. He woke willing to munch a piece of toast and was despatched home with his mother, a fitter, happier boy who certainly would have no fear of going into hospital again if he had to.

At the other end of the scale, an elderly friend of mine dislocated her replacement hip and had to spend Christmas and

New Year in **Mount Gould Hospital.** Not the happiest situation for anyone but the hospital was wonderful. Her 87 years old husband with his daughter and her husband were invited to have Christmas lunch in the ward and on New Year's Eve the husband was given a bed there by her side so that they could see the New Year in together as they had done in over fifty years of marriage. The care she was given, the patient understanding of her sometimes demanding manner, was far and away beyond the call of duty. She was well fed, albeit not always on her favourite foods.

My elderly next door neighbour lives alone. She is frail and cannot walk too easily but for her there is a daily attendance from a nurse, her doctor will always visit her whenever she asks and frequently pops in on his rounds just to make sure she is alright. It is only recently that he has become her doctor and if anyone doubts that there are medical practitioners who will look after the elderly, they only need to look at this practice and find a first class example of care of the senior citizen. The practice is Calder, Houston and Pickard in Beaumont Road, St Judes.

My family and I have always been patients of Doctors Dash, Macartney, Hopkins, Kitson, Donaldson and Bannon now at the new **Mannamead Surgery** in Eggbuckland Road. They have always been efficient and caring and never objected to house visits. Time is all important to doctors but the appointment service works for them and for their patients. The surgery is light and airy, the receptionists not ogres. Talking to my own doctor, who runs the business side of the practice, which is entirely computerised, he tells me that the challenge is rewarding but the amount of paperwork is alarming! He worries about standards being kept up and the patients of the practice getting the treatment they need.

This was a practice that was resuscitated in 1948 by Dr Neil Beaton, known to many for his great love of sailing. A former Commodore of the Royal Western Yacht Club, he died a few years ago and his first partner, Richard Maitland, has retired. I became a patient of their's when I returned to Plymouth in 1962. The surgery was at the top of Townsend Hill, now inhabited by my dentists, Rudge and Walker. In those days the area they covered was mainly Mannamead and Efford. Since then they have moved to Brandreth Road and on again to Eggbuckland Road. The practice now has five doctors and usually one or two in training as well - it has always been a training practice. Their 10,500 patients have changed as well. Today there will be as many on council estates as in what are known as the better residential areas of the city. Wherever you come from you get treated in exactly the same manner, with the same care and understanding.

The second doctor to join the original practice was Michael Dash, now the senior partner. It says much for the way the practice is run that the doctors who join seem to stay until their retirement.

There are practices which specialise in other matters, like drug addiction, and I am quite sure that the very best care is given to this very difficult problem. Sadly, it is on the increase in Plymouth.

Modern purpose-built surgeries seem to be becoming the norm and gone are the rather dreary, brown-painted, hard-seated waiting rooms. I have met many doctors over the years and at one time did market research for a pharmaceutical company. We had many good evenings in the Moat House, discussing new drugs and accompanying the conversation with some food and more than one or two glasses of wine. They were times when I got to know a bit more about the doctors themselves and how they spent their precious free time. Rugby and fishing seemed to go to the top of the list. I learnt that doctors were not persuaded to favour any particular company by such evenings or by any promises of free tickets for Twickenham or fishing weekends. They took the lead, when trying out new drugs, from the consultants in the hospitals rather than from any form of advertising.

Derriford Hospital is the hospital of the present and the future for Plymouth whereas Greenbank and Freedom Fields in the centre of the city will be gradually phased out. There are many who live in Devonport and in the city centre who are not happy about the casualty department being so far away from them, nor for that matter about having to go so far to visit the sick. On the bonus side Derriford is modern, spacious and far better equipped to deal with any kind of emergency.

I have fond memories of the casualty department at **Freedom Fields** where I seemed to spend a lot of time when my son was growing up! At one time I was such a regular visitor that the sister in charge threatened to issue me with an apron and put me to work. I found the same sister when I went to the casualty department at Derriford last year. She greeted me like a long lost friend and was quite horrified when I told her that the boy she remembered was 28. Time in the 1990s seems to fly past more quickly than ever before. Is it the pace at which we live, the fullness of our lives, or is it just that as you get older minutes no longer seem like hours?

Derriford Hospital will have its own £1 million body scanner before the end of the year. Consultants have been battling to get a 'Magnetic Resonance Imaging Scanner' for years. Hopefully it will be up and running by October, saving patients a 160-mile round trip to Bridgwater in Somerset for MRI scans. It is a significant development in the provision of health care in Plymouth from the diagnostic point of view.

Until the Department of Health finally agreed it was becoming more and more embarrassing and unacceptable for the hospital to be setting itself up as a sub-regional neurosciences centre without having MRI. An impossible situation.

The scanner is a giant computer-controlled magnet which enables doctors to see clear pictures of all internal organs, including the brain, spinal cord, joints and blood vessels. It means that once it is installed at Derriford, doctors can detect anything from cancer to a torn ligament without having to use potentially harmful X-rays or resort to restorative surgery.

Dr Wells who has led the fight to get this scanner says that 2,500 patients will benefit from it in its first year and he expects that figure to rise dramatically in subsequent years. The cost of this piece of equipment, £750,000, will be borne by the Department of Health and a further £250,00 for installing it will come out of the Plymouth acute unit's own capital budget.

These enormous costs really confirm what I was saying earlier about the difference in the cost of funding the National Health Service today and in 1947.

A recent installation at Derriford is a revolutionary new x-ray system which will benefit hundreds of patients. Designed by the Japanese company Fuji it means that patients will be exposed to lower radiation doses as more information can be shown on each X-ray. It is used for patients in the intensive care unit who are too ill to be moved to the hospital's x-ray department, and it has also been used for patients in the accident and emergency x-ray department.

I am an idiot when it comes to machinery but I understand that it uses high sensitivity phosphor plates, a laser scanner and computer-enhanced processing to produce clearer images of bones and body tissues, giving doctors access to more information about a patient's condition.

Plymouth desperately needs its own open heart surgery unit. Plymouth has the worst death rate from heart disease in the south of England and one of the highest in the UK. Only Devon and Cornwall are more than 70 miles away from a cardiac surgical unit.

Many heart patients have undergone traumatic journeys of up to 2,000 miles travelling to London for diagnostic tests and then surgery. It is an enormous expense for patients who have to travel.

Something that has been done to help the hard-working cardiologists at Derriford, is the installation of a two-way radio system which enables them to keep in constant touch with each other. It also alleviates the necessity to break away from patient sessions in order to answer conventional telephone calls.

The hospital's cardiographers undertake many diagnostic tests on patients affected by a wide range of serious heart conditions and are required to attend to patients in many areas of the hospital. While the conventional hospital telephone and 'bleeper' system works well enough for the great majority of clinical departments, the cardiographers have found the instant radio a Godsend. Co-ordinating the cardiac team effectively is a must and in an emergency speed is of the essence.

Plymouth patients with an acute mental illness are now treated in a superb new unit away from the Victorian and forbidding walls of Moorhaven which for so long has housed patients in a situation that leant itself to prejudice and stigma. Thankfully attitudes have changed and the new Glenbourn unit resembles an upmarket motel. Moorhaven nurses worked alongside architects to provide a pretty, relaxing colour scheme. The bright floral curtains hang against pale primrose walls, the floors are carpeted. Inside the facilities include a modern multi gym, beauty therapy and art therapy rooms, a woodwork room and a therapy kitchen. In the three wards, christened Harford, Bridford and Dunsford after villages in Devon, the emphasis is on privacy and comfort. There are four four-bed rooms, two twin-bedded rooms and five single rooms on each ward. Each room is partitioned from the next and has its own desk.

Thought has been given to mentally ill mothers with babies or toddlers. Cots have been provided on one of the wards so that the children may remain with them. This is a first for Plymouth.

The new unit will provide assessments and diagnosis for a wide range of mental illnesses, from severe post-natal depression to schizophrenia. It is hoped that with all the new facilities and treatments most patients will not have to stay more than a few days before they return home. Glenbourne is the central piece in the highly complex business of mental care.

Acute mental illness is now treated in new facilities at Mount Gould and Plympton hospitals and it is hoped that with the shutting of the doors at the old asylum at Moorhaven, the minds of Plymothians will be opened to help mentally ill people to become rehabilitated within society rather than being shut away and shunned by society in isolation.

One of the things that impressed me about Derriford in particular was the handling of what I call taboo illnesses: for example, the indignity and stigma that colostomy, ileostomy and urostomy patients feel. Each and every one has to come to terms with coping for the rest of their lives with a stoma - an artificial opening to enable the body to discharge waste. Imagine the fear and the dread. What will people say, how will your partner react? All this anguish is dealt with by a lot of caring and understanding people at Derriford. People from all walks of life and all ages suffer in this way. Every month there are some 20 new patients in Plymouth alone and they seem to be getting younger.

It is perhaps comforting to know that you are not alone and that there are people out there who do cope and realise that you can still feel good, look good and lead a perfectly normal life. Before surgery a patient has a stoma 'sited' to find out where it will be most comfortable. They are asked to sit and stand to see how it will feel when the patient is in a normal relaxed position. I discovered that there are many former patients who ski, swim, sail, abseil, hang-glide and climb mountains; so, horrid as the idea is, it is something one can learn to live with.

No one is going to claim it is easy, particularly in the beginning. Education and understanding are paramount at the time, just as love and support are vital in relationships. All of this Derriford helps you to find: part of this excellent hospital's caring service.

It was thirteen years ago that the consultant surgeon, Mr Wilkins, arrived from St Bartholomews - affectionately known as Barts to people all around the world. He realised that Plymouth was the only city of its size with a hospital that was not linked to a university. Nonetheless, the hospital did have a large number of graduates. Mr Wilkins felt that a **Post-Graduate Medical School** would be both opportune and necessary. He also firmly believed that such a school would establish a centre of excellence of care through teaching and research.

What he envisaged was a post-graduate school encouraging high calibre graduates to come to the hospital, plus high calibre consultants, leading to more graduates and developing an ever widening circle. He took his idea to what was then the Polytechnic and to Mr Knight, the Director, who favoured the idea. They researched, visited other establishment and finally got some initial funding for the project. The aim is for 165 postgraduates and the same number of consultants.

In October, 1991, Professor Karl Rosen, a Swede, was appointed Dean of the Faculty. This is a man who is both an academic and an inventor. He invented a baby rocking device which is on sale world-wide. A man of obvious academic ability but also one whose skills and sound commercial sense are all important. It had to be someone who could fight for funding. Someone whose desire was to stimulate people into asking questions and then if there was not a ready answer, look at the subject and see if it could be researched. He needed to be someone capable of building a community within the Post- Graduate Medical School and also someone who was able to make information available to the general public in terms that they could understand. The appointment was obviously a good choice.

The recent development of a Plymouth Science Park on the Derriford site provides an opportunity to build a Medical Research

Centre, linking medical research with industrial developments. Alongside the Medical Research Centre will be the House of Innovations and the centre for hyperbaric oxygen treatment. The building will give a strong focus on Plymouth -based research and the actual building work will begin in 1994.

The School is now seeking donations and sponsorship from local businesses, institutions and individuals, together with the medical industry. The aim is to raise £1m.

The Medical Centre, Derriford Hospital

The very word 'Cancer' frightens the bravest of us. It is a disease that not only affects the patient but the family as well. It looks as I write that Plymouth may well have a pioneering centre before very long to help both the sufferer and the family. Members of the Plymouth and Cornwall Cancer Fund are planning to set up a centre in a Victorian house near Freedom Fields. The house currently belongs to the Plymouth Health Authority but the fund hopes to buy it. The Cancer Fund is looking for a totally integrated service which begins to help the cancer patient from the moment of diagnosis and gives them the support that they and their families and carers need right the way through their cure or death. It would be wonderful for Plymouth, where such support is largely unmet.

To be told you have cancer must be devastating. Unfortunately once diagnosed it is almost impossible for the consultant to spend much more than 20 minutes with the newly diagnosed sufferer. I do not know how I or my family would react. I watched helplessly as my mother suffered from cancer in the last six months of her life. No one helped us, we just had to cope. This new centre will offer a telephone helpline information service on cancer and its treatment, counselling, relaxation, therapies and support group meetings.

Plymouth's leading cancer doctor, John Brindle, who heads the radiotherapy department at Freedom Fields, believes that such a centre will help look after the whole patient rather than just the physical illness.

The money will all have to come from charity donations but the fund members are confident they can raise the sum because so many people's lives are touched by the disease. About 2,000 new cancer patients a year are referred to the radiotherapy department.

The cost of this project is £100,000 to buy, convert and furnish the house in Woodland Terrace and a further £150,000 for the first two years' running costs.

Across the road from Derriford Hospital is the **Nuffield Hospital**, offering first class private patient care for those of us able to afford it. It is a first class hospital and every room is well furnished and complete with colour television to while away the hours. There is no doubt that it is a great benefit to determine, for example, when you will have an operation done rather than wait for your name to come up on the National Health list. The doctors and surgeons are excellent and so is the nursing care, but I doubt if it is any better or more caring than the National Health Hospitals.

My feeling has always been that if you can afford it you should have private medical insurance, not so much for your own convenience, but to alleviate the waiting time for National Health patients. One of the services Plymouth's Nuffield Hospital offers is something which would benefit all of us: a health assessment. Good health is an asset we all need to cultivate.

We would none of us dream about not getting our cars serviced. It is something that is costed into your budget, but what about a service for your body? Find out a little more about what is happening to you. The Nuffield Clinic at Derriford offers assessments designed to help the early identification of health risks. Confirmation that you are fit, as two thirds of people are, will bring peace of mind and renewed confidence. Alternately if it

Charles Church

The Guildhall and St Andrew's Church

Above: Spooner's Corner in the 1930's

Below: Debenhams on Royal Parade

Destruction viewed from the Guildhall

Above: An aircraft carrier in the Dockyard

Below: Devonport Dockyard

Leicester Harmsworth House during the Blitz

The ultra-modern Western Morning News building

identifies areas of concern, early detection is vital for successful treatment.

The CBI will tell you that 360 million working days are lost annually through illness at a cost of £8 billion to UK companies. An awful lot of money!

There is no guarantee that an assessment will stop an employee becoming ill but what it can do is to detect symptoms at an early stage. I always think about Liverpool manager, Graeme Souness, a very fit man who had regular check ups. It was one of these that discovered he needed triple bypass heart surgery. Had it not been detected he could have dropped dead at any moment. It is a fact that one in four men and one in five women start developing coronary heart disease at a time when they are entering the most productive period of their lives as an employee.

Women have slightly differing health concerns from men and Nuffield tests take this into account. For both sexes a full examination with tests and results is on offer and women in addition have the benefit of well-woman screening.

Remember: you service your car and that is replaceable, you are not! These assessments take no longer than two and a half hours. A worthwhile investment whatever your age.

The active **Royal Infirmary's** League of Friends has helped the **Royal Eye Infirmary**, Apsley Road, Mutley to obtain a new and much needed theatre. The necessary building work for the new theatre was paid for by Plymouth Health Authority but the League of Friends gave £35,000 to the project to buy equipment, £23,000 of which was spent on a hi-tech microscope. Public donations paid for some of the smaller items in the new theatre and its adjoining waiting room.

For Plymothians this new addition means that the gift of sight for thousands more of us will come sooner. The theatre can treat 350 patients a year more than the 1,400 treated before. It is the second theatre in the infirmary and enables surgeons to treat many disorders, such as cataracts and squints, within a day. Patients arrive in the morning for their operation and recover in the purpose-built five-bed day care area. Plymouth now has the best equipped eye treatment centre west of Bristol.

Just for the record, more than 50,000 outpatients a year are seen at the Royal Eye Infirmary, and pressure on the hospital is increasing as the number of elderly people in the area continues to rise.

The Royal Eye Infirmary

Newspaper headlines announced in November, 1992, that Plymouth was to lose its only city centre night-time casualty service. The news that the **Royal Naval Hospital** is curtailing its 24-hour accident cover outraged Plymothians. We have all benefited from the opening of its doors to civilians but, alas, this is the beginning of the end of the presence of this hospital as part of city life as we know it.

Surgeon Captain Mann, the Medical Officer in Command states that the decision is the result of a shortage of Royal Naval consultants specialising in accident and emergency. I suppose that is not unexpected when one considers the diminishing number of personnel serving in the armed forces. There is less need for a hospital of this size and for the number of skilled surgeons and physicians who have worked here in the past.

Perhaps I should have written about the Royal Naval Hospital in my chapter about the armed services but because of the affection the people of Plymouth have for it, I thought this was the more appropriate chapter.

The construction of the Royal Naval Hospital was revolutionary in 1758. It was built on the block system and was the earliest specimen of a hospital in this country with a limited number of patients in each block building. The reason was the desire to cut down the spreading of infection. I am going to take the liberty of quoting the description of the hospital written by Dr Farr, the first physician appointed - the staff then consisted of himself, his junior, Dr Walker, and two surgeons, Mr Geach, and his junior, Mr Fuge. In addition, they had the services of two assistants and a dispenser.

'The Royal Hospital for the reception of sick and hurt seamen and marines is situated at Stonehouse, nearly equidistant from the two towns of Plymouth and Plymouth Dock; a small arm of the sea which passes by Stonehouse, under the hospital wall, admitting of boats to land at the outer gate, by the time of half-flood tide.

'It consists of eleven large buildings, and four lesser, the whole forming a square but detached from each other, for the purpose of admitting freer circulation of air, as also of classing disorders, in such manner, as may best prevent the spread of contagion.

'The buildings are rough marble, raised in the neighbourhood, with Purbeck rusticated coyns, and in front is a handsome colonnade, supported by moor stone pillars, with a flat roof covered with lead, which serves as an airing ground for the convalescents in bad weather.

'Ten buildings (exclusive of the centre or chapel building) each containing six wards, in all 60; each ward will conveniently hold 20 cradles, and in the recovery wards, if required 25; so that with four underground wards, 1,500 patients may on emergency be accommodated.

'The ground-floor of the centre or chapel building, contains the dispensary, laboratory, surgery and dispensers apartments; the first floor, the chapel, council room, with apartments in that and the attic story for the matrons, assistant surgeons, assistant dispensers, etc. The area in the middle of the hospital is handsomely laid out with grass-plots intersected by gravel walks, which are kept in very good order; besides which there is a large airing ground, surrounding the whole, containing in all about 12 acres.

'At the higher end of the airing ground to the north is a large reservoir of water, which by means of a chain pump, throws the water into a leaden cistern, which being higher, conveys the water by means of leaden pipes, into every ward, for the use of the patients, cleansing the water closets, filling the baths etc, every building being furnished with a bath and copper for heating the water to the temperature required.

Patients on admission are washed and supplied with hospital dresses, and their own clothes carried to the fumigating house. A nurse is allowed for every ten men; the greatest attention is paid to cleanliness, and keeping the wards always well ventilated.'

If you walk around the hospital today, the lay-out has changed very little. It is a place of healing but run with efficient Royal Navy procedures. Civilian patients treated here will tell you that they prefer it to Derriford, Greenbank or Freedom Fields. Bringing patients to the steps in Stonehouse creek is a thing of the past, but the lawns are well kept, and cleanliness strikes you as you see the well-kept state of the wards. The buildings have grown mellow with age and in one corner against the outer wall leading to King Street, one block remains war damaged from World War II.

I do not think that the patients of today would be very happy with the menu prescribed by Dr Farr and his colleagues. It reads something like this:

1st Low Diet - Water gruel, panado, rice gruel, milk pottage, or broth and bread and butter if necessary. For drink, toast and water, tisane or white concoction.

2nd Half Diet - For breakfast, milk pottage; for dinner, half a pound of mutton, some light bread pudding, or in lieu of it, some greens; a pint of broth, one pound of bread, one quart of small beer; the men upon this diet to dine in their own wards.

3rd Full Diet - Breakfast as above; for dinner one pound of meat, one pint of broth, one pound of bread, three pints of small beer; supper in the two last named diets to be of the broth left at dinner; or if thought necessary, to be of milk pottage. Rice milk, orange whey, orange and lemon water, tamarind whey and water, vinegar whey, balm tea, sage tea. These to be discretionally ordered by the Physicians and Surgeons.

The thought that Plymouth is going to lose this historic hospital saddens everyone. We are fortunate that much of its history is recorded. Probably the most important event in the long history of the hospital was the arrival on the evening of August 27, 1795, of Captain Richard Creyke. He was appointed Governor of the Royal Hospital at Plymouth. The importance of this appointment was endorsed by his presence at a Levee and he was presented to King George III. He knew nothing of medicine but his diligence in getting himself briefed for the tasks ahead, and his tremendous vigour, guided the hospital through the difficult years of the Napoleonic Wars and beyond that. He was still in charge when he died at the age of eighty. He left to posterity a priceless document, his daily journal, embracing every detail of his administration covering a period of just over four years to 1799. Why he stopped we will never know but the entries that he made give a remarkable insight into the life of Plymouth at that time. What you discover on reading it is that during those four years he did not take a single day's leave and only missed Sunday Divine Service in the Hospital Chapel twice. Once, when he was in attendance on His Royal Highness, the Duke of York, on a visit to Maker Camp, and once when he was ill. I had no idea that a camp even existed at Maker in those days.

There are some very sad entries. In 1797 on December 11th the record reads, 'On the request of the Port Admiral gave directions that 2 coffins shall be sent to-morrow morning to receive the bodies of the two mutineers of the Saturn who are ordered to be executed on board the Marlborough in Plymouth Sound'.

That year was notable for the mutinies at Spithead and the Nore but it also shows that Plymouth was affected. Governor Creyke did report that 'No symptoms of mutiny appeared among the patients in the Hospital'.

The dedicated care of the staff of this hospital has continued through the centuries. Throughout World War I and World War II it worked to capacity and beyond. In the years that have followed casualties have come from Korea, Suez, Aden, Malaysia, Northern Ireland, the Falklands and the Gulf.

An integrated unit at Derriford Hospital is to be the future base for service personnel. I have no doubt that the care and treatment will be superb, but it is a sad thought that we are to lose a large slice of our history. The suggestion is that the buildings will be used as a campus for the University of Plymouth. It would be suitable, certainly, and at least the buildings would remain.

The diary of Governor Creyke is held in the Library of the Royal Naval Hospital, to whom I am indebted for their co-operation .

The Marlowe Medical Centre housed in 8 Ermington Terrace, Mutley, opened my eyes to the realisation of the dream by Dr. Nigel Gray whose aim here was to create a 'Complementary Medical Centre' where all the different applications are available under one roof. The Centre has seven practitioners, each independent. This is useful, not only in sharing overheads, but because each can refer patients to the other more readily. It has taken a long time for public acceptance of alternative medicine, but as the level of awareness widens so this busy establishment acquires more patients.

It is probably easier for me to tell you about each member and what he does than to explain the whole concept. Firstly, and what I have always believed is an essential to healthy living, is a 'Positive Mental Attitude'. P.M.A is now recognised as significant in illness recovery but more often than not difficult to quantify. Roy Castle is a prime example of someone who fervently believes in P.M.A; he truly believed he could win his fight against cancer and has done so.

Doctor Gray practised as a G.P. in south east England but wanted to live in the south west and concentrate on dietary medicine and food allergies. To do this he had to go 'private'. As Plymouth is effectively the centre of the south west he started his practice here. Dr Gray also specialises in the Candida therapy which deals with yeast allergies. It has taken time to get established, especially as it is very difficult ethically to advertise Complementary Medicine. The only way is by word of mouth. That he has been successful is proven. He started in one house in Ermington Terrace in 1989, and has now bought the next door property to cope with the expansion. His colleagues have varied interest and skills.

Mike Elliot concentrates on sports injuries, Philip Hartnell is a practitioner of osteopathy and cranial osteopathy while Iris

Robinson specialises in acupuncture. There is much reference to acupuncture in the press and on radio and television. However, people are still not sure what really happens and if it would be suitable for them. Iris Robinson explained much that makes it clearer and if what I write does not answer your queries she will be happy to answer your questions on the telephone.

All sorts of conditions are likely to respond to acupuncture including certain types of migraine, back and neck pain, muscle strain and injury. Stress-related problems are helped, as are some allergies such as hay-fever. Addiction is very common. It is when our pleasurable habits get out of hand that we need some help. Chocolate and too much of the wrong sort of food can make us overweight and unhealthy; self confidence goes. Caffeine and nicotine can make us hyped up and jittery. The substances taken with nicotine in every puff of a cigarette can cause lung disease, heart disease and general ill-health; they can also affect other people whom we would rather not harm. Acupuncture can help considerably over the initial period when withdrawal symptoms make us rush back to the thing we are trying to give up.

On the first appointment Iris takes a case history in general as well as the specific problem. An examination takes place. Restriction of movement, painful areas and tender points are noted. The tongue and the pulse often give valuable information. The latter have always been very important factors in traditional Chinese medicine. Needles are then inserted in acupuncture points. The needles are sterile and disposable so that each needle is only used once. There is no risk of infection. A well trained acupuncturist is used to using a good aseptic technique.

If you are afraid of pain you have no need to worry. Iris uses fine Japanese needles and the Japanese do not believe that acupuncture should cause pain! You will probably not even know the needle has actually been put in. Once in they may be manipulated gently. This causes a slightly heavy feeling radiating around the needle. In traditional Chinese medicine this is called Te-Chi, or the arrival of Chi. Chi is the energy which is said to flow through the 'meridans'. It is an imbalance of Chi which causes disease.

The meridans are invisible channels or pathways through which the Chi flows. They were defined in ancient times when it was realised that lines could be drawn up and down the body, linking various points. Each meridan has a special set of symptoms. Today, scientists believe that it is through our complex nervous system that acupuncture works. We still cannot provide a full explanation for its effectiveness. It is also gaining popularity in veterinary science.

The needles are left in for about 20 minutes. Sometimes they are warmed with a burning herb called Moxa. Sometimes a weak electric current is passed through the needles - this takes the place of the ancient way of stimulating a needle by hand about two hundred times a minute. This makes it possible to stimulate two or three needles at a time and is far less exhausting for the therapist! This method is regularly used in China. In certain conditions such as addictions, it is desirable to treat points between visits. This is done by putting small press-balls on a plaster over the acupuncture point in the earlobe. The patient can continue to give treatment. Sometimes acupressure is taught to the patient. It is not as effective as using a needle but can bring some relief of muscular pains.

Most conditions need a number of treatments. The longer a condition has been present, the longer the treatment it seems to need. On average, a course of treatment is between four and six visits. Occasionally there is complete relief of symptoms after one treatment. Sometimes it is necessary to have more treatments at longer intervals. Some people just enjoy having treatment a few times a year for nothing more than relaxation.

Susan Jones is a registered Iridologist and Reflexologist. I had no idea what Iridology is. Simply it is health analysis by studying the irises of the eyes: a science that has been recognised as far back as 1000BC by the Chaldeans, and also by the Chinese and Japanese.

The Institute for Fundamental Research in Iris Diagnosis was set up by Joseph Deck in Ettlingen in 1959. Annual international courses are run for medical and non-medical practitioners of many nations introducing them to the principles and methods of iris diagnosis. Thus, the knowledge and practice of this form of diagnosis is growing and is becoming a respected tool of health analysis.

It has been established that the iris reflects our genetic inheritance, complete with health weaknesses. We do not necessarily have to develop these weaknesses into full blown clinical conditions - a lot depends on our life style, how we live, what we eat and so on. This now recognised fact would have answered the question put by Ignaz von Peczely, the modern day founder of Iris Diagnosis, 'here the marking, where the ulcer'? An iris may show a genetic possibility of developing an ulcer, but depending on how the life is lived - it may or may not become manifest.

Susanna Terry trained in Homeopathy at the College of Classical Homeopathy and has been in practice in Devon for some years. She is a registered member of the Society of Homoeopaths and she has also received training as a counsellor. She describes the aim of homeopathy as gently assisting the body in its own natural tendency to heal itself. To this end the homoeopath does not merely treat a specific complaint or disease but prescribes for the person as a whole. Homeopathy takes special account of the fact that different people actually react in different ways to the same illness. Bearing this is mind the homoeopath does not regard the physical, emotional and mental aspects in isolation but as all being intimately connected.

Spinal Touch Treatment also comes into Susanna's capable hands. The benefit of Spinal Touch is that it is specifically aimed at encouraging the 'self-healing' which can only come from within the body's own intelligence. It gives the body the opportunity through corrective treatment to recover in its own time and in its own unique way.

During the treatment key areas of the spine are touched in such a way as to redirect the inner energies of the body so as to gently pull muscles into their more natural position. It is worth remembering that it is muscles which move bones. It is because of this that, provided the spinal structure is sound, Spinal Touch Treatment will bring more long-lasting relief than many other forms of spinal adjustment.

Lyta Humphries is a trained counsellor, hypnotherapist and pyschotherapist who treats stress-related disorders, relationship problems, depression, smoking and weight control, lack of confidence, as well as many anxiety provoking problems. Lyta feels that hypnosis is very beneficial and that stress plays a large part in many illnesses and that by the use of counselling and creative visualisation many conditions can be helped. The clients are taught self-hypnosis in order to reinforce the work done.

It is in the belief that well trained therapists can work alongside general practitioners, and can give clients more time to discuss stress related problems than the overloaded G.P. can deal with, that makes it beneficial.

Marlowe Medical Centre gives you a sense of purpose and positivity the moment you enter its doors which is enhanced by the super, friendly receptionist who inspires confidence in the centre. My conclusion is that if you have any doubts about yourself and are not sure who to see or what you need, come here and ask. The advice is free and genuine. For an appointment or for further information, telephone 0752 266200.

Drug addiction and alcoholism destroys so many people and their families with them. It is not a pleasant subject but it is not one that Plymouth can afford to sweep away with the tide. As a city we have both problems in abundance. We are fortunate in having dedicated people who tackle the problem with flourishing branches of Alcoholics Anonymous and Drugs Anonymous, but there are times when people cannot help themselves nor be helped by their families. It is at this low ebb that **Broadreach** comes into the scene.

This large house out at Roborough lives on a knife edge financially but if we were ever to lose it the result would be devastating. The government has said addiction treatment centres like Broadreach House are to loose their 'ring fenced ' funding status. Since 90 per cent of Broadreach's money comes from the Department of Health, loss of such funding would mean its closure.

Many addicts have nowhere else to turn to for help when they enter Broadreach House. The tough ten-week treatment is uncompromising but in the majority of cases it works and the inmates return to normal life which they face with the help of the many people who have preceded them through that front door. They know they can never touch another drop of alcohol nor take drugs ever again.

The strength of Broadreach is its ability to make its clients feel like one big family working not just for their own recovery but for everyone else's too. Patients are encouraged to openly discuss their problems in groups with fellow addicts. On top of this counsellors, who are frequently reformed addicts, encourage them to confront their problematic past and overcome the negative aspects that led to the original addiction.

Of course, the final outcome is up to the individual who must want to abstain, but Broadreach provides that firm foundation upon which they can rebuild their lives. For this reason no way should Plymouth allow such an asset be lost because of the lack of funding.

As you grow older and possibly lose a partner, living by yourself can be desperately lonely. It may also be impractical. The thought of giving up one's beloved house and moving into a home does not appeal, but there is so much to be said in favour of living where you will be well cared for and not lonely. I spoke to someone the other day who at 93 is happier than she has been for years. This lively lady fought her family before giving in to commonsense. She sold her home and moved into a delightful house where she has found people of her own age to whom she can talk and share the past. Plymouth is lucky in that it has several very good residential homes.

Connaught House at 15 Connaught Avenue, Mutley Plain, has been in existence since 1982. It is a large and gracious house with three comfortable and not too large lounges, and a conservatory which is very popular in the summer. There are facilities to make life easier, like a passenger lift and a stair lift, a bath hoist, radio-controlled call system, specialist care equipment and every visiting amenity possible.

The atmosphere is contented and cheerful. Residents give up only the minimum of independence when they come here. Connaught House takes care of the things that worry and perplex elderly people, such as house upkeep, the wherewithal to pay heavy heating bills and how to get to shops in slippery weather. It combats the very real fear and loneliness experienced and it remedies the lack of self-care that is all too often present. Outside interests are encouraged, outings are organised and the owners, Mr and Mrs Strong, help in any way they can to keep their residents aware of and interested in the world generally.

Mrs Strong told me that the 'Care' aspect has two things of major importance. First is the excellent and truly dedicated staff, many of whom have been on the Care Assistants' and Social Service Courses. They have a very good relationship with their doctors and community nurses, for whom nothing is too much trouble. Secondly the Strongs live on the premises, so that 95% of the time they are able to help immediately with any problem that arises. When someone comes to live at Connaught House the Strongs regard that as a commitment to themselves and in return they commit themselves to the care of the resident for as long as he or she desires. Residents' spiritual needs are a special care, and everything is done to cater for each residents' individual requirement.

Connaught House also caters for clients who require short term stays, either from necessity to build up their health or to give their carers a much needed break. In most cases help can be obtained with the fees.

Maureen Lawley who owns and runs **Ashleigh Manor** at 1 Vicarage Road, Plympton is a remarkable lady whose passionate belief in whatever she takes on is quite awe-inspiring. Divorced, with two daughters aged 16 and 8, she set up a hostel for one parent families in 1982. Her caring and sensible attitude produced success and before long she had six such hostels. Two of those she still has, but she wanted to go on from here and after a long search bought 1, Vicarage Road. It was a four bedroomed house at that time. Maureen obtained planning permission and with the help of an architect converted it to a 29 bedroom residential home for the elderly which opened in February, 1990, and has been fully operational since. It is a happy house and I doubt if anywhere this lady ran would ever be anything else.

I listened fascinated by her own story. She started as a housewife with no business experience. She worked closely with the Social Services in her original hostels but while she was waiting for her property she enrolled at the College of Further Education for an 'In Service Care' course. She thoroughly enjoyed it and went back the following year to do her City and Guilds for the 'Care of the elderly' and then the next year to do another in 'Advancement management in care'. When I spoke to her she was taking City and Guilds 7307 to become a qualified teacher. Because she is so keen on training she ensures that she gives her already trained staff ongoing knowledge to help them achieve higher standards.

In her spare time she manages to fit in being a member of the Chamber of Commerce, Governor of the local school, and an active member of the Conservative Party - she is standing in the May elections for the County Council. She teaches part-time at the College of Further Education about different types of care. She feels it is good to have a practical teacher and so she has students at the home for training and job experience.

There are thirty to thirty five on her staff so there is permanent on-going training. Her own assistant, Mrs Atkins, now goes to the College of Further Education to study physchology of the elderly. Maureen sees it as a means of keeping herself and her staff on the same wave length. That she succeeds is undoubted. Her home is one of the best I have seen.

Having a sense of humour in her job is all important and being able to cope with heaven knows how many happenings all at once. For example, on one Saturday one unfortunate lady had a coronary, another lady got stuck in the loo, it was the new chef's first day and two people came along to view the home! All going on at the same time.

I suggested that she must have many amusing incidents to talk about and she had no difficulty in providing me with some. Going to church one day, one of her residents lost her knickers. As she walked towards the vicar, the elastic went and they plummeted to the floor. Not fazed in the least she stepped out of them and a gallant gentleman just behind her picked them up and said ' Are they yours'. 'Oh yes' she said blithely, 'but you can bin them for me now if you would be so kind!' The vicar was more than somewhat non-plussed.

The installation of a new shower was causing problems when I was there. The age-old problem of the non-appearance of a plumber was driving Maureen mad. She had already been let down by four plumbers and the fifth finally seemed to be doing the job, but he had not put in an appearance that day. Maureen has champagne in the chiller waiting to have a celebration party with the whole home when the shower becomes operational. Any excuse for a party to break the routine is her motto.

Ashleigh Manor has its own annual fete in summer in the grounds and also an Easter bonnet parade. She also enters the home or its residents in other shows. They won a prize in the Colebrook Carnival and in the Lord Mayor's Show with decorated floats. No one could possibly feel old in this challenging but nonetheless tranquil environment.

A different kind of caring in the community is at **Astor Hall** in Devonport Road, Stoke, where the Plymouth and District Disabled Fellowship has been providing support and care for disabled people in the community for over 40 years. It enjoys a membership of approximately ninety disabled people who live in their own homes in the City and its outlying districts and these members find the support of the Fellowship's Welfare Officer to be of particular benefit. They and their carers draw extra peace of mind from the knowledge that they will be visited regularly by someone who can provide positive assistance.

Astor Hall is also a residential home for twenty-eight disabled people, from 18 years of age upwards, mainly from Plymouth but some from other parts of the country. The home is a member of the Residential Care Homes Trust and is registered with Devon County Council and fully accredited by them as a provider of care. The high level of support given to residents is supervised 24 hours a day by qualified nursing staff.

A full programme of daytime and evening entertainment and occupational activity is provided for the benefit of both residents and community members, who are transported by means of the Fellowship's specially adapted vehicles.

As a registered charity the Fellowship is a non-profit making organisation and the pleasant friendly atmosphere at Astor Hall makes it a very happy place to visit.

St Luke's Hospice, one of the best things that ever happened to Plymouth, is about living. It's not about dying at all. It is a place of true holistic nursing within a family atmosphere. No one could possibly doubt the genuine care, the laughter, the coping with stress. No one can pretend that people do not go there without problems and some of them will result in death, but when you have been a part of the enriching experience in this community, death will never be quite such a grim reaper. St Luke's deserves every bit of support from everyone in Plymouth.

St. Lukes Hospice

CHAPTER 12

By Land, Sea, Air, Train or Bus

There are few cities in the United Kingdom that have as much choice of methods of travel than ourselves. We sometimes feel we are a long way from East Anglia and even further from Scotland but each succeeding year it becomes faster and easier to reach the far corners of this country and the world.

The presence of so many distinguished car showrooms tells its own story. Within a short distance of my office there are no less than four. I have chosen to write about them in alphabetical order to prevent anyone thinking that I favour one or the other!

Grevan commands attention as it stands proudly on the junction of Western Approach and Union Street. The gentle, bald headed giant, Bob Grunsell runs this efficient and courteous showroom with the precision of a top class golfer about to tee off. He will take this as a compliment, the whole company is golf orientated. Bob, himself a Lord's Taverner, was Chairman of the Devon and Cornwall region which annually organised the Celebrity Golf Classic at St Mellion. Its purpose was to raise funds for handicapped children.

Entrusted with the BMW franchise for Plymouth and a substantial part of Devon and Cornwall, the showroom reflects the standard of the BMW image. The depth of experience of the Grevan staff would be hard to beat. Bob Grunsell and his co-director, Mike Evans, who looks after their Shrewsbury operation, have over 31 years involvement with BMW, and a further eleven members of staff have been with the dealership, or its previous owners, for a staggering number of years; well over 200, I believe.

Talking to Bob Grunsell, what comes over most strongly is his commitment to the team spirit, and this rubs off naturally throughout the business. It is not only the expertise with which the sales people talk to would-be purchasers, nor the competence of the technical people who deal with the maintenance and repairing of your car, it is the thoughtful and unexpected touches that make BMW drivers remain faithful. My son had a BMW when he got married and the day before his wedding he put it in to be serviced and valeted. It was ready for him on time and the valeting came with the compliments of Grevan - a wedding present.

When you are moving up from today to tomorrow you will want a BMW model with more similarity between your own style and that of your car - one that is exactly tailor-made to your new requirements. BMW cars are designed and built to fulfil the personal wishes of discerning motorists - as a more individual, outstanding and unique solution and at Grevan, they are always at your service to provide you with the fullest information and test driving facilities to ensure you are given every assistance during the selection of your new BMW.

There are 28 models in the BMW range - 10 in series 3, 19 in series 5, 7 in the 7 series, and 2 in the 8 series. Do go and see what Grevan have to offer - you will find them delightful people - and remember to take your golf clubs!

It just goes to show that occasionally one good turn does not deserve another. With the keen interest that Grevan have in matters charitable, they emptied their showrooms one Friday-Monday in order to raise money for the Saltram Rotaract. In no time at all rumours flew round Plymouth that Grevan had gone bankrupt. It took some time to convince people that Grevan was very much alive and kicking and merely doing their bit to help the needy!

A man who has earned respect throughout the motor industry, and has served Plymouth for over 41 years, is Ivan Lang, of **Lang's Honda**. As I write he has gone into semi-retirement and is off on a round the world trip which he won from Honda. He came 8th in the country against target figures. His recollections of his early days and the growth of the business make an interesting tale.

Born in Camels Head and educated at Camels Head school, his new site is just opposite. His philosophy in life and in business is that everyone has commonsense and ability but you have to learn how to use them! Certainly he has put what he preaches into practice.

His career, which started as an apprentice mechanic with Mumfords, has taken him a step along the road to success with each move - and there have been several. His first garage was part of the family home. He paid £5 for his first service van, an Austin 7. North Road, where he found a larger garage, came next. It stood where you wait to filter into the traffic at North Cross. By 1957 he was busy building Greenbank Service Station on a bomb site. Here he handled petrol sales for the first time and in 1959 took his first car agency. The busy Peverell Garage came next which in turn he sold to three existing managers. Eventually he moved to Albert road but realised the premises did not give him the potential to expand into the 90's with Honda. Several times he looked at his present site at Camel's Head when it was owned by a friend of his with whom he went to school. Nothing to do with garages, the business was a monumental masons.

The site was too good to miss, on a main road from the City Centre to Cornwall. He bought it, designed the building himself but within the parameters set out by Honda, including dimensions, corporate colour scheme etc. He has been a Honda man for over 19 years and has a deep faith in the style, the design, the performance, the service that are the ingredients of the respected Honda cars.

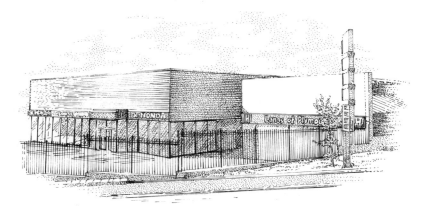

Lang's Honda

Honda have no control over his business, only a computer link between different branches in order to check the availability of parts or vehicles. Honda do train his staff but at a cost to Lang's.

Ivan Lang will tell you that the modern car gives tremendous value in reliability and service. Slightly different from the memory he has of an old Morris Cowley with a dicky seat that his father used to drive. Ivan and his brother sat in the dicky seat and if an oncoming hill was steep the boys would have to jump out and push the car the rest of the way to the top!

The belief that a dealership should offer a complete package of sales and service is applied constantly. When he built his office he had large areas of glass in it so that people could see for themselves that he was there, keeping a watchful eye over everything. His whole family work at the garage, including his wife, his daughters and his son-in-law. In fact, 90% of the staff are people who served their apprenticeship with the firm and have stayed loyally with Langs ever since. Ivan Lang believes this is common amongst Plymothians and he will tell you he considers Plymouth the best place to live in the whole world. I have no doubt that he will feel just the same when he returns from his world tour.

As I had heard elsewhere, Ivan Lang confirms that the days of big profits and quantity turnover are gone. Margins have been squeezed to the extent that there is very little leeway on price variations. With little price variation people start looking for better quality and service. That is where and when true recovery will come from the recession. Lang's Honda is a success story where the 'Near enough is good enough' attitude does not exist. Only the best will do.

Positive thinking is the philosophy of David Cornfield who has the **Mazda** dealership. His smart and purpose-built operation in Union Street, was opened in November 1991 and continues to flourish, thanks mainly to a tremendous team of people David has working with him and the innovative and unique nature of the Mazda franchise.

In landing the new dealership David fulfilled a lifelong ambition to own his own business.

After twenty three years in the motor industry he was chosen as the first person to be given the Mazda franchise under the Dealer Development Programme.

The Mazda scheme offered a once-in-a-lifetime opportunity for professional Managers who wished to run their own business, but could not afford the high cost of suitable facilities.

The discerning buyer who is seeking something a little different with reliability, quality and charisma, will find a visit to Plymouth Mazda most rewarding.

You only have to step through the showroom doors to feel the very positive and happy environment which exists and this is reflected in the way they look after customers.

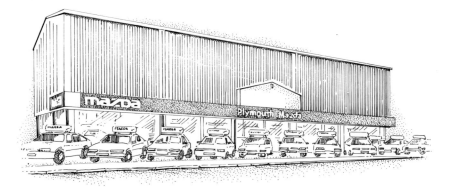

Plymouth Mazda

"Customers' expectations continue to rise" said David Cornfield, Managing Director "and it is our job to make sure we meet the high standards which are now rightly demanded of us".

"Our overall aim at Plymouth Mazda is to treat the customer fairly and do our utmost to satisfy their needs, both when buying a vehicle, and more importantly, in our attitude to after sales care".

Vospers has been synonymous with cars and service since it was founded in 1946 in Russell Street by Frank Vosper, father of the present chairman and managing director, Peter Vosper. In a very short space of time the motor business expanded and in the mid fifties held 7 agencies for new cars. In 1960 Vospers were appointed Ford Main Dealers and acquired their first premises in Millbay Road. In 1970, with the closure of Reeds, Vospers became sole Ford Main Dealers in the City.

This family business continued to grow and today is one of the leading Ford Dealers in the U.K. The interest was not only in cars but in other areas. In 1966 they became truck dealers for a large part of Devon and East Cornwall and are now Iveco Ford's

Main Dealer for that area. Motorcycles were an obvious market and again Vospers became a main dealer, this time for Honda Motorcycles.

Vospers Rental and Contract Hire has become an important part of the business. It runs over 2500 vehicles throughout Britain from its Plymouth base. Like everything else that Vospers does, it is an efficient and courteous service using a great understanding of client's needs.

In another part Vospers manufacture bodies for commercial vehicles for customers in all parts of the country. There is also a Marine Business in Sutton Harbour, representing many leading boat, engine and associated marine companies.

Vospers have a team of over 240 people working in Plymouth and 120 employees in their other dealerships, a total of 360 employees in all.

In 1986 Ford approved Vospers acquisition of the main dealership in Truro and have now asked them to provide an additional new dealership for the city at Marsh Mills. This is in anticipation of a new car market increasing from 2 million to 2.5 million by the year 2000. Total car ownership is expected to have doubled by then.

The Ford Mondeo at Vospers

The continuing success of the company and the leading market position of Ford has meant that the existing site at Millbay Road has been outgrown and because of development surrounding the site, it is not possible to expand the operation in the present area, so they are currently looking to relocate the main dealership to the site at Marsh Mills.

Vospers has always been a success story but it goes beyond that. The Vosper family have always associated themselves with the welfare of the city and take part in many charitable activities. Peter Vosper's mother and sister own the successful boutique, Francescas, in Mayflower Street, which I have written about in another chapter.

Wadham Kennings in Union Street have always served me well. I currently drive a secondhand Rover which I acquired from them and if the attention, care and service they offer to the purchasers of new cars equals that which I have received, I would happily recommend them to anyone.

Looking not so long ago to hire a car for a member of my family I approached **EuroDollar Rent A Car**, as much for the fact that I wanted to find out what the difference was, if any, since the days when they were Swan National Rentals. The change of name came when Swan National entered into a partnership with Dollar Rent A Car based in the United States. Dollar Rent A Car wanted a European partner and Swan National wanted to expand. The successful marriage resulted in a new international network throughout Europe for EuroDollar.

There are 105 EuroDollar branches throughout the United Kingdom making it possible to pick up a rental car anywhere and leave it at the point of destination. Customer care is all important and has many different guises. Foreign tourists, particularly Americans, book a car in advance of their arrival and forget the difference in the size of our cars to theirs. A Fiesta, for example when ordered unseen by an American is frequently useless; put in all their luggage and there would be no room for the passengers! There are many popular marques available including Vauxhalls, Peugeots and Toyota Previas. Lesser cars, too, but all of them well maintained and hired out in a spotless condition. With 12,000 high quality cars representing more than 40 models and 1500 vans, there is something to suit every driver and purpose.

The Plymouth branch of EuroDollar has its own unique qualities which have been recognised by the company's Gold award. A large percentage of the business in the Plymouth branch comes from service personnel who have built up a relationship with the company over a number of years. They need special handling because of the uncertainty of their movements. In addition the branch nurtures its relationship with local businesses as well as private customers. Courtesy and customer care is all important.

EuroDollar check on their branches by making telephone calls as potential customers and frequently sending their researchers to study a branch and report back on the way that they were treated. It keeps everyone on his toes but I am sure Plymouth would run as efficiently and caringly without the checks.

EuroDollar is currently the second largest vehicle rental organisation in the U.K. and leads the market in the corporate sector. They have plans for further expansion into Europe and it is hoped that before long it will be possible to hire one of their vehicles in Spain and return it to Plymouth, with the minimum of paperwork.

In nautical terms, the city is perhaps best known for its Ministry of Defence Devonport Royal Dockyard - the largest naval base in Western Europe and operational base for much of the Royal Navy Fleet. However, Plymouth is also the scene of a number of bustling and thriving commercial port activities.

Millbay Docks owned and operated by **Associated British Ports**, has been part of this scene for centuries. In the early days Millbay existed before Plymouth became Plymouth, because from the 12th century to the north, eastward of the present site, was a creek called Sourpole, which spread over the low lying land now occupied by the Octagon, Union Street, Phoenix Street and Rendle Street. It was here that Ralph of Valletort, an early member of that well known Plymouth family, granted to God and the Priors of Plympton a convenient place upon which to erect a mill. It was in early times that the inlet on the west side of the Hoe became known as Mill Bay.

At one time ships were accommodated as far inland as the Octagon for anchors have been discovered there. However, the first attempt at dock formation at Millbay appears in a map prepared in the late 1830s where the Union Dock is shown between Martin and Phoenix Streets. This dock was the property of three Plymothians, Richard Derry, David Derry and James Meadows-Rendel, who was a distinguished engineer. David Derry was Mayor of Plymouth from 1850-1851 and Derry's Clock in the centre of the city was given to the Corporation by a different member of the same family. Derry and Company were Cartage Contractors and Railway Agents, the company later being absorbed in the next century by the Great Western Railway.

The quarries, which can still be seen at West Hoe, were in full swing in 1840, steadily removing the famous Hoe in the recovery of limestone. The only other dock in the vicinity was the small West Hoe Dock situated in the quarries, and here the excavated stone and lime from the adjacent kilns was loaded into small vessels, which passed to and from the dock through a small channel located to the south east of the root portion of Trinity Pier.

Thomas Gill was Mayor of Plymouth in 1836 and the first person to hold that office under the Municipal Reform Act. He was the owner of the West Hoe Estate and proprietor of the quarries and it was he who realised the potential that existed within the Mill Bay for development. In 1840 he obtained an Act of Parliament which gave him powers to deepen the bed at Mill Bay and to erect at his own expense a pier and other works. This was the same year that the 'penny post' was introduced.

Several well known engineers were engaged in the construction of the docks at Mill Bay and the first of these was Mr Meadows-Rendel, also part owner of the Union Dock. He was ingenious and inventive. He designed Laira Bridge for Lord Morley; the first in England to be built of cast iron.

In 1840 the developers were given powers to take tolls in respect of the facilities they provided. Thomas Gill, as owner of the West Hoe Estate, was allowed to continue receiving tolls during the time of war in respect of prisoners landed at the new pier and passing through the estate to Mill Prison, which accommodated thousands of prisoners during the Napoleonic Wars and earlier. At this time the Royal Marine Barracks had a landing place for boats on the beach at the rear of Caroline Place. On the East Quay adjacent to the present Trinity Pier there was a drawbridge to enable vessels to pass to and from the West Hoe Quarry owned by Thomas Gill.

Thomas Gill was a wealthy man but he could not sustain the cost of developing Millbay. An Act of Parliament, called the Plymouth Great Western Docks Act, in August, 1846, authorised the expenditure of £980,000 to be subscribed in £20 shares and permit borrowing powers for a further £30,000. It empowered the new company to buy the existing works from Thomas Gill who became one of its directors. The building of the inner basin, and the provision of a dry dock, was part of the new programme. It was perhaps a prophetic inspiration for this dock company to be named Great Western because at that time the Great Western railway had only reached Bristol. The directors could have had no idea that 32 years later the dock would become part of that railway's undertakings.

Isambard Kingdom Brunel was appointed Engineer to the new Great Western Dock Company in 1846 and he used to travel to Plymouth in a first class GWR carriage which had the wheels coming up under the seats, a door between the two halves of the compartment and the luggage on the roof. He oversaw a great deal of work at this time. The inner basin and the dry dock were completed by the end of 1856.

An unexpected source of revenue came into the company via the dry dock; large quantities of fish became trapped in it and a record catch of mullet on the 16th October, 1875, was sold for a considerable sum of money.

When Millbay Docks were taken over by the Great Western Railway in 1875, a rock stood off the end of Trinity Pier. This was called Brunel's Rock because the great man had been compelled to leave it there when the pier was constructed: funds were not available to remove it. As a consequence vessels entering the inner basin had to pass through a narrow channel. This led to trouble. In 1880 the Company was faced with a lawsuit following damage to a grain vessel which struck the rock and defied the efforts of four tugs to move her. The company was required to compensate the owners not only for the cost of repairs but for the 45 days which the ship was out of commission.

Today's environmentalists would have been horrified at what followed. The rock was too expensive to retain and was blown up by explosives, killing or stunning thousands of fish. The seagulls had a field day!

In those days the docks were free from labour disputes although a labour agitator, Bill Sprow demonstrated his annoyance by pulling the Dock Inspector's beard violently in 1890. He was fined £2 10s 0d.

Over the years the docks were improved and further building carried out. For some time Plymouth had been the chief emigration depot for Government emigrants, and the ocean passenger traffic following in its steps began in 1850 with the introduction of the Cape Mail Union Line. Though the emigration traffic did not pass through the Great Western Docks, its development helped to show the shipping lines the value of Plymouth as a passenger port. In 1876 twenty five vessels left Plymouth with 10,194 Government emigrants for Australia and New Zealand. These were three vessels for Sydney with 1,118 passengers; two vessels for Queensland with 428 passengers; one vessel for Canterbury with 283 passengers; and nineteen vessels for Adelaide with 8,365 passengers. This figure did not include the large number of passengers who sailed regularly for America.

Emigrants, many of whom arrived by steamer from Ireland, would spend weeks at Plymouth waiting for the sailing ships to arrive. They were accommodated at the Emigrants Depot at Baltic Wharf where every adult was awarded a sum of money by the government to cover his travelling expenses to Plymouth.

With few exceptions, ocean liners never came alongside. Plymouth was only used as a port of call because a great saving of time could be achieved by the steamers anchoring in the Sound or in Cawsand Bay and tenders bringing the passengers baggage and mail ashore.

The busy tenders serviced all sorts of passenger ships and they themselves were a motley crew. Over the years there were paddle steamers, twin screw steamers and occasionally a purpose - built one like the 'Sir Francis Drake', built in 1873, and worked until 1903.

At a very early stage in the development of Millbay Docks it was realised the saving of time for overseas passengers and mail was a worthwhile benefit to be obtained. A government decision in 1849 to award mail contracts to steamship companies in open competition, thereby replacing the Admiralty Packet Services, led to the promotion of Plymouth as an overseas mail port. This was not altogether successful, with some disappointing times set on the runs, and eventually the Post Office cancelled the contract. Peninsula and Orient began calling at Plymouth in 1874 and this was the beginning of a regular service. In 1877 every passenger landing at Millbay Docks was charged 6d which covered his baggage. Even then some travellers were not satisfied and one wrote to the local newspaper complaining that he was charged any landing fee at all and said he considered 6d most exorbitant.

From 1879 onwards Plymouth became more and more dominant as a passenger port. By 1930 many famous ocean liners used Millbay Docks: the ' Mauretania', 'Bremen', 'Lusitania' and 'Ile de France', were calling here. The 'Normandie' called on her maiden voyage in 1935, and the following year the 'Queen Mary'. They were exciting times. The advent of World War II halted all this.

Millbay Docks was rapidly involved. In September, 1939, fourteen survivors from the 'SS Kensington Court' were landed after being rescued off the Scilly Isles by seaplane - probably the first recorded case of a ship's crew being rescued by a seaplane. On October 15th, 1939, four hundred and forty four survivors were landed from a number of different ships. In January, 1940, the 'SS Pacific Shipper' arrived in Millbay Docks in a damaged condition and was berthed at West Wharf. She had 8,000 tons of general cargo including fresh fruit, canned goods, timber and pig lead. This was only one of a steady flow of damaged ships arriving throughout the war.

From 1st to 28th June, 1940, not a single day passed without a contribution to the war effort. It is impossible now to imagine how the work force coped in those days with pressure of work, anxiety over members of their families fighting on the Continent and the injuries and exhaustion that they must have seen that summer month when refugees and troops passed through the docks.

Between June 11th and July 7th, 1940, over 67,000 members of the British and Allied troops disembarked from France. 45,000 were British and the rest a mixture of French, Belgian, Polish and

Czechoslovakian. Between the 22nd and 28th June almost 3,800 refugees from France were disembarked. France capitulated on July 15th, 1940, and the 'SS Penchateau' on passage between two ports in France was diverted to Millbay Docks with her cargo of military stores, bread, oats, hay and wine.

We gave each Plymouth air raid a number and Number 61 occurred on the 27th August, 1940 destroying a car, doing extensive damage to the tender 'Sir John Hawkins' and holing the pontoon and buildings on Millbay and Trinity Piers. By the 15th December the tender 'Sir Walter Raleigh', anchored in the Sound, was hit and a number of the crew injured. By the 13th January, 1941, Plymouth was experiencing air raid No.273 between 6.38pm and 9.35pm. At least 200 incendiary bombs fell in the docks area, and so it went on. On the 19th February a high explosive shell fell on number six shed on North Quay close to where the digital readout weighbridge is now located. The most sustained damage occurred just after King George VI and Queen Elizabeth had left the city on the 20th March. In the docks, Jewsons timber yard, Shed 76 and Shed 81 were burnt out. Clyde Sheds badly damaged by a high explosive bomb, and two cranes at Clyde Quay badly damaged. A high explosive bomb felled the operating gear of West Outer Gate. The SS 'Marie II' and two naval tugs were sunk at West Wharf plus two crabbers which burnt and sank in an inner basin. Worse was to follow. Even greater damage was done on the following night.

The heavy bombardment of Millbay Docks was repeated on the 22nd and 23rd April, 1941, when the estimated cost of the damage was £143,400. These two nights wreaked havoc on the buildings in the dock area and it demanded a very special kind of courage to report for work and endure bombing night after night for hours at a time. I can vouch personally for the uncertainty and anxiety we all felt. When you left home in the morning you had no idea whether your home or your workplace would be in existence by the evening. Yet we got through it and smiled for most of the time. I could write on for pages listing all the damage but suffice it to say that it was considerable. It did not stop work being carried out every day.

In 1943 the Admiralty started building the grid in the corner of the outer basin which is still visible from the corner of East Quay near the present workshop. The silo which still dominates the

Plymouth skyline was first used in February 1943 and camouflaged the following month.

On the 17th January, 1944, the Prime Minister landed at Millbay Docks at 11.18pm accompanied by Mrs Churchill and their daughter Sarah, who was in the WAAFs. They were returning from the Teheran Conference during which Winston Churchill was severely ill with pneumonia.

The intensive preparations for D - Day brought untold work to Millbay Docks. There was intensive preparation and rehearsals and once again the docks were in use for the return of wounded men and women, or the landing of prisoners of war. Even the Nazi flag was seen at West Wharf when a captured German hospital ship was berthed on September 20th, 1944. A week later the 'SS General Black' also berthed at West Wharf and took on board 1,000 German prisoners of war for shipment to America.

In October a French trawler lay alongside East Quay with 16,000 bottles of wine on board which three French wine merchants wished to exchange with the British Government for arms to be used by the Free French but the offer was declined!

With the war nearing its end it was a time for counting the cost. For most Plymothians it was a time of hardship but I suspect that for those who had worked in and around the docks throughout the war years, the horrors of war were even more deeply engrained. Casualties passed through in large numbers in very short periods of time and the cost of life and human suffering was very apparent. In January and February, 1945, there were over three thousand casualties.

The first Ocean mail and passenger liner returned to Plymouth on the 19th June, 1945, after a period of almost six years. In August, 1945, the King arrived at Millbay Docks in the royal train, on his way to welcome President Truman on board the battleship, HMS Renown, which was anchored in the Sound.

In June, 1946, all the tenders were returned to their peace time occupations with civilian crews, and the enormous contribution of Millbay Docks and its staff to the war effort came to an end.

Times had changed by the end of the war. Air travel was becoming a faster means of moving around the world, and in 1958 the 'Ile de France' made her last voyage calling at Plymouth as she had on her maiden trip 31 years earlier. P & O who, through companies which it had absorbed, could trace its links back as far as 1850, was persuaded to resume calls with its Australian vessels in 1962. In 1963 they also stopped.

The fact that Millbay Docks remains successful in spite of its chequered career is largely due to the hard work and innovative thinking of the people who work there. This adaptability was highlighted at the beginning of the 1970s when Breton producers decided to alter their transport arrangements to the United Kingdom by introducing a Roll-on Roll-off operation to ensure goods were not repeatedly handled. As Breton produce formed a large part of the business it was imperative Millbay Docks was capable of handling the traffic by the revised method. Facilities were constructed during 1972 and brought into use in January, 1973, coinciding with Britain's entry into the European Economic Community.

At first there were only three sailings a week but it eventually increased to one a day. For part of the year vessels arrived during the evening so produce could be delivered to fruit and vegetable markets ready for sale the next morning.

In the beginning only freight facilities were provided, but interest from the general public was so strong that during 1973 limited opportunities were made available for passenger movements, and almost 14,000 passengers were carried in that first year. It became obvious that substantial growth could result from obtaining passenger vessels and providing shore based passenger facilities. This part of the activity at Millbay Docks has grown significantly and services for both passengers and freight have been extended to cover Northern Spain.

Before 1978 when the Spanish route was introduced, the then British Transport Docks Board (later to become Associated British Ports) had identified the possibility of linking Plymouth with Northern Spain. The savings on steaming times, and utilisation of hauliers' vehicles, was to prove attractive and the service came into existence in 1978 with two sailings each week predominantly for passengers. Limited amounts of freight were carried until in June, 1980, an additional ferry was obtained by Brittany Ferries to provide extra accommodation for freight vehicles.

Brittany Ferries has become very much a part of the life of Plymouth just as Millbay Docks has been since it was a creek called Sourpole in the 12th century. I have no doubt it will continue to grow and prosper as Plymouth does.

A.B.P. at Millbay Docks are responsible, too, for the services which have brought a number of cruise liners to Plymouth. For eight years or so **Cotswold Travel** have been running a programme of cruises from here to the Canary Islands drawing their passengers from all over the United Kingdom.

Cotswold Travel who hail from Bearland House, Longsmith Street, Gloucester are a well established and highly respected company who have brought much business to the city but who freely admit that their life has been made easier by the co-operation and efficiency of Associated British Ports. Send for their brochure and discover where you can go in the world starting from Plymouth.

In my enthusiasm for the history of Millbay Docks I must not forget the importance to Plymouth of Cattewater Harbour. Today the main activities centre on Cattedown Wharves, chiefly involved in the import of petroleum products, and Victoria Wharves, specialising in dry bulk. Between them more than a million tonnes of cargo is handled in a 175 hectare stretch of sheltered water which includes the original port of Plymouth, where the Phoenicians were among the early traders.

Brittany Ferries offices and reservation centre are based in Associated British Ports ferry terminal building and the company's increasing presence in Plymouth, benefits the city. Recently the company has become major shareholders in Westcountry Television, who started transmitting at one minute past midnight on January 1st, 1993.

Naturally, one of the worries has been how much business will be lost with the advent of the Channel Tunnel, but the head of Brittany Ferries confidently predicts that the firm's two new super cross channel vessels will head off the challenge of the tunnel.

In 1992 Brittany Ferries took delivery of two new cruiseferries Normandie and Barfleur. This year sees the introduction of the biggest ship in the fleet, the £70 million, 31,000 tons, Nils Holgersson which will operate out of Plymouth from June.

The feeling is that the introduction of these large cruiseferries will persuade holiday-makers to steer clear of the Dover-Folkestone tunnel when it opens. It makes sense because Brittany Ferries serves the western channel and so more than two out of three of the firm's current passengers would have to make a detour to get to the tunnel. Passengers would save little time and money using the tunnel as they would have to drive further in France, paying for petrol, tolls, meals and even overnight accommodation.

Brittany Ferries offers a first class service to its passengers and the 23,000-tons Bretagne won a five star rating for the quality of its crossings to Santander in Spain and Roscoff in France in 1992. Only five other vessels, including a second Brittany Ferries vessel, in Britain earned such a high rating.

The Bretagne

On the Plymouth to Santander crossing there is plenty to do on board to suit all kinds of travellers no matter what their budget.

I understand that a selection of top class performers have been retained to entertain, including strolling musicians, pianists and groups playing a variety of music from jazz to classics. On some sailings the company will provide games for children, fashion shows and a series of quiz and deck games. Obviously entertainment will vary from ship to ship depending on the size of the vessel and the length of the sailing.

Caring for the passengers is all important, a bevy of attractive and smartly dressed young women greet the traveller and cope with every imaginable question. It is efficiently done and without fuss.

Plymouth benefits enormously from Brittany Ferries. Passengers frequently stay overnight and this means the hotels and the restaurants gain. Perhaps the city centre shops and stores as well but that is slightly less tangible. Working together for the benefit of us all should be the aim of every business and Brittany Ferries certainly point the way.

Proving that small is beautiful is probably the best way of introducing the little passenger ferries and pleasure cruisers which are so much part of Plymouth life. **Tamar Cruising** operates the ferry that crosses the river from Admiral's Hard in Stonehouse to Cremyll and Mount Edgcumbe on the other side. I use it regularly in the spring and summer when I take my grandchildren to discover the joys of Mount Edgcumbe Park, the property of the city and Cornwall and free to us all.

All day every day the Armadillo goes to and fro taking people who live on the other side to and from work and to link up with the buses that regularly leave from Cremyll for Cawsand, Whitsands, Millbrook and Torpoint. I used the ferry when I was a child on my way home from school to Cawsand. That was sixty years ago and the same ferry, the Armadillo, is in service.

Nothing has changed really except that there is a car park on the Plymouth side where visitors can leave their vehicles, and on the other side the buses are modern. It is a peaceful, delightful crossing with the elegant, handsome Royal William Yard on one side and the busy Mayflower Marina on the other. It is still a slippery landing on the Plymouth side at low tide and the gangway which is run out for landing on either side is just as rickety. The Armadillo makes the same noises and the crew are friendly and caring.

I was delighted to be given an account of a journey in 1698 and thought you would like to read it as well.

The Journey of Celia Fieans to Cornwall
Her Account of Crossing Cremyll Ferry

'From Plymouth I went one mile to Cribly (Cremyll) Ferry which is a very hazardous passage, by reason of three tydes meeting; had I known the danger before, I should not have been very willing to have gone it, not but that is the constant way all people go, and saved several miles rideing; I was at least an hour going over, it was about a mile but indeed in some places, notwithstanding there was 5 men rowed and I sett my own men to row alsoe, I do believe we made not a step of the way for almost quarter of an hour, but blessed be God I came safely over; but those ferry boates are soe wet and then the sea and wind is allways cold to be upon, that I never faile to catch cold in a ferry-boate as I did this day, having 2 more ferrys to cross tho' none so bad or half soe long as this; thence to Millbrooke 2 mile and went all along by water and had the full view of the Dockyards.'

Not much has changed. The tides still meet but are counteracted by the power of engines and the crossing takes a bare ten minutes. It can be cold and wet but there is a cabin and it certainly saves many miles if you want to get to Cawsand or Millbrook.

Judging from several yarns about the Tamar crossing which appeared in the Evening Herald before 1946 things were not too different then either. I hope the Herald will not think this piracy if I quote one.

'To Cawsand folk who sail the seas
From Cremyll to the Hard
To me seem very hard to please
And apt to disregard
The vast amount of fun they get
When sailing to and fro
They always have a chance to bet
On 'Will it stop or go?'
But when they have to cross in fog
That's when the fun begins,
And every soul is all agog
And thinking of past sins
Up in the bow like sheep they crowd
The skipper to advise

Although this should not be allowed
This right they exercise.
Some tell him he should go to port:
Whilst others favour starboard
And ancient mariners have sought
That he should steer to larboard.
In spite of this we oft arrive
Right at the spot we aimed for.
And if we don't the rest contrive
The skipper all to blame for.

And having reached the other side
We bravely breast the slope
And put on speed with every stride
To catch the bus we hope.
But as we get near Durnford Street
It dashes past like smoke
These busmen have no boat to meet
And love this little joke
And then we have the Turnstile Stakes
For those who're homeward bound.
Each one in hand his life he takes
As up the ramp we pound.
The leaders wildly storm the bus
Then proudly sit in state.
The panting losers stop and cuss
They have to walk or wait.

And when the ferry plies no more
And all of us are fliers,
Our wretched offspring we will bore
(Tis said 'All men are liars')
With gruesome tales no man could crown
No tall yarn being barred -
Of how we ran the Armadillo down
From Cremyll to the Hard.

In 1993 we are not fliers and the Armadillo still serves us faithfully.

In addition to running the Cremyll Ferry, Tamar Cruising operate regular cruises up and down the Hamoaze to see the warships and on to Calstock; a supremely beautiful trip which gives you a totally different view of Plymouth. You can also go the other way towards Newton Ferrers and the River Yealm which is equally beautiful. It is something no visitor to Plymouth should fail to do and Plymothians, too, need to be reminded by a gentle voyage like this, how beautiful is our heritage. We all need reminding from time to time.

Special occasions and evening trips are part of the itinerary with Tamar Cruising. Throughout the season there are all sorts of different trips with supper or a barbecue as part of the fun. The boats are licensed. It is good fun and not too expensive.

Torpoint Ferries have been the backbone of Tamar crossings for a very long time. The advent of the Tamar Bridge in 1960 eased their burden but without them crossing regularly from Devonport to Torpoint, many miles would be put on people's journeys. For the visitor the short crossing is an interesting experience. You can abandon your car and climb to the top deck which gives you a splendid view of the activity in the Hamoaze, a clear appreciation of the number of Royal Naval ships tied up alongside the Dockyard wall, the enclosed Submarine and Frigate complexes where ships undergo repairs and refits. The fight to maintain these refits has sparked off one of the longest and most acrimonious debates that Plymouth has ever encountered with the Ministry of Defence. The outcome is still undecided as I write. If Devonport Dockyard does not win the battle and the Dockyard at Rosyth is the victor, the economy of the whole city and businesses all over the South West will be severely affected. There is not one of us who does not support the struggle.

Plymouth without an airport would be worse than Easter without eggs! The city could have found itself in this situation in 1975 when property speculators did everything in their power to prevent **Brymon Airways** from taking over **Plymouth Airport**. They did not succeed and the company has a long lease which should secure its future.

Way before the 1939-45 war the City fathers had been brave enough to look at the question of air transport out of Plymouth. As far back as 1923, the Chamber of Commerce had the concept in mind to take mail which had crossed the Atlantic by ship, from Plymouth to London. From there it could be transferred to a regular air service to Europe, within seven hours of arriving by sea. It sounds very tame now but in those days it was quite a feat.

From a small grass plot at Chelston meadow - now the refuse tip for the city - Alan Cobham, who became one of the best known airmen ever, took off on a proving flight to Croydon. This was successful and the city council started looking for a suitable site. Roborough appeared to be the ideal spot and from then onwards the airport has grown.

After the war it was used by small airlines and had resident planes belonging to Britannia Royal Naval College who used it for training. Dennis Teague, who is an aviation historian and has written some first class books on our local aerodrome, said to me when we met one day, 'It might be fair to say that Roborough played a more important part in the Falklands conflict than it did in the war, because every Naval Sea Harrier and helicopter pilot received his basic training in the Chipmunks based here.' Not many people know that !

It is the success that Brymon European Airways have made of the City Airport that has brought much business to Plymouth. They persevered where many fell away. The service offered is efficient and enables people to make a trip to London and return the same day with speed and comfort. They have consistently introduced new routes although, sadly, Brymon Eurpoean are unable to expand much further in Plymouth. They do operate out of Bristol which provides new routes and aircraft.

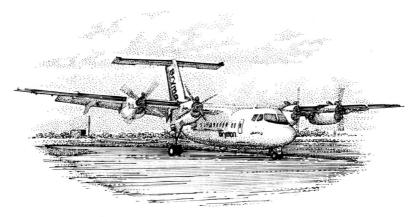

Brymon European Airways

British Rail have invested large sums of money recently to make Plymouth Station's concourse attractive and efficient. My family and I use British Rail quite regularly and so one tends to notice the differences between one station and another and how well or badly one is treated by the station staff. Plymouth can hold its head up high. It is not perfect but a very real effort is made to ensure the well being and comfort of the travelling public.

Perhaps we do not recognise sometimes the many factors and reasons for redesigning something like Plymouth station, for example. Originally built in 1960 the station looked old and it no longer met the high standard that InterCity required for its customers. The new design has created a focal point under the station's main roof made from a series of translucent sheets of material. Fashioned into geometric patterns, they create the effect of a ship's sails. To add to this visual appeal, the sails are draped over taut wires and resemble the rigging strung between four vertical columns that look like tall masts.

The main aim was to change the cluttered appearance of the main customer circulating area and provide a clean crisp look - this they have achieved admirably.

Other factors were taken into consideration as well. Buildings in Plymouth are relatively low and punctuated by towers of the churches and Smeaton's lighthouse. The station mirrors internally what the city skyline is like externally. The whole enhances the amount of natural light in the building. Retail outlets have been remodelled and Hertz Car Rental, Spar convenience food store, Traveller's Fare buffet and W.H. Smiths complement the whole concourse.

From the customers point of view it is far nicer, but more importantly, six new ticket windows are in use which reduce customer waiting time. No one needs to wait more than three minutes during off peak periods and five minutes during peaks.

Intercity from Plymouth offers a speedy service to Paddington several times a day. The Golden Hind Pullman, for example, leaves at 7am and takes only three hours to reach London. Every First Class Pullman offers unrivalled levels of welcome and service, with a choice of light refreshment or full breakfast, lunch, afternoon tea and dinner, beautifully presented at your seat.

Services to the north and to Scotland are equally efficient although less frequent.

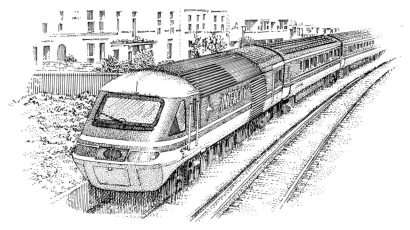

Intercity

For businesses the Intercity Business travel executives are trained to provide customers with all the travel requirements obtainable from a BR Travel Centre and more. Travel planning and travel arrangements can be tricky but a simple telephone call can sort it all out for you. They will co-ordinate your arrangements from car parking in Plymouth to travel on the London Underground and the return trip as well. It could not be simpler. Tickets can be sent to you or collected at the Travel Centre without the need to queue. I have used the service and it works.

My five year old grandson has a great passion for trains and stations and through his eyes I have discovered how many different sorts of trains, engines and locomotives come and go from the station during the course of the day. Local services abound, goods trains trundle through and the regular long distance trains pull in and out more often than not on time, and sometimes they arrive early.

The Sunday local service to Gunnislake and back, the Tamar Line, is a favourite outing. This delightful journey takes you on a winding route through lush countryside, beside the river, through small hamlets and villages, stopping from time to time at stations which one had forgotten existed. This is a service that attracts visitors and Plymothians. You see familiar faces who travel the line regularly, a bit like a club. Young Angus loves the fact that he can sit right up front behind the driver who is invariably kind enough to answer his endless questions. The conductor, too, treats all the passengers like long lost friends and is a mine of information.

Nothing to do with British Rail, but fascinating for all railway buffs of any age, is the **Dart Valley Railway** which runs a service from Buckfastleigh to a halt just outside Totnes. It is enchanting. Old G.W.R carriages and steam engines take you along one of the prettiest routes in the whole of the county. Sometimes during the summer they have Thomas Tank Days when the normal engine is joined by a whole variety of other steam engines, each with a Thomas Tank face. If you are an expert like my grandson you soon learn to look for Henrietta or Percy, the Fat Controller or Thomas. It is a great day out because not only do you get to travel on the train, you also have the opportunity to see and explore the other engines, go across the bridge and enjoy the adventure park and finally, probably exhausted, have tea in the cafeteria or picnic.

At Christmas we travelled on the Santa Special, with Father Christmas on board and a whole host of nursery rhyme characters. Every child had a present, and the adults - mulled wine and mincepies.

On a more serious note, British Rail plan to invest £3.5 million in developing Plymouth's Laira rail depot as part of a new night-train Chunnel link connecting the city with Brussels and Paris. The choice of Plymouth apart from allowing a through train service to and from Continental Europe is a great boost for the city. It should be operational by November, 1994, and will certainly help Plymouth business people to succeed in Europe. It will also attract any businessman who wishes to set up in Plymouth.

I talked for quite a long while with David Thomas, the enthusiastic, efficient and likeable station manager. He is full of plans for the future, both for Plymouth and for his staff. He told me about new approaches to marketing methods which will help Plymouth realise its aspirations to become the South West leader for conference venues, the arts, recreational activities and exhibitions.

InterCity are keeping a close watch, for example, on plans for the proposed National Marine Aquarium which would attract thousands of people to the city and would enable British Rail to lay on many more trains. This is one of the reasons why British rail invested £1.5 million in improving Plymouth Station which is already the highest revenue earning station in Devon and Cornwall.

When you are walking underneath the station to reach Platform 7 or wherever, take a look at the murals on the wall, two of which have been painted by Peter Trim, a railman, the others by local schools and art colleges. One of the things that struck me about David Thomas was his keen interest in the people who work with him and a desire to help any one of them. He believes it is as important to encourage their interests as it is to have them working efficiently. Happy and fulfilled people are more productive and usually pleasanter colleagues!

Plymouth has one of the best public transport systems in the country. It is plentiful, covers the city thoroughly and while it is not cheap it is better than many places. The bus station at Bretonside is an eye opener. If you sit there long enough you will see buses and coaches departing at regular intervals for destinations as far away as Scotland and as close as Plympton. It is also the starting point and the destination of many tour companies who whisk you away to magical places for a package holiday in Europe or an afternoon's mystery tour not too far away from Plymouth. The booking service is efficient and when I did a sort of mini, market - research with coach and bus users I found that 90% had no complaints whatsoever, and of those who had, I found that in general their problem had been resolved amicably.

One small instance I can quote is of two elderly ladies waiting for a bus in Looe to take them back to Plymouth. It was the last one of the day on that particular route. The ladies maintained the bus had left early leaving them stranded. They had to get a taxi back to Plymouth at a cost of £16. Not good for pensioners. The company concerned was the **Western National**. When they were telephoned and told what had happened they sent two inspectors to see the ladies, took statements and went away to investigate. The ladies were convinced that they would hear no more but before very long the inspectors were back with an apology, a refund of the £16 and two return tickets from Plymouth to Looe to be used whenever the ladies wished.

When I talked to Western National about this incident they told me that not only was it very important to maintain good customer relationships but it was equally important to ensure that drivers did not leave even half a minute before the scheduled time. I was impressed by their courtesy and efficiency and I would add that they had no idea I was writing this book.

In June 1982 Plymouth Corporation bought the Plymouth Tramways Company and so began the history of what is one of the most go ahead and efficient bus companies in the country, **Plymouth Citybus**.

When you see the compact, well - designed minibuses travelling the city from one end to the other all day long, it takes more than a little imagination to paint a picture in one's mind of the days in 1872 when the trams were drawn by horses and the tremendous step forward when the Corporation's line was electrified in 1899. The last horse-drawn tram ran on June 21, 1907. By 1915 Plymouth Corporation had acquired the Devonport and District Tramways and the Plymouth, Stonehouse and Devonport Tramways Company. It was not until 1922 when all three systems came under the one ownership that work began to properly co-ordinate the network. By 1928, with a total of 127 trams it was at its height. The first bus service began in 1932 with 20 vehicles covering four routes. The first double deckers arrived in 1930 by which time the trams were fighting a losing battle and in 1934 only two circular routes were left. The last route, from Old Town Street to Peverell via Mutley Plain was abandoned in 1945.

Trams on the electrified line

Milehouse has always been the headquarters and over the years it has been modernised until in 1985 the new engineering complex was opened, making it one of the most modern facilities in the South West.

In that same year the Transport Act changed the way the company operated. From being a department of Plymouth City Council, Plymouth Citybus emerged as a commercial company in the council's ownership.

The Act also de-regulated bus services, which led to a major overhaul of routes. And it led to the introduction of minibuses on a large scale. In October, 1986, Plymouth Citybus put 85 minibuses on to the streets of Plymouth, representing some 70% of the fleet. Today we have comfortable, streamlined minibuses working all over the city. It makes you stop and think when you realise that the weekly fleet mileage is 87,000 miles.

The bulk of Citybus routes are run on a strictly commercial basis but a number of routes are subsidised by Plymouth City Council where the social need has to be considered. The company does believe that it has a duty to the city and is delighted when they are able to do things like refurbishing two double deckers to meet more adequately the needs of disabled, handicapped and frail people. The buses have low steps, non slip floors, more bells and handrails and they are marketed under the banner of Easybus.

Community involvement also includes charity work. The drivers nominate charities, and money is raised by all sorts of means. I can remember a special Mufti Day in a Christmas period when drivers wore fancy dress and management dressed as drivers. Together they raised £1,500 in one day for the Devon and Cornwall Child Development Centre at Scott Hospital. At other times there have been events including a bus-pull. Apart from being worthwhile these occasions do have the benefit of team work which rubs off on the daily routine. You get the sense of belonging and pride when you go to the depot. Brian Fisher, the managing director, is a man of great passion when it comes to Plymouth Citybus. He is an organised, dynamic guy whose burning desire is to make an ever increasing success of his company and also to pass on his ability. He is currently the chairman of the South West section of the Chartered Institute of Transport which has 300 members in Devon and Cornwall. He is a communicator and continued efforts are made to ensure that members of staff, at all levels, speak to each other. The regular staff bulletin carries official news but also welcomes letters and comments from staff, and includes quizzes and competitions which offer attractive prizes.

Brian Fisher believes in an open door policy which provides staff with easy access to managers at all convenient times.

The increasing Citycoach operation which takes people all over Europe, is one of Plymouth Citybus' great successes. The fleet has luxury coaches smartly painted with the company livery. Frequently they work in conjunction with the Western Evening Herald offering tours that are snapped up very quickly.

For smaller parties there are nippy 21-seater mini-coaches and the Infobus is the mobile exhibition unit especially designed for local businesses. You can go out to potential customers without waiting for them to find you!

Most laymen will not appreciate the work that is done by the car and commercial department. They do repair work of all kinds and their sights are firmly set on winning new business. Their capabilities cover anything from the private motorist to heavy commercial vehicles and fleet operators to the light van sector. It is an impressive array of skills in the fields of repair and maintenance, electrics and electronics, spraying and signwriting, in body work and specialist engineering services.

The Citybus Driving School has professionally trained instructors who have an excellent pass rate. In addition to on-the-road training, the company's classroom tuition covers such vital areas as the Highway Code, Drivers' Hours Regulations and Tachograph Training. They offer courses of up to three weeks duration as well as pay-as-you learn lessons on most types of training.

PSV Training for Class 1 and Class 3 public service vehicle licences are available, using Leyland PD2 or PD3 and Renault Dodge minibuses respectively. Semi-automatic vehicles can also be dealt with.

The school operates Plymouth City Council's Taxi Driving Assessment which is something all new and prospective taxi drivers must pass before they can be licenced. There is HGV training and Fork Lift training. In fact a fully comprehensive driving school.

For me one of the best things that Plymouth Citybus does is the guided tour on their open-topped double decker which goes round the city. The bus is comfortable and the commentary excellent. I learnt all sorts of interesting bits and pieces. For example did you know that in 1797 three United Irishmen were executed on the Hoe by firing squad for treason, or that on the front of the Hoe there is an area where bulls were deliberately baited in the belief that it would ensure their meat was tender? I learnt that Friese-Greene, a pioneer of the motion picture, had a shop in Union Street where the Two Trees pub now stands. I had forgotten too that Stanley Gibbons, whose name is synonymous with stamp collecting, had a shop in Treville Street on Bretonside opposite the bus station where the taxi rank is today. He moved, I believe, to North Hill for a time just above the reservoir.

This is an excellent way to see the city and I would recommend it to all Plymothians as well as to visitors.

The City Council's joint venture on 'Park and Ride' from the car park at Home Park has been very successful. The park and ride scheme operates from 7.30am to 6.15pm with buses running every ten minutes during peak periods. Specially marked park and ride bus stops are at Western Approach, Union Street, Royal Parade, Exeter Street, Charles Street and Coburg Street.

Plymouth Citybus

With travel uppermost in my mind throughout this chapter it seems appropriate to end with one of the most successful and helpful travel agents in the city. **Peter Goord Travel** is a family business and run for a clientele who are independent minded. Those who wish to take package holidays are well catered for as many brochures not seen in other travel agencies are available at West Park. The company personally checks out as many destinations and accommodation as possible.

You will find the company based at West Park which is a convenient geographical situation for anyone in Plymouth. Peter Goord himself is a Plymothian and his first business which is still in existence was insurance. That was over thirty years ago and this ex- Devonport High School boy now has his two sons as partners. Peter is the travel consultant for Radio Devon and has a fount of knowledge about travel throughout the world that is invaluable to his clients.

He tells me that Cyprus from Exeter is one of the biggest attractions for Plymothians who seem to like the idea of being able to fly direct rather than have to go to Heathrow or Gatwick. This reluctance has its drawbacks because it does not always represent the best choice. Certainly there is a move away from Spain, for example. More people go to the States, and Turkey is on the up and up. I was looking for a cruising holiday, which I still hope to be able to take before the end of this year. Peter Goord recommended several different options but was equally kind enough to suggest that I waited as long as possible before booking because frequently good offers came up at the last minute. Certainly worthwhile if one is not tied down to a definite date and does not have rigid ideas about the destination.

It was probably the courtesy, the understanding and the commonsense which made me select this travel agency to write about although Plymouth has several very good ones.

CHAPTER 13

The Time, The Place and The People

I would doubt that few cities can boast the number of outstanding people who are either natives or have become Plymothians by adoption. Drake, Hawkins, Raleigh and Grenville are names that even today conjure up visions of greatness. Their exploits have become the epitome of all that Plymouth stands for: courage, determination, adventure and vision. I have no doubt either that if one dug too deeply into their methods and their successes, present day moralists would say they were nothing more than pirates. Hawkins for example was the first Englishman to engage in the foul trade of slavery, a business that had general approval of the highest and the lowest in the land. No one thought ill of him for this brutal venture. A trade from which Britain enjoyed great wealth for two centuries to come and then spent another stamping out the evil. Nonetheless for me they will always be the most colourful men in Plymouth's long and distinguished history. Richard Barnfield wrote on the death of Hawkins:

'The waters were his winding sheets, the sea was made his tomb
Yet for his fame the ocean bed, was not sufficient room.'

I find no difficulty in seeing them in my mind, as they walked the streets of the Barbican to Sutton Pool on their way to board their ships. Incredible that in those little ships they took on the might of unknown oceans and undiscovered territories. Robert Blake, the greatest of our admirals next to Nelson, and Martin Frobisher who played a heroic part in the scattering of the Armada, died in Plymouth. Their hearts were buried somewhere near the chancel steps of our mother church, St Andrews - a simple stone marks this fact. Drake is forever immortalised. His statue on Plymouth Hoe looks out over Plymouth Sound and within his sight lies the English Channel. This,

'fellow traveller of the sun
Whose shippe about the worlde's wide waste
In three yeares did a golden girdle caste'

was a hard act to follow but the succeeding centuries have given us many great men and women. Sir Joshua Reynolds' work needs no introduction but I wonder how many Plymothians know that he made his first painting when he was twelve, on a piece of sail with the paint the local boatmen used for their boats. By the time he was nineteen he had settled in Devonport painting portraits of naval officers. One of them, Captain Keppel, took him on a cruise to the Mediterranean which enabled him to study the Old Masters at Florence, Venice and Rome. On his return Lord Mt Edgcumbe encouraged him to set up a studio in London and although he was still a young man, wealthy people competed to have their portraits painted by him. He strove hard to discover the secrets of the colours used by the Old Masters, the way they were laid on canvas and the materials they used but somehow that which he used in his painting, whilst giving brilliant colour at first, became pale wrecks as the years went by. This has never detracted from his great genius and his portraits are still wonderful today. You can see them at Saltram House, where he often stayed, at Mount Edgcumbe and in the Plymouth Art Gallery.

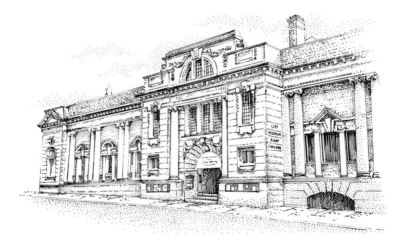

The Mesuem and Art Gallery

No matter how famous he became he still loved Plymouth and when in 1773 he was elected Mayor of Plympton he said it gave him more pleasure than any other honour he had received, and they were many, including his knighthood. He was a man who had a host of friends, many of them famous.

Fame does not always help the talented. This was the case with the brilliant Benjamin Robert Haydon, born in Plymouth in

1786. He was educated at Plympton Grammar School, where Joshua Reynolds' father was a master and he a pupil, and from there he went to London. At the age of 21 he found success with his picture of 'The Flight into Egypt'. He was a difficult man, always quarrelling with people, and his row with the Royal Academy over the hanging of this picture caused a breach which was never healed. He was always in debt and never free of his creditors. His pride in many ways was his downfall. He could have mended the bridges with the Royal Academy but instead he chose to hold exhibitions of his own which were not always successful. His pride took an especial hammering on the day when he wrote in his diary:

Tom Thumb had 12,000 people last week; B.R. Haydon 133½.
Exquisite taste of the English people.

Modern Plymouth also has its share of artistic brilliance. The genius of Robert Lenkewiecz is undoubted. An odd man who seems to have covered the whole spectrum of the artist's canvas. I have seen his exhibitions over the years and either been stunned by their beauty or filled with repugnance. Prudish maybe, but personal choice does come into it. Then there is the irrepressible Beryl Cook who has found worldwide fame with her paintings which are an expression of the fun and the pathos to be had out of life. Brian Pollard, a Plymouth G.P., is an emerging painter of whom I expect we will hear more. Then there are the exciting coterie of artists who show their work under the auspices of one of Plymouth's most interesting restaurateurs, Steve Barrett, of Barretts in Princess Street. One of their number is Karen Pawley, whose brilliant handling of colour and the third dimension makes her a young talent from whom we will surely see many more paintings.

William Cookworthy, born in Kingsbridge, may also be claimed by Plymouth for it was whilst he was living in Number 58 Notte Street that he discovered china clay in Cornwall from which to make English porcelain. In 1796 he started the Plymouth china factory at Coxside but it lasted only two, years when it was transferred to Bristol. Perhaps Plymouth ware is not of the highest importance but the charm lies in the fact that when it was manufactured it was done with great difficulty and it took Cookworthy more than twenty years of singleminded, unaided research to discover the method.

What more courageous Plymothian can there ever have been than Robert Falcon Scott, who was born at Oatlands? Here was a delicate boy, who overcame his disabilities to become first and foremost a sailor. He found naval life to his liking and even as a young midshipman of no more than eighteen years he attracted the notice of Sir Clements Markham, who marked him down as a man who would make a fit commander of a voyage to discover Antartica. When the expedition was organised Scott commanded Discovery and was away two years. He and his fellow explorers discovered that the great ice barrier was the gateway to the Pole and no more and no less than a barrier resting on the water. From that point there was no way by ship, only over a plain of ice stretching 360 miles south, and beyond that a mountain range and a desert of snow. Scott and his men explored this hostile land and the story of their journey is one of the great epics of Antartic travel. After Scott returned he was asked if he would do it again and he said he would go back tomorrow. He did and was never to return.

He reached the Pole in January 1912 with Wilson, Oates, Bowers and Evans, only to find their rival Amundsen had beaten them by 35 days. The disappointment must have been terrible. He writes, ' All the day dreams must go: it will be a wearisome return.' It was worse than that. Blizzards blocked their path, Wilson strained a tendon, Evans broke down and died, their feet were frostbitten and Oates could barely walk but they struggled on. On March 17, Oates showed unbelievable courage when he told them he was going out and might be sometime. He walked into certain death hoping that his comrades without having to carry him, might fight on and live. They were only 11 days from safety but the blizzard continued and Scott's own words serve as his epitaph:

'For four days we have been unable to leave the tent - the gale howling about us. We are weak, writing is difficult, but for my own sake I do not regret this journey, which has shown Englishmen can endure hardships, help one another, and meet death with as great fortitude as ever in the past.

'We took risks, we knew we took them; things have come out against us, and therefore we have no cause for complaint, but bow to the will of Providence, determined still to do our best to the last.

'But if we have been willing to give our lives to this enterprise, which is for the honour of the country, I appeal to our countrymen to see that those who depend on us are properly cared for.

'Had we lived, I should have had a tale to tell of the hardihood, endurance, and courage of my companions which would have stirred the heart of every Englishman. These rough notes and our dead bodies must tell the tale.'

It was eight months later that an Englishman found the tent and opening the flap saw a sight that will never be forgotten. Scott lay with one arm over his life-long friend, Wilson. Bowers was on the other side and near him were his diaries and the bundle of letters he had written whilst the three of them lay dying. A great cairn was built over the tent and a cross, made out of skis, marked the spot. No trace was found of Captain Oates but a smaller cairn was built at a point near which he walked out to die.

A great Plymothian and a hero for all time.

Then there is the extraordinary parson, Robert Stephen Hawker, Hawker of Morwenstow. Born in Plymouth, he was baptised in Stoke Damerel Church and buried in Plymouth cemetery. Plymouth is strongly Devonian but none of us deny that we do have links with Cornwall. Hawker's Song of the Western Men, still stirs my heart and sets the adrenalin flowing when I hear it sung whether at Twickenham or in Songs of Praise from Truro Cathedral quite recently when the Cornish choirs raised the rafters with:

> A good sword and a trusty hand
> A merry heart and true.
> King James's men shall understand
> What Cornish men can do.
> And have they fixed the where and when?
> And shall Trelawney die?
> Here's twenty thousand Cornishmen
> Will know the reason why.

Trelawney's men and women have had a hard time in the recession, as indeed has Plymouth, with the fight for the survival of the Dockyard still raging as I write, but Hawker's song says it all for both sides of the River Tamar. You have only to change the words a little and ask:

> A good sword and a trusty hand
> A merry heart and true.

355

Elizabeth's men shall understand
What Dockyard men can do.
And have they fixed the where and when?
And shall the Dockyard die?
Here's three hundred thousand Plymouthmen
Will know the reason why.

By adoption, Plymouth owes much to the great architects John Foulston (1772-1842) and Sir John Rennie (1826-35). Foulston left an unmistakable stamp everywhere in what were then the three towns, Plymouth, Stonehouse and Devonport. It was not until he was forty that Foulston took up residence in Plymouth and for the next thirty years he devoted himself to building on the grand scale and the domestic with equal skill. His work in Devonport survives in the Guildhall and the Naval Column. The Column was never completed. It was supposed to have a vast statue of George IV on the top but the funds ran out. My favourite is the unique Albemarle Villas just above the College of Further Education. The houses are charming, elegant and have superb views. Dame Joan Vickers, the M.P. for Plymouth Devonport for so many years, now a Life Peeress, lived in one of them.

In Plymouth not much remains of Foulston's work; most of it was destroyed by the bombing in World War II but here was a man who dreamt of creating buildings and in addition to designing most of the terraces in Plymouth. He constructed nearly all the public buildings with the exception of the Customs House, which was designed by Laing. He shaped Union Street with the Octagon at its centre, Athenaeum Street, Lockyer Street and The Crescent. Even after his reign came to an end builders continued in the same vein.

If you look back at some of the photographs of old Plymouth you will see the old Theatre Royal, the Royal Hotel and Assembly Rooms, The Athenaeum, the Proprietary Library and the Royal Union Baths. All Foulston's work, they are no more but he will always be remembered. So too will Sir John Rennie whose Royal William Victualling Yard at the end of Durnford Street awaits a new use. This must be one of the finest 19th-century buildings in England. Hidden away from the general public it is little known by Plymothians. It is almost Spartan in its severity but has a dignity and grandeur that is fabulous. Every house or building in the complex is built with the precision of an engineer. Even the lamp-

The Crescent

posts are sited with exactitude. Everywhere there are immaculate lawns and even today, with still an uncertainty about its future and buildings that are in dire need of maintenance, it has an air of wellbeing.

The Breakwater was begun in 1812 and finished by Sir John in 1840. An incredible feat of construction. It is a mile long and lies just about two miles offshore. 4,500,000 tons of limestone was used to build it. Just think of the logistics of taking the materials to the site. It would be difficult enough now but one hundred and fifty years ago without modern equipment it must have been a nightmare. The lighthouse on the end was first lit in 1844 and in the centre is a large fort which is actually a separate structure. This was an achievement that provided Plymouth with one of the safest anchorages in the world.

This is the moment to return to the Royal William Yard and to tell you what is happening there at present. **The Plymouth Area Groundwork Trust** has taken up residence in one of the buildings at a low rent.

First though I must tell you how the Trust got off the ground in the Plymouth Area.

It is all down to a very effective partnership for action between the local authorities in the area, the Department of the Environment, a wide range of local businesses and the dedicated staff who work for the Trust.

357

I am sure that the work of the former Executive Director, Charles Howeson and that of his colleagues will go down in the annals of Plymouth history as one of the great achievements of the 1990's.

The Plymouth Area Groundwork Trust, the 26th of its kind in the country, acts as a catalyst to bring partners together to help them improve and conserve the environment of Plymouth and its surrounding area.

Initially the Trust brought together a small group of local specialists, including an ex naval officer, a landscape architect and a rural resources manager, to establish the Trust. It was clear that a headquarters would be required and the Trust sought a site which would be as accessible as possible as well as reflecting the varied interests of the City.

One such place was the magnificent Royal William Yard which was hardly used and in need of re-development but still owned by the Ministry of Defence. The Trust was able to secure the use of one of the beautiful houses within the grounds.

A low rent was agreed in return for the Trust repairing the premises they were to use and work began to restore the building and to establish the Trust itself. The staff were soon joined by a small army of volunteers, secretarial and maintenance staff, a Deputy Director and an Environmental Scientist.

Some twenty seven windows, much wall-papering and painting, rewiring and maintenance later the building has become the centre for a flurry of activity. Walk into it today, with its attractive interior, and you might wonder where it all came from. Once again the Trust has been active in partnership with local companies and a lot of the furniture and equipment has been donated by people who, through the good offices of the team, have become enthusiastic participants in the work of the trust.

British Telecom donated the telephone system, Komet Karpets helped with the carpets and Toshiba donated the televisions and video equipment. Every bit of the decorating was done by volunteers.

In between times they found moments to plant new trees, to clear the derelict gardens and lawns and to recreate the nurseries and gardens which generally take the Royal William Yard back to the time of John Rennie.

It was therefore a proud moment for the staff and volunteers of the Trust when, on a sunny day in May 1992, Groundwork House was officially opened by Her Majesty the Queen. The 25th Groundwork Trust in the nationwide network of partnerships was truly ready for anything.

I wish I could show you the staff lists of the Trust. Headed by the Executive Director there are eighteen paid members of staff but I defy anyone visiting the Trust to know which members of the staff are volunteers. There are over one hundred people involved from secretaries to botanists and they all work like beavers, frequently commuting considerable distances, at their own expense, to work in such a stimulating environment. All of the staff, whatever age and from whatever background, pull together and the offices hum with a sense of pride and professionalism. The dedication to the Trust is astounding.

Unusually, sustainable and high quality environmental improvement projects have been undertaken by the Trust from the very outset and successes have already been achieved, usually a Trust would take at least a year before these were attempted.

Job opportunities feature highly on the Trust's agenda and as well as skills training and the chance to hunt for jobs, the Trust offers an opportunity for people who are unemployed to get back into the habit of working and to feel that their contribution is worth something. It restores their professional pride and their self respect, and all the time they are working they are adding to the CV's which will eventually help them obtain a satisfactory post.

In addition to the in-house staff, there are hundreds of other people involved with the Trust's work. Over 150 different groups and organisations work with the Trust in a variety of ways and more than 100 private sector companies have offered their assistance by way of sponsorship in some way. The Trust has more than 200 listed projects, and to date, over 53 schools and 1300 school children have been involved in schemes all over the area.

Statistics prepared by the Trust for their first Annual Review, show that almost a quarter of a million pounds of 'external' grants have been attracted to the area, and over 200 people have regularly been involved as volunteers on conservation projects. If you count all the shrubs and trees planted by the Trust in the last year, you would come to the staggering figure of almost 21,000. Over 36km of footpaths have been developed or improved by the Trust and 30 projects have been completed in the last year. This represents a remarkable achievement in so short a time.

The Trust is proud of the powerful support it has from the five local authorities with which it works. Plymouth City Council has been joined by South Hams District Council, Caradon District Council and both Devon and Cornwall County Councils in their support for the Trust.

In addition, a growing number of businesses who at first became interested, now actively support the Trust either financially or through other benefits which will all go towards improving the environment for everyone in the area. The Trust has certainly raised awareness of environmental problems by working with the community on practical solutions and through the formal education system.

There is always room for keener awareness of the environment as it is something we can all become involved in. The Plymouth area does not present the image of dereliction often associated with heavy industry but the City has experienced considerable changes which provide plenty of scope for the environmental benefits that the Plymouth Area Groundwork Trust can bring. If we do not look after our environment - who will?

Everyone can do something, no matter what their age or experience and ideas are always welcome. The Trust gives us the chance to make things happen.

If you are interested in joining the Trust as a volunteer or taking an active part in one of their many projects, please seek them out at Groundwork House, No 2 Royal William Yard, Stonehouse, Plymouth. Telephone (0752) 254444.

The Plymouth Area Groundwork Trust is a partnership between every Plymothian seeking to improve this wonderful City. How lucky we were that the Groundwork Foundation saw Plymouth as a prime site for a Trust.

Plymouth has a remarkable history in its selection of Members of Parliament. The city seldom seems to have been without a leading parliamentary figure and frequently one or more holding high office. From the days of Sir Joshua Reynolds onwards we have been well served.

I was privileged to take tea with the leader of Plymouth City Council, Councillor John Ingham in the drawing room of Number 3 Elliot Terrace, once the home of Lord and Lady Astor, who bequeathed it to the City - more of that later. Our conversation was to a certain extent in general terms but we did get round to talking about the various Members of Parliament we have sent to the House in the last sixty years.

I started talking about the strong women who dominated politics in the City for some time. Nancy Astor being the most outstanding. What a woman. Not even English but an American from the South, Virginia to be precise. She married Waldorf Astor and when he inherited his title and was no longer eligible to sit in the Commons, Nancy stood in his place. The ensuing twenty five years were good for Plymouth. With Waldorf increasingly involved in local politics and Nancy championing the City at national level, I doubt if we have ever been so prominently represented.

Lady Astor was never backwards in coming forwards! A strict teetotaller and a Christian Scientist, she did her best to correct the drinking habits of the armed services in the City. A hopeless task but she was never daunted. With her husband, Lord Astor they became Lord Mayor and Mayoress throughout the war years with the consent of all the political parties. Both worked tirelessly in their efforts to assist the population during the stress of the bombing. Later they worked equally forcefully and successfully to help Plymouth rise from the ashes. On her becoming an Honorary Freeman in 1959, Plymouth was gifted with 3 Elliot Terrace and inherited some wonderful silver, many fine pictures and a mountain of memorabilia some of which can be seen if you get the opportunity to visit 3, Elliot Terrace. The other wonderful gift she gave the city was a diamond and sapphire necklace that she literally used to wrap around her neck. On the day she was made an Honorary Freeman of the City of Plymouth, an honour which had been bestowed on Lord Astor in 1936, she took the necklace off and placed it around the neck of the Lady Mayoress, Mrs

Washbourne, saying that it was for the use of Lady Mayoresses to wear during their term of office. The present Lady Mayoress may only wear it six times a year, to satisfy the insurers. It has been modernised and can be worn at any length with wrist bands and earrings to match. It is stunning and I imagine every Lady Mayoress must enjoy its six outings each year.

The Victorian house, No 3 Elliot Terrace looks right out over Plymouth Sound. It is gracious and elegant but essentially a home. Visiting it one wonders how the council could ever have thought of turning down this generous bequest to the city. Her idea was that it should be used as a Lord Mayor's residence during his term of office. This was totally impractical and possibly was the reason that the gift was only accepted by the narrowest of margins. Thirty six councillors voted for acceptance and thirty four against. Has it been a drain on the civic purse? A question that is constantly asked. The answer is simple: Yes if you count the money that is required for its upkeep but a definite no if you balance it by recognising that this is a house used for occasions that the general populace know nothing about and from which millions of pounds are acquired for the City.

Elliot Terrace

Let me paint one picture of what happens for you. I went to talk to Graham Stirling of the Barden Corporation, a large employer in Plymouth and an American company. The Plymouth operation needed more funding for expansion. The American parent company could not see the advantage of investing more in a city so far away from London and almost unheard of. Eventually after a lot of transatlantic telephone calls the American board decided that they would pay a fleeting visit to Plymouth when they were next in the U.K.

How to entertain them and how to make them realise just what we had to offer became all important. It was suggested to Graham Stirling by the then Leader of the Council that perhaps the city might entertain them to dinner in Elliot Terrace. This was done and the Americans were entranced by the house, the view, the meal and the company. Before the end of the meal the senior director informed the company that they would be delighted to invest further in the Plymouth factory. This brought several millions to the city, more jobs and therefore more spending power down the line. That one dinner virtually paid for the cost of running the house for at least a year. An example of co-operation between business and the city fathers and what can be done by pulling together.

There can be no doubt that the purchase of **3 Elliot Terrace** and the Astor's position as leading lights in both political and social life at national level, brought enormous benefits to Plymouth. They brought so many dignitaries and politicians to the City, to enjoy their hospitality and to let them see what Plymouth had to offer. It was here that many secret meetings took place. Sometimes it would be to consider the future reconstruction plans for the blitzed city with a personal friend, Professor Abercrombie, and John Paton-Watson, who worked on the scheme. Winston Churchill came on more than one occasion, Montgomery on another. From another walk of life, George Bernard Shaw was a welcome visitor, Lawrence of Arabia, Charles Chaplin, Queen Marie of Roumania, King Peter of Yugoslavia, General Eisenhower and John F. Kennedy. King George VI and Queen Elizabeth honoured them with their presence for a typically wartime meal after which they went upstairs to the first floor drawing room to enjoy the spectacular view from the balcony across the Hoe and Plymouth Sound. It was only a matter of hours after that visit that the Plymouth Blitz began. Plymouth as we knew it was about to crumble before our eyes.

Nancy Astor lived up to her reputation of fearing no one or anything. She is reputed to have seen through the rear windows of Elliot Terrace, the flames enveloping the city. Some of it was too close for comfort. She donned her tin hat - we all had them and accompanying gas masks in horrid cardboard carrying boxes - and climbed onto the roof to see what the damage was. Windows were shattering, glass was flying everywhere but above the din came her fairly strident voice saying 'Where in hell are the buckets of sand for the roof?'

No. 3 Elliot Terrace has had the benefit of Rex Roberts and his wife, Marion, for some years now. They are the custodians of the house, Rex acting as butler and his wife as cook and Housekeeper. Rex has a thirst for knowledge and a joy in imparting it, and this is apparent if you talk to him. He will tell you all about caring for the High Court Judges who stay in the house when they are visiting Plymouth. He is the soul of discretion but you are quite likely to be told little snippets of information which are fun. One particular Judge loves baked beans, another liver and bacon. Both of the Roberts take very seriously their responsibilities for the day to day running of the house. They are required to look after all the Lord Mayors resident guests as well as the judges. Rex has to co-ordinate all functions, dinners and luncheons. Between them Rex and Marion keep a book showing what menus have been used for what occasions. They are meticulous about remembering peoples' likes and dislikes. An ideal couple for this demanding post.

Rex is at his happiest when he is escorting people around the house. He has become an expert on the lives of the Astors and their families. Much more memorabilia has been brought back into the house in the past couple of years due to his good offices, mainly pictures which were stored in the vaults of the Plymouth City Museum and Art Gallery. His use of words paints a vivid scene of the lifestyle and work of Lord and Lady Astor. You will learn how the Astors were one of the richest families in the world in the 1800's. How in 1905 Waldorf and Nancy met on a liner crossing the Atlantic and fell in love. Waldorf's father did not attend the wedding in 1906; he was annoyed that his son was marrying a divorcee. Nancy had been through a disastrous marriage with Robert Shaw, a drunkard and a womaniser by whom she had one son, Bobby. Waldorf owned the great Cleveden estate. When in 1908 he decided to become an M.P. he did not choose a safe seat but the anti - Conservative Plymouth Sutton. It took him two attempts to succeed. In 1917 his father was created a Viscount and died in 1919 forcing Waldorf to become the second Lord Astor and to sit in the Lords. He tried to disinherit the title but could not and so Plymouth Sutton became vacant. Nancy however could sit in the House of Commons. On the 28th November 1919 after one of the most dazzling election performances she was duly elected M.P. for Sutton and became the first lady to be an M.P. although not the first lady to be elected. Baroness Markiewicz of the Sein Fein Party had that honour. She, with thirty five others from that party refused to swear an allegiance to the Crown and so they did not become M.P.'s.

Plymothians should feel proud of this house, learn to know a little more about it and realise what an enormous asset it is to the City.

Due to tight security, which is necessary to protect the priceless collection of Astor memorabilia, people wishing to visit must first book with the Tourist Information Centre in the Civic Centre. Armada Way, Plymouth.

Arsonists virtually destroyed another famous house in 1991. **Pounds House** at the Peverell Corner end of Central Park is one of the jewels in Plymouth's architectural crown and its restoration has been welcomed by every Plymothian. Built in 1825 for local banker and merchant William Hodge, it remained in the family until 1927 when it was purchased by Plymouth Corporation. The setting is wonderful, an oasis of peace in the midst of the busy city. It is used for wedding receptions and other functions but by no means to its full capacity. All sorts of uses have been suggested for it and one hopes that they will be taken up. I read of someone suggesting that

Pounds House

it could be used for the West Devon Record Office giving them respite from their cramped quarters in Coxside. This would make records more accessible, too, for the growing number of people researching family history.

Nancy Astor's work amongst the poor and needy will go down in history. **The Virginia House Settlement** came about because of her good offices. The building was bought by the Astors in the 1920's and included what is now the **Arts Centre**. The objective was to provide facilities for the community - people of all ages - of the Barbican, Coxside and Cattedown.

This venture has grown so much that it would be beyond her recognition today. I can remember helping there in the early days of the War in what was I suppose the first nursery school in Plymouth. The children were all underprivileged, and coming from a sheltered and comfortable lifestyle it woke me up to the realities of how poor people lived. A salutary lesson. Contrary to some of the opinions I have heard, Nancy Astor did not treat this venture as one of patronage. I have seen her roll up her sleeves, don an apron and get down to work in what were not the most salubrious of conditions.

The role of Virginia House today continues to do what Nancy Astor started. It is to enhance the well being of the communities of Sutton in particular and the City of Plymouth in general by the provision of services, facilities, and enabling action, to promote social justice, welfare and education in the areas of the greatest need.

The place buzzes with activity all day and all night. It engages in a wide variety of initiatives both in Virginia House and outside of it with most age groups and varied independent organisations.

Services today include an Under Eight's Centre, Pregnancy Testing, BeFriending, Crisis Counselling and Training and, the agency serves the entire city as well as its immediate area.

Community development has always been close to the heart of Virginia House. Traditionally they have been engaged in this work with local communities. This remains central to the development of neighbourhood services and, they are open to collaborative projects with other organisations city-wide.

Virginia House Settlement provides a home for many independent organisations, large and small, who are all providers of services for people in Plymouth and often for people outside the City. For example they work with people over 55 with a large number of activities and classes that are grouped together under the title of the 'Lighthouse Club'. Run by two redoubtable women, Doreen Naish and Jan Martin who are also responsible for other services to this age group including home visiting, the Hyperthermia Prevention Project, foot care, Home Hair Hairdressing, day trips and holidays.

Traditionally Virginia House has worked with young people in the Barbican, Coxside and Bretonside areas. They operate the Barbican Junior Youth Club which offers a diverse programme of activities for young people up to eleven years of age. Youth Link, an initiative that provides young people up to the age of eighteen with a planned programme of training in skills such as video making, sound recording, photography and radio broadcasting, operates weekly. There are play scheme for children in most holiday periods. In fact it is almost impossible to find an activity they do not cover.

One of the outstanding people working in the Settlement is Kay Isbell, a community worker who has made it her task to seek out and care for the Barbican Archives. This started as an oral and social history project aimed to bridge the gap between the generations by focussing on the areas of similarity between them and the communities within which they grew up in. It has a superb collection of pictorial records of Virginia House Settlement itself, the Barbican area and Barbican families. Increasingly it is developing work with young people and schools in particular, including non-school attenders.

Kay and her team now work within the Settlement in collaboration and partnership with C.S.V. Media Network which enables them to provide a wealth of audio visual facilities for training and various other initiatives. C.S.V. Media Network is an independent national charity that provides training in a range of media and communication skills for people of all ages. They also deliver high quality training for voluntary organisations in dealing with the media and promotions.

Devon Training for Skills occupies quite a large part of Virginia House and is concerned with the 'Options for Learning

Scheme'. This is about opportunities for people who, for one reason or another, have been out of a job for six months or more and are between the ages of 18-59 years. It is also for those people with disabilities which restrict their chances of finding a job and for women who want to get back to work. In Virginia House it is particularly concerned with people wanting to learn or fine - tune their secretarial or computer skills. The length of time is designed to enhance the aims of those who join. It can be as little as one month or as long as two years. Training includes the time spent with an employer

As a result of the enormous development programme which has been carried out, and is still going on, as a result of over £675,000 being raised from local authorities, charitable Trusts, loans and other sources, this old building which dates back in parts to 1704, has been given a new lease of life. It can offer now space within the Settlement for meetings, training events, functions, conferences and activities on a regular, or occasional basis. Rooms can accommodate up to 35 whilst the newly furbished main hall which is adjacent to a fully equipped commercial kitchen, can seat 150. Visual aids and catering equipment can also be provided to enhance meetings.

Nancy Astor would be delighted if she saw what had been done. She cared deeply for Plymouth and its people.

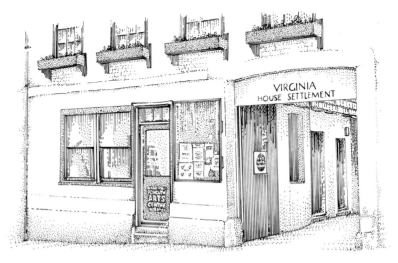

Virginia House Settlement

Not in the same mould as Nancy Astor, the now **Baroness Vickers**, once Miss Joan Vickers, became M.P. for Devonport in the 1955 General Election amazing everyone when she toppled Michael Foot. Not only did she gain the seat then but she held it for the next 19 years. This stylish, blue - rinsed lady, always wore a hat which matched her smart, businesslike but feminine suits. She says quite modestly that she achieved success because she so badly wanted to be an M.P. It was much more than that: she did not have a car so she set about getting to know Plymouth by bus and finding that in so doing she was getting a chance to talk to all sorts of people. She got to know Dockyard men, the crews of the buses and many others who were won over by her straightforward, no nonsense attitude. She did not harangue those of a different persuasion. When she called at houses she explained that if she was going to ask for their vote the least she could do was to visit them personally and they certainly did not shut the door in her face. Her victory was sweet and especially to the Conservatives in Devonport, having fought a hopeless campaign in the previous election with Randolph Churchill, Winston's son as candidate - not a popular man in this City.

Baroness Vickers disliked Nancy Astor who behaved quite horribly to her. Nancy tried to make a fool of Joan Vickers in public. She made catty remarks about her hats and was not at all pleasant. They never got on well together. Jealousy probably because no one was more annoyed and disappointed than Lady Astor when she was persuaded not to stand in the election immediately after the war, by her family. They recognised that the country was ready for change and she might well lose her seat. They were right. Labour got in by a landslide.

The baroness was none too fond of David Owen either. He defeated her by 437 votes in the 1974 election. She saw it as a cold calculation on his part when he decided to drop Sutton when boundary changes were made which would have made it harder for him to win it. He moved over to the safer Devonport seat.

Following her defeat she might well have been a European M.P. had Mrs Thatcher not persuaded her to take a seat in the House of Lords instead. In her remarkable career she espoused many and varied causes. Giving Falklanders the right to British citizenship, effective ways of dealing with kerb-crawlers and prostitution, the threatened closure of the Royal Marines band, support for fish farms and the continuing development of Devonport Dockyard. She lives now in Pusey in Wiltshire but keeps her ties with Plymouth.

When she was made a Freeman of the City of Plymouth with her one time political foe, Michael Foot, I wonder if she thought of Nancy Astor at that time and said 'What kind of fool am I ?'

If I were a betting person I would lay odds on Plymouth - born **David Owen**, or more correctly Lord Owen, being the next person to be given the Freedom of Plymouth. Here is an extraordinary and larger than life man in many ways. A great servant of the people and a master of diplomacy as he is proving in the impossible task of trying to get the Serbs, the Bosnians, the Croats and all the other former members of Yugoslavia, to reach agreement and stop their killing wars.

It is not often that such a character is thrown up on the political arena. He is a bit like Nancy Astor, inasmuch as he fears no one and is his own man. Incidentally as M.P. for Devonport he sat in the House just a few days longer than that great lady. Like her he has always had the ability to be extremely controversial. Few people would have chosen to move their political position as he did. Indeed I heard it mentioned in quite reliable political circles that when his role with the Bosnians et al is completed he may well become a cabinet minister in this Government. Crossing the House again? It would not be surprising and certainly we can well do with men of his outstanding ability. I would prefer to see him as British Ambassador to the United Nations. His qualifications are impeccable.

I met him for tea one afternoon in the Royal Western Yacht Club. He has loved the water and boats since childhood and one of his big complaints against Plymouth is that it is slowly but surely taking away all the free places where locals can slip their own boats into the water. I mentioned this fact to the Plymouth Area Groundwork Trust who said that Lord Owen had already talked to them about it with the result that the Trust has put out a very useful little pamphlet called 'Landfall' showing all the places that are available.

It struck me that while we were talking - and this was just before the General Election and after he had announced he was not standing again - that here was a man who was an achiever in spite of the loss of the S.D.P which must have hurt him badly. His qualification as a doctor of medicine was really only the preliminary to his desire to help people. He talks movingly about his personal life, his family, his love of poetry but underneath it is a ruthlessness and determination that marks him out as a cut above many. He is a restless creature. The carpet of the Royal Western took quite a hammering as he paced up and down, occasionally stopping to gaze out at the sea. I asked him what he was going to do when his role as an M.P. came to an end. 'Not a clue' he replied 'Except that I will be offered a seat in the House of Lords - they always do that for ex-Foreign Secretaries. After that - well, a job will turn up for me to do somewhere'.

He cannot have foreseen the Yugoslavian scene but how right he was. Plymouth has need of him if he ever has time. Derriford Hospital would like him, so would Plymouth University. A man for all seasons - I think so.

I was reminded by the Leader of the Council, John Ingham that the renowned Lucy Middleton was another woman who had stood successfully for Plymouth - the only woman Labour member, I think. Then there was the remarkable Albert Medland who firstly was a revered councillor and then at a late age became an M.P. and very influential. His knowledge of Plymouth, its post war problems, and rebuilding projects made him a respected authority as far as the Government of the day was concerned. There were few members who had been through the experiences that Plymouth had produced during the years of the war.

Further back, Plymouth also had the late **Leslie Hore-Belisha** as an M.P. The modern generation will have no idea who he was but others will remember him for the Belisha Beacons which flashed on and off at road crossings. The first acknowledgment of the dangers that the increasing motor traffic was causing pedestrians. Now we have the traffic light crossings as well.

Isaac Foot and his sons will always be remembered by Plymouth. The great Isaac was almost as good an orator as his son, **Michael Foot**, the Leader of the Labour Party. Isaac was an ardent Liberal and a staunch Methodist. This outstanding family has also given us Lord Foot, a senior partner with Foot and Bowden, the diplomat Lord Caradon and M.P. and Q.C. Sir Dingle Foot.

Dame Janet Fookes has achieved great things in the House and is now one of the Deputy Speakers, a role she was honoured to accept. But I wonder if Plymouth realises quite what restrictions this has put on this redoubtable lady. It means that she cannot voice any public opinion on such issues as the battle of the Dockyards, Devonport and Rosyth, for example. She must remain neutral. It galls me when I see some of the letters from uninformed people who think she is doing nothing to ensure that Devonport wins this monumental battle without which a great portion of the West Country will suffer financial disaster. Of course she is fighting for them behind the scenes and because of the length of time she has served the constituency so well, she has learnt how to wheel and deal in the corridors of power for the benefit of Plymouth. This lady was not created a Dame for doing nothing but because of her dedicated work and her parliamentary skills.

When Dame Joan Vickers, as she was then, suggested to Janet Fookes that she might care to stand for Plymouth Drake, she was gratified naturally but did not think for one moment the selection committee would choose her. Dame Janet tells a lovely story about her final visit to the selection committee. Never one for travelling lightly generally, this occasion she decided to be different. It was just for one night and only one appointment. She chose her outfit with care, a suitable pair of shoes and an overnight bag. The train arrived in Plymouth on time at 5.20pm and as she stepped off the train, briefcase and overnight bag in hand, she caught the heel of her elegant court shoe and it broke off. Flashing through her mind was the time of day, the thought of appearing either barefooted or with one leg shorter than the other before this committee and the certainty that Dame Joan would not approve! She cursed travelling light - and never again has done so - rushed almost hopping to the taxi rank and directed the driver to find the nearest shoe shop with the utmost speed. Bemused, the poor man drove fast against the rush hour traffic and arrived in the then unpedestrianised New George Street outside one of the many shoe shops just as the clock was reaching the half hour. Dashing into the shop, which was just closing its doors, Dame Janet, purchased the first pair of likely shoes she saw. Whether the selection committee noticed them history does not relate. They would certainly have been surprised if she had been sufficiently unconservative to be barefooted! The result: Plymouth Drake acquired another first class female Member of Parliament. A fact that many of her constituents will bear witness to.

I voted for **Alan Clark** throughout his years in the House but not until I actually met him when I went to talk about this book did I decide I did not really like him very much. I wondered afterwards if I would have voted differently if the meeting had been years before. Do we vote for the person or the party?

This was a man who had been here for years. Wealthy, privileged, highly educated and the Minister of Defence, yet he seemed to be without any real depth of feeling for this city. We talked about many subjects and I enjoyed his rapier mind but what I did not like was his declared policy of not getting himself involved with local matters. Plymouth as a place seemed to be almost a mystery to him. When he arrived he made straight for the Forte Posthouse, if he was staying overnight, or to his offices in Addison Road if he were not. He had no idea about the geography of the city and was the only member who did not have a residence either in Plymouth or in close proximity. How can you represent people if you have not their true interest at heart?

In his favour I have to say he worked hard at the Ministry of Defence, but like Janet Fookes as Deputy Speaker this took away his right to openly fight for the needs of the armed services and the Dockyard. That he fought for Plymouth's interests behind the scenes, I do not doubt, but not the doughty fight that Dame Janet is continuously pursuing.

It was probably this meeting that was in my mind after the general election when we had two new boys in the House. How were they going to make a mark? They both have, their platform the issues of whether it should be Devonport or Rosyth that has the refitting of the nuclear submarines. Both of them have shown that they are not men of straw and whatever your politics their efforts should be recognised.

David Jamieson who took David Owen's old seat, is an ex - schoolmaster who was not able to spare time to talk to me. He stands as a Labour Member in a traditionally Labour seat. It was only David Owen's personality that kept and won it for the S.D.P.

The new boy for the Conservatives in Plymouth Sutton is **Gary Streeter**, once a supporter of David Owen and the S.D.P. This former city councillor is a family man with high ideals and the will to carry them out. I enjoyed meeting him one Saturday morning after he had dealt with his constituency surgery. I wanted to know what it felt like walking through the doors of the House for the first time. He said it was like ones first day at school; daunting and lonely. There is so much to get to grips with. The procedures are all strange and the protocol quite unique. What he did confirm was that once you enter those hallowed portals you start the process of addiction! You get hooked on the lifestyle, the buzz, being at the centre of everything British. The danger lies in becoming too protected by the easing of paths when you are a Member of Parliament and getting too big headed. Gary Streeter says there is no chance of that: he has a wife, and children who bring him back to earth every time he comes home.

One of the bonuses occasionally is the opportunity to travel to otherwise unlikely places as a representative of the government or the party. Recently Gary Streeter went to Israel. The added pleasure for him in this trip was that the Israelis had invited wives as well. A rare chance for them to spend time together and to do what he feels is very important for a Member of Parliament; learn about the culture and the workings of other countries.

Another question I asked was whether being in Parliament was affecting his family life. Very much so, was the reply. Living away all week is not good and the weekends tend to get involved with constituency matters and duties but Gary does have something which protects him and his family. It is a very strong faith in God. This is a side of his life that is all important to him. It colours everything he does. A year ago with another family he started the Barbican Church in New Street on the Barbican. A place to meet and worship, a place from which to spread the gospel literally. It is a place of worship that has caught the imagination of many over the last twelve months. The church is growing and as it does it reaches outwards taking the Gospel to the people. Faith is a living thing in Gary Streeter's daily life. He practises what he preaches, and he firmly believes that working as a Member of Parliament is what God wants him to do.

'We are such stuff as dreams are made on' comes immediately to mind whenever I think about Trevor Hall and his **Ambulance Museum**. Just a few years ago he was a member of the Ambulance Service, a man with a desire to get children to have a better understanding of what the service did. He found and bought an old ambulance and started taking it to schools, in his own time and at his own expense. Once there he caught their attention and imagination. It was not long before a teacher told him she knew where he could get another ambulance. Someone else told him where he could lay his hands on equipment to fit out the inside. The germ of the dream was sown. Before long the possession of a number of ambulances dating back as far as 1830 took too much of his spare time and so he made the brave decision to resign from the Ambulance Service and start activating his dream - a full scale Ambulance Museum.

His ambulances were housed in an old barn at Plympton but the farmer needed it so he had to move. He found, with the help of the Council at a peppercorn rent, an old building down beside Stonehouse Creek at the back of Stonehouse High Street. By now he had several enthusiastic volunteers to help him and the number of ambulances was growing but so were the costs. Every ambulance offered had to be purchased, nothing was given to him voluntarily. He scrimped and saved, got a little sponsorship from some local companies and tremendous help from Black and Decker. By now he was taking ambulances to fetes and shows from which he acquired donations. Not enough though because every time a machine leaves its base it costs at least £60.

Writing letters to every Television and Theatre Production Company was time consuming but it has produced results. The producers of Indiana Jones used a 1938 Opal Blitz ambulance which had seen service in the Spanish Civil War. A 1928 Guy Wolf, the only one ever built, found its way into Agatha Christie productions, a 1951 Bedford ML2 was used in one of the Miss Marple series. The ambulances have found their way into the House of Elliott and Doctor Finlay. It has taken persistence but this remarkable and growing collection is the only one in Europe, if not the world. Many of the ambulances are the only ones of their kind in existence.

If you take a look at this incredible collection, lovingly restored and maintained, you will find a contraption that carried hammock stretchers dating back to 1830. There are Litters used in 1854 in the Crimea at Scutari. No doubt Florence Nightingale would have soothed the brow of many an injured and dying man lying on them. From the Boer War there is an ambulance carriage - officers for the use of only - never mind the poor old Tommy. The crude 1914 Thorneycroft and 1915 Humber were used by the

R.A.M.C. in World War I. 1922 produced a Clement Talbot - the first ever to be built. One of the most prized of the collection is a 1933 Fordson 51 which film buffs will recognise as the one used in Genevieve.

Few of us know that Sulky Litters were dropped by parachutes at Arnhem. Sadly few of them were ever used. In 1942 the Bedford produced the ML, and in the museum is the only survivor which was built for Elastoplast. There is a 1949 Daimler DC 27 - the Rolls Royce of ambulances. The 1951 Ford F3 built for the Swedes gained fame in the films, the Godfather and Superman IV. A 1957 Alvis Saracen came from Malaya, and so it goes on until you come to a 1978 Landrover 101 which was used in the Gulf War and a 1977 Landrover series 2A which worked hard in the Falklands conflict.

A 1949 Daimler DC 27 Ambulance

As I write there are 57 ambulances in the Museum plus three old Police Cars and 3 Fire Engines. The reason for the diversification is to show an overall picture of rescue services and their roles. It helps children enormously to have a 'hands on' approach to vehicles that they might otherwise fear. The exhibition is also designed to stop hoax calls.

Schools are enthusiastic supporters of Trevor Hall's dream and so are his volunteers. Sadly Plymouth cannot offer him a big enough site and so later this year he is hoping to move to the old Tate and Lyle site at Tavistock on the Okehampton road. Here he will be able to display everything. The Guides will be dressed in the costume of the time,he will have a souvenir shop, a cafe, open up nature trails, display old railway carriages on tracks, and make a visit to the Ambulance Museum, a day out for the family and for everyone who is interested.

The dream is becoming reality. We should be grateful for this kind of enthusiasm and proud that a Plymothian has had the vision to achieve it.

A four storey **Age Concern** centre on the site of the former Astor Institute at Mount Gould owes its being to the generosity of the widow of a Barbican boy, William Venton, who became a noted architect and retained his love for the area and Plymouth generally, all his life. The gift, £3.5 million to Plymouth Age Concern, is the single biggest donation ever made to any organisation in the city.

The building, overlooking the River Plym, provides residential care for 25 active people over 60, giving them their much cherished independence. Each resident has a comfortably furnished bed-sitting room with kitchen facilities, separate bathroom and toilet. For companionship and for meals there is a private dining room, a large restaurant or a coffee lounge where anyone is welcome to drop in. This one gesture will benefit Plymothians for many generations to come and is not the first time Plymouth has been on the receiving end from the generosity of the Ventons. In 1988 Mrs Venton gave £55,000 towards the building cost of the Plymstock Age Concern centre which was named after her.

William Venton spent the first fifteen years of his life on the Barbican where the fishing boats 'adopted' him and he spent many happy times, never to be forgotten, out with the crews. In spite of living firstly in London and then in Durban, South Africa, he never forgot the happiness of those early years.

Charitable people abound in this city, and there are so many unsung heroes and heroines. You have only to read one of the local papers to see that every day someone somewhere is doing something to help fellow Plymothians. Not so long ago I watched twelve trainee firemen scale the Theatre Royal six hundred and thirty one times by ladder, equivalent to the height of Everest. They took two hours and forty one minutes raising £1,000 for Cancer and

Leukaemia in Childhood. At the end of this gruelling event the fire service flag flew proudly from the roof of the theatre.

St John Ambulance Service can boast 32,000 volunteers throughout England and Wales. They spend something like 4,000,000 hours each year caring for others in the community. Plymouth has a very active membership with some 120 adults. We see them at all sorts of occasions, football matches, concerts etc where there skill is relied upon. How few of us know that they give their time freely to train and carry out their duties, often paying for their uniform and equipment out of their own pockets.

The role of the St John Ambulance has changed considerably in recent years. It used to be First Aid but now they are finding that their talents and training are in demand to provide support to elderly and handicapped people living at home as well as in the provision of transport for those attending day centres. They often provide friendship and support to housebound elderly people by organising days out and trips to the theatre.

Youngsters are encouraged to join as early as six, when they will learn much more than basic first aid. The emphasis is on having fun together and, at the same time, learning about life and the care we should give to each other. From the age of ten these youngsters become cadets and join with St John adults in carrying out first aid duties at public events, a skill and confidence which will stand them in good stead for the rest of their lives.

This is an organisation that really puts caring into practice. They are often to be found working behind the scenes as major providers of first aid training in the world of business, commerce and industry.

The St John Ambulance relies entirely on our support to make sure it can continue so if you would like to know more about them or contribute you will find them at St John House, 2, Bedford Terrace, North Hill, Plymouth. Telephone number 0752 665842.

A band of more than 1,000 volunteers in Plymouth selflessly give their time each day to the **Plymouth Guild of Community Service**. Since 1907 the Guild has been providing a listening ear for city people. They not only provide volunteers to help with Age Concern, Relate, the Citizens Advice Bureau and Riding for the

Disabled but have a number of projects of their own to help the needy in the city.

The Guild owns two homes in Plymouth for battered wives and their children providing an escape in one for some of the women and children who are being abused in their homes. The second is mainly used as a secondary home for women and their children who are no longer in need of crisis intervention but who are still awaiting the outcome of court hearings, court welfare reports or resolution of tenancy agreements.

Most of us think we will never need some of the services that the Guild offers but we none of us ever know. Many of the volunteers help in people's homes - not counselling but the practical things like maintenance around the properties. Volunteers at the Centre in Buckwell Street run a regular lunch club for the elderly and form a taskforce which travels around the city gardening, decorating and doing odd jobs for the elderly and disabled.

An advice centre which is one of Devon's newest charities is also staffed by these volunteers. It offers help with enquiries housing, finance, transport and any other matters which relates to a person with a disability.

The Guild also runs a community transport service which has more than eighteen volunteer drivers who carried something like 10,000 passengers in 1992 on over 30,000 journeys. They really do have a remarkable record and tend to be far too reticent and modest about their work and their achievements.

Fortunately there are always people wanting to do something for others even in this sad world we live in where crime, aggression and depravity are commonplace. If you are interested in becoming a volunteer or in the work of voluntary organisations of any kind please contact the Guild in Buckwell Street. Telephone: 0752 226082. You will be welcomed with open arms.

I have always had a great deal of time for the work of the **Y.M.C.A.** and the **Y.W.C.A.** For young people between the ages of sixteen and twenty five coming to work or study in Plymouth, the Young Women's Christian Association has a place in Lockyer Street. Unlike the Y.M.C.A, which is mainly a club for young people, the Y.W.C.A is a hostel where youngsters, particularly young girls, can find somewhere safe, pleasant and comparatively inexpensive to live. Gone are the days of rigid discipline and strict rules. Plymouth's Y.W.C.A is a bright, cheerful establishment which can accommodate up to one hundred at a time either in hostel rooms or in the twenty four self-catering flats. The rent is inclusive of light and heat, the use of a fully fitted laundry room, lounges, games room, sauna and sunbed.

The residents include a complete cross-section with students from the University, people starting jobs, the unemployed and even some refugees. The likeable staff are trained to cope with all sorts of problems and are very approachable. The aim is always to have more women than men with bedrooms for the different sexes on different floors.

If I were a parent with a youngster needing accommodation I would be more than happy to see an offspring settled in the Y.W.C.A. For further information ring Plymouth 250144.

A little under a year ago **Plymouth's Association of Retired Persons** met for the first time in the **United Service Officers Club** at Mount Wise. It has a membership of some 500 people and meets a real need. People over 50 for whom the club caters have more spare time and probably less responsibilities than younger people. Meeting others of a similar age and making friends becomes more important than ever. The club aims to introduce people with similar interests. The growing membership shows its popularity. I do not have a contact number but if you ring the United Services Officers Club they will be able to help you.

Whilst I am writing about accommodation and sanctuary it is a moment to tell you about an example of the selflessness of Plymouth people to those in need of help. I know there are many such people in the city but only from experience can I speak of one. Fionnuala Macready-Bryan owns a house in the Greenbank area of Plymouth in which for years she has cared for those down on their luck whether from crime, drink or drugs. Her courage in coping with some of the hair - raising incidents that have occurred over the years make a story that to most people would be unbelievable. She has on several occasions faced death when she has been confronted by a crazed , drug ridden man wielding a knife. Her calm, matter - of - fact manner has somehow saved the day. The police, the social services and many organisations have reason to thank her for taking in people that no one else would tackle.

Over the years dealing with eccentrics of all kinds has taught her a tolerance and with it a keen interest in the human mind. This led her to explore the realms of transactional analysis. From being a quick learning student she has become a University Lecturer in T.A. teaching classes in Plymouth and the outskirts and more recently in Cornwall and Exeter.

One of her students was Christine Robinson whose young son, Matthew, was brutally murdered last year. It was to Fionn that Christine and her husband, Alan, went for sanctuary. This remarkable woman housed them and stood quietly and supportively behind them throughout the ensuing weeks, right up to and through the trial of the man responsible, neither seeking thanks or recognition. It was harrowing, an experience she will never forget. Fionn says ' I'd like to think it was a merging of energies that brought Christine, Alan and myself together - that it was fate and meant to be.'

That steadfastness brought her a nomination in the South West finals of the first Red Cross Care in Crisis Awards, an award that she won for her compassion. An award that I know all her students and her friends, eccentric or otherwise, will feel is richly deserved.

There are not enough pages in this book for me to write about all those who day in day out care and enable Plymouth to be the great city that it is. This tribute I have paid to Fionnuala Macready-Bryan, I hope, will be accepted by all those who do such wonderful and generous work.

Watching over us all with just as much compassion is the **Police Force**. They have a physically tougher role and frequently suffer mental torture seeing the aftermath of tragedies. We are lucky. We have a dedicated, high morale force, led by determined and skilled officers. Plymouth is seldom behind the times with innovative ideas when it comes to policing. I spoke with Chief Superintendent Anthony Berry when he was kind enough to spare me time at the Crownhill headquarters. A busy station, equipped with every kind of modern device for security purposes. One story he told me painted a picture of the differing roles the police play. It was about the Duchess of York. Security is always a nightmare for any force having to protect a Royal. The Duchess was visiting on the outskirts of Plymouth and wished to stop for lunch in the Plymouth area. One major headache for the protection squad: where was a suitable spot. If a hotel was used it would have to be searched from top to bottom before her arrival taking up valuable time and tying up officers who were needed elsewhere. A restaurant or a pub was equally difficult. The answer was to offer her lunch at the Police headquarters in Crownhill. Security was in place, no extra men needed. Lunch was laid on which the Duchess enjoyed. She was able to relax away from the general public and have a rest before she continued on her busy schedule. A question of good management and housekeeping by Crownhill police and an example of the understanding that the Royals endeavour to show the people who look after their safety.

Of the 330,000 people under the watchful care of Superintendent Berry's 'E' Division, 30,000 of them were victims of some sort of crime in 1991. A horrifying number and one that the police are desperate to reduce. They are mainly burglary and car thefts. One recent innovation which has helped considerably is the introduction of closed circuit television cameras in the city centre to monitor activity. Police statistics show a fall of 46% in the crime rate in the two and a half years since the cameras were installed. Tapes taken from these cameras, which were shown to councillors, recorded two youths kicking in a shop window in New George Street. It showed also the arrival on the scene of security guards who made a citizen's arrest whilst waiting for the police to come.

There are 26 cameras positioned in and around the city centre and 43 in the Theatre Royal and Western Approach car parks, all of which record 24 hours a day. They are monitored between 7pm and 4am every day by a trained security guard with a radio link to two colleagues on foot patrol and a direct connection to the police. A mobile car park patrol also operates 24 hours a day. Police are pleased with the results which have led to arrests which would not have been made if the cameras had not been in position.

More new equipment is to be installed in 1993 at Crownhill when touch screen equipment arrives in the new control room. For the first time officers in each of the city's three sub-divisions will be able to keep in touch with each other on a citywide incident channel. This might be when a stolen car was moving across the

A Police Helicopter at work

boundaries of Devonport, Crownhill and Charles Cross. It could be
the policing of a demonstration, a march, a royal visit or a murder
enquiry. Every new installation takes Plymouth's police force
further into the twentieth century and will help to stem the tide of
rising crime. One hopes it will also help to make the job safer for
these men and women who are so vulnerable in our service. The
number of times a police officer is subjected to attack, even in
Plymouth, which we have all believed to be less violent than many
other places, is unacceptable and anything that can be done to
make it safe for anyone of any age to be able to walk abroad and to
be secure in their own homes must be welcomed.

The city is blessed with dedicated men and women in all its
public services. The **Fire Service's** annual 'Open Day' at
Greenbank is a thrill for children and for their elders, when they
show off their paces, their equipment, allow children to climb all
over the engines and generally give everyone a good time, whilst
putting over the message of the dangers of fire. It is a day when
charity benefits and a day which is planned skilfully from one year
to another.

The Ambulance Service has its team of para - medics who are
promptly on the spot when they are needed. A cheerful band of
professional people whose praises are seldom sung. Even our
traffic wardens deserve a mention. They tend to use common sense

far more than some of the vicious ones I have come across in my travels around Britain. Of course they have a job to do but even receiving a ticket is more palatable if it is accompanied by courtesy and a smile!

The Old Police and Fire Station in Laira

CHAPTER 14

What's in a name - 47 Plymouths worldwide

'O dear Plymouth town, O blue Plymouth Sound,
O where in the world can your equal be found?'

The answer to that couplet in the eyes of a Plymothian is nowhere. Our Plymouth is the mother of cities and she belongs to history but we should never forget the compliment that all these other Plymouths have paid us.

'Despite the current economic climate, Plymouth County has enjoyed unprecedented economic growth in the past decade. Average annual employment in Plymouth increased by more than 42,000 jobs between 1980 and 1989.'

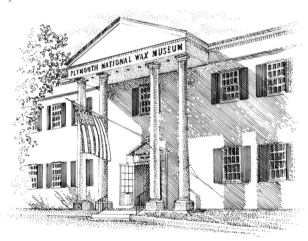

Plymouth National Wax Museum

So reads the Plymouth County Business Update which was sent to me from Plymouth County, Massachussets. I read on through a report from the Business Colony and it told me that Plymouth serves a wide variety of businesses. Virtually all categories of commerce are carried on from high-tech to light manufacturing, to retail, tourism and recreation. Sounds quite like Plymouth, Devon, doesn't it?

This particular Plymouth is easy to place on the globe and has an international profile because of her unique history: the pilgrim's landing. Boston is 40 miles to the north, New York 220 miles to the south and within a 500 mile radius are the marketplaces of Baltimore, Hartford, Providence, Buffalo, Washington D.C and Philadelphia.

Known as the 'gateway to Cape Cod', Plymouth is the perfect base for a New England vacation. The world famous 'living muse', Plimoth Plantation is there and it realistically depicts life in the Plymouth colony of 1627. You can take a look at Plymouth Rock, the Mayflower II, Pilgrim Hall and the historic homes and landmarks of 'America's Hometown'.

Plymouth's attractions are far more than just historic. There is warm sand on White Horse Beach, the Blue Spruce Motel, great golfing at Plymouth Country Club, deep sea or fresh water fishing, sailing, whale watches, cruises to Nantucket or Martha's Vineyard and dozens of excellent restaurants for every taste and budget. Apart from the whale watches I could have been writing about us. There is something very special about this Plymouth. To travel its 100 square miles is a tremendous undertaking in time and beauty. It is a town of communities, neighbourhoods and housing options that range from $110,000 to $139,000.

My quest when I started this book was to link up with Plymouths throughout the world but sadly some of them were not in the mood to respond to my letters. The ones that did were very friendly and very interested in us. I have tried to tell you a little about each of them and to tell you that they all, without fail, feel a link to Plymothians.

A delightful lady, Dorothy Wales, who is the town historian for Plymouth, New York State, wrote to me and sent me a clipping about this little place. This told me that 'Plymouth NY, is a rural town with dairy farming as the main occupation. The population is 1,344. There are no major businesses in the township nor are there incorporated villages or other municipalities. The town is governed by an elected supervisor and elected town councilpersons. Area children attend Norwich schools, in a nearby community. Plymouth residents also go to Norwich for shopping, doctors and police protection. Plymouth does have an active fire department and emergency squad, a post office and a Methodist church. Of historic interest, the Plymouth Historical Society has restored the original depot of the Auburn Branch of the New York and Oswego Midland Railroad which ran through Plymouth from 1869-1891. museum.'

I did appreciate her help and wish that I had time to find out more.

Plymouth, Minnesota, has a Communications Coordinator, Helen LaFave, who was kind enough to furnish me with information about this busy place which can trace its history back to the pre-Colombian period, 1400-1500AD. The original inhabitants were the Wahpeton Sioux. Their encampment was at the north end of Medicine Lake. Indian burial mounds are still visible there.

It was not until 1848 that the first settler arrived. Antonine LeCounte was a guide and explorer and he carried mail from the Red River country to points south, trading trinkets and other goods to the Indians for horses on the way. Le Counte built the first cabin on East Medicine Lake Boulevard.

The town started growing from 1855 on the northwest shores of what is known as Parkers Lake. New settlers arrived and began organising themselves. The decision was made to call the settlement Plymouth. The name nearly did not survive because during one lot of elections it was decided to change it to Medicine Lake. It was recorded once at a town meeting but for some reason it was never used again.

The Sioux did not take kindly to the settlers and an uprising in 1862 caused the townspeople to form a militia. Schools and churches were built and a post office. By 1863 there were hotels as well. Farming became the trade of most of the settlers and with the building of roads Medicine Lake became a tourist attraction.

Today it is a well-heeled town with a population of some 50,000 and covers 36 square miles. It is both residential and business. The location, combined with Plymouth's lakes and rolling, wooded terrain, continues to attract new residents and businesses, making it one of the fastest growing communities in the metro area. Sounds a nice place.

Maybe it was a small booklet entitled 'Discover the historic Amador County wine country', that made me attracted to Plymouth, California. It is right in the heart of this wonderful wine making area. Numerous wineries can be found along Shenandoah Road in the Shenandoah Valley just east of Plymouth. Explore the D'Agostini Winery started in 1856 - a wonderful experience. From here you are not far away from Sacramento to the south, Nevada City to the North and Lake Tahoe to the west. You are also in California's Gold Country which is rich in recreation, entertainment and the arts.

Local historians still question whether Pokerville, Puckerville and Plymouth sprang up at different times, at the same site where Highway 49 meets Main Street today. No matter really, for the town was finally born in 1871 when the Empire Pacific and Plymouth Consolidated Gold Mines promised big dividends. Today, Plymouth is the site of the Amador County fair, started in 1938.

Plymouth Township, Pennsylvania is 307 years old and proud of it. Although English settlers from Plymouth, England, first bought the land from William Penn in 1686, their holdings were purchased by Welsh Quakers before the end of the 17th century. It was the Welsh who were principally responsible for starting the Village of Plymouth Meeting which spans the line between Plymouth and Whitemarsh Townships. The original Meeting House, built in 1712 was destroyed by fire in 1867. The present one dates from that time.

On Germantown Pike, opposite Hickory Road was situated the Hickorytown Hotel, which was a prominent road house. The village of Hickorytown developed in the vicinity of this centre of activity. In the beginning of the 19th century it was a training place for the 326th Regiment of Pennsylvania Militia and the Second Battalion of Montgomery County. The Friendship Company for Protection against Horse Stealing was organised there in 1807. Hickorytown got its first post office in 1857.

Today's local residents probably are not aware that they live in what used to be Hickorytown. The completion of the Pennsylvania Turnpike with a major interchange at Germantown Pike has motivated considerable development in the vicinity including a large shopping mall known as the Plymouth Meeting Mall.

In the mid-19th century, Plymouth Meeting was a well known station on what was called the Underground Railroad, the road to freedom taken by escaped slaves. George Corson built Abolition Hall on his property for holding meetings condemning slavery. Toward the end of the century the hall became a studio for George's daughter and her husband, Thomas Hovenden. Hovenden's most famous painting was 'Breaking Home Ties' which may be seen today in the Philadelphia Museum of Art.

Plymouth, Connecticut is not so far from Bristol or Manchester! And so it goes on. Carolina has Plymouth in Washington County; Florida, Plymouth in Orange County; Idaho, New Plymouth in Payette County, Illinois, Plymouth in Hancock County. Marshall County is the home of Plymouth in Indiana, and there is a Plymouth County in North West Iowa and in Cerro Gordo County. Plymouth is in Lyon County, Kansas and Louisville, Kentucky. In Maine it is Plymouth, Penobscot County, and it was a governor of our Plymouth, Sir Ferdinando Gorges, who was appointed the first governor of Maine in 1635. He died in 1647 and a table monument to him is to be found in St Budeaux parish church. Michigan has a Plymouth in Wayne County, and in Mississippi it is in Pontotoc County. Jefferson County has the honour of Plymouth in Nebraska; Grafton County in New Hampshire and Chenango County in New York State. Ohio has no less than four Plymouths in Ashtabula County, Fayette County, Richland County and New Plymouth. Pennsylvania has both Plymouth Meeting in Montgomery County and another in Luzerne County. There is Plymouth Park in Dallas, Texas, Plymouth, Box Elder County, in Utah. Windsor County has a Plymouth in Vermont and another called Plymouth Union, while in Virginia there is Little Plymouth in King and Queen County. Finally in the States there is Plymouth in Benton County Washington and Plymouth Sheboiygan County in Winsconsin.

Reminds me of Genesis and all the begats. Certainly Plymouth, England, begat much!

I discovered that Canada can also boast some Plymouths in Yarmouth County and Pictou County, Nova Scotia and one in New Brunswick. In New Zealand there is a delightful New Plymouth in North Island, a place I would love to visit.

Perhaps the most unlikely ones are in the Caribbean where there is a Plymouth in Trinidad and Tobago Island and finally there is a Plymouth in Monserrat discovered by Christopher Columbus in 1493 who named it after Monserrat in Spain because of its resemblance. Colonised by the Irish in 1632, the island was twice occupied by the French. In 1967 the island chose to remain a Crown Colony.

   This 'Emerald Isle' is one of the Caribbean's Leeward Islands and lies about 27 miles south-west of Antiqua and 30 miles from Guadeloupe. The climate is pleasant all the year round, its beaches are beautiful, volcanic, and full of glistening sand. Like our Plymouth it is situated in a wonderful place.

Plymouths around the world

CHAPTER 15

The Villages within the City

When you start looking up the history of a village or indeed anything about the past anywhere it is sometimes a shock to the system. I do not consider the 1950s to be so far in the past but when I read a description of **Plympton St Maurice**, for example, I realised that time was almost in another world. The description taken from W.G. Hoskins' well loved and respected book on Devon said,

'Plympton St Maurice lies on a by-road half a mile south of the busy main road from Plymouth to Exeter. Those who have a special feeling for the small, ancient and decayed boroughs of England will be delighted with Plympton. It has been left on one side in the past two hundred years or so, and one smells cow-dung in the streets instead of petrol fumes: the immemorial life-giving smell of the land from which the little town took its birth in the 12th century.'

It is not recognisable from that description today. The twin villages of Plympton St Maurice and Plympton St Mary are both still there and so is Colebrook, but the insidious growth of Plymouth has built new houses, new estates and new industrial areas all around them until they have become part of the city. All of them still have great charm in the older parts. The Roman Ridgeway still runs through it and it is a popular place for shopping today.

A business that is very much of the present time but housed in a beautiful terraced property is **Skin Deep Hair and Beauty Salon** owned by Nicola Polson. This lady is very much of the nineties and enjoys the village sort of life that Plympton still retains. It helps her business in many ways because from a residential point of view more and more people have moved out to this side of Plymouth in the last decade.

Nicola Polson believes that you must not only be competent and professional in today's business world, you must also be able to offer something different. Here she has small, intimate and relaxing areas for different aspects of her trade. Ladies and men's hairdressing have their own space and so does the beauty salon and sunbed room. She has proved to her clients since she opened in 1987 that she offers a complete service which is as good, if not better, than anything they will get in the centre of the city without having to worry about parking or any other hassle. Skin Deep has acquired a reputation as a specialist hair salon. It is one of the few Redken agencies offering the Trichoanalysis Hair Unit. This looks at hair through polarised light under magnification. This enables an analysis of the hair to show exactly what is wrong and therefore allows Nicola to give the correct treatment. This is extremely accurate.

The staff of seven in this attractive business give you immediate confidence. Nicola makes sure they are all professionals, and to help her look after clients, she has brought her mother into the business as the receptionist. If you want beautiful hair then this must be the place to go. The recipe for shining, perfect hair, is the avoidance of stress and the correct shampoo to put right anything that might be wrong.

I am sure when Nicola got married last year it was for love, but you cannot help wondering when she tells you that her husband is a production chemist who has already been converted! He is now training in hairdressing so that he can join the business and she is looking forward to him offering new aspects for the business. With his background, who is to say that they will not produce their own products? If they did they would certainly be of a high standard and have to match Nicola's own desire for perfection.

There is a little rhyme that says,

> 'Plympton was a Borough Town
> When Plymouth was a vuzzy down.'

Very true in many respects. The stately church of St Marys was the mother parish church of Plymouth. Its 15th-century grandeur still impresses us today as it stands in a lawn-like churchyard. Hearing the melodious peal of bells which hang in the fine 108 feet tower is one of the pleasures of visiting Plympton. It has parts that date back to the 14th century and no one should miss the rare beauty of its vaulted roof. The church is rich in monuments. Under a canopy lies the armoured figure of Richard

Strode of Newnham, who died in 1464 leaving instructions for making this beautiful tomb. I have already written about the 16th century Newnham where his descendants live and where we can share in the delight of the estate if we take part in some of the activities held annually.

An Augustinian priory was founded at Plympton St Mary in 1121, but a collegiate church of St Peter and St Paul existed here from the time of Alfred. It was very rich and among its property was the site of Plymouth, and to its priory we owe the city we have today.

Plympton St Maurice we will always remember for its famous son, Sir Joshua Reynolds. His father, Samuel, was the vicar of St Maurice and master of Plympton Grammar School which bears the name Sir Joshua Reynolds' School today. What is less widely known is that this small country grammar school has the unique record of having four famous artists among its scholars, two of them Presidents of the Royal Academy: James Northcote, a pupil of Sir Joshua was head boy in 1801, Benjamin Robert Haydon was another and his pupil, Sir Charles Eastlake, learned to draw here. He is the man who saw Napoleon, a prisoner on the Bellerophon in Plymouth Harbour, and from sketches he made at the time he painted a remarkable portrait of the fallen Emperor.

Plymstock goes back a long way. A small number of manors existed here as early as the Norman Conquest - Goosewell, Hooe, Staddon and Staddiscombe. They are all now part of this busy suburb which has also brought a reluctant **Elburton** under its wing. Oreston has extensive quarries of limestone from which the stone for the Breakwater was taken between 1812-1841, some 4½ million tons in all. Mount Batten which for years has belonged to the R.A.F and which I remember, with affection as a sea-plane station, has been a place of discovery. Relics of Roman times have appeared over the years showing that a native trading settlement existed on the south shore of the Cattewater throughout the greater part of the Roman period. During excavations of the present Fort Stamford in 1864, a late Celtic cemetery was discovered.

It is the present day Plymstock that I want to tell you about and more importantly the tremendous facilities offered to the people who live here and sometimes those who come quite a distance to do their shopping. Plymstock Broadway is purpose built and has adequate parking space behind it, making it simple for shoppers. The wide shopping area is pedestrianised and attractive. It has every sort of shop including its own **Woolworths**. It is the individual shops too that make it such a pleasure.

Perhaps because I am a writer I love browsing in bookshops but seeing the number of people there are always to be found in these places, that cannot be the only reason. There is something that makes you feel good when you handle a book. Claire Dolton, who owns and runs **Plymstock Bookshop** in the Broadway, understands this feeling and tells me that she has many regular customers who come in just to see what is new or seeking a book on a specialist subject. The range of books she has covers almost every subject and she is not only a supplier to the individual, she supplies schools as well.

In addition to the books this is a place where you can buy any sort of greeting card for any occasion, sometimes pretty, sometimes austere and frequently amusing. Claire has postcards, gift wrapping paper and assorted items of stationery. The shop is attractive and I understand that Claire hopes to extend her activities to take in local arts. Plymstock Bookshop is friendly and the service excellent.

Not far off in Church Road, there is a friendly pub, the **Plymstock Inn**. This is a Bass house and the beer superbly kept by Barry Turner who runs it with his wife, Sharon. Plymstock Inn is a good traditional pub, spacious and comfortable and just the place to stop after shopping. The service is quick and the food good pub fare. You can have anything from a well filled sandwich, freshly cut to a hot bar meal or a succulent steak with all the trimmings. The staff are polite and efficient and the price is right. There is a separate restaurant if you have children with you and do not want a bar meal.

Beacon Electricals should probably not be written about in the Plymstock part of this book but the owner, Chris Higgins, has a habit of popping up all over the place and here in Plymstock, just off the main Plymouth-Kingsbridge road, he has one of his shops. The business was established to provide and supply electrical equipment to both the trade and private customers. His main store is in Beacon Park close to Plymouth Albion's ground.

Here is another man who saw the need to find an occupation away from the Dockyard where he was a draughtsman. He left in 1979 and set up this flourishing business. He sells televisions, videos, washing machines and every other machine but his core business is lighting from bulbs to fittings. In the last couple of years he has built a completely new showroom for low energy lighting, namely lighting that gives the equivalent of standard light bulb's output but at a fraction of the power consumption. He and his staff are able to advise, design, install and service a complete lighting system, both interior and exterior. They also provide equipment in bulk to the trade, including light bulbs to a very well known and rather large yacht which shall be nameless.

The Plymstock shop is small but efficient and capable of dealing with anyone's needs in the field of electrics. Chris also has a shop in Totnes. I asked why on earth he wanted to go that far away when he was busy anyway. The answer was simple. 'It is because I have been going to Totnes to Ticklemore Cheese to buy cheese. They persuaded me that Totnes was just the sort of environment that I would enjoy trading in. They were right.' I understood what he was saying because I visited Ticklemore Cheese when I wrote 'Invitation to Devon'. Sarie Cooper and her husband have been making cheese for twelve years. It is cheese with a difference, made from sheep's milk. It is not only Chris Higgins who has discovered them; the demand for Ticklemore cheeses grows every day and they deliver as far away as London. The backbone of their business are the local hotels and restaurants whose customers in turn ask where they can buy the cheese.

I wandered a bit there but this is the effect this energetic man has on one. He has interests in all sorts of places but mainly in sport. He believes that people who are in a position to do so should plough as much as possible back into the city to which they belong. Sport is a great leveller and enables people from all walks of life to take part or at least spectate. He has sponsored Plymouth Argyle and sponsors smaller local teams in the leagues. He has established a trust for youngsters which gives money to schools to help talented children. He openly admits that sponsorship has its rewards as far as his business is concerned.

Beacon Electricals has a wonderful old van that drives through the city, adds a splash of colour and never fails to be noticed. It is not quite as old as one would think but that is of little importance. It has been used in the Lord Mayor's Day Procession and for fund raising events.

Beacon Electricals' van

Chris Higgins is a Plymothian born and bred and has both faith and enthusiasm for the future of the city; something that comes across when you walk into any of his shops - the staff are equally enthusiastic.

Elburton just about joins onto Plymstock but its residents are a village community. In Springfield Road is **Elburton Patisserie**, a remarkable business run by Gordon Smith who has been a baker for 34 years. The smell as you walk in through the shop door is wonderful. Bread is baked on the premises and pasties too. The pasties are famous throughout the world; they are sent regularly to Jersey and to Australia. In 1991 he won the West of England British Bakers award. A well deserved accolade for this super business. He has got all the ingredients right. The products are superb and his happy smiling staff obviously enjoy working there; so too does a ghost called Jasper!

The Patisserie was once a farm building, and Jasper has managed to outstay any alterations to the shop. He is mischievous and turns off the ovens at night. Slamming the shop door when there is no one about is another of his favourite tricks. One cannot blame him for staying; he must enjoy the sight of all the delicious bread, pasties, cream cakes etc even if he cannot eat them.

This is not Gordon Smith's only business, he has a large wholesale and outside catering business which operates from Pomphlett Farm Industrial Estate.

Lorna Brace and Diane Trerise had for years dreamt of owning their own flower shop and one day they noticed that the old Smithy in Haye Road South was being cleared out. It had stood empty for 25 years and was almost derelict. Rumour had it that the council were going to pull it down. Lorna and Diane could visualise it as a Florists cum Gift Shop and the realisation of their dream. The people of Elburton and Elburton Residents Committee fought for it to stay. A long lease was bought from the council, who own the property and the two ladies set about restoring it.

With the retention of all the old features, the **Old Smithy** was opened as a florists and gift shop in May 1985. Here these two Elburton - born ladies, run a successful and outgoing business. I use the word outgoing because this is exactly what they do for weddings. They decorate the churches , provide the bouquets and buttonholes and have been known to help with dressing the bride. Their delight in their work spills out of them. Every flower is beloved and their arrangements are very special. Not so long ago when the Prince of Wales was in Plymouth at St Lukes Hospice, they made the Plume of Feathers - all in fresh flowers. They have also done bouquets of flowers for the Princess of Wales on two occasions.

It is a very personal service that these ladies offer, both with their flowers and their gift shop. As much as possible they use local suppliers for both. Their reputation has grown steadily and the Old Smithy is charming.

Going towards the moors one skirts the edge of Crownhill, another thriving community with a group of shops all clustered together away from the main road. Watched over by the **Tamar Hotel**, a lively hostelry run by two equally lively publicans, the Lovells. It was reputedly once a coaching inn although this is difficult to see today. The Plymouth Leat used to run past its doors bringing water to the citizens of the city and in the time of the Civil War, a battle raged outside.

There is no battle today in what has become the village street. It has banks, the second busiest Post Office in Plymouth, a building society or two, a chemist, newsagents, grocers and **Village Fayre Delicatessen** run by the able and likeable Phil Dart. This man has been a butcher for over 23 years and had his first shop in Plympton but moved to Crownhill in 1984, converting an old garage into this very acceptable shop. He still buys traditionally and has whole animals to butcher himself. He prepares the meat in front of his customers and you can see and ask for exactly what you want. It is an art that is fast dying out. Phil goes to a free range farm in Dawlish to pick out his birds for Christmas. He has well in excess of four hundred to dress at that time of the year.

With the number of butchers declining as the supermarkets take their toll, Phil believes that he must concentrate on giving first class service to his customers. This he does admirably but you might be slightly surprised if you stood back and listened to some of the conversations he has with his customers. Boxing seems to be the predominant subject. When I asked why, I discovered that he himself is a boxer and represented England four times at full international level. He could have turned professional but chose the financially more secure way and stayed an amateur. He is still involved with Devonport Boxing Club - the biggest in the West Country, and helps in the sponsorships and money raising efforts. If you look around the shop you will see several boxing photographs and a small display case containing two pairs of boxing gloves and a larger case with an England vest on display.

I am quite sure that with the presence of the banks, the post office and the excellent shops which all offer good, personal service, Crownhill village will continue to flourish as a shopping centre.

Tamerton Foliot is a delightful village on the outskirts of the city, with a singularly beautiful old church and some good pubs about which I have already written. My interest this time took me to **Lukes Fruit Farm**.

Five generations of Lukes have farmed in this valley and until the late 50's they were traditional farmers. It was then that Mr Stanley William Luke, father of the present farmer, Ron, tried strawberry farming at Porsham Farm. It was successful and in 1961 he began farming strawberries on 65 acres of the present Great Trehills Farm. This is where the story takes a twist. In 1970 a lady arrived at the farm for some strawberries which she had not ordered in advance. There were none available. She was desperate and hadn't time to call back when more fruit had been collected. There were no staff available to do it immediately and so she offered to fetch her own strawberries from the fields and did so. When she returned to have them weighed she had picked far more than she intended but bought them all and she described it as 'a wonderfully invigorating experience.' This got Ron's father thinking and very shortly afterwards he opened up the 'Pick Your Own' scheme with which we have all become so familiar.

From strawberries, Stanley Luke expanded into other soft fruit and became known locally as the Strawberry King. His expertise and drive continued in retirement; he became a soft fruit consultant.

Ron Luke took over the farm when his father died in 1982. His brother still farms Porsham Farm of 130 acres plus another 50 acres, all in the same valley. The soft fruits now include raspberry, blackcurrant, redcurrant, gooseberry, tayberry, blueberry and a new one available for the first time this summer of 1993, the jostaberry, a cross between blackcurrant and gooseberry.

The pioneering and adventurous spirit of his father remains in Ron. He tries everything new as it comes along which is why he is so successful. He provides certified plants for other growers, he has developed a picnic area and a tea room. There is a small valley for walks and a farm shop which sells vegetables as well as his fruit and cream. He amused me when he was talking about the six varieties of potatoes he grows. His wife, Hazel, likes the different types and so Ron thought if he had to grow them for her anyway he might as well sell them.

Hazel Luke is a tremendous support to her husband. She comes from Edinburgh from a non-farming family and started at Lukes Fruit Farm as a fruit picker. She ended up marrying the boss' son and providing him with two stepsons at the same time. She runs the farm shop skilfully and with enjoyment of her products and her customers. Their own family are now grown up, the younger son Nigel works for the NRA but occasionally helps out; Jonathan works full time on the farm whilst stepson, Derek, a local policeman, and his wife are a tremendous help in the season. Family get-togethers are great. They all sit round the vast kitchen table where I sat to glean all this information.

The whole enterprise is a family concern and while they are professional farmers they have no intention of allowing it to become too commercialised. When Ron's father started Pick Your Own, there was a 5-6 week season. Now with the different fruits and different strains of plants the season has expanded to six months. They endeavour to be organic, restricting alternative chemicals to a minimum. It is Grade 3 land so it does need feeding. Fortunately there is a dairy farmer next door so his farmyard manure is used. This is not cheap with the price of haulage, but it is worth it, Ron says.

Pick Your Own means you pick the quality you want at a lower price but the therapeutic value of picking fruit seems equally important. One day last year a man said to Ron 'Do you realise that you have had six peers of the realm on your farm today picking fruit?' On the other side Ron always knows when there are V.I.P's in the area; there are phone calls for fruit to be delivered. As a result Ron can say confidently, 'Prince Philip likes raspberries but the Queen Mum prefers strawberries!

In a building, in a small lane just off Albert Road in Stoke, is **Trevor Burrows Photography**. Named after the man who literally rebuilt the building which is now studio, office, darkroom etc. This talented, professional man has just that something extra that makes people seek him out rather than having to look for work himself. It is to him that I am indebted for the picture on the front cover.

He will tell you that being a successful, commercial photographer is much more than just taking a photograph. It is a question of balance, in other words knowing about electronics, people, creativity, a business sense and your own limitations so that you get the best results for yourself and your client. Trevor Burrows has proved this is true. In conjunction with the main thrust of his work within advertising, PR, industry and commerce, he does a lot of work for the local tourism agencies such as the Plymouth Marketing Bureau and Devon Tourism, amongst others, generally promoting the area. His work over the years has given him a library of photographs which he calls Image File and consists of filing cabinets full of transparencies which can be used as stock shots for brochures and a hundred and one other uses.

Plymouth was lucky that he came here. It was pure chance, he and his wife wanted to come to the South West, put a pin in the map and the place pinpointed was Plymouth! He worked for some time in the Plymouth Polytechnic Media Unit, working his way up from a junior position until he found himself in charge. His business sense and organisational ability made him able to implement several worthwhile changes, he wanted to work on his own however and the result is Trevor Burrows Photography. It was certainly the right move, something that was emphasised in March of 1992 when he won a Merit Award from the British Institute of Professional Photography at their South Western Region Annual Print Awards. He was particularly delighted to have won the award because the example he sent them was the only one he submitted!

Down the road from Trevor Burrows, in Exmouth Road, is **Exmouth Social Club**. This is another success story and again because of the initiative and hard work of the owners, Diane and George Borg. Diane is a Plymothian who married George, a Londoner, and moved away. Her parents owned the Stoke Social Club, and in 1973 a phone call from Diane's mother saying that her father was ill brought them back to Plymouth where they helped ease the strain and ran the club until he died in 1980. Without Diane knowing it George had leased the top room of their present club and they ran it for a year until they were able to buy the freehold of the property. I remember it as a Cabaret Club but this was way before the present time. It more recently had been used as a fruit machine factory. Since 1981 it has been the Exmouth Social Club with a membership of over 1,000, mainly middle-aged people with a three year membership.

George has good contacts in the entertainment field and they put on shows quite frequently mid-week using artists from the 50's and 60's like The Platters, Ivy League, Foremost and Ricky Vallance. It is a risky business, though, because it costs so much money and you have to be sure you can fill the club.

A totally different activity on Thursday evenings is catching on fast. It is Auction Time, held in the lower hall. People with items to sell leave them there during the day and then they are sold that evening. Every Sunday is devoted to Country and Western and at the other end of the scale Exmouth Hall is used as the Headquarters of Plymouth Boxing Association and also for Rugby Clubs.

One of the most important functions of the club and this enterprising couple is their ability to put on superb functions. The 'Wedding Special' for example, offers a fully inclusive price of £15 per head for a reception which includes Sherry or Bucks Fizz on arrival, a glass of Liebfraumilch with the main buffet, a glass of champagne to toast the Bride and Groom, a super buffet, and then in the evening, a disco and another buffet. The disco is included in the price and so is the use of a Rolls Royce for the Bride and Groom. If the booking is for over 100 people then the wedding cake comes with the compliments of the club. Fantastic value.

George and Diane have only had to advertise twice in the last ten years which speaks for itself. They are doing more and more receptions and parties purely by word of mouth. They will even allow self-catering functions, providing the club has the bar. You do not even need to be a member to take advantage of this super service.

Living on the premises has no doubt helped this remarkable couple to control everything. One end of the building used to be a shop which the Borgs have converted into a large kitchen/diner and lounge while what used to be a restaurant upstairs is now bedrooms and a bathroom. Hard work, a liking for people, a sense of humour and a spirit of adventure is what makes this couple tick and the Exmouth Social Club a place to remember.

Stoke village is the hub of the community: a busy shopping area and the scene of an annual carnival. There is every sort of shop including a large Plymouth Co-operative supermarket. **Carolyn Louise** is an established and respected hairdressing salon for ladies. Owned by Carolyn, her staff are as well trained as she is and have been with her for a long time. In fact during the sixteen years she has had the salon the only reason people have left her is because they are having children. This sense of continuity is all important in hairdressing. The female sex get attached to their hairdressers and hate changes. It is not just the question of someone getting to know and understand your hair; it is a sense of trust and knowing that if suggestions are made on styling they are done with good reason.

The casual, natural look is all the rage at the moment but for people who want something more these professional ladies can deal with anything from the longest hair to the most outrageously 'dressed' head.

The salon is spotlessly clean, the welcome is friendly and the results obviously very good. People in Stoke have been coming to Carolyn Louise for years.

Present Company is a fascinating shop run by an interesting lady with the occasional help of her husband and daughters. I found it as a result of a recommendation. I wanted a necklace restrung and to find someone willing and able to do it these days is quite difficult. When I went into the shop I found all sorts of other things to interest me. Well designed jewellery, much of which Sue Heslop, the owner, makes herself. In fact that is how it all started. When she first arrived in Plymouth with her husband and family from Derbyshire, she took a job with Mr Minit and on her days off took her jewellery to the Victorian Market at Tavistock. This sold well and she decided to open her own shop. In addition to the jewellery the shop now has a stock of unusual gifts, most of them under £5 and seldom over £10. There are silk scarves, scented candles, a good selection of dried flowers and some unusual cards and wrapping paper. It is certainly a shop I will remember and not just because my necklace was so well re-strung.

Ashley and Margaret Newton bought **Brimbles**, a bakery at 1,2 & 3 South Hill, Stoke, six years ago. Once three old cottages which were knocked down, the National Trust who owned them built the present shop and store as a butchers roughly thirty years ago. After that it was converted into a bakery. Ashley and Margaret are restricted in any improvements they wish to make because the shop lies in a conservation area.

They were neither of them young but they wanted the challenge. Ashley has been a baker all his working life, working for several Plymouth bakeries but this time it was for himself and Margaret and what a success it has turned out to be. They now deal with 700-800 customers a day - more than they did in a week at first. Their daughter, Janet, works with them and they employ 3 bakers and 5 shop assistants in the shop over the lunchtime period. 300 filled rolls are sold every day in addition to the normal bread, special breads, breadcakes of various types, hot pies, sausage rolls, pasties and pizzas. They also do hot soup and hot jacket potatoes with various fillings. Even fresh popcorn.

It is a pleasure to watch them at work. The majority of their customers are known by name and frequently they know what their order will be before they ask! It is a tough life, Ashley starts at 4am and Margaret and Janet are in the shop by 7.30am. The shop closes at 6pm.

Ashley sees a bright future for Brimbles. So do I. People will always want first class fresh bread and confectionery and especially when it is baked and served by such welcoming people.

How good it is to see people with the guts to have a go for themselves at running businesses. I have just written about several examples and here at **Pippin** is another. This fruit and vegetable shop is an enjoyable escape route for Susan Harry who was getting very bored at home while her husband worked and her children were growing up fast. The family joke that the real reason is because her husband got fed up with buying new vacuum cleaners to replace the ones she wore out cleaning an already spotless home!

Sue told me that her husband has his own scaffolding business and while he was happy for her to branch out on her own he needed to be sure that any business she went into would not have to carry too much stock and would be cash orientated. A fruit and vegetable shop answered this criteria. This is obviously a well trained husband. Sue gives him a list of the shop's requirements each evening and on the following morning he gets up early without even disturbing her and goes to the wholesale market to buy whatever is required, delivers it to the shop and comes home for breakfast.

The sensible way of running this kind of business is to buy little and often to make sure everything is absolutely fresh. This Sue does and has a steadily growing number of customers who know they can rely on fresh produce at reasonable prices. I was particularly impressed with the range of marmalades, jams, pickles and chutneys which she gets from Saltash and which have no preservatives or additives. Her flowers and plants come from a man in St Dominic, daily in summer but at weekends only in winter.

My grandfather had a saying which has always stayed in my mind. 'From the seeds of adversity grow greater benefits'. You cannot always see this when life is treating one unfairly. My next visit in Stoke village was to **Austin Carpets**, where the owner Kevin Duke knew all about rough knocks in life. Without warning he was made redundant from Courts and even more harshly without the comfort of redundancy money.

With a depth of knowledge about the carpet industry after 20 years there was only one way forward and that was to strike out on his own. He had no money, no stock and his company car had been returned to Courts when he left. He worked from his home in Austin Crescent - hence the name of the company - and in his first week sold £300 worth of carpet. This rapidly rose to between £3-4,000 a week. Success was now a nightmare. Kevin was storing his stock in his small garage and had to juggle deliveries. He had nowhere other than the communal garage area to spread his carpets out to cut roughly to size. Naturally the neighbours, sympathetic at first, found the growing business a nuisance. By March, 1992, he had found the shop in Stoke Village. Funnily enough this caused a drop in trade which Kevin could not understand. He eventually found out that people stopped responding to his advertising because he was using a shop address and they thought his prices would no longer be competitive. In fact no prices went up and a number came down because Kevin could now buy some lines in bulk and get better discounts.

What is so special about Kevin Duke and Austin Carpets is that he is prepared to take samples to your own home for you to look at if that is more convenient. It means he has to work in the evenings when the family are at home but he does not mind a bit. He is equally prepared to call at weekends.

If you ring him he will ask you several pertinent questions to try and narrow down the samples he brings. His range is too big to bring them all. He does offer a first class service which is professional from the sale of the carpet to the fitting.

Kevin was interesting on the subject of the ratio of his business. Sixty per cent comes from the general public from whom he gets many recommends. The other 40% comes from business via insurance companies. Kevin does the estimates and on acceptance fits the carpet and bills the insurance company direct. This was not an easy market to break into. Eagle Star in particular were reluctant to use him until one day on a normal visit he found that his client was the manager for Eagle Star. Two days after the carpets were fitted he received an enquiry for a claim valuation for Eagle Star and has done work for them ever since.

The aim of Austin Carpets is to fit a carpet within a week of the customer placing an order.

A totally different kind of business is **Inn and Tavern Design**, housed in The Lodge, Stoke Damerel Business Centre, Church Street. Two quantity surveyors, Brian Cooper and Mike Yendall, formed the company in 1985. Both experienced men; Brian was a partner in Haughtons of Plymouth, and Mike the quantity surveyor with Halls Brewery. Their role in life is what the name of the company implies. They are interior designers for pubs, clubs, inns etc. They acquire a lot of work from architects and big firms, mainly because they have proved their worth both in design and the efficient manner in which they work. They have just finished the Dartmouth Golf and Country Club where Nigel Mansell is the President, and one of their first jobs was the attractive Kings Head at Kingsbridge which features in my 'Invitation to Lunch, Dine, Stay & Visit in Devon and Cornwall' book, the second edition of which is out in May 1993.

I have a great deal of admiration for Mandy and Mike Duignan who had the courage to take on the **Masonic Inn** in the village quite recently. This free house had been closed for two years and was in a desperate state of repair. They moved from the comfortable Pear Tree Inn which they had run for a short time as their first tenancy and where they had upped the barrellage by 2½ times. This new pub was a challenge but one in which they were joined by many of their former customers who wanted to be part of this new enterprise. The interior of the Masonic has been stripped right down and brought back to its original brickwork. The theme is brick, wood and cork with real solid brass bar fittings. The flooring, the bar, the curtains, the fittings, the furniture and the toilets are all new. It is warm, comfortable, friendly and has already acquired a great atmosphere.

In the short space of time that Mandy and Mike have been at the Masonic, 5 pool teams, a euchre team, a ladies' darts team and 2 men's darts teams are all up and running having transferred their allegiance from the Pear Tree. It is certainly a good pub to visit at any time and you will be warmly welcomed.

The little parish church of St Budeaux epitomises this part of Plymouth for me. It is one of the loveliest churches in the city and it was here that Francis Drake married Mary Newman. The atmosphere inside the church is quite wonderful and conjures up the essence of the past. St Budeaux has changed tremendously over the years and with the bypass has recently been allowed to settle down into a more peaceful existence, but its village is no more.

The Parish Church at St. Budeaux

Like St Budeaux, Devonport, too, has been swallowed up by the rapacious appetite of Plymouth but more easily does it hold on to its own identity because of its association with the Royal Navy. Marlborough Street has always been the main shopping area here and has a goodly selection of shops.

Perhaps the biggest 'village' of them all today is Mutley Plain and the surrounding area of Hyde Park and Peverell. I have always thought of Mutley Plain as the entrance to the city centre but people who use it regularly would probably rebel at this description. Its wide sweep that stretches from the base of North Hill to the beginning of Townsend Hill, just beyond the island-sited Hyde Park inn, is a shopping and banking centre for those working and living in the area.

Just off Mutley Plain in Belgrave Road, is one of the oldest businesses. **Evans Fireplace Centre** has its origins in William Street, Devonport, 100 years ago. Felix Evans, the founder, was a blacksmith and used to make hoops for children. He was well known as a local preacher and a vegetarian - a practice the family still adhere to today. Colin Evans who now runs the business with his wife, Peggy, can remember living on the top of a three-storey building in William Street and the business having three lorries and their own petrol pump. Because of the nearness to the Dockyard it was inadvisable for the family to remain there at night during World War II and every evening they used to set off for Bere Alston and comparative safety. The inevitable happened, one morning they returned to a pile of rubble instead of a house.

After working for a while renovating farms and barns in Bere Alston, Felix's son George acquired a property in Albert Road and opened a shop and stove works in which not only were new grates and stoves sold but old ones were renovated. A move to Pennycomequick came next, where Torex Hire is now. This had a vast sales area with great displays of fireplaces, firebacks and accessories etc. The next move was to Mutley Plain where Gateway is today - the rent at that time was £20 per week! Eventually this business was sold to a Mr Russell, better known to many older Plymothians as the 'Biscuit King' - he pioneered the idea of selling biscuits on a 'Pick 'n Mix basis'. He moved it to the end of Mannamead Road where it is known as Evans Ironmongers and still thrives.

Mr Russell had no desire to carry on the fireplace side of the business and this is when Colin and Peggy decided to open a fireplace business for themselves and carry on the family tradition. The business has now acquired another generation of the family. Daughter Alison has taken an interest and she with Kathy Hicks-Jane carry out the daily business. There are 50 fireplaces permanently on display, with a gas coal effect fire in one corner connected up and working aptly to display their wares.

It is good to see old Plymouth businesses continuing.

Another long established establishment is the **Geraldine Lamb School of Dancing** in Connaught Avenue which seems to have been there forever! There must be generations of Plymothians who all went to this delightfully Victorian establishment and learnt far more than just dancing. Miss Sylvie and Miss Valerie still reign supreme and were totally charming to me when I called one afternoon to see them. Their pupils have gained fame worldwide and still do. Wayne Sleep was a pupil there - on the other end of the scale so was I and my twin daughters who are now in their thirties.

Old fashioned it may be in one way but there is nothing old fashioned in their teaching methods nor their knowledge of what is required today. Yes, they do miss the more gracious days but the youngsters of today are lively, competitive and not afraid of self-expression. I hope that the school will go on and on. It has every chance because there are younger members of this family in the wings.

Yvonne's, a pretty florist's, has been at the North Hill end of Mutley Plain for many years. Yvonne Floyd started in floristry in the present shop in 1965 and bought the business in 1969 renaming it Yvonnes. It was only half the size then, the other half was the Western Morning News office which for a short time during the war had been their main office. I remember it when it was Bishop's pram shop where Yvonne's mother bought her daughter's pram!

In addition to the masses of beautiful flowers one can choose from, there are all sorts of ancillary bits and pieces which are useful. Dried flowers are very popular and silk flowers. The really useful Oasis without which none of us would be able to arrange flowers today, glassware with an application for floral displays. Basically Yvonne supplies whatever anyone asks for. Yvonne reminded me of the crazy law that still existed in the 70's which enforced shopkeepers to close for a half a day a week, or at least part of it. People could buy plants and flowers but not pots or compost!

The shop is a member of Interflora and I had not appreciated that this organisation was not open to everyone. Strict standards have to be maintained and Interflora do five yearly inspections of all their member shops. One great improvement that has been made over the years is the Interflora fax machine which allows an original message to come through in print and prevents some of the misunderstandings that arose when messages were passed verbally by telephone.

Yvonne uses local growers wherever possible but she finds that flowers which traditionally came from Holland come now from Kenya, Columbia and Israel, flown in fresh every day. There used to be seasons for flowers but now virtually any bloom is available at any time of the year - only the price varies.

The days have gone when Yvonne used to deliver to the liners and stay open on Friday nights for Dockyardies coming home by bus, but business is still buoyant and she is doing more special arrangements than ever.

One can never say that there is not a diversity of business on Mutley Plain. At 2-4 Mutley Plain, **Cycle City** is a very successful cycle sales and repair business. Mountain bikes are the 'in' thing and in this shop you will find anything from the bottom of the range to the most expensive including the Bacini range from Viceroy Cycles - one of their best sellers.

Cycle City also has a same day repair service. Repairs include wheel straightening. A free six week service is included on the purchase of all new cycles and a three month guarantee on frame and forks for second hand cycles.

Dominic Reeves owns the shop and works with his wife, Sarah and his brother Warren. You will find them knowledgeable, caring and helpful. During the summer you can hire bikes.

For years I have seen the bikes displayed outside **Damerell's Motorcycles** on the corner of Connaught Avenue and Mutley Plain and the motorcycle enthusiasts who gather round the shop. There is no doubt that it is a well established company and known far and wide.

It all started 50 years ago when Steven Damerell's grandfather worked in the clay pits near St Austell and sold push-bikes part time. Then along came Cyclemaster - an engine on the back wheel of a cycle, followed closely by Lambrettas and Vespas. The interest was great and the business became full time. Steve's father joined the business and acquired the Yamaha agency and the Yamaha spares distribution, supplying agents throughout the country. By 1973 they also had the Honda agency.

Steve served his apprenticeship in the workshops at St Austell after three years at Camborne Technical College obtaining his City and Guilds Motor Mechanic certificate. He also did a course in salesmanship and then joined the firm in its new premises on Mutley plain in 1978.

Surprisingly enough it is important to have a main road site. It catches people's eyes and they come looking at the latest bikes. Clients used to be youngsters but now the age range is 25-50 and among them quite a few women customers. The days of the little 50cc get-to-work bike seems to have gone, probably because of the very few apprentices being taken on in big firms who used to buy these bikes.

Most of the time, Steve says, the bike is a secondary form of transport and more of a luxury but there is certainly the nostalgia factor with older clients. It usually takes people three or four visits before they decide on the bike they want to buy.

Damerell's in Plymouth is linked by computer to St Austell and everything needed for repairs is obtainable very quickly. For the Yamaha and Honda range they cover not only the bikes but workshops, clothing, spares and full diagnostic facilities.

Tim Parkins is a franchisee of **Weider** who are experts in the body building field. He operates his franchise on Mutley Plain just a bit further up from Damerells going towards Townsend Hill.

While he was not born in the city, Tim has been here since he was seven years old, leaving it only during his time in the army when he was a Guardsman. Once he was married he decided that army life and the separation it entailed was not for him so he re-trained as a commercial diver. Success in this profession meant he was constantly in demand and pulled him from home once more. So he looked around for a business which would allow him to go home at night. He has always been keen on fitness so when he saw the Weider franchise advertised he thought it was a way in which he could work at something he enjoyed and enjoy family life.

He trained in Weider procedures by working in their shops in Bristol and Manchester. Most of the technical details he already knew and soon found himself more than able to talk to people with knowledge and advice. This is a specialist business and advising on equipment, clothing and special foods is all important. At the moment he majors on clothing but this will soon be equalled by equipment and foods. He is an interesting man who believes

Plymouth needs his expertise because it is so poorly represented in this field.

Just next to the Swarthmore is one of my favourite bookshops, In **Other Words**, run by two delightful and interesting ladies, Gay Jones and Prudence de Villiers. I hope they will forgive me if I say that meeting them takes one back into another era. It is not because of their age; they are young. It is because they have the charming and courteous approach of another generation. Perhaps it has something to do with handling books because I find that the old established publishers frequently have the same approach.

Certainly I find a visit to their shop which is housed in an unusual building, full of nooks and crannies, is therapeutic. The range of books is vast and catholic. If you fail to find what you want then it is never too much trouble for In Other Words to acquire the title for you. If you want a gift, wrapping paper, postcards and greeting cards with a difference then you are equally in luck. The shop is small and maybe that is what makes it so interesting although Prudence and Gay would love to have somewhere bigger to show off all their wares and branch out into some of the bright ideas that Prudence conjures up without difficulty.

I would recommend In Other Words to anyone.

Almost directly across the main road is **Threshers**, an established shop selling fine wines, spirits, sherries and every sort of alcoholic beverage as well as all the non-alcoholic ones. Why would I use this shop in which to buy wine when there are others in the vicinity and certainly in the supermarkets? The answer is simple: the staff care. Of course it matters that the range of wine and spirits that they sell covers every palate and pocket but that is comparatively unimportant to the average customer. Most of us like to be helped when it comes to buying wine especially. Here, whether you are served by Roy Hambly, the manager, or Pat Pinch, one of the helpful assistants, the service and the knowledge is excellent. I have a liking for Australian and Californian wines but on several occasions I have been persuaded to try a Chilean or a New Zealand vineyard. I have never been asked to spend too much or regretted the purchase. You cannot get that sort of service in a supermarket.

I have already written about my bank, Nat West on Mutley Plain, but I should tell you that all the main clearing banks have branches here as well as several building societies. There is a large post office, Gateway Supermarket and a Plymouth Co-op store on the other side of the road. There are three pubs, bakers, newsagents and chemists, a shoe shop, hairdressers and opticians. In fact just about everything and one old and established building houses the **Mutley Conservative Club** which moved to its present site close to Mutley Baptist Church in the early 1920's.

Conservative political opinion is a supposed requirement of membership but this is not always the case. It is more of a social club than overtly political. It has always tried to move with the social trends and women were accepted into the club for the first time in the mid 70's. The club is comfortable, well furnished and very popular with its members. The only thing wrong with it according to the Treasurer, Ray Fordham, is that the members tend to be in the older age group. It is a standard joke amongst members that the flag is always flying at half mast!

Snooker is one of the popular games in the club and Ray Fordham is involved with the local social clubs' snooker league comprising 45 clubs in and around Plymouth. One of the members of the club is Frank Oliver who is the owner of the Belgrave Snooker Club, just off Mutley Plain which I remember when it was a small cinema and a place we all used to visit to see films we had missed first time around. I think I saw 'The Battle of Britain' six times with my then small son! The Belgrave is a popular place in its role today as well.

If you talk to the regular users of the Mutley Conservative Club they will tell you they go there for the companionship, the well-kept, low-priced beer and the food which is equally inexpensive. It is an institution and Plymouth would be poorer without it. Let us hope that new, younger members can be encouraged to join. It only needs one or two to set the ball rolling.

The little shopping centre directly opposite Hyde Park School is always busy. I have been getting my greengrocery for years from **Hyde Park Fruit Stores** where the likeable and helpful owner, Dave Slade, is always willing to deliver to his customers. What a Godsend that is. Close to him is a busy newsagents which is almost overrun at the beginning and end of the school day both from

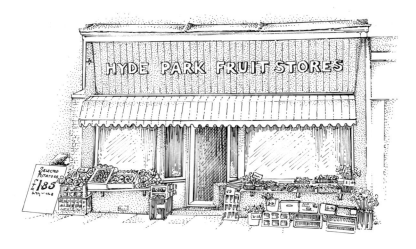

Hyde Park Fruit Stores

Hyde Park and from Plymouth College. **Leachs Electrical Centre** is at number 71. Run by Monica Leach, who is Cornish, this is a super shop to know about because not only does it sell electrical goods of all kinds including cookers and washing machines, they also do repairs to appliances and will tackle anything, even very old items, making parts if possible when the spares are no longer available.

I learnt about the difference between reconditioned and graded products from Monica Leach. Reconditioned is what it says but if you are offered a graded product it means that it will have a scratch or two or even a dent but it still has its manufacturer's guarantee and is cheaper to buy. A useful tip.

Monica and her husband, who is a qualified electrician, came to Plymouth in 1989 from Launceston, basically because they wanted a good education for their daughter. Not the first couple who have told me this. Plymouth can be proud of its reputation in this field. Richard, Monica's husband, has to cope with Muscular Dystrophy and he is an example to anyone. Recognising that his days of crawling about lofts and working under floorboards were over, he took a retraining course to teach his own trade but has ended up teaching 16-18 year olds with behaviour problems. Slightly different! He helps out in the shop occasionally and finds himself being presented with all the awkward fiddly repair jobs that no one else wants to do!

414

Two electricians are employed full time by Leachs Electrical Centre and for the last six years they have handled contract work on Christmas lighting as well as summer lights on the Hoe. However it is repairs that are in great demand and Monica is looking for another outlet or workshop although she will stay in Hyde Park. It is convenient; she lives around the corner.

Good, competent service is undoubtedly the hallmark of success in this business.

At number 51 Hyde Park, there is a totally different business, **Paws for Perfection**, which started as a mobile service when the owner, Debbie Byrne, was only nineteen. The start-up capital came from a grant from the Princes Youth Business Trust and the Enterprise Allowance Scheme.

This bubbling and enthusiastic girl deserves success and is delighted to talk about it quite openly. She told me how nerve-wracking it was to go before a board consisting of Peter de Savary and others in order to get her Princes Trust grant. She obviously did well and in March, 1990, was able to open her shop.

A year later she was chosen as a representative of the Princes Youth Business Trust to make a speech in the Pavilions when Prince Charles was present. Her two dogs accompanied her on to the stage and were extremely well behaved while she made her speech but afterwards Prince Charles remarked that ' You were taking a chance - one should never work with children or animals!'

Debbie operates a collection and delivery service for her Dog and Cat Grooming Salon. All breeds and cross-breeds are clipped and styled to the customer's requirements. Nails are clipped, ears cleaned, glands cleared, as well as bathing, fluff drying and styling. Her rates are competitive and almost always because she is such an extrovert her customers become her friends.

Like many people the paperwork side of a business is a chore. Debbie openly admits she finds it very hard to sit down at the end of a tough day's work and get on with it. It is a discipline which she is working on. A little while ago her bank was refusing to take her seriously. Perhaps her account was not run in the pristine way the bank required but they on the other hand would not sit down and discuss the matter or give her sensible advice. Their attitude was that her business was not viable and it was up to her to sort the matter out.

Debbie's landlady, at **Hyde Park Florist**, who is an astute and respected business woman - and a first class florist - banked in the same bank. She took Debbie to see the bank and told them quite firmly that if they did not stop being so silly and actually talk to Debbie, she would move her account. Then they listened and now the relationship is good.

Paws for Perfection is a good business and Debbie is undoubtedly talented. This year she takes and will pass her final City and Guilds in Grooming and then there will be no stopping her. Thank goodness for the Princes Trust in the first place and the help of a friendly landlady. Young people need to have confidence shown in them. They are the future of Plymouth.

Jacqui Pike is the inspiration and the driving force behind 'A Touch of Class' at 57 Hyde Park. This is its latest resting place. The first was in the shopping parade at Bretonside Bus Station and was opened by Debbie Owen, wife of David Owen. The opening date coincided with David Owen being in the City and he had an ITN film crew following him who, in turn were followed by a crew from Time International. The long and short of it was that because Jacqui and her team were local people they found themselves having the benefit of the opening of 'A Touch of Class' appearing on News at Ten. A big exposure for any small business. Since those days she moved to Millbridge, to 59a Hyde Park, and finally to the present premises.

There are two sides to this business; Touch of Class is the manufacturing side and Classic Design is retail. The original concept was to make evening dresses for service wives abroad and supply on a mail order basis. Any service wife would appreciate this because formal occasions remain much the same as they were several years ago and evening dresses abroad are not the easiest things to acquire.

Her partner, Mr Jennings, met Jacqui when he was running the 'Start your own business' courses at Enterprise Plymouth and thought she was one of the liveliest people he had met. He was invited to help her launch the business and for general advice. This he gave her and also used the DTI initiative for the benefit of the business. This led to Jacqui asking him if he would like to be part of the business. He has become so, but not full time, and still remains a management consultant.

In 1988 Jacqui was offered the contract of making the Mess Dress for the Womens Royal Army Corps which she did outstandingly well. About 2 years ago the army re-organised and redesigned the uniforms. The contract was lost because there was no longer an approved Mess Dress. Eventually the Army approved several of Jacqui's designs and one would have supposed things would have been straightforward from there on but that is not the case.

The rules are incredibly complicated. A 17th-century tradition lays down the rule that the Colonel of the regiment is responsible for clothing his men. Whilst this no longer applies in practice, the decision on which design to adopt is still with each Colonel. A further complication is that the streamlining of the Army has caused 5 regiments to be united into one, but even so the Colonels now have to agree on which design to adopt. This has created delays but it will be good business sometime in the future.

A Touch of Class does make other uniforms and eighteen months ago started making evening wear and ball gowns for the larger lady - the 18+ size. This is good news for those of us who are not petite and dislike the idea of only having the most uninteresting materials and designs on offer. Jacqui finds a large part of her business is manufacturing and supplying nationally to ball gown hirers and of course special orders. It was quite sad to realise that most of the materials used come from Spain, Italy and Germany because there are so few manufacturers left in this country. The materials are wonderful, they look expensive and luxurious and to feel the heavy brocades and the rich silks, takes you into a fantasy world.

The concentration is on the top end of the market which is not the biggest opening but it is less volatile and is quite big enough for A Touch of Class to handle. Within the range there are all sorts of different orders; new robes for the Mayor of Tavistock as a gift from Lloyds Bank, a full set of Elizabethan costumes for the Armada Experience.

It is an exciting business and a challenge that Jacqui Pike relishes.

417

Modern up-to-date marketing methods have made a success of **Animal Magic** at 6, Peverell Park Road. If any pet owners have not discovered this excellent pet shop then they should make a bee line for it. Mr Bowden had managed nine pet shops in Surrey before he made up his mind to return to Devon where his father is a vet at Horrabridge. He loves this part of the world although he feels that if anyone can make a success of a business in Plymouth it would be child's play elsewhere!

Animal Magic

Having established his business here in 1988, and been successful, he opened a second shop in Exeter in late 1992. This was a struggle at first but is now building very nicely. He was quite surprised to find that a number of Cornish customers come to Exeter by-passing Plymouth.

Like many people who have moved here, or who have returned, he feels that the massive potential of the city is not being exploited. While I would have agreed with him a few years back I firmly believe that Plymouth is taking up the challenge of the future, tackling the internal problems and showing the world that it is a major city with a leading role to play in the United Kingdom and in Europe.

In researching this chapter and writing it I was excited by the number of individuals who have successfully gone into business for themselves. This has to be good news for Plymouth.

CHAPTER 16

Commerce and Industry - the future of Plymouth

One of the difficulties in deciding the market at which this book was to be aimed became even more complicated once I started researching and interviewing people. Plymouth is a deceptive city, even to Plymothians. We wake each morning and go out and about seeing people driving cars, vans, lorries, getting on and off buses and on foot. It had never occurred to me to wonder where they all went, what sort of work they did and how many different industries and businesses made up the whole. Even now, over twelve months later, I have only scratched the surface of the range of skills and enterprise. As I have delved further, and written each succeeding chapter, I have become more and more excited about what Plymouth has to offer, both for those who live and work here, and for those who would wish to relocate, use all that is on offer for a conference or enjoy a first class holiday.

The Western Evening Herald ran a 'Wake up Plymouth' campaign not so long ago. They need have no fear: Plymouth is wide awake and the sleep has left its eyes.

I found that the City Council, led currently by John Ingham, a quiet, far seeing man, had put in an enormous amount of spade work to attract new businesses and, in its turn, Devon County Council also played a large part. I am quite sure that the background work is constantly being done and it is something that the layman like myself never hears about. But what caught my imagination was the work of one or two individuals, Mike Wharton, the Commercial Marketing Director of Devon County Council, Graham Jones, Peter Burrows of Plymouth City Estates Department and Roger Matthews of **Plymouth Marketing Bureau**. It is the activity of these men working in the interests of the city that has brought so many new firms here in the last few years.

Part of their job perhaps, but if I give you examples of what the heads of firms who have moved from other parts of the United Kingdom to Plymouth say about these men, then you may understand that here we have men who go way past the normal confines of their jobs.

One man, who shall be nameless, told me that he applied to the North, to Wales and finally to Plymouth, for help in relocating his business. The North did not even bother to reply, Wales told him he could call on them if he thought they could be of help, but Plymouth responded with an immediate telephone call which led to an arranged visit to the city the following weekend. The man and his wife were put up in the Moorland Links and throughout the weekend were driven around to various possible sites for the business, taken to meet some people from the Chamber of Commerce, shown the various schools available, and introduced to estate agents. In addition, they were told also what help they could expect from the City if they decided to make the move.

It was not a hard decision for them to make, aided and abetted by the fact that the weekend was warm and sunny and Plymouth Sound looked at its magnificent best. The firm is now successfully established here and my informant tells me that it was the best thing he ever did. His family loves the area, he has a contented work force, some of whom came with him, but mainly local people, and even in a time of recession his business is more than holding its own. He also went on to tell me that every possible help was given to him and his family to make sure they settled happily.

I have heard the same story from conference organisers who have found the hoteliers and the council agreeable, efficient and the city a wonderful place to visit. The men appreciate the conference facilities and if their wives are with them, the women enjoy the shopping, the restaurants, the theatre and the various trips that are almost always arranged for them in which they get to see the surrounding area.

It is the work of the council, with the assistance of people in business and industry, who have managed to win so much money to breathe life back into Plymouth's economy. The Urban Development Corporation has £45 million to be spent over five years and has targeted the Royal William Yard, RAF Mountbatten and Mount Wise for revamping. Admiral Sir Robert Gerken has been appointed head of the Corporation with city council leader John Ingham in the vice-chairman's role. Then there is the £1.8 million cash grant awarded to Plymouth in the Government's Urban Partnership Fund which was higher than that given to any other council in the country. The city scooped the largest share of £20 million pounds that was divided among 46 authorities.

This funding, which is vital to Plymouth, is matched by a further £1.8 million from Plymouth City and Devon County councils. That total of £3.6 million is doubled when it is matched by European Renaval funds - making a total spending facility of £7.5 million. This money is earmarked for crucial access roads into the Cattedown, Coxside and Millbay areas. Of course, it has other benefits than the finished product - it produces jobs along the way.

Some time ago I spoke to Tony Holland, the senior partner of Foot and Bowden, who was the chairman of the City Challenge Bid, and to Gary Streeter, who both agreed that it is the partnership that the Council has built up with the private sector that impressed Whitehall. Working together the whole future of the city is exciting and a recipe for success.

Dr. Geoffrey Potts, the instigator and director of the National Marine Aquarium project, welcomes this investment in the city. It brings his dream of a marine aquarium on a waterfront site at Coxside, overlooking Queen Anne's Battery and Plymouth Sound, into the realms of possibility. It reduces some of the enormous sum that has to be raised to get the aquarium scheme off the ground. As I understand it the largest sum of £740,000 is towards a new car park at Coxside which will support the proposed Aquarium with all the benefits it will bring to Plymouth.

£630,000 will go towards the cost of providing new access roads in the Prince Rock and Shapters Field area of Cattedown. This will unlock land for new industrial areas where more than 1,000 new jobs could be created. Then there is £290,000 for a link road from Gydnia Way to Coxside, where more development sites supporting 1,400 jobs could be created. And there is money for a new access road and highway improvements for Millbay which, in turn, will stimulate private sector investment and help Associated British Ports improve the ferryport as an important European gateway.

What is important for Plymothians to know is that all the work by the dedicated people who put forward the schemes in the City Challenge in 1992 has been justified. We might have lost out on that bid but the council resubmitted the proposals when the Government launched the £20 million Urban Partnership Fund.

When I talked to **Devon and Cornwall Development Bureau** at Derriford, I learnt of a different aspect. They work to promote the two counties abroad. The Bureau has an office in Tokyo and another in Boston, U.S.A., both of which work hard to entice companies to come to Devon and Cornwall and with remarkable results for Plymouth. I was quite amused when I learnt that they always try to arrange for visiting potential investors to come to Plymouth last after they have been to the North and to Wales or Scotland. By this time the visitors are all tired and not inclined to be too enthusiastic until they see how superb Plymouth Sound is and how awe inspiring the ruggedness of Dartmoor. Add this to a traditional cream tea and possibly dinner in 3, Elliot Terrace and there is no contest - Plymouth has won!

It is not quite so simple as that but who can deny that Plymouth is a wonderful place in which to live and work?

The Development Bureau does its share of encouraging people to come to Plymouth as well. Every effort is made to increase the city's £80 million annual income from the tourist industry. The Bureau also works in Japan and has a promotional brochure in Japanese which is available to the public in Tokyo. The brochure paints Plymouth as one of the 'elegant cities' by emphasising its maritime character and historic heritage. Part of the brochure is taken up by a personal message from Yoshitsugu Fujiwara, managing director of Estover - based electronics firm, **Murata**. He outlines the city's features and attractions which persuaded him to move and settle in Plymouth.

The Japanese market is one of the fastest growing and most lucrative in the world and one we need to attract. There is no way we should rely on the Americans although that has always been a good market place for the city.

Yoshitsugu Fujiwara was kind enough to spare me some of his valuable time when I went to see the Murata factory. We took tea together and he expressed the great pleasure that he and his wife got from living here. That would not have been sufficient though if the rest of the package was wrong. What Plymouth had to offer was entirely acceptable to the Murata Manufacturing

Company Ltd., whose headquarters are in Kyoto, Japan. They are a world leader in the production of electronic components and the many tens of millions of pounds original project was the largest ever inward investment into Devon.

The arrival of Murata demonstrates the success of the partnership approach employed in Devon to attract new investment.

In this case it was a two-year operation by the Devon and Cornwall Development Bureau which succeeded in bringing Murata to Plymouth, but in this it had key assistance from the City Council. The Council had secured the Texas Instruments' site two years earlier in readiness, rather than letting it go for warehousing or distribution services, until a new job-creating project could be attracted to replace the employment lost when Texas Instruments closed its Plymouth operation.

Mike Wharton of Devon County Council himself shows how the partnership operates in Devon, working as he does not only for the County Council and the Devon and Cornwall Development Bureau, but also for Plymouth City Council as its commercial marketing director.

Murata purchased the former Texas Instruments' plant from Plymouth City Council and set about refurbishing the 47,000 sq ft factory to the high standards required by Murata. From the small staff of 150 in 1990 it is expected to grow to several hundred in the near future.

The gentle colour schemes and the peaceful atmosphere within the building belie the amount of production that is achieved here. Murata is one of the largest manufacturers of ceramic capacitors in the world; indispensable parts of virtually every electronic circuit.

I always thought ceramics had something to do with pottery! I have now been taught differently by the quietly informative Mr Fujiwara. Historically mankind has created various civilizations. Each civilization was driven with 'basic materials'. There was the Stone Age, the Age of Earthenware, the Bronze Age and the Iron Age. Today three types of materials in particular support modern civilization. They are polymers, metal and ceramics, surprisingly the newest material on the list, yet also one of the oldest.

Today's ceramics are called fine ceramics. They are inorganic substances, with the exception of metals, and because of this they are the most plentiful of all resources on earth and in the entire universe. Though in the past they were often used for utilitarian purposes, now they are in the spotlight as the latest technological discovery serving today's rapid progress of the electronics industry. Their features include what conventional materials lack, and they have become one of the most widely used materials in every type of electronic equipment, from household appliances to industrial machines.

Murata supplies an amazing number of ceramic-based electronic devices. To come to this factory is to enter the wonderland of electronic ceramics.

Mr Fujiwara talked to me in his slightly halting English, for which he apologised, although I have no idea why he needed to do so. We as a race would never make the strenuous efforts to learn another language as he has done. I found out that one of the reasons that Murata was attracted to Plymouth was the cleanliness of the city and the green surrounds, and another was the availability of high calibre labour. He was also very happy with the way in which he and his Japanese colleagues had been welcomed into the life of the city.

It was from Graham Stirling, the chief executive of the **Barden Corporation** in Estover, that I learnt of the existence of the unobtrusive but immensely powerful **Plymouth Manufacturing Group**. This group consists of 25 members who are represented by their Chief Executives. The requirements are that they must be manufacturers, they must have over one hundred employees, and that whatever they talk about is totally confidential.

This group does not have an office, but they do have a secretary, who at the time we met was about to retire. Over coffee in the Forte Posthouse, Alan Macfarlane told me that the group meet over lunch, each time at a different venue, six times a year. They also have social occasions but the main purpose is to talk about generalities in their world without betraying the individual confidentiality of each company. The conversation will range over current trends, the consideration of annual wage increases, new regulations and any other topic which is beneficial to the group. They also unite as a pressure group to encourage the city or the county to act in a way they think is necessary for the good of the whole. There is no question but that they are immensely powerful. Quite rightly, when you consider that between them they spend in excess of £30 million annually on goods and services provided by other businesses within the city.

It is known that every job in manufacturing creates another four in other services, including sub contracted work. We should also remember that a great deal of the new investment in supermarkets and leisure facilities would probably not have taken place without this new wealth injection into the local economy.

To return to the **Barden Corporation (U.K.) Limited**, where Graham Stirling is the Managing Director and a sincere fan of the virtues of our city. It is a subsidiary of FAG Kugelfischer Georg Schaefer of Germany and part of the Barden Corporation of Connecticut, U.S.A, a world leader in the manufacture of precision ball bearings.

It was Graham Stirling who with the help of the council and a splendid dinner at 3, Elliott Terrace, convinced his originally reluctant American parent company to invest £3 million more in an expansion programme as part of an export drive. Once again underlining the value of this former home of Lord and Lady Astor to Plymouth.

Barden is the only U.K. producer of super precision ball bearings which have applications in many industrial sectors, including textile machinery, high performance vacuum pumps and machine tools. The company machines to near frictionless perfection, providing an engineering service which is the envy of other European ball bearing manufacturers. Barden's advanced bearing technology is specified throughout the aerospace, medical and computer industries. More than three quarters of the £3 million investment has gone towards buying production machine tools, costing £300,000, to produce the bearings. The plan which was supported by a Department of Industry grant, provided at least 20 new jobs for skilled and semi-skilled workers.

The company's underlying principles are product quality, precision, excellence, performance and availability, and that is repaid by the loyal workforce in terms of versatility and adaptability.

The decision of the parent company to go ahead with the plan was a tremendous confidence-boost and consolidated their position in Plymouth.

One factor that Dr Stirling pointed out to me was the lack of absenteeism in Plymouth and the almost non-existent stoppages which people experience in other parts of the country.

Dr. Stirling also praised the united efforts of the DTI Regional Office, Plymouth City Council and the Devon and Cornwall Development Bureau for all that they had done. Barden, like several other companies, is quite often the host when possible new investors come to take a look at the city. He readily assures them that Plymouth has a great deal more than most places to offer. When I asked him if he had any advice for an inwardly investing company, his response was immediate, 'Tell them to come, they will never regret it.'

It was very pleasing to walk into the office of the Director and General Manager of **Gleason Works Limited**, also in Estover, and find that he was a Plymothian. Robert Ball is a man who, having left the Dockyard, looked for a company which could offer an exciting and challenging career.

Gleason were currently based in Watford, and in 1964, needed to expand but because of Government restrictions this was not possible in that area. They had to find a Development District and visited every area in the United Kingdom recommended by the Board of Trade. In each locality an in depth survey was carried out and Gleason met with the local Board of Trade representatives, councillors, industrialists and, where appropriate, trade union representatives.

At that time, everywhere available in England, Scotland, Wales and Ireland offered government grants and local incentives but this was only one of the considerations in choosing an appropriate site. Such a move, by a company whose skilled operators and engineers manufactured a high precision product, necessitated the re-location of a nucleus of key Gleason employees.

An attractive area was important and Gleason wanted to ensure they chose the best location which met, not only their present needs but those for the foreseeable future. Therefore they compiled a shopping list:

1. A green field site on which to build a factory and office with land for future expansion.

2. An area of unemployment without being depressed.

3. A pool of labour which would become a committed and loyal workforce and who would be willing to be trained, spending several months in Watford prior to the move.

4. An area with good employee relations.

5. A helpful and co-operative local government.

6. A college or organisation qualified to assist in the training of apprentices.

7. Council houses available until employees found their own homes.

Plymouth became the yardstick to which all succeeding areas were compared. Nowhere achieved the same standard. Plymouth was not actually on a government list of places available but, the City Council were so keen to have Gleason move to the county, they moved heaven and earth to achieve this.

Gleason, for their part, liked Plymouth, liked the site on offer at Estover, found the Council extremely co-operative and other local managing directors helpful in outlining the advantages and also the disadvantages in the area, such as communications.

In August 1967, the factory was transferred from Watford to Plymouth and Robert Ball was one of the engineers who returned to Plymouth with the company. Gleason have never regretted the move. That was just over 25 years ago and the Plymouth plant is now the major gear tooling and cutter blade manufacturing site for the entire Gleason Corporation.

The history of the firm is quite interesting. It was established by William Gleason, who began his apprenticeship in America in

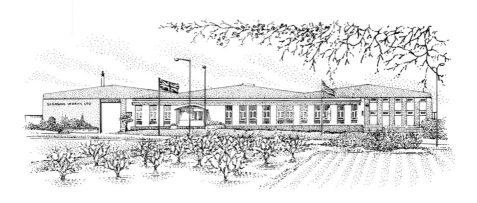

Gleason Works Limited

1851 on arrival from Ireland. He worked in a Rochester, New York, machine shop and when the Civil War broke out took his mechanical skills to Colt's Armoury in Hartford, Connecticut. He returned to Rochester in 1865 and formed the firm of Connell and Gleason. From his invention of the bevel gear planner, the company grew to world leadership in the production of gear making machinery. In 1919, the first Gleason cutting tools were manufactured in the United Kingdom under licensing agreement with Buck and Hickman, long time representatives of Gleason.

We already know of the move to Plymouth and from that time onwards they extended their area of business from Europe to the Far East and as more and more machines were brought in. In 1969 it became necessary to extend the factory by a third. By 1973 the decision was made to build an extension at the rear of the factory across all three bays.

Gleason Works Limited was one of the first companies in Britain to obtain the National Training Award and in 1989 received the British Standards Award, BS 5750, in recognition of its quality standards.

In 1991 three separate product groups were created to further improve and strengthen Gleason's position in the market place. These were the Standard Products Group, the Special Products Group and the Tooling Products Group.

Robert Ball, who by now was the Director and General Manager at Plymouth, became Vice President of the Tooling Products Group responsible for operations worldwide.

The Plymouth plant is now the major gear tooling manufacturing site for the Group, with the Rochester part of the Group concentrating on the manufacture of workholding equipment and cutter heads. CNC technology and computerisation increasingly play a part in consolidating the forward thrust of the Plymouth operation, as does the design, research and development of tooling equipment.

Gleason have carried out extensive re-design work on its products and recently were granted major patents with more pending. This together with major investment in manufacturing equipment, will ensure market leadership.

The streamlining which has taken place on both sides of the Atlantic has placed Gleason in a very strong position in today's volatile and competitive marketplace. It is quite clear that Gleason responds quickly and effectively, not only to present, but also to predicted customer demands, and as a consequence, now exports more machines and tooling to Japan than any other company in the world. The Plymouth operation exports 95 per cent of its production, with about 30 per cent to the Far East, 40 per cent to the USA and 30 percent to Europe. The UK accounts for about five per cent.

Gleason is a true creator of wealth in the Plymouth area since raw steel is the only bought in part of the product. Even the steel is supplied from the UK.

The company also invests heavily in the training of its employees through apprenticeships and ongoing training. It takes a great interest in welfare and education in the city and the Gleason Memorial Fund has donated to various local organisations and schools, such as the RNLI, Age Concern and have provided a technology room at Southway School. Also, as I wrote about in the chapter on education, the Memorial Fund donated £47,000 to Coombe Dean School for a business centre equipped to train pupils and adults in the type of skills needed for the high tech future.

The centre houses an information technology studio equipped with fully IBM - compatible personal computers and industry standard software. The PC studio is the heart of the centre and is used extensively for the IT courses on offer, but is available for hire at certain times. There is a 30 seat conference suite for lectures, seminars and meetings which is also available for hire.

Part of the requirements Robert Ball of Gleason put on his shopping list when he was searching for a new site for their factory was repeated on **Wrigleys** list when they needed to move from Wembley. They had expanded the Wembley factory three times between 1953 and the mid-1960s and had reached a point where they either had to build a totally new factory or set up a subsidiary plant. The decision was made to build a new factory, and a firm of management consultants was brought in to survey the country. Wrigleys needed to have access to engineering skills, because about a third of the employees in the factory are associated with engineering of one kind or another. Wrigleys build their own high-speed wrapping machines. They needed help with housing their key workers and they wanted to be sure the people they wished to bring from the London area would like the new situation. Another vital requirement was clean air. Chewing gum quickly absorbs obnoxious odours from the atmosphere.

Plymouth was an obvious choice, during their negotiations with the city council for the Estover site, a clean air covenant was written into the agreement. This requires the council to confer with Wrigleys when industry is brought into the surrounding area to ensure there is no contamination to the production process. Wrigleys will tell you that Plymouth City Council were fantastic when the firm came here and have been ever since. Only one of the employees who made the move with them disliked Plymouth and returned to London.

Wrigleys have enough land for the next thousand years for making chewing gum so they will never find themselves in the same situation as they were in Wembley. Wrigleys has been one of Plymouth's success stories in recent years and has achieved five consecutive years of record production. In 1992 I believe they produced in excess of 200 million packs of gum!

I was given a write - up about the firm which I am going to repeat here. It tells of the history of the company far more succinctly than I am able to do. The story of the growth of the Wrigley Company is one of a man with a mission and $32 to carry it out with. William Wrigley went to Chicago in the spring of 1891, and with the only other commodities he possessed, energy, enthusiasm and salesmanship, he started Wrigleys Scouring Soap from out of a basket.

The enticement he gave to purchasers proved to become more popular than his initial product. He switched to selling baking powder and began offering two packets of chewing gum with each can of powder. Everyone loves getting something for nothing and the gum overtook the product it was supposed to promote! Though at the time there were already a dozen or more gum companies, William began marketing it under his own name, carrying on with the principle of offering free gifts with purchases.

In 1907 business in the USA experienced a general slump and slashed expenses, including marketing activities. William Wrigley was a pioneer in the use of advertising to promote sales and instead of cutting back, he saw that spending more and increasing this activity would put him above the competition: by 1910 Wrigley's Spearmint Gum was America's most chewed brand. There is a story told about William Wrigley that sums up his philosophy. He was travelling on a train to the West Coast of America with a young accountant who questioned the large sums the company was spending on advertising. The accountant suggested that Wrigley's bottom line profits would improve considerably if the advertising budget was reduced.

William Wrigley responded by asking the young man how fast he thought the train was travelling. About 70 miles an hour, retorted the accountant. 'What do you think would happen if they took the engine off?' asked Wrigley. 'The train would come to a dead stop,' replied the puzzled accountant. That explained exactly what would happen to the Wrigley business if there was a cut back in advertising. One of the things William Wrigley always used to say was: ' Tell them quick and tell them often', meaning it was essential to keep your name in front of the public all the time. That policy is still adhered to. Wrigleys in the UK spend about £8 million a year to keep the famous Wrigley Spearmint and all other brands of chewing gum it produces in the public eye.

Factories were established outside the USA and business boomed until the breakout of World War II meant the drying up of the top grade materials used to make the gum, and the entire output of gum was shipped to the troops abroad. Even then, although no gum was available for sale to the civilian market, a unique advertising campaign featuring an empty wrapper with the slogan 'Remember this wrapper', ensured that Wrigley remained in the forefront of people's minds if not in their mouths!

The site at Estover covers 45 acres, although only six were built on. 80% of production is sold outside the South West, but as the product is small and compact, freight charges are not that great so Plymouth is an ideal location. Land availability and a good supply of skilled workers were two of the major reasons for choosing Plymouth.

The Wrigley family are still in control of this vibrant business which grows and grows and has always managed to weather economic storms without ever resorting to the wholesale layoff of the employees. In fact, it is just the opposite. In January, 1992, at the height of the recession Managing Director, Philip Hamilton announced a £5 million investment at Estover following record production of 870 million packs of chewing gum in 1991. Wrigleys has an excellent reputation as an employer and its products are undoubted.

Even dentists favour the idea of chewing gum because it removes debris from between the teeth and reduces plaque acid which causes tooth decay. The idea has become even more appealing since the introduction of sugar - free brands, including Wrigley's Extra and Orbit.

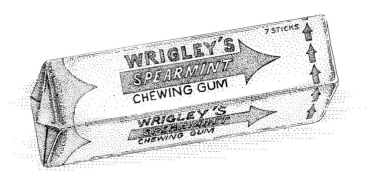

Wrigley's Spearmint Chewing Gum

Every year thousands of Plymouth people support Wrigley's gala day - a highly successful fundraising event. About 7,000 people converge on the Estover site to enjoy a fun day in the sun.

432

Different things happen every year. It is a day of laughter for adults and children as they take part in organised fun races, ski on a dry ski-slope, or perhaps take to the skies in a helicopter. Nearly always the Royal Marines and the Royal Navy take part. In 1992 the Royal Marines abseiled down the factory wall and Devonport Field Gun crew showed off the skills they hoped would win the Royal Tournament at Earls Court.

Scores of staff join in, including the managing director, Philip Hamilton, who became the Burger King for the day. Wrigleys are an example of the many companies in this city who have made themselves part of the community.

Stafford Miller are also at Estover and they are investing in a multi-million pound expansion programme in Plymouth, to create a modern high-tech distribution centre for its U.K., European and Middle Eastern markets. The company, a subsidiary of the Block Drug Corporation based in new Jersey, U.S.A, which manufactures dental, pharmaceutical and household products worldwide, plans to bring the new centre into operation towards the end of 1993.

250 people are employed in Plymouth with Stafford Miller who have been based here for 20 years. The company manufactures Sensodyne, the world market - leading toothpaste brand for sensitive teeth.

The company is buying seven acres of land with premises adjoining its existing facility to accommodate the expansion. Over the past two years, Stafford Miller has invested heavily in a programme to update and renew its buildings and machinery.

Operations director, Mike Perry, is enthusiastic about Plymouth and says that they see the whole site as an expansion opportunity for their plans and activities, certainly over the next ten years.

British Aerospace is always in the news and few people would doubt its success and stature. The products and the range of BASE in the air, at sea or on land cover everything from aircraft and missile navigation systems, flight recorders, gunfire control systems, electro optic tracking instruments to Steadyscope and security systems. Their building at Southway is a familiar one and their presence in the city appreciated.

The Southway site at Plymouth, now the Business and Engineering Centre of BASE first became a British Aerospace location in 1982, when BAe acquired Sperry Gyroscope Company. Sperry themselves had taken it over from Remington in 1975 and had established Plymouth as a manufacturing facility for its main business centred in Bracknell.

British Aerospace acquired the freehold of the Plymouth site in 1983, and it continued primarily as a manufacturing facility until, in the restructure which followed the formation of BASE, it was decided that Bracknell should be closed, and Plymouth should become the centre of BASE.

Since then the working population has more than doubled, and the site development has been virtually non-stop. The old style administrative building at the front of the site was completely modernised, with a new reception area, board room and office facilities being installed during 1989. Begun in the same year and completed in the Spring of 1990, was the construction of D Building which houses some 300 engineers as well as a single-status restaurant and some administrative functions. This building was opened in June 1990, in a ceremony conducted by the then Minister of State for Defence Procurement, Alan Clark, and watched by many BASE employees.

The development and expansion at Plymouth have led to increased demand for facilities other than offices, and in Autumn

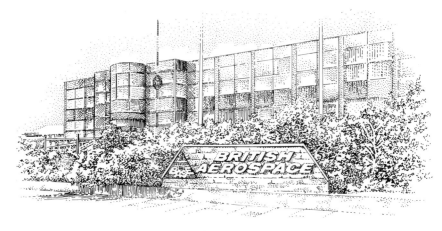

British Aerospace

1990, an adjoining field was purchased and used to provide additional car parking. In January 1991, BASE became British Aerospace (Systems and Equipment) Limited, a stand-alone company within the British Aerospace group.

It is a company which has shown and continues to show interest in the welfare of the community as a whole, providing perpetual shields for scholastic events and, in one case, backing a young woman, Susie Beaman, in a day nursery which also provides places for the children of working mothers at British Aerospace. I wrote about this young lady in the chapter on education.

I find everything about the computer industry mystifying but if anyone can unravel it for me it would be **JAD**, one of the longest established and most broadly based computing companies in the South West. David Tomalin, the managing director, is an enthusiast and believes that training at all levels to help both beginners and more advanced users get the maximum benefit from their equipment and software, is a must. JAD has devised a series of top quality training courses for clients and staff. These range from an introduction to basic principles to training on specified packages.

JAD was set up in 1976 by specialist staff of Rockwell International when the company decided to cease commercial operations in the UK. They immediately began to lay solid foundations of expertise with Apple, Commodore and North Star microcomputers. Then in 1982, when IBM entered the microcomputer field, JAD was ready. It was one of the first to meet their stringent standards, and became an authorised dealer serving the South West. Three years later it won the coveted IBM Marketing Excellence Award.

The company is well known for its excellent accounting systems, having gained much expertise from over 350 successful installations for large multi terminal systems, to smaller single user systems, all backed by their famous support service and training facilities.

Manufacturing software is an area in which JAD specialises. The team can take you through the manufacturing administration scenario by computer, including systems for large or small companies.

There are other important software packages they are able to supply and fully support from the leading Word Processing, CAD, Spread Sheet and Data Base suppliers. Their Networking and Unix Team offer the highest standards available for both installation and training courses. They also customise software to client requirements.

JAD's modern offices at Dark Lake View Industrial Park, Estover, are equipped to the very highest standards, and run their own diagnostic test facilities. They are staffed by professional engineers trained by the manufacturers of the hardware on which they specialise. Repairs can be undertaken on an 'as-and-when' basis, or can be programmed into a comprehensive maintenance contract designed to eliminate unscheduled down-time. Whichever suits the client best.

I found this a very honest, straightforward company who genuinely wanted to help their customers. David Tomalin loves Plymouth and the South West although sometimes he does get irked by the laid back attitude of Plymothians! However over the years he has learnt that it is good to take life at a slightly slower pace and he certainly enjoys the environment.

In November, 1988 the **Algram Group** joined the increasing number of successful, expanding, small companies who have relocated their businesses from the overcrowded South East to a new home in the South West. The Group is a UK leader in prototype toolmaking and injection moulding, pattern making and vacuum forming. It is an important supplier to the aircraft, motor, defence, telecommunications, electronic, medical and domestic appliance industries, often acting as an extension to their own design, research, development and model making departments.

Algram produces the tooling and mouldings for design and pre-production models of many well - known products. It also specialises in the production of small batches of often complex mouldings, using some of the most demanding top line materials for the aerospace, defence and other industries.

It provides a full computer - aided component design service as well as a range of other services, including GRP hand lay up and the production of jigs and fixtures and engineering and space models. It has been quality approved to BS 5750 part II, ISO 9002, and EN29002.

'Our decision to move' says Algram's founder and Managing Director Alan Cox, ' can be summed up in just four words, "Space, costs and labour."

He adds, - "We had been very successful in building our business in Marlow but we had no room for further expansion. The concentration of industry around the M4 west of London had also created a severe shortage of the kind of labour we needed and the cost of industrial land had escalated. If we were going to continue to grow, especially in export markets, we just had to move."

"Once we had decided that, it made sense to look for a completely new location, well away from the problems of the overcrowded South East."

Algram's search for a new location was governed by four main requirements. It needed:-

A site that would be big enough for its future expansion plans.

A good supply of suitable labour.

A good communications network.

It also wanted a good environment in which to live and work.

'Having decided what we wanted, says Alan Cox, ' we started looking. We wanted to leave the South East so it seemed logical to head west along the M4 and M5. We considered a number of locations along the way but it wasn't until we reached Plymouth that we found everything, including a very helpful local authority, that we needed.'

'The City Council's Estates Department did everything they could to assist us. They offered us a six acre site that met all our requirements, helped and advised us on the availability of grants and in many other practical ways. their assistance was a major factor in our decision to move to Plymouth.'

The other factor influencing Algram's final decision to move to Plymouth was the design and construction of its new headquarters. It was clearly one of the important considerations, in terms of both cost and timescale, in the decision to move to Plymouth, and had to be considered at an early stage in the discussions with Plymouth City Council.

Algram's specifications for its new headquarters called for the design to provide:

An aesthetically pleasing, yet practical, building that made maximum use of the available floorspace and reflected the company's reputation as a market leader in industry.

A building that could be readily extended to meet future needs.

A building that would be cost effective to construct as well as a sound financial investment.

Alan Cox said, ' We were faced with the decision of how to best achieve our objectives. Should we opt for a traditional approach, employing an architect and then going to tender before placing a contract or should we use a specialist design and build contractor, with its own in-house architectural design department, who could undertake every aspect of the design and construction contract?'

'We chose the latter which gave us the opportunity to discuss alternative designs with almost immediate information on the cost implications and the security of having a guaranteed, fixed price at an early stage of our planning. By selecting a South West - based contractor, Westframe Construction, we were also negotiating the design of our new building with the people who had first hand, local knowledge of the site and of the local planning, fire and building requirements. Ultimately it enabled us to reach a contractural situation and complete our move in a much shorter timescale than would have been possible with a traditional building contract.'

'Westframe's experience in regularly dealing with the end user meant that they fully appreciated manufacturing industry's costings and design criteria for new developments and were able to offer us practical help and advice on the relationship between cost and design. I am sure that, by opting for design and build, we have achieved a good balance between cost and an attractive practical design.'

Alan Cox told me that he has never regretted the decision and finds Plymouth a great place to live and work and he sincerely hopes they are here to stay.

Moving the whole company was a mammoth undertaking. 400 tons of heavy plant and machinery had to be moved. Around 100 new staff had to be recruited and trained from the Plymouth area to join the 25 or so key employees who moved with the company. The new headquarters are delightful and a splendid working environment. It has enabled Algram to expand and diversify their production, particularly in export markets where they have won new first time contracts in Sweden and Germany since the move. They employ over 90 people, around thirty more than they did in Marlow and this should increase significantly in the years to come.

The move certainly presented the City Estates Department with a challenge but Algram has the kind of vigorous, thrusting image the city wishes to encourage, and with considerable goodwill and help from Westframe Construction the requirements were met. It is a prime example of what can be achieved by close co-operation between a local authority and the private sector.

It is not only the industrial giants who work in Estover. **Adam's Bakery** in Dark Lake View is another of Plymouth's success stories for small businesses. Dianne and Paul Adams have built a business of which anyone could be proud. They moved to Estover because their premises grew too small for the expanding firm which now has a staff of 23 and bakes twenty four hours a day. 6,000 doughnuts find their way from the bakery each week as well as bread to local health shops, Captain Jaspers, the College of St Mark and St John, the Head Post Office, Woolworths and the local law courts as well as some city schools and various smaller outlets. Their products are also to be found on Paul's own and his father's stall in Plymouth Market. Four vans can be seen travelling and delivering round Plymouth every day. They use no additives in their bread and keep to the recipes of bygone years which is why their bread is so good.

Paul Adams worked for several local firms before he decided to step out on his own. His first venture, a bakery and shop in Glenholt, proved so successful that he launched a second unit in Plympton. This is his third move and he has had the opportunity now to install state of the art equipment. The Koma retarder prover for example has an alarm system that can raise him from his bed when he is needed at the bakery. He now produces large crimped pasties which were not possible at Plympton but he states that he is definitely going back in time after acquiring a lot of old recipes. Modern equipment is wonderful but the recipes our ancestors used take a lot of beating.

The rules that govern baking and associated products is in danger of killing off one of the best things about Plymouth and Cornwall - the pasty trade! By 1995, Mike Furzeland of **Ashford's** Bakery in Union Street tells me, bakers will not be able to supply other shops with hot pasties, they will only be permitted to sell them on the premises where they are made. The others will have to be chilled to 3-5 degrees centigrade. Then the retailer will have to heat them up himself to be able to sell 'hot' pasties. Yet we read that hospitals who pioneered this system are now saying that cook and chill systems can cause more problems!

The present law also says that extra wrapping has to be provided, so for example a box which will hold 10 pasties costs 29p which means that 3p has to go on the price of each pasty. They are not allowed to use animal fats in pastry but vegetable fat with half a dozen E numbers and potatoes must be sanitized before use. It is no wonder that the older ones among us think that nothing tastes the way we knew it in our younger days!

Ashford Bakery looks little more than a doorway in Union Street but it is deceptive. The business was started by Mike Furzeland's uncle in 1934 but he believes that it dates back into the last century. His parents inherited the business in the 1950's and then in 1968 Mike took over. Work starts here at 3.30am and opens up its doors from 7.30am-12.30pm. The main business is wholesaling to shops and schools. Everything has to be fresh and there is a very limited time in which to produce what is required. British machines in 1974, when Mike wanted to increase his production, could only provide him with one that would turn out 1800 pasties per hour at a cost of £7,000. Eventually he bought a machine from a Chicago company for £30,000 which was designed to turn out 12,000 apple turnovers per hour. It took Mike Furzeland 12 months to get the machine acclimatized to pasties! He thinks it will produce 12,000 per hour but has never had to run it more than 8,000 per hour, although on a day-to-day basis it runs at 4,000 pasties an hour which is infinitely better than the best British machine.

Ashford Bakery employs 11 people in the bakery, most of whom have been there for years - 2 of them worked for Mike's parents. Cleanliness is the hallmark of Ashford's Bakery - a must as we all know. The pasties are some of the most delicious made in Plymouth.

Most Plymothians will know of **Feneck's**, the Naval Outfitters, in Union Street, and because the shop is so close to Ashfords it brought to my mind a story about one of Plymouth's best loved characters, Joe Feneck, who died not so long ago. He was known and respected by so many people. His beloved shop and the caring for customers was quite the most important thing in his life. When he died he was cremated but he was not going to let his grandaughter and partner who now run the shop, or anyone else forget him. His ashes have been put in a casket and placed in the cabinet of the shop so that he would be able to watch over what was going on!

With Wrigleys, Gleason and the Barden Corporation, I have already written about three members of the Plymouth Manufacturing Group. Now for some more. The great name of Toshiba has dominated Plymouth for quite some time. Not only are they considerable employers but they also play a large part in the welfare of the community. That was an aspect that especially appealed to me when the managing director of **Toshiba Consumer Products (UK) Ltd**, George Williams talked to me a few months ago. Care of their own staff has always been the keystone of the enormous Toshiba Corporation. The staff are encouraged to contribute to the successful running of the company by talking over ideas and being made to feel that they are an integral part not just people there to collect a wage packet.

Supporting charities is one of the philosophies of the company and sensibly handled it is. The worthy causes can be almost anything but they must be beneficial to the catchment area in which the Toshiba staff live. This is excellent and you find that frequently donations are made to causes that otherwise would get nothing because they are not well known.

However, that does not deal with the reason that Toshiba is in Plymouth and has two factories, one at Ernesettle which makes television sets and the other, opened by His Royal Highness the Duke of Kent, at Belliver which manufactures air conditioning. Toshiba has invested over £30 million in its operations and over half the output from both plants is exported to mainland Europe. From its Plymouth base, firm business objectives are set for both businesses.

A Toshiba Television

While the company is Japanese and has many of the good points from that country, it is today very British in its outlook. Nonetheless it runs with an efficiency that is an example to everyone.

Within Toshiba Consumer Products there is an active policy of participation and involvement. The contribution of all employees is recognised as being essential to the future well- being of the company and its staff. While the necessity for close teamwork is essential, ample scope is given for individuals to realise their potential. To support the manufacturing operations, the administration, purchasing, personnel and technical functions have been brought together in one large open plan area. The factories are laid out in a spacious manner with a clean working environment.

There are no individual offices, ensuring efficient communication and close relationships between all departments. Every month without fail, the managing director chairs a meeting of the Company Advisory Board. The members of the Advisory Board are elected from the workforce as representatives of all Toshiba Consumer Products employees. The subjects discussed at the meeting include business plans and investment, trading performance, operating efficiency, manpower plans, and terms and conditions of employment including salaries and benefits and working conditions.

The Toshiba Group of companies based on their total commitment to people and the future, are determined to help create a higher quality of life for all people, and to do their part to help ensure that progress continues within the world community.

They endeavour to serve the needs of all people, especially their customers, shareholders and employees, by implementing forward-looking corporate strategies while carrying out responsible and responsive business activities. As good corporate citizens they actively contribute to further the goals of society.

By continually developing innovative technologies centring on the fields of electronics and energy, they strive to create products and services that enhance human life, and which lead to a thriving and healthy society. They constantly seek new approaches that help realise the goals of the world community, including ways to improve the global environment.

One of the things that impressed me when I went to Toshiba to see George Williams was that he himself came down the stairs to collect me. This is a man who is unassuming, yet I understand that quite recently he received the ultimate accolade of the Institute of Management. He was nominated as a Companion of the Institute, an honour bestowed on individuals who have demonstrated particular ability in the practice of management or administration. Only 1500 people of the organisation's 75,000 members had received the honour.

Wandel and Goltermann Limited, based at Burrington Way, Honicknowle, fascinated me. When I asked the managing director, Victor Parsons, to tell me what the firm did, his reply was simple: 'We take the crackle out of telephones'. Sounds simple but obviously it is far more than that. They are manufacturers of tele-communication test and measurement equipment. 95% of its products are exported and they also supply British Telecom, one of its main UK customers.

Seldom does one meet a man of Victor Parson's calibre. He told me how he came to join Wandel and Goltermann. It was quite by chance. He came to Plymouth to try and buy an electronic company which was about to go out of business. He wanted to buy it because he was bored. He had sold a successful company of his own and decided to retire. For a while messing about in boats down at Pin Mill in Suffolk, where I used to live, kept him happy but it was not enough. He went hunting and thought he had found the answer but Wandel and Goltermann beat him to it and acquired the company first. He like the sound of Wandel and Goltermann and when they suggested he might run the operation in Plymouth for them he agreed. From there retirement went out of the window. Within a short time it was decided that the factory was of no use and would have to be pulled down and rebuilt so he turned to the council and asked for an adjacent site. It was a weekend and he wanted a decision within forty eight hours. Having got over their shock the council responded magnificently and by the Monday morning, agreement had been reached. Wandel and Goltermann with Victor Parsons at the helm were in business.

This is a man who never seems to do anything yet he achieves more than most people I have ever met. He is laid back but motivates his staff to achieve impossible heights. The operation here has succeeded and since then he has set up a Canadian operation for the parent company and was off to India to repeat the same purpose. His energy is incredible.

I enjoyed hearing about Mr Wandel and Mr Goltermann who started the business as students in Germany before World War II when they mended radios to make a bit of extra money. The business grew from there and remains still firmly in the hands of the two families. It is a tale of hard work, persistence and an astuteness that is superb. They were lucky when they beat Victor Parsons to the draw. His skills have assisted the parent company to trade worldwide.

In recent years Victor Parsons and the company in Burrington Way have developed strong links with John Kitto Community

College to whom they present Science and Technology Awards every year. The winners, in addition to their prizes, are invited to visit the company and view its facilities. The company is keen to encourage young people into the field of electronics. To this end they have become one of the first companies in the region to be recognised for its commitment to staff training. In October of last year the company was presented with the Investors in People award after reaching a national standard for effective investment in staff.

The award is part of a national scheme, administered locally by the Devon and Cornwall Training and Enterprise Council. Victor Parsons said that the company was merely continuing its same lifelong commitment to staff training to win the award. But there was some hesitation when the firm was first approached by the TEC.

They were slightly anxious that the TEC and Wandel and Goltermann might not have the same objectives. In fact it has worked out well and the criteria for the award did reveal a few areas where the company, which uses staff training courses across the country, could improve. Victor Parsons firmly believes that encouraging people to go on training and educational courses means that Wandel and Goltermann have a workforce, including himself, which is better equipped to deal with the changes in the industry. It has another benefit inasmuch as training also enables staff to develop through the company, and makes them more suited to look at new job prospects which may arise within the firm. With the advances being made in the telecommunication field, Wandel and Goltermann is eager to keep its staff in readiness to cope with daily changes.

With the same commitment to the welfare of the city that other members of the Plymouth Manufacturing Group have, Victor Parsons is also a Governor of the University of Plymouth and in that role encourages the young and those slightly older to seize the learning opportunities that are available. It was his encouragement that persuaded my 27-year-old son, who left school without academic qualifications, to apply for the MBA course in Business Management at the University. The initial reaction was that if you do not have A-levels of some kind, you cannot be considered but this is not so. Providing you show an aptitude, a desire to learn and pass a personal interview, the door is open.

Whatever happened to retirement and messing about with boats?

Tucked away at the bottom of Burrington Way is a much smaller company than Wandel and Goltermann but here is a success story both for the company, and for City Estates and Devon County Council, who persuaded them to come here: **Kestrel Injection Moulders Limited** headed by Howard Thornton.

A keen commercial interest and more than twenty-seven years experience in injection moulding led Howard Thornton and his partner, George Henry to establish the company in Plymouth. It was the help given to the company by Plymouth that made them move here from the Home Counties. From the outset Kestrel's emphasis was on quality. Howard Thornton told me that 'There was nobody in the region taking the market seriously. We built Kestrel on the principle that we would do things right or not at all.' That they have done things right is unquestioned. Seven years later with the turnover over £3.5 million from a carefully nurtured client list, which includes some of the best known names in the automotive, telecommunications, TV and consumer goods market, Kestrel is proud of its reputation. Toshiba and Ransomes Consumer, both companies I am writing about in this chapter, are just two of their clients.

Kestrel has invested over £2,000,000 in new equipment over the last five years and have the latest microprocessor machinery ranging from 30-350 tons. Their service is among the most complete and technically advanced available to industry. It covers product development from concept to finished product and includes material selection, moulding tool design and manufacture, moulding production and a variety of assembly, welding and printing techniques. Complete assemblies and sub-assemblies, incorporating bought in components are also carried out.

On site Moldflow 3D finite element flow analysis i.e. Computer Aided Engineering (CAE) methods for studying the design and production of Thermoplastic parts is utilised to both improve the quality of the part and reduce manufacturing costs.

From the delivery of raw materials to the final end product there is total commitment to quality at Kestrel with 24 hour coverage by qualified inspectors. First off, batch and last off inspection of mouldings is normal procedure and detailed inspection is carried out on a computerised 3D axis co-ordinated measuring machine.

Quality at every stage from design to delivery, that's how Kestrel is moulding its reputation.

I mentioned the **Ransome Consumer Group** just now. Here is a company that is based at Bell Close, Newnham Industrial Estate at Plympton. I read an article about them in a magazine in November, 1991, which I thought was one of the best examples of positive thinking. This market leader of petrol lawnmowers and garden tractors was on a high in 1988. For the third year consumer spending was rising. There were good times ahead and there was an obvious need for manufacturing expansion. The company bought companies in France and in Italy but then in 1990, while holidaymakers in Britain and Europe celebrated record sunshine levels, Ransomes Consumer Division found itself facing falling orders as its dealers found supplies stockpiling.

The problem was simple: as the rain stopped falling so the grass stopped growing and the following year it did much the same thing. Reeling slightly after an unprecedented two years of drought, Roy Ashwell, the managing director, and his team did not waver from their purpose. They strove for new markets and produced a range of four new Westwood tractors in a new bright red livery which has proved to be very successful. They also produced a machine that is tipped as likely to be one of its biggest successes over the next decade. It is called the Mountfield Muncher which answers a growing market need. It munches garden refuse so it can be recycled as mulch. No burning is necessary. No dumping in land-fill sites - which in the US has already been banned because it gives off harmful gases. Their biggest advantage over traditional shredders, however, is the quickness of operation compared to other machines on the market today.

The development of the above new products, as well as two fun carts, has taken over 2½ years, and in addition a seven model 'Budget range' of mowers has been produced for the 1993 season. It is an investment for the future and a mark of faith within the company in its ability to achieve its aim of being the leaders in its field on the European stage.

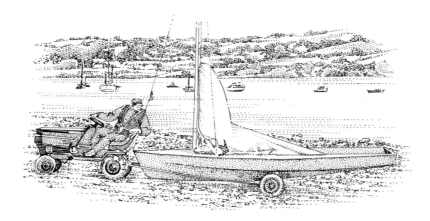

A Westwood Tractor

The company also invested £1.5 million in a 40,000 sq ft extension to its Plymouth factory including new offices. This is a strong positive company and another example of the excellence of industry in the city.

An outsider might question the viability of such manufacturing when the market was sluggish but Ransomes has always been a seasonal business. Its products sell most between March and June and its production systems are geared to take account of peaks and troughs.

Its staff consists of some seasonal workers, for example, and they are trained as production needs rise.

Ransome's actions have placed them in a strong position to take advantage of the growth in interest in gardening throughout Europe but they have recognised that they are in a business where sales are allied to house building, buying and selling. When people move house they tend to buy a new mower or garden tractor, so the slump in the house market has had a knock on effect, but stock piles are clearing and the machines are on the move again.

If you read a company profile on **Becton Dickinson** whose U.K site is based at Belliver, it will say 'Products: Evacuated blood collection tubes and laboratory equipment.'

That rather cold statement gives no-one an insight into how this giant American manufacturer of health care products started.

The story is simple. Maxwell Wilbur Becton and Fairleigh Stanton Dickinson met on a sales trip in 1897. Noticing that bright sunshine pouring through a dining room window was bothering Dickinson, Becton pulled down the shade. The appreciative Dickinson invited him to breakfast, beginning a lifelong friendship.

Within months, the pair formed Becton, Dickinson and Company in New York City. From imported fever thermometers, their line expanded to include hypodermic units and other supplies.

Several years later, to ensure consistent product quality and supply, they moved to a new factory in East Rutherford, New Jersey, one of the first U.S. plants to make hypodermic units. In a few years, Becton Dickinson was producing and marketing a full range of high quality products.

During World War I, the company produced all-glass syringes, a significant improvement over the metal units of the day. Becton Dickinson also developed the ACE brand bandage, originally an acronym for 'all cotton elastic.' For his contribution to the war effort, Dickinson was commissioned a lieutenant colonel in the Medical Corps and thereafter was called 'the Colonel'. Steady growth followed the war. People who were to make an outstanding contribution joined the company. These included Andrew W. Fleischer, always called 'Doc' even though he did not have a medical degree, and Dr Oscar Shchwidetzky. Brilliant inventors, they headed the company's medical products research for decades. Fleischer modernized the stethoscope and invented the first accurate instrument to measure blood pressure. Schwidetzky developed special hypodermic needles and other devices.

In World War II the company was awarded an Army/Navy 'E' for Excellence, for providing quality medical equipment for the armed forces. Dickinson and Becton were instrumental in establishing Fairleigh Dickinson Junior College, now a university.

Following the war, Becton Dickinson continued to develop innovative new products such as a glass syringe with interchangeable parts and a device to collect blood in sterile tubes for laboratory analysis. This instrument sold under the Vacutainer brand, opened laboratory medicine to the company.

After the founders died, control of the company's future passed to their sons, Fairleigh S Dickinson Junior and Henry P Becton. Product lines were broadened and new production capacity built, while international expansion, which had begun in Canada continued.

From the 1950s to the 1980s, Becton Dickinson acquired such leading firms as Bard-Parker who developed the first two-piece scalpel; the Baltimore Biological laboratory, which produced dry culture media in which diagnosticians grow microorganisms for tests; Clay Adams, manufacturer of surgeons' supplies and laboratory instruments; Johnston Laboratories, which developed the BACTEC microorganism detection instrument; and Deseret Medical Inc, a leading provider of catheters, protective gloves and surgical products.

The advent of the disposable hypodermic syringe and needle, introduced by Becton Dickinson in 1961, completely changed the company. This product significantly differed from the traditional reusable type. The needle had to be permanently bonded to the syringe, glass barrels were replaced by more cost-effective plastics and enormous volumes had to be manufactured. This meant huge investments in new equipment, packaging and distribution. Becton Dickinson became a publicly held corporation and in 1963 was listed on the New York Stock Exchange. The family partnership was over, replaced by a new responsibility to thousands of stockholders.

The corporation has remained innovative and today is a leading, diversified, transnational health care corporation with sales of more than £2 billion and more than 20,000 employees at 74 locations in 20 countries. The company brings to millions of people modern medical technology, products made with meticulous attention to quality and a real sense of caring.

This is the legacy of an act of kindness and a shared breakfast over one hundred years ago.

Plymouth is one of those locations and here with a multi-million dollar investment, on a 27 acre site in July 1982, Becton Dickinson, Plymouth, was officially opened by HRH Princess Margaret.

Becton Dickinson based its decision for investing in Plymouth on the market potential that lay in Europe and the assurances that were given on the quality and reliability of the workforce. This confidence in the City and its labour force has been justified by the excellent performance of the plant.

A further £10 million has been invested in the city allowing the company to incorporate a 70,000 square foot distribution centre to serve the entire UK with products manufactured by the company throughout the world, and a 110,000 square foot manufacturing and office complex. This allows British made goods to be exported to all parts of the world.

John Hanson heads Becton Dickinson in Plymouth and he confirms that the rapid growth has to a certain extent been made possible by the quality of our Plymouth workforce and the positive cooperation of the local business and civic community.

Every year a large American contingent from the parent company comes to Plymouth. On Saturday, October 26th, 1991, they came to celebrate the 10th Becton Dickinson, Plymouth, Anniversary. It was a splendid occasion made memorable for two reasons. The first, obviously, was Becton Dickinson's own occasion but it was also the first banquet staged by the newly opened Plymouth Pavilions. The Americans were very impressed and enjoyed every moment.

Becton Dickinson in Plymouth

G.E.C Plessey Semiconductors caused a great stir at Roborough with their new site. Prince Charles condemned it as an eyesore and an insult to Dartmoor but when one watches the growth of the trees and the blossoming of the hedgerows, its stark and somewhat unusual appearance will soften and become part of the landscape.

The Roborough plant uses the world's most up-to-date technology to produce chips of the type known as CMOS (complementary metal oxide semiconductor). These chips require significantly less power than other types and with their densely packed circuitry are especially suited to the demands of communications and computers.

Roborough went into operation in November 1986, processing six-inch wafers of 2-micron CMOS chips (with circuits etched on their surfaces only 2 thousandth of a millimetre across - 50 times thinner than a typical human hair). Since then it has moved on through to 1 micron processes to produce sub-micron chips.

The advantages these ever-smaller and more complex circuits bring are better performance, lower power consumption and a dramatic reduction in the size and cost of some key equipment. Because of the density of the G.E.C Plessey Semiconductors process and the complexity of the circuits, wafers will contain more than 20m components.

Eventually the plant will mean a tenfold increase in G.E.C Plessey Semiconductors capacity to manufacture metal oxide semiconductors, and is the world leader in high-speed bipolar circuits, which it produces at Swindon.

Roborough sets a new bench-mark for what can be achieved by a British company employing the best people it can find and determined to exploit new areas of technology. Some 450 high-calibre engineers and other specialists work at the plant. Automation means that only about 40 people are needed at any one time in the fabrication area at Roborough in order to keep the plant running 24 hours a day seven days a week.

Roborough provides a total in-house production capability including wafer fabrication, assembly and testing and employs the latest computer-aided engineering, design and manufacturing techniques. Quality assurance procedures are built into the manufacturing routines. Rigorous environmental testing of products includes, checks at extremes of temperature and for thermal shock, humidity and mechanical performance.

Most of the wafers produced at Roborough are sent to the Far East to be assembled into packages. They then come back to the plant and are subjected to a final electrical test and inspection. The whole process, from raw silicon to completed chip, takes about 13 weeks, although prototype semi-custom arrays in sizes up to 1 million transistors are offered in only six weeks from completion of design.

The whole building is cleaner than an operating theatre. It is a place of no smoking and no drinking - I have a story to tell about that in a minute.

Semiconductor manufacture demands extraordinary measures to remove dust and other impurities that might impair the performance of a chip. The entire 22,600 square foot wafer fabrication area at Roborough is many times cleaner than an operating theatre - to Class 10 standards (fewer than 10 microscopic particles per cubic foot, compared with several billion per cubic foot in a typical office.)

A series of powerful fans changes the air inside the total clean room area 600 times an hour, or once every six seconds. Air is circulated by both vertical laminar flow and side wall return, enabling any operation to be placed in any manufacturing bay, as distinct from isolating just critical areas such as photolithography.

Ultra-pure water needed for manufacturing processes comes from a de-ionisation and purification plant. This produces electrically inert water containing no particles, either organic or inorganic, larger than 0.1 micron at the point of use, and has an output of 100 gallons a minute (expandable to 150 gallons). There is also a high purity specification for key process gases of less than 0.4 parts per billion for all contaminants.

Critical environmental conditions such as defect densities, temperature and humidity are recorded by an array of detectors in each manufacturing bay and monitored at a computer-controlled central facilities monitoring station.

Needless to say I was completely out of my depth, but fascinated. The high calibre workforce, many of them graduates, were by no means all from Plymouth but had been delighted to have the opportunity of working and living either in or around the city. GEC Plessey Semiconductors have an excellent Sports and Social Club which is a good base for socialising but no one has found it hard to integrate with Plymouth. The company sent its personnel officer out on what is known as the Milkround to its favoured universities seeking the right graduates for the job.

Stuart McIntosh is the Director of Operations, responsible not only for Roborough but also for Swindon, Oldham, Lincoln, Scotts Valley - California, Farmingdale - Long Island and Tours in France. He has been here nine years and lives at Yealmpton but there was a time when he wondered if he would survive the first year!

When the building was still being erected he had his office in a Portakabin in the grounds. He was informed that he was to be visited by the then Chairman, Sir John Clarke, who was known for his low threshold of boredom and also reputed to enjoy his food and drink. The date was fixed and Stuart was told to keep a watchful eye on the Chairman who if he got bored would play with his fob watch. That would be the signal for Stuart to suggest adjourning for lunch.

With limited facilities in the portakabin and the ruling that no alcohol was allowed on the site, Stuart laid on a buffet, soft drinks, tea and coffee. Sure enough around about noon the fob watch was on the move. An adjournment was suggested and accepted with alacrity. Sir John eyed the buffet with a certain amount of disfavour and asked for a drink. When he was offered something non-alcholic his face fell and he turned to Stuart asking where was the nearest good restaurant! A black mark for Stuart McIntosh.

When the official opening was to be arranged, with HRH Prince Charles doing the honours, Stuart was still in charge but he received a memo from Head Office which advised him of the date, the protocol and everything else, but ended up by saying that there would be no need for him to bother himself about the catering; Sir John was arranging it!!

It is interesting to note that G.E.C Plessey Semiconductors could increase its turnover from £200 million to £2 billion as further funds are invested. This is a tremendous challenge in such a volatile market.

Marine Projects (Plymouth) Ltd, is a company of which Plymouth is intensely proud. It grew from a little acorn twenty five years ago into the giant it now is and astonished its founders along the way. David King, the managing director told me that when they started they thought they might sell a small number of boats every year but so well were the boats made, and so popular were they with the sailing and cruising fraternity, that before they knew it they were building and selling 1,000 annually.

This group of craftsmen came together to build the very first Marine Projects production cruiser. Five years later, having already achieved considerable success with their early models, the first Princess was launched. This introduced a new name to the boating public, a name that was to become one of the most famous and most highly regarded in the world of power cruising.

Today, the Princess range is the most successful in Europe. Princess power cruisers are widely acknowledged as the leading craft in their class and can be seen in all the major yacht harbours from Scandinavia to the Mediterranean.

The reasons are simple. Over the last two decades Marine Projects has been responsible for more major developments and innovations in power cruising than any other builder. Princess has frequently been the first with new technical advances, design improvements and styling innovations. A commitment to continuous development and a constant search for new ideas and initiatives ensures that the Princess range will always remain well ahead of the competition.

The same commitment to high standards of quality and service is followed worldwide by Princess distributors. Whether arranging a viewing or demonstration, assisting in the search for a mooring, providing efficient after sales service or simply offering advice, their distributors are experts in their field.

As more and more owners experience the pleasure and satisfaction of owning a Princess, the reputation of Europe's leading power cruisers continues to go from strength to strength.

The Princess 65, for example, came about very much in response to customer demand. Existing owners wanted to trade up, but did not want to leave the make, a brand-loyalty that exists right the way down the range. In fact it is probably fair to say that without this pressure Marine Projects would not have produced a 20m (65ft) boat. The whole scale of the vessel is of a far greater magnitude than anything they were successfully doing before, with a price nearly double that of the next boat down the range. Also new was the sheer complexity of the systems that are installed into what is a small ship rather than a large motor boat. However the company accepted the challenge, and used it as an opportunity to develop their new ideas on interior styling. The fact that the first two years' production of the Princess 65 was sold out 12 months before the boat ever touched the water shows the correctness of that decision.

In styling, design, technology, and craftsmanship, today's Princess sets an example that others can only aspire to. The advanced hull forms have won international acclaim for their consistently outstanding performance, exceptional all-weather handling and economy.

Developed from the well-proven deep 'V' form with its excellent seakeeping qualities, designer Bernard Olesinski has created the unique modified 'V' exclusive to the Princess. This combines the fine entry section that performs so well in head seas with a gradual reduction in deadrise towards the stern, giving better planing performance, improved economy and precise directional stability. It makes the boat much easier to handle in awkward beam and following seas, and gives the smooth ride of a deep 'V' without the need for such high powered engines.

All Princesses now have either the new extended stern profile with its integral bathing platform, or a reverse sheer to the transom. Both of these design features effectively lengthen the hull planing surface, lifting the boat onto the plane more efficiently at lower speeds and also improving performance and fuel efficiency. Precision-designed spray rails also assist in this respect, as well as helping to give a very dry ride.

One of the most important considerations in the design and performance of a powerboat is correct trim. It's a matter over which Marine Projects takes particular care, in order to achieve the best possible ride, handling and drive efficiency. For this reason every new Princess undergoes a painstaking programme of development and sea trials to establish the optimum choice and layout for engines, shaft geometry, propellers and weight distribution. Few other builders can match the depth of development undertaken by Marine Projects in relation to this critical factor, and the outstanding performance that results is probably the single most important element in Marine Projects' reputation as one of the world's leading exponents of power cruiser engineering.

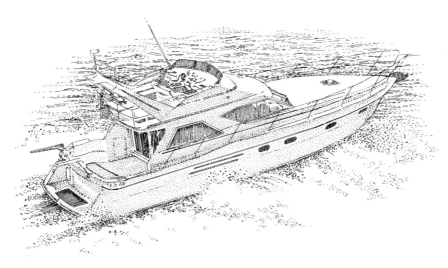

A Princess 398

In this age of mass production, it is unusual to find a major boatbuilder building each craft from start to finish with a single team of craftsmen. The Princess style of team responsibility for each boat means there is a considerable personal pride in maintaining high standards of craftsmanship, with a tangible benefit to the owner in terms of quality and finish.

For equipment and fittings, experience has shown that the best way to ensure consistently high standards of quality is to produce as much as possible themselves. That's why all hull and superstructure mouldings, interior joinery, upholstery and most window assemblies are all manufactured within the company. We insist on the highest standards - who better than Marine Projects to ensure they meet them?

GRP moulding of hulls, decks and superstructures is carried out in Lloyds-approved moulding shops under strictly controlled conditions of temperature and humidity. For the maximum resistance to water penetration, hulls are moulded using a very high quality isophthalic gelcoat backed by a special powder bound glassfibre matt. It is a more time-consuming process than common moulding practice, but it produces a very high quality moulding with a considerably enhanced lifespan.

A matrix of longitudinal and transverse foam cored ribs and stringers are integrally bonded into every hull to create the massive strength and structural integrity for which Princesses are so well known.

Deck and superstructure mouldings are built using a sandwich construction with a pvc/balsa core. This method not only gives exceptional strength for minimum weight, it also provides good thermal and sound insulation for the whole of the interior. This feature, with flexible engine mountings and couplings, extensive engine room insulation and specially designed exhaust systems make Princesses among the quietest cruisers on the water.

Safety at sea is a paramount consideration at Marine Projects. The greatest care is taken over all aspects of design, testing and assembly for onboard systems in order to achieve the very highest standards of operational safety.

Copper gas pipes are sheathed in polythene to provide a double line of defence against leaking. Electrical power comes from generously specified heavy duty batteries with automatic double diode charging circuitry. This ensures that engine starting batteries always receive priority charging, and the chances of being completely immobilised due to low battery power are minimal.

Circuit breakers are used in place of fuses wherever possible, so overloads can be easily reset in seconds. Hydraulic steering lines are copper, affording better protection to hot (sometimes flammable) hydraulic fluid than the more common synthetic hose.

When completed, every Princess, is thoroughly tested to check that every item of equipment and every fixture and fitting is installed and functioning correctly. In addition, all conventional drive craft are put through a full sea trial to verify that handling, trim, performance and top speed are all up to specification.

The care that goes into building a Princess means that every boat they produce is not only a source of immense pleasure and relaxation to its owner, it is also an object of lasting value. Princess motor yachts will always be sought after throughout Europe and around the world, and experience has shown that, as a result, resale values can be much higher than the average. So the Princess owner can enjoy his cruising secure in the knowledge that his investment is surprisingly well protected.

Because they put more into a Princess, you can expect to get more out of it. Better handling, better performance, greater strength and higher reliability all make their contribution, and of course every onboard facility is thoughtfully provided to make life afloat as luxurious, relaxing and enjoyable as it could possibly be.

Is it any wonder that Marine Projects is so successful, even in these difficult times?

On the other side of Stonehouse Creek from Marine Projects, in Richmond Walk, is another, smaller but world renowned company, **JPW Loudspeakers Ltd**. They design and make Hi-Fi equipment which they export to 35 countries worldwide. Peter Wanstall started this exciting business in 1979 with his wife who still helps him in the business today, with fellow director Charles Greenlees. It is a company which has won more awards than most, including the Queens Award for Exports.

This is another company which was helped greatly by the City Estates office and Peter Burrows in particular, when they needed bigger premises in order to expand. I am not knowledgeable about any of this equipment but from what I have been told it is better than almost anything else in the world. Certainly the company's Swedish distributor thinks so. He brought sixteen of his top dealers firstly to Huntingdon to see another company and then to Plymouth to see JPW on an all expenses paid trip.

JPW recognise, too, the value of good staff and enter their shop floor people for the Nat West Shop Floor Employee of the Year. JPW's man won the award and the prize was a trip round the world to the company's overseas distributors.

You get the feeling of energy, drive and success as you walk into the building. There is great motivation and the increasing international stature of the company says the rest.

Another Plymouth company, **Silent Channel Products Ltd**, based at Langage, in July 1992 became one of the first companies in Europe to drive off with a top Ford quality award. They were presented with the QI award after engineers designed a special seal and trim system for American Ford's Crown Victoria and Marquis cars. The company were thrilled but regard it as only the beginning of bigger and better things.

Ford North American Automotive Operation Worldwide Quality Assurance QI status award is only made to companies which can meet particularly tough and stringent quality tests. The award is made by the US arm of the company for component manufacturers, and has been revised into a tougher test.

Silent Channel, which employs 430 staff, came to Plymouth in January, 1990. It is a subsidiary of the American firm, Standard Products, of Cleveland, Ohio, and also has a technical licence with the Japanese firm Nishkawa.

Several factors contributed to their making the decision to come here. The first was the massive grant available, the second was no lack of suitable labour, and the third, and by no means the least, was the greenfield site offered to them.

The company has been a rubber components supplier since 1931, designing and manufacturing extruded rubber and plastic sealing/trim systems for the car industry. Its secret of success is a highly trained workforce, attention to detail, keeping up with modern breakthroughs, and involving employees in the running of the firm.

Silent Channel's Gerald Buckingham is known as the 'Waste Wizard'. He joined the company two years ago as its waste co ordinator and promptly set about saving the firm a massive £336,000 by reducing its waste disposal bill from £32,000 a month to just £4,000. In so doing he put a scheme in place which provided work for additional employees who set up a business within Silent Channel to clean rejected glass for re use in the factory. With the help of Devon County Council he also found other firms which would accept the waste rubber and materials produced by the company for recycling.

All this economic activity has led to more recognition for Silent Channel. The company was presented with the Devon Recycling Award by Brian Wills-Pope, chairman of the DCC recycling co-ordination working party.

This commitment to waste minimisation is typical of the attitude of the company and one that sets an excellent example for other companies.

From a company comparatively new to the city to one which has been a steadily growing influence, **Johnson and Baxter**. The original company was formed by the late Mr A.L. Johnson in the summer of 1945, when he purchased the small plumbing section of David Sale Limited, who in turn were a subsidiary of Rowe Bros; at that time a large Bristol-based builders' merchants.

Mr Johnson changed the name of the company and brought in W.M. Baxter, a local chartered accountant and business friend, although Mr Baxter was only a nominal shareholder for a few years. The company he had purchased had a staff of only five people, which included a blacksmith, a tinsmith, two plumbers and an apprentice, who were housed in very dilapidated premises off Fore Street, Devonport, an area which is now part of the Dockyard.

One of his sons, Bryan, then joined the business and became managing director in 1968 and chairman when Mr. A. L. Johnson died in 1983.

In need of an office they leased very modest accommodation in what was then Princess Square and shortly afterwards they purchased an old chapel in Mount Street, Devonport, which was converted into stores and workshops. These premises allowed the company to expand apart from their normal mechanical engineering installation work, they diversified and turned to the manufacture of copper coal scuttles and hods in quantity. These were virtually hand-made, using very primitive machinery, and those that survived have reached the status of being antiques!

They also manufactured and sold in some quantity, complete house service units, which consisted of a sheet metal box, into which they installed a hot water cylinder and connecting pipework, cold water connecting pipework, drain and waste pipework, all of which was preassembled and fitted to prefabricated houses, which were exported overseas. The integral system that was supplied allowed the local plumbers to join their water and waste connections from the bathroom and kitchen to the unit, which Johnson and Baxter provided. This was quite an innovation in the late 1940's, but the market lasted only a few years, and then totally disappeared.

This did not stop the growth of the company. They moved offices again in 1949 to Ebrington Street this time where they remained for several years.

1957 saw the company on the move again, this time to Wedgwood Villas, Ford Park and here they stayed until 1960 when they bought their existing premises, Eagle Works, Clare Place, Sutton Road, which had combined offices and works facilities and so allowed the company to move its stores and workshops from the old chapel in Mount Street where it had been since 1947.

The Eagle Works premises consisted of old buildings, which apparently had started life as a ship building factory, and on the first floor of the main building they covered in the openings that allowed the builders to erect masts of ships they were constructing on the floor below.

In 1945, the centre of Plymouth, as we know it, was virtually non-existent. One of Johnson and Baxter's first major projects, was the replacement of the central heating system in St Andrew's Church and the Guildhall, closely followed by mechanical services in many of the offices and shops in the new City Centre, including the new buildings for both the Prudential Assurance Company and the Royal Insurance Company. These were followed by many other projects, including Western Trust and Savings, Y.M.C.A., Royal Sailors Rest, Westward Television, and others.

As the city developed, so Johnson and Baxter, working closely with the architects and consulting engineers, installed mechanical services in many of the more recent major developments that have taken place, including the award winning Plymouth Dome on the Hoe. Contracts were won, too, for the installation of services in many schools.

462

Through its reputation for good quality and reliability, the company has become established on all the local government contracting lists, as well as those of health authorities, county councils, Home Office and Property Services Agency.

In 1967 Eagle Developments (Plymouth) Limited was formed and a year later started work on the development of a long-term luxury housing project in the coastal village of Thurlestone in the South Hams.

Over the past years more than 120 quality houses, bungalows and flats have been built, which has seen the village grow in a measured way that has not spoilt its original quality.

In 1972, the Group purchased W.G. Heath & Co Ltd., an old established electrical contracting company, who had been operating in the Plymouth and surrounding areas since 1898. Several of Heath's staff had been with the company for many years, and their knowledge and experience has been of great value to the Group.

Many Plymothians will remember Mr W.G. Heath, the founder of this company who died in 1961 and was a pioneer in the electrical industry. His company were the first to install electric street lighting in Plymouth, and also fitted the first electric motor to be used in the city.

W.G. Heath was instrumental in installing electrical generating plants for the first electricity supplies to many small towns in Devon and Cornwall, at such places as Buckfastleigh, Plympton, Okehampton, Tavistock, Saltash, etc. Later some of these generating stations were taken over by other companies and those in West Devon were incorporated in the West Devon Electricity Supply Company, of which concern he was a director.

He even had a hand in broadcasting, providing the accommodation for the first wireless broadcasting station, 5PY, in the South West at Plymouth under P.P. Eckersley of the British Broadcasting Corporation. There was almost a stampede as people crowded Heath's shop to listen to the inaugural broadcast in George Street in 1922.

From a Plymouth business which has grown successfully to one that I can see achieving great heights in the future if determination, application and a high standard of workmanship has anything to do with it: **S.R. Vosper**, Electrical Contractor is the name.

Born and bred in Plymouth, Stephen Vosper served his apprenticeship with T. Clark and Co., of London and joined the Dockyard in 1978. A little over ten years later there was a great deal of unrest within DML and the threat of many redundancies. Stephen decided to ask for voluntary redundancy and then set up in business for himself. The redundancy was refused but his mind was made up and so he left with just a week's pay in his pocket.

They say that behind every successful man is a good woman this is certainly the case with Stephen. Karen, his wife has given him every possible support from day one. She drew the line at digging trenches and chasing walls but she does all the bookkeeping for the company and deals with the suppliers.

It is his straightforwardness and ability to complete a job skilfully and on time that has won him many contracts - not all of them in Plymouth. He has found that life is tough, the hours long and not much in the way of time off but that one week's wage packet has been put into an excellent investment. Of course, there are bad days but when he comes home he is offered sympathy and understanding and a willingness to listen.

At one time Stephen Vosper was regularly to be seen playing rugby for the Ministry of Defence, Plymouth Albion and Old Tech's but those days have gone and it is his eight-year-old son, Matthew, who is following in father's footsteps and before long 4½-years old Adam will be in the thick of the scrum! His father's leisure-time and frequently Karen's, too, is taken up with the Plympton and Plymstock Round Table, helping with their work. He is currently their Chairman.

Being a Plymothian through and through he looks to being part of the growth of the city and giving as much to the community as he takes out. It will be interesting to take a look at Stephen Vosper, Electrical Contractor, in ten years time.

Devon Co-operative Agency helped five men set up **Beta Blast** in 1988. They had all taken voluntary redundancy from the Royal Naval Dockyard at Devonport, in order to fully exploit the perceived potential in the abrasive cleaning market. It was clear that the majority of other firms were using mainly unskilled labour and offering a service that could be improved. Beta Blast knew that they could offer a more competitive service in terms of price, quality and flexibility. They also have the capability to call on ex M.O.D shotblasters and paint sprayers to make their service complete.

It was explained to me that Beta Blast offer a comprehensive mobile shotblasting, metal and paint spraying service. In addition to this the facilities of machine chipping and high pressure water jetting are available to the customer if required.

In most, if not all, areas of industry surfaces are present which tend to corrode: i.e. steel will rust, concrete weather, paint systems break down etc. These surfaces then require cleaning or stripping back to bare metal. There are many processes which can do this including machine chipping, paint stripping, sanding and burning.

Shotblasting, however, is the quickest and most effective cleaning process of all. This, combined with a hot metal and paint spraying capability to respray prepared surfaces, completes the service offered to customers.

In January, 1989, they expanded with the opening of Wixenford Farm, Plymstock, for the shotblasting, metal and paint spraying of more intricate work that did not need to be carried out on site. They have the facilities to handle anything up to two tons, that is girders, pipes etc.

There is no doubt that these highly trained men have made Beta Blast successful. They give their customers a first class service and it is a company policy to only use labour that has undergone levels of training similar to those that Graham Horne, Ernie Prout, David Barlow, Paul Prouse and Mike George went through while they were in the Dockyard. These courses included Hodge Clemco Abrasive cleaning course, Metco metallisation course, Harben High Pressure Washing course, Dockyard 'in house' courses on spraying and application techniques.

Safety is all important and working in a nuclear complex demands that the highest safety standards be observed. The Royal Navy and Royal Fleet Auxiliary contracts, indeed all contracts, were performed with health and safety standards being rigorously observed. The discipline instilled by such procedures has been translated to all Beta Blast's operations. All personnel are fully conversant with the Health and Safety regulations that are pertinent to the industry.

In addition to the work that was carried out on ships of the Royal Navy including work on submarines, both nuclear and conventional, embracing fuel tanks, freshwater tanks, chemical and ballast tanks and torpedo tubes, these men have specialist abilities in paint application whether it is by brush, roller, spray - airless and airmix. One capability they have is something few firms do on site and that is metallisation techniques including molten zinc spraying and molten aluminium spraying. Their specialist blasting skills include the ability to blast masonry, aluminium, wood, glass reinforced plastic and steel.

Beta Blast are currently one of the major contractors to the South West's fishing fleet, contracting individually to trawler owners. This is an expanding market for them in other areas and other fleets. The boatyards of Philip & Son, Ltd. and Mashford Bros. at Cremyll, are also customers of this successful co-operative.

I was saddened to read of the death not so long ago of the venerable Sid Mashford who must have been well into his eighties. **Mashford Brothers'** boatyard at Cremyll has been synonymous with craftsmanship ever since it built its first boat. The brothers Sid and Sam Mashford set up in partnership in a small sea-front workshop on the River Tamar at Saltash in 1920. They employed three boatbuilders and two apprentices. Sam was a trained boatbuilder while Sid was a seaman cum general factotum and his role was to take care of the books.

They spent some ten years at Saltash building dinghies, Admiralty whalers, sailing boats and launches up to 26 foot in length. With a workshop situated on the wharf they could berth and work on yachts of up to 60 tons. One of the first ones they ever worked on was the gaff cutter 'Jolie Brise' owned by Robert Somerset. This charismatic man sailed the 'Jolie Brise' in the Fastnet and Santander races in 1929 and won both of his particular classes. Sid Mashford crewed for him on one of these occasions. Sadly, Robert Somerset was drowned in later years.

In 1930 the shipyard at Cremyll came on the market to let. The Mashford brothers wanted it badly but although they had plenty of determination and guts, they had no money. Nonetheless they took it on. It was a time of trade depression with little or no work in the yard and no money in reserve. This was either a bold or a crazy step to take but it was a family decision after a lot of discussion. Sid had seven sons aged between 21 and ten. Sam had three sons and two daughters. With both wives and children around the table they decided that if all of them were prepared to put their backs into it they could succeed. Sid Junior joined the firm as a boatbuilder apprentice and for a while ran the Saltash yard but eventually moved to Cremyll with the small staff.

The yard at Cremyll had been used mainly to build and repair steel vessels but before that it was run by Waterman Brothers who employed six boatbuilders and about 40 apprentices who were all expected to wear bowler hats while they were working!

When Sid and Sam and their families moved in to the yard they took on what was little more than a scrap heap with only a couple of open-ended sheds left to work in. One of the first jobs in the yard in 1930 was the overhaul of the Plymouth Lifeboat ON 696, Robert and Marcella Beck. She was 60ft long and it was considered an honour to be trusted with a contract from the RNLI.

As the years passed more RNLI work came along, with repairs to lifeboats from Fowey, Torbay and Salcombe, and this work continues. The yard also overhauled their three largest vessels of 70ft and have had boats sent from as far afield as Scotland and Ireland.

When Sid Mashford died in 1931 his place was taken in the partnership by Sid junior. With no cash in the kitty, the years ahead were a hard struggle, but with the help of the bank and the assistance of a few friends, the firm weathered the storm, ploughing everything available back into the business.

As the years went on all the Mashford sons came into the business - ten in all! New sheds took shape when money came available and at the start of World War II Mashford's was asked to build some 112ft 'B' class Fairmile ML's so a shed had to be extended to lay down two of these together. Other craft came along as well and the business flourished. Private work stopped but the staff increased to a maximum of 120. It was slightly different work from the development of a range of motor and sailing cruisers that they were building every year. They could produce an 18ft carvel sloop for £100 and dinghies were only £1 per foot. I hate to think what they cost today.

One hull of a 23ft sloop was all that was left of the pre war boats and this was sold to a bachelor yachtsman in 1945 who had it completed to his bachelor requirements. He used it for a season and then Ann Davison came along and bought it with the intention of sailing it single-handed to America.

Modifications were carried out and in 1950, with no previous sailing experiencel Ann Davison made the first transatlantic crossing by a woman. The boat was the 'Felicity Ann'.

Mashfords is very different today. Peter Lavers, the son in law of Sid Mashford Junior, and Maurice Mashford, are the joint managing directors. Peter was kind enough to show me round the yard and as we walked he told me about other famous single handed voyages which started out at Mashfords. Gipsy Moth III, IV and V all came here. Sir Francis Chichester owned all three of course. The first one won the first Transatlantic race ;n 190 beating Blondie Hasler whose idea it was. The time taken was 40 and a half days. Sir Alec Rose, Chay Blyth and Eric Taberley all sailed from this yard in single handed races and the lovely old ketch 'Kathleen and May' was refurbished there.

In recent years they have built commercial fishing craft, yachts varying in length from 30-50ft, carried out maintenance of HM Customs launches, and made life rafts for the Admiralty and private use. The work of maintaining the NLI boats still takes up a large part of the work programme.

The yard has always built boats of wood in the traditional manner but there have been no contracts for wooden hulls since the building of the 54ft 'Lone Star' in 1983. Peter Lavers has fond memories of that boat when he took a trip in her with her American owner and went from the Virgin Islands to Texas via Jamaica and Mexico.

Today Mashfords continues to carry out fishing boat repairs and yacht maintenance, besides work for the Dockyard, the RAF and the Lifeboat Service. There is a very special feeling about this yard which smells of the sea and creosote.

Good advance planning has been very much the cornerstone upon which **Kevin Cooper Motor Factors** has been so successfully built. The company which deals in motorparts and motor accessories, had the foresight to create a ring of shops around Plymouth, believing that customers with broken down cars would appreciate a shop near their locality.

In 1980 Kevin Cooper returned to Plymouth after a career in the motorparts business in Hampshire. Plymouth was a city well known to him since part of his childhood had been spent in the city and he still had relatives living in the city.

The company's main branch is situated in Martin Street, off the Octagon, close to the city centre. The shop was the first one opened by the company in 1980, and formed part of a motoring centre with other garages and allied services, grouped together in what had previously been the old Octagon brewery. As the company grew, the main warehouse and offices had moved out of the city to Lee Mill, where a new store had been built, but space restrictions still hampered the expansion of the Martin Street shop. By one of those strokes of fortune the freehold of the whole Martin Street building became available in 1980 when Kevin Cooper acquired it, allowing the whole company to come back together under one roof.

Having opened shops in Plymstock and Plympton on the eastern side of Plymouth, each of which was very productive, the company decided to look for suitable premises to the west of the city centre in the densely populated St Budeaux area. 99 Victoria Street was the chosen site and it opened as the company's tenth branch in July 1987.

Another chance for expansion in Cornwall came when the proprietor of a motor factors business in Bodmin approached the company with an offer to sell. By January 1988 Express Auto Parts of Bodmin had become another Kevin Cooper branch.

With a population of 250,000, Plymouth obviously offered the largest potential business and having now established a presence first on the eastern side at Plymstock and Plympton and on the western side at St Budeaux, the possibility of finding suitable premises in the northern area was investigated. It had been in this part of the city that most housing development had taken place and where there seemed to be most of the population now living. A building which had previously been used as a garage had long stood empty on the corner of Crownhill village. This was investigated and found suitable, and the Crownhill branch opened on this site in February 1988.

Continuing the expansion programme in Cornwall, the Company sought and obtained Planning permission to convert a furniture storage building into a shop in Bude; three months after the Crownhill shop got off the ground Kevin Cooper opened in the popular holiday resort of Bude. The company has expanded in Devon and Cornwall and now has established outlets in Okehampton, Tavistock, Launceston, Ivybridge, Totnes, Liskeard and St Austell as well as nearby to Plymouth, at Torpoint and Saltash.

The business flourishes largely because of the expertise and hard work of the owner and his staff and because of the company's early computerisation. Kevin Cooper has developed, if not invented, their own computer catalogue giving instant information for all models of British and foreign cars and light vans irrespective of their manufacturer, with each model and engine variation listed separately. This data-base gives a powerful tool to the counter staff who have access to parts, not only for current models, but for older models which have been removed from the manufacturers catalogues.

In a changing and ever more sophisticated world Kevin Coopers have employed the very latest techniques to give their customers the best possible service.

Westcom in East Street, Stonehouse, is an interesting business, the brainchild of Nick Strachan who wanted a business where he was in total control of the quality service it offered. Initially he thought of Telecommunications but his experience in that field was 20 years out of date, and he accepted that the market was well catered for. So when the new cellular technology was launched, he decided to establish a mobile phone business. Offering a high quality back up initially cost Westcom dearly, but he accepted the principle that reliable service was a vital ingredient for company growth. An example is their 'Two Hour Pledge' which basically promises the client that he can he back on 'air' within two hours of bringing a faulty phone to either of their service centres during business hours. This policy is typical, since their aim is to offer the kindest after sales care available. In consequence Westcom enjoys a very high proportion of new business simply by word of mouth.

Westcom for instance were the first company in the U.K to be endorsed by the R.A.C. in a television advertising campaign. Mr. Strachan explained that for a small firm to receive such an endorsement from one of the U.K's highest profile companies, who themselves flourish purely from delivering high quality service, was indeed confirmation that Westcom were going in the right direction. The R.A.C. agreed to the T.V. campaign about eighteen months after Westcom solved the technical problems of installing 'Hands Free' carphones on R.A.C motorbikes. Providing solutions is becomming a niche for Westcom since they now also manufacture the 'Tecfone' which provides contractors and wideload drivers temporary communications to the police from contra flow road works, in locations where B.T. landlines would not be cost effective.

Westcom Fazing and Westcom two way radio were set up in 1992 so as to offer the complete mobile communications range. Mobile communications is a fast developing market place and Westcom look forward to offering products and service in the new technologies which are shortly to be available throughout Europe.

Finally, I have decided in this chapter to write about the extraordinary building in which Leisure in Print, my publishers, have their office and warehousing **Quickstore** in George Place is a vast warehouse with just three offices plus the manager's office, and innumerable small lock-up steel storage rooms. In this vast warehouse all sorts of people from the banks to H.M. Customs and Excise store everything from boats and cars to books and furniture. Private individuals can rent space for whatever purpose - legal that is! I have seen the contents of houses being stored here, boxes of all kinds. There is a carpet warehouse and many more things. Quickstore are efficient and the whole place is secure. It is inexpensive, too. You can rent a store from as little as £12 per week plus VAT and it is accessible whenever you wish between 8.30am and 5pm Monday to Friday and 8.30-1pm on Saturdays.

Leisure in Print is a busy office bringing out a book just about every two months in its 'Invitation to Lunch, Dine, Stay & Visit' series and other publications in between.

Vision Home Improvements are Leisure in Prints' next door neighbours. This friendly, family run business has more than fifty years of experience in the fitting of UPVC windows, doors patios, porches and conservatories. Run by Brian and Sandra Calder they are not tough double glazing people at all. Their reputation has been built on quality and service at sensible prices.

Brian was telling me that the recession has hit them like many other businesses but they did the sensible thing and upped their advertising budget rather than cutting it and so have kept the business running steadily. With their team they operate in Exeter and Torbay and into Cornwall as far as St Austell.

In the ten years that Brian has been in the business he has seen many changes: companies come and go and fewer houses need windows, but the positive mental attitude is always to the fore. Some older types of double-glazing needs replacing and more and more people are enjoying the luxury of a porch. There is always business out there ;f you are prepared to look for it and once having achieved it, honour the contract to the letter. This way produces personal recommendations which are worth their weight in gold.

Next door is another local company, **Select Vending**, serving local organisations like ourselves and bigger, with a quality vending service. One based on the philosophy that quality in ingredients combined with quality service from local people will invariably prove the least expensive in the long run.

Select Vending specialises in machines manufactured by Wittenborg, Europe's largest manufacturer of Vending Equipment. Machines that are technologically advanced, superbly designed and engineered to last, market leading machines that are selected by many of the world's leading employers for their quality, reliability and longevity.

There can be absolutely no doubt that the quality of the taste you get from a vending machine depends entirely upon the quality that is put in. So if the taste you end up with is any less than you settle for at home - colour, strength, richness, aroma, then somewhere along a compromise has been made.

Select Vending believe that the real key to customer satisfaction is totally efficient, reliable and dedicated service. Dedicated to responding in the shortest possible time. Dedicated to maintaining the equipment in first class condition. Dedicated to the customer's needs at all times.

This is why the company only operate in a relatively small localised area. They can react fast and so keep their promises and provide one of the best and most efficient quality vending services to be found anywhere.

They offer the service on several levels. They will simply supply and service the machines if this is what you need. But they can supply the quality ingredients of your choice. Plus all the consumables such as cups, filters and cleaning materials. The Customer Care Contract makes them responsible for everything - machine, servicing and maintenance, ingredients, sanitising and cash collection. It leaves you free to concentrate on what you do best. I know of many satisfied customers who use Select Vending.

If I had not been convinced of the healthy future of Plymouth before I wrote this chapter, I would certainly be so now. There is so much talent, brainpower and sheer enthusiasm in the companies that I have talked to: it is stimulating and exciting.

CHAPTER 17

Within easy reach of Plymouth

One of Plymouth's greatest assets is the additional benefit of wonderful countryside, beaches and the moors within easy reach. It does not matter whether you strike out towards the ruggedness of Dartmoor, seek out the gentleness of the countryside and villages of the South Hams, or collect your passport to gain entry into Cornwall by crossing the River Tamar by ferry to Torpoint, or the sweeping structure of the Tamar Toll Bridge to Saltash: everywhere has its own charm and its devotees.

The main road from Plymouth to Tavistock will lead you very rapidly to the beginning of Dartmoor. You either love or hate the moor: there is no half measure. Most people fall in love with it and it is a bit like a good marriage: sometimes turbulent, sometimes inexplicable, mysterious, exciting, infuriating, but always beloved. Within its encompassing arms you wake in the morning never knowing what the day will bring.

People who live on the moor are a breed apart, generous enough to want to share their love affair with outsiders and astonished if your reaction is not the same as their's. No intrusion of man, since prehistoric times, has managed to conquer the wildness of this granite mass, some 130,000 acres in all.

There are fundamental lessons to learn about Dartmoor before you start exploring. It is a National Park, but that does not mean you have unlimited access. For example, it is an offence to drive a car more that 15 yards off the road.

You are asked not to feed the ponies because it encourages them to stray onto the road, putting themselves and road users into danger. There is a severe fine for those who do not heed this request. One other important point is to take note if red flags are flying on the north side of the moor. This means the army is at work. Disobey the warning and you could get shot.

It is not a place in which to take chances. People die of exposure on Dartmoor. The weather can change in minutes from glorious sunshine to impenetrable mists. On a summer's day it looks as if butter would not melt in its mouth. Do not trust it. It is easy to get lost and very frightening. In heavy rain it becomes almost sinister.

If you have only a little spare time to explore, a round trip that will take you from Yelverton to Princetown and Tavistock and then back through Horrabridge to Yelverton again, is ideal. There is constantly changing scenery, rugged moors, isolated small moorland farms, rough coated ponies and grazing sheep belonging to these hardy farmers. In places the land is lush, in others sparse and riddled with gorse and heather. You will see the tors and the valleys as you wend your way until you arrive at isolated and forbidding **Princetown**, the home of Dartmoor Prison. These forbidding walls were first raised in 1806 by French prisoners-of-war who were forced to erect their own gaol. It must have been appalling. Even on a summer's day Princetown is never the warmest of places and in the swirling mists of winter, penetrating rain eats into one's very soul, so these poor devils must have hated the guts of every Englishman.

In 1812, the French prisoners were joined by hundreds of captured American sailors, who built the church. Its beautiful east window lights up the greyness of the interior. It was donated by American women in memory of two hundred of their kin who died in captivity. There is also a memorial inscribed to Sir Thomas Tyrwhit 'whose name and memory are inseparable from all great works in Dartmoor'. It was this wretched man who suggested Dartmoor prison should be built, a memorial of which Devon is not proud, and a prison sentence for the offender to this barren fortress, sends shudders down the spine of the most hardened criminal.

There is happiness in Princetown and that is to be found in the welcoming warmth of the **Plume of Feathers** where James and Linda Langton have wrought miracles since they arrived there in 1968. James is the son of the man who started the **Rock Complex** at Yelverton, now operated by James' brother. The Plume was the first building to be erected in Princetown in 1785 during the reign of George III.

Here you will get good company, good ale and super food. The beamed ceilings are the originals and with slate tables, copper lamps and log burners, it has a thoroughly comforting atmosphere.

Without in anyway detracting from the antiquity of the pub, the Langtons have a camp site for Dormobiles and tents just across the car park. It is the only one on the moor. In a sort of hostel, known as the Alpine Bunkhouse, you can stay in what are effectively two dormitories with ten beds in each, a kitchen, dayroom, toilets, showers and drying room - something you will find essential on Dartmoor. If you prefer something a little more sophisticated there are letting rooms at the Plume. Children are welcome and a special adventure playground has been designed for them.

A wandering road will take you down into **Tavistock** a fine Stannary town and the birth place of Sir Francis Drake. Here is a place steeped in history which will give you a great deal of pleasure, whether you explore the parish church with its magnificent windows and its great sense of history - Drake worshipped here - wander amongst the array of shops and the market or pop into **The Bedford Hotel**, now a distinguished part of the Forte empire. The river runs at one end of the hotel and on its banks are the ruined walls of the abbey. I love the shops and especially Crebers, an old fashioned grocer's that smells of sugar and spice and all things nice and has an array of some of the unobtainable delicacies not to be found in Plymouth.

The Abbey to all intents and purpose governed the little town and its markets so when Henry VIII gave the Abbey estates to his friend, John Russell, the first Earl of Bedford, it must have meant considerable change. By this time the trade in wool had brought the town new life and prosperity, and everything went swimmingly until the Civil War when the town was held for Parliament by the Earl of Bedford but changed hands no less than six times.

You can still see the stones in the heart of the town around the square laid out by the Duke of Bedford, who spent his mining royalties in doing so.

In the vicarage next to the hotel are the most picturesque fragments of the abbey and the Great Gate with the abbot's prison in the ruined tower above it. Betsy Grimbal's Tower is also here. She was a nun who was loved by a monk. He, perhaps from a sense of guilt, perhaps from rejection, murdered her.

The abbey saw much history in the making. One of the young abbots became so great he was chosen to crown William the Conqueror. One of the first printing presses in the country was set up here, and in the medieval church I have witnessed the sadness of death when a young American friend of mine buried her mother beneath its wonderful pinnacled tower, wide nave and glorious gables. One of the three aisles was built for the Clothworkers' Guild, with a lovely roof of carved beams and bosses. The font is 500 years old; who knows, Drake might have been baptised in it. The church is a place of peace and exploration and worthy of your time to look at its treasures.

Just up the road from the church, the unpretentious **Cornish Arms** in West Street is an excellent spot for lunch. I didn't think from the outside that it was a pub; it looks more like a restaurant. I liked it and so did my purse.

If you have time to spare before you start the journey back to Plymouth you might drive out of Tavistock on the Okehampton road and take a look at the two Tavys, Mary and Peter. Twin villages which grew out of the settlements on either side of the River Tavy. Each has a church linked by a bridle path and a little bridge. **Peter Tavy** has an old and very attractive hostelry which provides good food, warmth and a great atmosphere.

Just a little further up the hill and on through **Mary Tavy** you will see the engine house of Wheal Betsy, which was part of the extensive workings of an old lead and silver mine. Women worked on the surface of this mine breaking up the ore. They were known as Bal Maidens. Bal is an old word for mine which is more often in use in Cornwall than Devon.

At one time Mary Tavy housed Wheal Friendship, the largest copper mine in the world, later producing arsenic which was exported from **Morwellham Quay**. A day's outing to this fascinating place which takes you back in time is something you should try to do. You will find people there in period costume and a wealth of interesting things to see and explore. It is another world. You will find it well signposted on the Tavistock-Callington road.

I am tempted to take you further into the moor towards **Brentor** where Gibbet Hill was once the gruesome place at which wrongdoers were hung and left dangling at the end of the gibbet as a deterrent to anyone thinking of stealing sheep or becoming a highwayman. The condemned were kept waiting for their execution in a cage at the foot of the hill on the Brentor road.

This road leads you across some of the most beautiful stretches of the moor and before very long you will see Brentor church high up on the tor as near to our maker as you can possibly get. A strangely beautiful place with a dedication to St Michael de Rupe. There are several legends about how it came to stand, 1100 feet above sea level, and only accessible after a difficult climb. My favourite is the one where the church was being built at the foot of the hill but every night the stones that were laid were removed and rebuilt at the top by the devil, because he reckoned that no one would love God enough to climb the rugged tor for worship. It took 700 years for him to be proved almost right! Now there is a chapel in the village itself and the church on the tor is seldom used.

In **North Brentor** lives a lady who may well interest you. Her name is Sally Wetherbee and she owns a small nursery, specialising in cultivating a wide selection of culinary, fragrant and medicinal herbs. She started it with her husband in 1983, when they both knew he was dying of cancer. The result is a wonderful living memorial to a courageous man. There is nothing morbid about Sally Wetherbee. She is a practical, hardworking lady who has built a successful and interesting business which she is more than delighted to show you on her open days. Herself a skilled cook and with a great knowledge of dairy products, she is often to be met at wine and cheese tasting evenings when she is either displaying or talking to those who want to learn. Frequently the cheeses she uses will have come from the Hungry Palate in Frankfurt Gate which I have told you about already.

Another place you might seek out whilst you are so far out is **Countryman Cider** at **Felldownhead** where a fascinating couple, Bob Bunker and his wife, Anne, tackle making some of the finest cider in the Westcountry. It is a business that was almost non-existent when they bought it but with the same resolution that Bob Bunker showed when he was one of the first men to tackle the single - handed transatlantic crossing way back in 1964, he and Anne cleared out the rotting barrels, rejuvenated the presses and fought long and hard to obtain the right size and shape containers which hold the exact measurements laid down by the E.E.C. That was a surprisingly difficult task. I learned from them that even if you are successful in finding a supply there is no guarantee that delivery will be on the promised date. This is a malaise that damages a growing business and, surely with all the people out there unemployed, there must be someone who would tackle supplying pots of the right shape and size to firms such as Countryman Cider and many more who need such a product throughout the country.

The danger in writing a book like this is that one gets carried away and wants to describe some of the many wonderful places that really are within striking distance of Plymouth but if I do the book will be too big, so restraining myself we will return to Tavistock and take the pretty, leafy road back to Yelverton via **Horrabridge** and stop there at the **Leaping Salmon** in the village. This delightful pub looks out onto the River Walkham, the second fastest rising river in England. It can be swollen by heavy rain to several feet in depth and within half an hour be back to normal.

Pino and Eileen Di Bello have been at the pub for some years and have always hoped that the brewery would eventually sell it to them but no such luck. It is too good and the brewery are determined to hang on to it. Born of Italian parents in Ethiopia one wonders how Pino arrived in the quiet backwater of Horrabridge. Apparently he met his wife Eileen, who came from Barnstaple, whilst he was working in London. After they married they went to live in Barnstaple and as their children grew up they looked around for a nice pub and eventually found the Leaping Salmon. Although Pino's mother tells him he used to speak fluent Arabic he now only remembers the swear words and how to count from 1-10!

You will find that inside the Leaping Salmon it is almost like two pubs. The public bar, used by locals, has three darts teams, two euchre teams and two pool teams and following this enthusiastic sporting side, the establishment sponsors two football teams.

In the lounge bar/restaurant which has 60 covers, the emphasis is on food. Pino will tell you that people come to eat and not to play pool or darts. This is understandable because the food, which covers everything from a freshly cut sandwich to a huge mixed grill, is beautifully cooked, fresh and appetising. The daily specials blackboard can be full of surprises. How often do you see tripe and onions on the menu today? Another rarity is barracuda steak which is very popular.

Open from 11am-11pm with meals every day of the week, Pino and Eileen concentrate on giving value for money. They firmly believe that if you do this and not get too greedy on profit margins, which so many people do, the business will thrive. This is certainly the case here and consequently the recession has affected the Leaping Salmon hardly at all.

Onwards to **Yelverton** where you will find the village divided - not against itself - but because the main road to Tavistock has created the barrier. Tucked away in one section is Leg O'Mutton Corner where the **Bangkok Palace** is one of the finest Thai Restaurants in the country. People come from miles just to savour the food and the atmosphere.

Outside the restaurant you will see that Suree Stanton, the owner, has placed a shrine from Thailand in honour of Phrad Narai. The god Narai is said to have powers to grant all sorts of wishes, from a male child to a successful business. Believers offer garlands of flowers, incense sticks, and carved wooden elephants to please the spirit, and if their wishes are granted they often sponsor performances of Thai classical dance in gratitude.

Each evening a fresh glass of water and small bowl of rice are placed on the shrine. You will see also many garlands, small wooden elephants and horses which have been left to please the spirit.

Once inside you are enfolded in the gentle atmosphere of Thailand. This is an exotic country in the heart of southeast Asia, a land where the past and present meet to produce a kaleidoscope of stunning attractions, coloured by a unique culture and enduring traditions. Giving life to this enchanting world are the gentle and hospitable Thais; indeed a country of golden places and smiling faces. Nothing is hurried and the waiting for the superb Thai food only heightens the anticipation.

It may be that while you wait you will talk to some of Suree's family who help her. They are always happy to talk about their homeland and give advice, if required, to anyone thinking of visiting Thailand, especially if they are not going with a package tour. In fact you do not even have to be a customer here to have a chat; you are welcome to call in or ring up and ask questions.

The Thais' love of good food ensures excellent dining nationwide in their own country. The cuisine is distinctive thanks to the liberal use of spicy ingredients and combines the best of Chinese and Indian culinary traditions - noodles, curries, sweet and sour dishes, lengthily cooked and fast-cooked ingredients, exotic spices and condiments - while retaining its own very special character.

Since the majority of Thai dishes are either soft or soupy, chopsticks are not used at a Thai dinner; a spoon and a fork are usually the only utensils provided.

Most of the trade comes from regular customers and from word of mouth. It is a truly memorable place in which to enjoy an evening out. Suree is opening a second Thai Restaurant in Elliot Street in Plymouth in time for Easter 1993, to be looked after by her husband. I am looking forward to it as I am sure many other people are.

One of the things that always brings me to Leg O' Mutton Corner is the **Yelverton Paperweight Centre**. On my first visit I had no idea what to expect as I walked through the door into a room full of well-lit cabinets and showcases, housing paperweights of every conceivable shape and size. It was the radiance of the colours that first struck me. Then I began to take more notice of each individual piece and wanted to know more.

This is where the Yelverton Paperweight Centre becomes so special. Kay Bolster owns the business, and with Susan Portchmouth, now her right - hand woman, worked for the late Bernard Broughton, whose collection forms the base of the Centre. He was an incredible man who first started showing his collection in St Tudy, Cornwall in 1968 and later moved to Yelverton. His love for these beautiful objects and for the history of paperweights rubbed off onto Kay, who had little knowledge at all when she started working for him. It was her instinctive love of beautiful things which had surrounded her in her formative years, that developed in the years they worked together. When he died, Kay bought this unique business and with the invaluable help of Susan, she has built a tremendous following all over the world. These two charming and knowledgeable ladies will talk to anyone and make a point of doing so, showing the uninitiated like myself some of the facets of the world of paperweights.

The Yelverton Paperweight Centre is celebrating its 25th anniversary. The collection today has some 800 paperweights on permanent exhibition and is reputed to be the largest private collection in Europe. Among these beautiful objects are many from the factories of Baccarat and St Louis who make the finest French paperweights. Both the casual visitor and the serious collector are fascinated by the beautifully handcrafted Millefiori and abstract designs.

I fell in love with the Millefiori weights, which consist of a great variety of ends of fancy canes cut sectionally, at right angles with the filigree cane to form small lozenges or tablets. These, when placed side by side, and massed by transparent glass, have the appearance of a series of flowers or rosettes. If you think I have suddenbly become an expert on paperweights, I have to confess I am cheating. When I left I was so enthralled by what I had seen that I read avidly anything about paperweights that I could find. When you see all the different types, the flowers, the whirls, the butterflies - even reptiles - all encapsulated in beautiful glass, I am sure you will be as eager to learn more as I am.

Collecting paperweights need not be a costly business, although the most expensive one in the world costs £99,000 in 1990. Here one can start from the modest price of under £5 rising to somewhere over £1,600.

The Yelverton Paperweight Centre is unique. As far as I can discover there is not another one in the country. It attracts collectors from all around the world. Admission is completely free; there is also free parking.

It is open from two weeks before Easter until the end of October, Monday to Saturday 10am-5pm. Sundays from the end of May until mid September 10am-5pm. Winter Wednesdays from 1pm-5pm and Saturdays 10am-5pm. From the first of December until the 24th it is open Monday to Saturday 10am-5pm - a wonderful place in which to buy a special Christmas present or two. Kay is delighted to welcome parties over 25 providing she is telephoned first. The number is 0822 854250.

A paperweight from the Yelverton Paperweight Centre

From Leg O'Mutton Corner you can virtually see **Harrabeer Country House Hotel** in Harrowbeer Lane. Owned by Ron and Patsy Back they run it as they would their own home, which so happens to bring them in a little income as well. It works splendidly. Many business people come to stay and rapidly become friends, bringing their families back to stay at a later date. It is not only people from this country who find Harrabeer House. Patsy told me that on one night they had Germans, French, Swedes, Welsh and English.

This is an hotel to which you can bring your pets free of charge - all the Backs ask is that you will leave a donation for the local animal rescue.

Delicious home-cooked meals are always available for residents , and by prior arrangement for non-residents. There is a comfortable lounge but it does tend to get neglected because everyone tends to congregate in the bar area which has an enormous log fire.

I have a different memory of this fine house. It used to be the Officers' Mess for the R.A.F squadrons flying from the aerodrome which took up all the land around and was the cause of many houses in Leg O'Mutton Corner having to lose their gabled roofs and replace them with a flatter variety - the planes needed the height to land on the runways. Many good parties were held in the house, and some sad occasions when pilots did not return.

193 Squadron, who flew Typhoons, were based here and they had a duck as their mascot. The duck was taken every evening for a trip to the nearest hostelry - usually The Royal Oak at Meavy. Here the duck would dip his beak into any beer mug he could get too and frequently end up absolutely pixilated. I understand he never suffered from hangovers!

Memories are very important and I am quite sure if you choose to stay at Harrabeer Country House Hotel you will have nothing but fond memories of two very nice people, the Backs and their helper , a Yelverton lady, whose family have lived in the village for years and is a fountain of knowledge. You will also never forget the gigantic breakfast offered to you each morning.

A good many people come to Yelverton to ride across the moors and they get their mounts from the well established **Crossways Riding School** in Axtown Lane. Once a racing yard, Alex Howard and her husband, Bob, bought it in 1984 and have steadily developed it into the highly respected establishment it is today.

They both have a basic love of horses and people - I hope they will not take offence when I say that I believe the horses come before people! They have twenty five horses, with school horses and liveries.

Dartmoor gives a lot of options for the rider, depending on the weather, the time of the year and the level of skill the pupil has. Alex likes to think that Crossways is a riding school with old fashioned values, not a trekking centre as so many stables are. Crossways gives instruction to B.H.S exam level and has working pupils training for their certificates.

As well as themselves, the Howards have two qualified instructors in their staff of six. It is very much a team, all working together for the good of the horses and the stable. People are made very welcome and not in the least cliquey as so often happens in the horsey world. They are particularly good with new and nervous people and with small children.

I was interested to find that Crossways has 'Stable Days' in which people are introduced to the art and skill of stable management rather than riding. It is very popular and quite rightly so with such professional people running it.

The art of riding side-saddle has come into its own again and here you can get instruction in this elegant style. Several of the Crossway horses can carry side-saddles and a visiting instructor is available.

If you are worried about making a fool of yourself if you have never ridden before, you truly do not have to worry here. They are practical, sympathetic and will laugh with you rather than at you. A great place.

One important role Crossways plays is through the South Dartmoor group of Riding for the Disabled Association. The stable offers both riding and driving instruction. We are talking about traps, not cars, incidentally. One trap is specially adapted to take a wheelchair. Lessons for the able - bodied who want to drive a trap, are also available.

I learnt that before a pony can qualify for use by the disabled, he has to be put through a two hour test.

The Moorland Links is on your way back to Plymouth from Yelverton. I have told you about this splendid hotel already but you will be able to see it for yourselves if you just turn off the main road to the right where it is signposted.

If you were leaving Plymouth on the Kingsbridge road, en route you would come to **Yealmpton**, and the **Kitley Estate**. This has been in the same family for generations and one of its great attractions, **Kitley Caves**, attracts thousands of people every year. I talked to Mark Bailey, the marketing manager for Kitley Estates who has been instrumental in turning the enterprise into such a success. I will tell you about the 'Farm Shop' first. This started as a small business in a shed set up to sell the produce from the estate. This quickly developed into a substantial business and is now a very large shop selling a wide range of produce, including honey from bees who find the fruit crops ideal! There are some speciality goods and what is really a delicatessen although I do not suppose Mark Bailey would describe it quite like that. Whatever one names, this enterprise is superbly run. It is clean and absoultly professional but not quite what I envisage as a 'Farm Shop'.

Attached to the shop is an enormous conservatory housing winter and summer bedding plants for sale. It really is an absolute must for gardeners. You can wander round here to your heart's delight, getting advice if you need it and remain dry even if the weather is a little inclement.

I am told that between 35-40,000 people come here every year and the number is growing, thanks largely to Mark Bailey's ability to get things moving. He keeps house and thoroughly enjoys living in this area although he hails from Shrewsbury. He has every intention of staying.

Also under his aegis are Kitley Caves which were undiscovered for many thousands of years until local quarrymen accidentally uncovered a cave entrance whilst blasting for limestone in the early 1800's. Since then much has been discovered and is being discovered; about how the caves were formed, the extent of the system, about the creatures that have lived in the caves and those who have died, even about the quarrymen and the part limestone played in the local economy.

It is one of the most fascinating places to visit in the area and a splendid booklet, written by Mark Bailey, is available for you when you visit. It is able to trace how the caves were formed. It is interesting, if a little unnerving, to realise that the limestone from which Kitley caves were started off as the skeletons of billions of living creatures. Caves such as those at Kitley are the result of acids contained in water dissolving the rock and carrying the solution away: typically caves start as tiny holes dissolved out of the rock and as these grow so they can carry more water which in turn can dissolve greater volumes of material.

Throughout much of the period of cave development animal and plant debris found its way into the caves. There are still bats there today but it is suspected that other animals actually made their homes in the caves. It could have been hyenas and bears; the fossil remains of both have been found on the site. Kitley Caves are endlessly exciting to scientists because of the information they unveil about themselves, the ever changing environment and because of the light thrown on cave development. For laymen it is equally enthralling, the colours of the calcite formations are exquisitely beautiful - sectionalised formations are on display in the museum.

Excavation is still continuing. The cave passages illuminated and safe for visitors, form only a fraction of the cave system at Kitley. The caves sit on a block of limestone covering an area of over two square miles and from the evidence of trial digs and geological surveys, the area is honeycombed with cavities.

Kitley is set in beautiful countryside and the Woodland Trail through the woods starts just outside the museum. The first thing you will notice is the boulder field, draped in ivy; a great jumble of massive boulders which stretch as steeply upwards to a rock peak known as Wester Torrs. It looks as though it has something to do with quarrying but that is not so. It is entirely natural and was caused by the action of temperature fluctuations alternately freezing and thawing water in fissures within the rock and consequently splitting chunks away from the bedrock.

At one point you will see a steel gate blocking the entrance to a cave which is too dangerous to admit anyone but a serious caver. In here in the summer of 1987 a number of flint tools were discovered. These would have fallen in from the surface and do not suggest that the cave was inhabited by prehistoric man although we do know that there was a human settlement somewhere in the woods. Stone Age men lived in numbers in South Devon.

The path winds its way among vast beech trees which I am told are coming to the end of their natural lives. There are wild animals, birds and insects along this route for you to see. The larger animals that live in the woods around Kitley Caves are unlikely to be seen in daylight but in the stillness of the night foxes and badgers are quite a common sight in the light of a full moon.

Finally the children's playground comes into view below the trail on the other side of the river. As you walk along the riverside back to the car park take time to stand on the wooden bridge which spans the River Yealm and take stock of the beauty that surrounds you. In summer it is peaceful but in the winter months storms can turn the trickling river that flows some ten feet beneath the bridge into a raging torrent that rises to within three feet of the wooden walkway. Whole trees are caught up and swept down in the frothing angry cataract. The rise in the water level also has its effect on the caves' interior where sections become inundated.

The River Yealm rises in the foothills of southern Dartmoor and the source of the Yealm is itself a notable beauty spot, particularly attractive to those fond of walking in rugged and beautiful seclusion.

Back at Kitley Caves and past the second lime kiln, an underground or cave stream joins the river through a hole in the bank. This is known as a resurgence. Following the River Walk downstream, past the brick towers that once supported the railway bridge which carried trains on to Plymouth and the Yealmpton branch line, past a series of magnificent oak trees on the river bank, there is a shallow weir with a hut on the far side and a calibrated post on the near one linked by wire ropes. This is a Water Board guageing station used to measure the Yealm's rate of flow, which on average is thirty six million gallons a day.

At one time many salmon were found in the Yealm but now, sadly, hardly a salmon makes its way upstream to spawn. The salmon population was devastated by salmon disease, much in the same way that myxomatosis rabbits. Thankfully the disease is on the wane. The life cycle of salmon is disrupted by widespread netting both inside and outside the estuary mouth which has hit the Yealm especially badly. You may still be lucky enough in the autumn and winter to see a salmon swimming powerfully upstream to a suitable gravelly spot in the headwaters where it makes a shallow depression, called a redd, into which it lays hundreds of eggs. There are still trout to be seen which attract the avid kingfisher - the most spectacular angler of all the birds! The river is always entertaining and always beautiful no matter what time of the year just as Kitley is. A day spent in this extraordianry place will stay in your memory for a very long time.

Kitley Caves are open Good Friday till the end of October, (or end of half term, whichever is later) from 10 - 5p.m. Last admission at 5pm. Adults £2.90 Children £1.50, discounts for Students and OAP's.

Leave Yealmpton and only a short way along the main road towards Kingsbridge you will see a turning that points you in the direction of the **National Shire Horse Centre**, a place in which you can happily spend a day. It has steadily grown in size and stature over the years. Here you can see the gentle giants of the equestrian world, the Shire Horses, with their new foals, a Falconry Centre with flying displays, the Butterfly House and the amazing freefall slide. There are special play areas for children of different ages. A horse drawn cart will take you on a pleasant amble through the centre. Patient archers teach people this ancient art, you will find a Blacksmith working at his forge, there is a craft centre with a saddler and a glass engraver. It is a day filled with excitement.

The Centre opens from 10am-5pm seven days a week and every day at 11.30 there is a parade of Shire horses in the main arena. At 1pm, weather permitting, the same arena is used for a falconry flying display, and again at 3.30pm. The main event of the afternoon is the special parade of Shire horses in the arena. It is called 'The Age of the Horse'. Wonderful to watch and at the end you are encouraged to go down into the arena to become acquainted with these truly magnificent animals. Finally at 4.15pm there is another short parade of Shire horses.

You will find several restaurants and bars, ice cream stands and a takeaway. It is a good value day out.

The owner, Mr Flower, was telling me about his plans for the future which include putting up a huge complex on the land to include a hotel, a new stable block and a 300 - seat cinema. There would also be a new covered display arena and an expansion of the Falconry Centre and a Museum. It is a plan welcomed by the West Country Tourist Board and Plymouth Marketing Bureau.

The National Shire Horse Centre

The narrow roads leading on from the Shire Horse Centre would take me to one of my favourite places in Devon, **Alston Hall Country House Hotel**. It was not built until 1904 but has all the hallmarks of a gracious country house standing in four acres of grounds. The whole has an Edwardian character complete with croquet lawn. The only concession to the modern days is the outdoor swimming pool. The house belonged originally to the Sayers family who have done so much for the county and for the preservation of Dartmoor. Dame Lucille lived in this treasured home for over fifty years and became a renowned expert on peonies. It is her love and knowledge of gardens that can still be enjoyed today. Her memory lives on in the house in the restaurant which is named after her.

I remember this hotel with affection as far back as the beginning of the sixties when I used to take my children there for a super cream tea and a swim in the pool on idyllic summer afternoons - at least in one's memory one always thinks of wonderful summer days. Since then I have been there many times but it was not until the last four years that its rebirth took place. During this time every bedroom has been refurbished and made en suite, the wonderful library bar has not been changed but given a face lift. The Great Hall is magnificent and welcoming, whilst the minstrel's gallery running around it just waits for the players. Everywhere has been lovingly restored until you have what it is now, probably the best country house hotel in this part of Devon.

Tim Pettifer, the general manager, will tell you it is the only true country house hotel in Devon. This man's leadership and drive has achieved recognition in the shape of an AA rosette. Previously unrated, it already has AA three stars and is striving for four.

Conferences and corporate business sustain the hotel during the week and at weekends there are parties and individuals who have learnt and experienced how good it is to stay or dine here. Guests can enjoy membership of the leisure club during their stay. Facilities include a large indoor heated swimming pool, gymnasium, solarium, sauna, and all weather tennis courts.

This is an hotel that is sufficiently flexible to be able to undertake all sorts of different occasions. Recently Tim held a party for secretaries of the managing directors of many of our Plymouth and surrounding area companies. Not only did the guests enjoy it but it was much easier for them to see what was available when their bosses wanted some sort of occasion organised.

In the restaurant there are regular promotions. Every Thursday is devoted to 'A Taste of Italy', which includes an authentic two course Italian dinner with fresh pasta and a half bottle of wine. Sometimes it will be 'The Taste of the East' perhaps Japanese, perhaps, Thai or Indian. These are great evenings and at sensible prices. Sunday lunch is a 'Dip and Dine' attraction. You can enjoy a swim and the leisure facilities before or after a full three course meal and coffee.

It is value for money that is the criteria on which Tim Pettifer runs Alston Hall. This does not mean it is cheap - it is not - but the surroundings are wonderful, the service terrific and everything about it is right. Alston Hall Country House Hotel should not be missed.

Ivybridge just ten minutes up the A38 from Plymouth is one of the fastest growing small towns in Europe and yet not so long ago was a quiet village. Its growth has allowed many things to happen and brought business to some interesting places.

I have an affection for the **Hunting Lodge** which you will reach at Cadleigh just before you come to Ivybridge. My first interest in it was because of the proprietor, Richard Odgers, whose ability to take on the challenge of establishments that were suffering and turn them within a year into thriving and successful venues, says much for his tenacity, courage and personality.

The Hunting Lodge was his first venture into ownership. Before he had been a 'troubleshooter' going to pubs that were in need of better management. His last task in this role was at the Hunting Lodge where the previous owners were near to retirement. He agreed to stay slightly longer than his norm, on the understanding that he would get the chance of buying it when they retired.

It was nearly three years before the deal was done, by which time he had been able to assess the potential and decide what needed doing to improve the place. The bars were altered and intriguing stencils appeared on the walls. Old stonework was uncovered, the small dance area was changed. New loos, attractively decorated, took over from the rather tatty ones. In short, he has turned it into one of the nicest pub restaurants in the area.

At lunchtime the big restaurant is shut, but in the large, interesting bar good pub food is served from 12 noon until 2pm. It is excellent value as people in the nearby industrial estate have discovered.

It is at night that the Hunting Lodge sparkles. The candlelit restaurant is open, complete with its beams and rafters. The menu is not extensive but it concentrates with great success on first class grills to which one can add an extra sauce if required. Live music and dancing are part of the entertainment on Saturday nights.

If you have ever organised a staff outing or an office Christmas lunch you will appreciate the efficient way in which the Hunting Lodge works. Organisers take on the task willingly and know that they will have satisfied customers on the day. How is it done? Simply ensuring that constructive discussions take place early on. Everyone orders the meal of their choice in advance and then Richard ensures that a copy of each person's choice is given to the organiser, with a copy for the guest; the final copy remaining with the Hunting Lodge. A coach is available if it is required to ferry people - indeed every little detail is covered.

I discovered new things about the Hunting Lodge quite recently. A meeting of the Dolphin Association was taking place. Who are they? People who are as fanatical about clinker built boats as vintage car owners are about their mechanical beasts. Apparently this is their regular meeting place.

Richard has also added what he describes as 'Country Style' accommodation. What he really means is comfortable bedrooms, where you will sleep well, be warm and come down to a breakfast equally as good as the previous night's dinner. Great for people touring or for those of us who want to dine well, enjoy the wine and definitely not drive.

Just behind the Hunting Lodge is one of the most popular sporting venues in Devon. **Dinnaton Sporting and Country Club** has just about everything and it is great fun to belong. Owned and run by Graham and Carole Powell with the help of a very efficient and caring staff, Dinnaton has two different purposes which are also integral pieces of the jigsaw that make up this successful place.

For local people wanting somewhere to enjoy sport whether it is to play golf on the 9 hole course which presents a challenge to even the most experienced golfer, or, maybe it is somewhere to take the family to swim. One of the main and most popular features at Dinnaton is the 25 metre indoor swimming pool. The pool water is kept at an enjoyably comfortable temperature within the fully air conditioned surroundings. If you want to work out every modern facility is available. A versatile gymnasium equipped with its Powersport Multigym and Power Jogger allows for everyone's keep fit requirements - from females in need of light exercise and 'tone up', to the experienced athlete training for competition.

Before you work out on your own a qualified coach is available to provide a valuable short course of instruction if required. There are sauna, steam and solarium suites which have the best in modern day equipment. The relaxation area will allow you to unwind or, perhaps, enjoy the beauty care and massages available. You can play squash on one of the four courts, which include three glass backed Perstorp Championship Courts and on the same semi sprung wooden floor two Badminton courts wait to be played on.

For snooker players there is a match play table in a specially designed room. Dinnaton truly has everything.

I sat talking to Graham Powell in the coffee lounge which overlooks the swimming pool. Here you can relax with a drink or enjoy a light meal which is available throughout the day.

All this is only part of what Dinnaton is all about. In addition behind the sporting area there is a delightful block of buildings nestling around an attractive courtyard. Here you can stay in comfortable rooms, use the facilities and enjoy the fun of the club. Also The Courtyard contains The Haywain, a complex of a Restaurant and various rooms fully equipped for business conferences or seminars. It is also used in total for weddings and other functions - the courtyard makes a wonderful place for photographs with the colourful walls of the building making a perfect backdrop.

The Haywain restaurant is open all the year round, especially to non-members. Here you can dine in atmospheric and charming surroundings. The menu is always interesting, beautifully presented and fits comfortably into most people's budgets. Sunday lunch is traditional and for a modest fixed price families can enjoy a three course meal starting with a choice which will probably include the Chef's mousse or pate of the day - quite delicious. The roast beef or pork perhaps as well as the Chef's special of the day, served with crisp roast potatoes, boiled potatoes and three seasonal vegetables is quite liable not to leave room for you to enjoy a choice of dessert from the trolley. Follow this with coffee and mints and you will leave the table delighted but in need of a little of the exercise that Dinnaton provides.

The Haywain can accommodate up to 100 people and has the benefit of its own private bar. It is a delightful venue and somewhere I am happy to recommend.

Perhaps after lunch instead of swimming or playing squash you might decide to take the family to the **Dartmoor Wildlife Park** at Sparkwell. The park is situated on the south western edge of Dartmoor in thirty acres of beautiful Devon countryside, three miles from Plymouth and one and a half miles from the A38. It has been developed in the grounds of Goodamoor House, an old country mansion which stands in the centre of the park. This was the home of the Treby family for many years and they also had the village inn at Sparkwell named after them - the Treby Arms, somewhere you should visit.

Sparkwell has one of the most comprehensive 'Big Cat' collections in the South West, a falconry centre second to none and a very successful animal breeding programme. If the weather is not too kind the barn is the venue for 'Close Encounters of the Animal Kind', a 'hands on' talk, touch and learn session, which is fun, informative and educational. Children of all ages respond to it.

I enjoy the two acre 'walk in' enclosure where you can wander at will and mingle with friendly birds and animals. There are pony rides for children, an adventure playground, picnic areas and much more. For the exhausted parents or elders there is a large licensed restaurant and bar in which to revive your flagging spirits. The car park is free to both private vehicles and to the coaches who come from quite a distance. Dartmoor Wild Life Park is open every day of the year from 10am until dusk.

Ivybridge itself is a bustling place which has somehow managed to cope with its fast growth and not lost the feel of a village. One business that I went to see is really traditionally the essence of village life - a bakery. Man may not be able to live on bread alone but it is essential and what better smell is there than bread as it comes out of the ovens? In the centre of Ivybridge, May and Ray Dunn with their son Trevor run **Dunn's Family Bakery**, a hive of activity from the early hours of the morning. Trevor starts the ball rolling at 2am in the bakery where he is joined an hour later by Ray. Here they prepare and bake the range of enticing loaves and rolls. By 6.30am May is there, too, preparing to open up the shop at 7.30am when you can be sure she will be very busy making and selling freshly filled rolls and sandwiches to workmen who know this is the only place open in the area. Everything is prepared and cooked on the premises, including their own meats. Freshness is the key to everything this hardworking and enterprising family do.

They bake about 200 loaves a day, fifty percent of which are white, and the others various health type breads. It is a fascinating operation. Four small shops and an equal number of pubs in the area have discovered the excellence of their products and so the business is growing. Ray also ices celebration cakes. He will tell you, modestly, that he is self taught and is not an expert, but customers keep on coming back, so he reckons he must have got it right!

Dunn's Family Bakery is a fine example of what can be done with a small business today.

On my way back in to Plymouth having been to the bakery I called in at one of my favourite places, the **Endsleigh Garden Centre**, which has something new everytime I go there.

One tends to think of a garden centre being a nursery where you can buy plants but not so here. It is a world all of its own in which you can enjoy the magic that it conjures up. This eight acre site has been skilfully utilised to cover comprehensive needs. There is a central sales area of some 30,000 square feet, with a two acre outdoor plant sales area on the south side. Specialist franchises are almost all on the north boundary of the site. Car parking is easy with space for about 500 cars. People come here regularly from Plymouth, Torbay and Exeter to enjoy the Centre, and get advice on the many aspects of gardens and gardening.

Robin Taylor is the owner and the driving force of what must be the most successful enterprise of its kind in the area. Originally Robin and his brother bought just four acres in 1972, in order to establish a garden centre outlet for plants raised on their father's nursery at Endsleigh, Tavistock, but it has grown. Enlargement to twice the acreage could have meant a hotch potch, instead of which it is laid out superbly and logically.

I am always impressed when I go there by the helpful, intelligent staff who are to be found everywhere and in the four information centres. These are people who do not mind a simpleton like me asking questions which are quite trivial. They are as helpful to my small needs as they are to the serious gardener spending a lot of money. This team work is part of the philosophy taught by Robin Taylor who is insistent that courtesy is shown to all customers. He is the sort of man who does not expect anyone to do anything he would not do himself.

Talking to him, one would expect to find an ardent gardener, but he will tell you quite openly that it was not his love of plants that brought him into the business but strictly as a viable economic proposition. I believe it was this approach to it that has brought him so much success. He is objective and not a dreamer.

It is this objectivity that made him look seriously at the benefits of employing selected specialists on a franchise basis in order to ensure that Endsleigh could offer a comprehensive service to its customers. There are several such enterprises now covering aquatics, ponds, pools, saunas, garden buildings, conservatories and horticultural machinery, as well as an aviary and animal centre, where I spotted chipmunks!

Catering is also franchised and in the main sales area you will find an attractive area in which you can get excellent home-cooked food. Sitting there you will be fascinated by the enormous collection of teapots on the surrounding walls, with pretty jars of conserves and other things. I am a collector of teapots and quite often go there just to see if I can find something new for my collection.

Before I take you over the River Tamar to some of my favourite places just into Cornwall, I should tell you about **Saltram House** as a place of great beauty and also tell you something of the traumas that beset those who care for our heritage - in this case, the National Trust.

You approach it along a sweeping drive which prepares you for the wonder of this Grade I listed Georgian house, built in the 18th century by the Parker family.

The National Trust does not like to think of Saltram as a museum, but as a home. It is their wish that visitors should feel that they have arrived whilst the family is out. Everyday silver is left out, as if it were going to be used, and everything has been arranged in the house as it would be if it were lived in. You can wander along the stone flagged floors, marvel at the beautiful and ornate pieces that adorn the walls, ceilings and floors. It is quite blissful but a nightmare for those who have to care for it.

The administrator will tell you that the National Trust is changing its ways and becoming more commercially aware. It is quite obvious that increasing sums of money are needed if we are to conserve our national heritage. The sad thing is that the greater the public's interest in our wonderful houses, the more people visit them, and the influx of people can cause more harm than monetary gain because of the resulting damage to the buildings and their contents.

How are the National Trust handling Saltram? Well, treating it in many ways as families would have done in the great days of country houses. Often they were only lived in for a few months of the year and the remainder of the time shutters were closed and furniture covered. Practically the same thing occurs at Saltram today. The house is open from April or Easter, whichever is the sooner, and closes for the winter months from October.

Saltram over the years has suffered much wear and tear, more so now with such an increase of visitors the previous decade. A lot of the furnishings have been damaged by sunlight. The silk wall hangings, Chinese wallpapers and original carpets are very fragile. These carpets cannot be walked upon so special carpets are laid down for the visitors.

To protect the colours of carpets, upholstery, paintings and textiles, the windows are fitted with ultraviolet filters and the light is controlled by drawing Holland blinds. Every evening the shutters are closed and all the silver is put away. Every morning, just before opening, the shutters are opened. this is just one way of conserving these wonderful historical artefacts.

The humidity of the house has to be kept constant all year long. It has to be monitored every day. If the level rises suddenly this can result in untold damage.

The house is spring cleaned from January until opening time by specialists taking the utmost care. One of the servants in the time of the Morley's (the last family to live at Saltram) is now one of the Parker residents of the house and she can remember when the nine carpets used to be dragged outside in the early morning, turned over and dragged across the dew to clean them. There is no use of ordinary furniture polish, which contains acrylic and would ruin the wood. Special polish is used just once a year. Scaffolding is put up to clean the high shelves and ceilings. The vacuum cleaner has a piece of netting attached to it to catch any precious pieces that might fall off the ceiling, ornaments or paintings. The offending piece is then rescued and taken to the restoration room for repair.

Contingency plans against any eventuality have been taken by the National trust. The library contains irreplaceable material, the oldest book being the Nuremberg Chronicle, and there are some superb Rembrandt etchings to add to everything else of beauty and antiquity. If, God forbid, they were damaged by water following a fire, then Saltram has the co-operation of a blast freezing company who would blast-freeze everything that was damaged by water and remove them to cold storage until such time as the conservationists could use their special techniques to dry them out. I had no idea what a complex task it was caring for this sort of property. It was an eye opener, and has made me even more appreciative of all that is done to allow the general public the sheer joy of sharing the wonder of our heritage.

One of Saltram's major assets is the park. As the house becomes more and more fragile, entertainment is transferred outside. Saltram has hosted Anglo-American fairs, paid for by the organisers. The Lions Club, one of Plymouth's very active fund raisers, takes advantage of the setting, too, on occasions and pays for the privilege, of course. The courtyard and stables are an attraction and this is enhanced by the possibility of a carriage taking visitors round the estate. On most days the park is free for use by anyone, but it is closed from dusk to dawn.

The National Trust have been imaginative and hard working in seeking monies to help maintain this beautiful house. One of their fund raising enterprises is a series of concerts, mainly of classical music, held either in the Saloon by candlelight or in the Orangery. Imagine the tones of a harpsichord playing Mozart, fragile light flickering over breathtaking scenery, with the stillness of an autumn evening catching every note. Parts of the house are lit by candles for these splendid occasions and visitors are allowed to look around. It is quite magical.

Saltram House

Crossing the River Tamar can be done by several means but I am going to take the little passenger ferry from Admiral's Hard in Stonehouse across to Cremyll on the edge of the Mount Edgcumbe estate.

The journey takes only ten minutes and you pass to your left the magnificent, historic, Royal William Yard and to your right the modern, busy Mayflower Marina with yachts of many different countries moored along its pontoons.

Looking at **Mount Edgcumbe House** rising majestic above the tree-lined avenue from Cremyll, is quite wonderful and it is almost impossible to believe that you are looking at a building that lay in ruins,a victim of the Second World War. Over the last thirty years it has been rebuilt and once again its grace adorns the park. It is equally interesting and quite moving to know that it was the vision and determination of Kenelm, sixth Earl of Mount Edgcumbe, and his architect, Adrian Gilbert Scott, that caused the ancestral home of the Mount Edgcumbe family to rise, like a phoenix from the ashes. I am always moved because Kenelm did it knowing that he had no son to inherit and the line would pass to the New Zealand branch of the Mount Edgcumbe family. Kenelm's son was killed in World War II and is remembered in the private chapel of the house dedicated to him some two years ago. I like to think that the whole restoration was started by Kenelm and continued by others after his death in memory of Piers Richard who was killed at Dunkirk in 1940. It was such a courageous act of Kenelm. With no direct heir, he could have walked away from the ruins.

My first memory of the Mount Edgcumbe family was in the thirties when, as a child, I was occasionally taken sailing with my father in the sleek dark green, ocean - going yacht which lay at anchor just off Cremyll, belonging to the 5th Earl, another Piers. Afterwards I would be given tea in the big house, perched on a chair with my small legs trying hard to reach the floor. I have nothing but happy memories of this great house.

Now I walk through the formal gardens towards the house, I love every moment: the English garden, so called because it is the picturesque shaping of the beds that earns its name, not the exotic plants. Then what is now the Italian Garden containing the Orangery where you can get a very good cup of tea and excellent home-made cake. The marble fountain, the stairway, the statuary, all make it enchanting. The French parterre garden, all of them protected by large hedges of evergreen, oak, laurel and bay to provide essential shelter.

The great green sweep of manicured grass takes you up the drive to the house and through the Earl's garden which surrounds the house. This was probably laid out sometime in the early 18th century and now consists of lawns, terraced walks and shrubberies. The lawn area to the east has been returned to its mid-Victorian beds, and one of the three summer houses within the Earls Garden has been beautifully restored by the 'Friends of Mount Edgcumbe'. This is the Cedar Seat which looks across Barn Pool to the Hamoaze and Plymouth Sound.

The Shell Seat, a fragile dome like structure in the Earl's garden, has been restored. Shell grottoes were much in vogue in the latter part of the 18th century and because of Cornwall's interesting geology and its many mines, a number of grottoes and seats were built using a mixture of both minerals and shells for internal decoration. Sadly now only two remain in the county. The Mount Edgcumbe Shell Seat is all the more precious for this reason.

There is no way that I am going to have space to tell you all that I would wish to do about Mount Edgcumbe Country Park which belongs to the people of Plymouth and Cornwall and through which they can wander, picnic, sunbathe and enjoy the fabulous scenery, wildlife, and birds that are all an integral part of this fine estate. Philip of Spain promised it to his Admiral, Sidonia Medina, if he was successful with his Armada.

Mount Edgcumbe House has stood looking out over Plymouth Sound for over 400 years and in that time kings, princes, poets and painters have all enjoyed its hospitality. Now we are able to enjoy the restored house. Not with all its treasures because so many of them were destroyed but under the responsibility of Plymouth City Museum and Art Gallery, the hall, library, drawing room and dining room are all magnificently restored.

Mount Edgcumbe House

When you walk into the entrance hall you will find some interesting pieces of furniture, two tables thought to be of the 18th century, cannons of the 17th century and a small George III cannon used for signals. There are late 17th century chairs, straight backed and upholstered Coronation chairs used at the Coronation of Queen Elizabeth II. This really gives you an immediate insight into the collection of furniture that has been gathered to furnish the house. Much of the furniture was saved and this was later augmented by additions from Cotehele and the Edgcumbe's London house. It all has an interest and is set off by the lovely, warm colours on the walls, apricots and blues, showing off the fine plasterwork. There are some fine portraits but none to compare with those lost when the Germans destroyed the house. The house then contained an oval dining room hung with portraits of the family going back in unbroken succession to Piers Edgcumbe of the Civil War. Only one of these survived, Richard, the second Lord Edgcumbe (1716-1761), who had been the black sheep of the family - his portrait was stored in the basement and survived to outlive his more respectable relatives. Three beautiful seascapes by William van de Velde are probably the best of the other pictures to survive.

It is the joy of wandering through this house and catching glimpses of the stunning views that makes it so appealing and in another sense it is the great effort that has gone into recreating the original house for the benefit of Plymouthians. I just wish more of them took the trouble to visit the house. Even the park does not get the number of people it should and yet it is free. For those of us who do use the park and love it, we are probably blessed with the fact that it is not crowded. Here you can walk for miles and seldom see anyone.

There are many walks. Cremyll to Redding Point for example, will take you about 1½ hours and goes via the Avenue to Barnpool, Milton's Temple and Lady Emma's Cottage, originally a small thatched house built in the 'picturesque' style of the early 19th century. Emma was the daughter of the second Earl of Mount Edgcumbe (1764-1839) and she used it to entertain her weekend guests. It was rebuilt about 1880, and is now leased to a private resident. From here it zigzags uphill to the Earl's Drive and Redding Point, returning to Cremyll Lodge Visitor Centre via the top of the Amphitheatre.

The least hard work is the three miles around the coast via Maker into Kingsand and Cawsand. One I often took as a child but I doubt if then I appreciated the beauty around me; I would have taken it for granted! Follow the track towards Maker and you will see Maker Church, sometimes referred to as St Macra's. It is first mentioned in 1121 but during the second half of the 15th century it was almost entirely rebuilt. The 70ft tower is a landmark for miles around and was used as an Admiralty signal station in the 18th century when its own crew passed messages by semaphore to Devonport Dockyard and to Mount Wise.

Before long you find yourself looking across the Sound to the Mewstone jutting out of the water near the Devon Coastline. Follow the track as it slopes into Hooe lake valley - a misnomer because there is no lake! Almost immediately you get a superb view of Cawsand Bay ahead of you surrounded by the eastern coastline of the Rame Peninsula, and terminated by Penlee Point with the fog warning station below.

You just keep going, passing Hooe Lake Cottage, originally a huntsman's home, now a private house. From the road the view back to the left includes the Breakwater and the Lighthouse, and in the meadow nearby is a white navigational beacon. Opposite the cottage there is a stile on the left hand side of the road. Cross the stile and follow the path around to the right, where you enter a dense copse of evergreen oaks, known locally as Dark Trees. This track is part of the Earl's Drive which extends from Mount Edgcumbe House to Penlee Point, where in the 19th century there was a liveried gatekeeper.

Coming out of the copse you have a clear view of Kingsand and Cawsand. Between Cawsand and Penlee Point a terrace of what were once coastguard cottages stands out. A few hundred yards further on you pass by a footpath branching off to the left. This gives access to the tidal Sandway Point and the beach below. It is here you will see the remains of some of the old fish cellars where catches of pilchards were sorted and packed in cases for overseas shipment.

Before you reach the village of Kingsand you will climb the steep slope of Minadew Brakes rising to over 400ft at a point inland just beyond the still threatening walls of the now disused Grenville Battery which dominates the skyline. Pass through the gate, turning sharp right almost immediately opposite the road Lower Row, onto Devonport Hill. As the summit is approached the views of Plymouth Sound, Staddon Heights, Bovisand Bay and Wembury are unsurpassed and behind them the rolling Devon Moors.

Your reward for this walk, if the beauty was not sufficient, will be a visit to the **Rising Sun**, an inn which is not only hospitable but has some of the best food, including crab dishes from local crab caught mainly off the headland or the Eddystone Rocks, that you will find anywhere.

Reputably a former Customs House, the Rising Sun, is a listed building, dating back to the 1700's, when the Royal Navy 're-vitalled' from Cawsand Bay to avoid the temptation of the flesh pots of Devonport for the largely 'pressganged' sailors. Henry Tudor is said to have used the path outside during his clandestine visit to England whilst in exile. Kingsand is believed to have derived its name from this visit and the fact that during the 1700's and 1800's the Kings Men or Revenue men as they were better known were based here to patrol Cawsand and Cornwall - Kingsand in those days was in Devon.

The adjoining villages of Kingsand and Cawsand are so much part of my life that I tend to go towards them like a homing pigeon. I spent the greater part of my childhood there in a house on the hill, overlooking Cawsand Bay and leading into the Square. A blissful life for any child. I had my first boat, a small rowing dinghy with lightweight oars by the time I was five and progressed from there to a larger dinghy with sails. Every free moment was spent in that boat. I remember lying at anchor under the lea of Penlee woods whilst I studied for my School Certificate as it was in those days. I remember the young midshipmen from the the giant aircraft carrier, Hermes, and the battleship, Rodney, sailing their whalers into the bay at weekends and usually taking several of them home for tea.

Whenever I go there it is always a case of I remember. I will never forget the sunlit mornings when the sound of the waves, gently lapping, were the first things I heard when I opened my eyes. I remember the storms when the wind blew so strongly that one could not stand up on the hill and the rains would come tumbling down the hillside, right through the backdoor until they found an escape at the front. I remember the old fishermen, the

Hancocks, the Williams and Sam White, a great character who taught me how to fish. I remember the occasion when we caught a small shark in his nets and had to bring it ashore. The nets were ruined but Sam and I thought up a scheme whereby we took it into a yard by Cawsand Beach, mounted it on a trestle, polished the now very dead shark, and then opened the doors to the public charging them one penny a time to look at the monster! I can also remember helping him with his ice-cream stall on hot summers' days. The pay: as much ice-cream as I could eat in wafers that always ended up a soggy mess before the ice-cream was finished. Wonderful! I remember going to church in St Andrews and sometimes in the little Norman church at Rame Head, which to this day has no electricity and is the most atmospheric church I have ever been in.

Sundays would have been a lot happier for me if I had been allowed to go to the Congregational Chapel in the village, especially on Sunday School Sundays when the children all had special, frilly, brightly coloured dresses and wore straw hats with flowers and ribbons. To dress similarly was always my ambition but my attire was far more austere and the Church of England did not have these wonderful Sunday School specials with the outings as well. Strange what one remembers.

Just close by the old chapel, across the narrow street, the Old Ship Inn still stands. This was owned and run by a colourful character called Fred Eteson whose fame in my eyes was his friendship with Gracie Fields, who came to stay regularly.

Because of the geographical position neither of these two villages has ever suffered too much from the twentieth century. The streets are still narrow, the houses and cottages charming and the people who live there seem to be able to stand back from the 1990s and enjoy life. Of course the position was the most wonderful place for smugglers who carried on their nefarious trade almost unscathed. Every house in the villages was in some way part of the activity. I believe there are still tunnels leading from Cawsand beach into caverns, blocked today, of course.

My late father, who was a total pillar of society and declared absolutely everything from his travels abroad, thought nothing of a little smuggling in my childhood days. He would not have considered it so. He merely carried on a tradition started by his father and grandfather before him. The French crabbers sailed into Cawsand Bay regularly and when they came ashore they brought water casks. They would arrive at our house, the contents would be decanted into suitable containers, the water casks filled with their rightful contents and the Frenchmen would depart with a smile and some money. My father's dinner parties were renowned for fine wines and brandy!

There is a bus service which will take you back to Cremyll and the ferry if you do not wish to walk but whichever way you cross the water you must not miss these two villages which have won 'The Best Kept Village in Cornwall' for the last two years.

If I had come across the Torpoint Ferry to reach Cawsand I would have driven through the winding leafy lanes up to Tregantle and then taken the coast road to Rame and down into Cawsand. This gives you quite the most stunning seascapes of Whitsand Bay which stretch right round as far as Downderry. The cliffs drop fairly steeply below the road and it is quite a climb down to the beaches but the long stretches of golden sand outweigh the energy expended.

Had you not taken the fork at Antony to Tregantle, the road would have taken you on through winding roads, with sudden and unexpected glimpses of the creeks of the River Lynher, through Sheviock with its splendid church, the old village of Polbathic and then to a point where the road joins the main Plymouth-Liskeard road at Trerulefoot.

There you will see on your left **Windy Ridge Eating House**, a remarkable business which has grown from the time when it was just a stopping place for lorry drivers, into a good, inexpensive restaurant, where the food is plentiful and it is ideal for families. Not only can you eat well here but businesses in Plymouth are now able to benefit from the efficient sandwich delivery service from Monday to Friday. The choice is wide and the bread and rolls crisp and fresh. Just something for you to bear in mind.

If I am wanting an evening out in a special place then I would choose **Heskyn Mill** down from Trerulefoot at Tideford, just nestling in the Tiddy Valley. It is a beautifully converted 19th-century corn mill and the unusual restaurant is a unique and highly acclaimed venue for lunch or dinner.

Part of its charm is the machinery which is still intact and in working order. The large chimney beside the building was to aid a steam engine, housed in the adjacent barn, which used to keep the mill wheels turning during water shortages.

A wood burning stove gives a warm welcome to a very cosy bar area, where a small menu is available at lunchtimes. Upstairs, amongst the wheels and machinery, is the restaurant, where a full a la carte menu is served all week apart from Sundays and Mondays. The menu is mouthwatering and innovative - the chef is without doubt dedicated. Whether you are entertaining business colleagues or just visiting the area on holiday, this is a perfect venue.

Continuing into Plymouth, perhaps having looked at the charms of St Germans first, you will go up hill and down dale until you come to the Saltash bypass and there before you will be two great feats of engineering, the modern Tamar Bridge linking the two counties by road, and one of Isambard Kingdom Brunel's masterpieces, the Brunel Railway Bridge built in 1859.

The Tamar Bridge and the Brunel Railway Bridge

INVITATION TO PLYMOUTH
INDEX

511

Name	Address	Telephone No.	Page
Lukes Fruit Farm	Tamerton Foliot	785022	398
Masonic Inn	Stoke	562541	406
Mutley Conservative Club	Mutley	663358	413
Old Smithy	Elburton	492874	397
Paws of Perfection	Hyde Park Road	661976	415
Plymstock Book Shop	The Broadway, Plymstock	403672	394
Present Company	Devonport Road	607062	403
Plymstock Inn	Church Road, Plymstock	402127	394
Pippin Fruit & Veg	Devonport Road, Stoke	563238	404
Tamar Hotel	Crownhill	771445	397
Skin Deep Hair & Beauty Salon	Ridgeway, Plympton	344258	391
Threshers	Mutley Plain	664435	412
Trevor Burrows Photography	Stoke	564216	400
Village Fayre Delicatessen	Crownhill	789607	398
Weider	Mutley Plain	253884	411
Yvonne's Florist	Mutley Plain	664864	409

CHAPTER 16 - COMMERCE AND INDUSTRY - THE FUTURE OF PLYMOUTH

Name	Address	Telephone No.	Page
Adams Bakery	Estover	695901	439
Algram	Langage Industrial Estate	342388	436
Ashfords Bakery	Union Street	663410	440
Barden Corporation (U.K.) Ltd	Estover	735555	424
Becton Dickinson	Belliver Industrial Estate	701281	448
Beta Blast	Kings Tamerton	396570	464
British Aerospace	Clittaford Road	695695	433
Devon & Cornwall Development Bureau	Derriford	793379	422
Feneck Naval Outfitters	Union Street	665763	441
G.E.C. Plessey Semiconductors	Roborough	693000	452
Gleason Works Ltd	Estover	739661	426
J.A.D.	Estover	696000	435
J.P.W. Loudspeakers	Ocean Quay, Richmond Walk	607000	459
Johnson & Baxter	Sutton Road	664231	461
Kevin Cooper	Martin Street	673573	469
Kestrel Injection	Kestrel Park	793073	446
Leisure in Print Publications	Stonehouse	256957	472
Marine Projects	Newport Street	227771	455
Mashford Bros	Cremyll, Nr Torpoint	822232	466
Murata	Estover	696696	422
Plymouth Marketing Bureau	St Andrews Court	261125	419
Quickstore	Stonehouse	223337	471
Ransome Consumer	Bell Close, Plympton	346555	447
Select Vending	Stonehouse	257666	472
Silent Channel	Langage Industrial Estate	346580	460
Stafford-Miller	Estover	730311	433
Toshiba Consumer Products	Roborough & Ernesettle	785411	441
Vision Home Improvements	Stonehouse	250100	472
Vosper, Stephen	Cumber Green, Plympton	335661	464
Wandel & Goltermann	Burrington Way	254314	443
Westcom	Stonehouse	667100	470
Wrigleys	Estover	701107	430

CHAPTER 17 - WITHIN EASY REACH OF PLYMOUTH

Name	Address	Telephone No.	Page
Alston Hall Country House Hotel	Holbeton	075530 555	490
Bangkok Palace	Yelverton	0822 852939	480
Bedford Hotel	Tavistock	0822 613221	476
Cornish Arms	Tavistock	0822 612145	477
Countryman Cider	Felldown Head	082 287 226	478
Crossways Riding School	Yelverton	0822 853025	484
Dartmoor Wildlife Park	Sparkwell	075 537 209	494
Dinnaton Sporting & Country Club	Ivybridge	892512	492
Dunns Family Bakery	Ivybridge	892523	495
Endsleigh Garden Centre	Ivybridge	892254	495
Harrabeer Country House Hotel	Yelverton	0822 853302	483
Heskyn Mill	Tideford	0752 851481	506
Hunting Lodge	Ivybridge	892409	491
Kitley Caves & Estates	Yealmpton	880202	485
Leaping Salmon	Horrabridge	0822 852930	479
Mount Edgcumbe House	Cremyll, Torpoint	822236	500
Morwellham Quay	Tavistock	0822 832766	477
Moorland Links	Yelverton	0822 852245	485
National Shire Horse Centre	Yealmpton	880268	488
Plume of Feathers	Princetown	0822 89 240	475
Rising Sun	Kingsand, Cornwall	822840	504
Saltram House	Saltram	336546	497
Windy Ridge Eating House	Trerulefoot	0752 851344	506
Yelverton Paperweight Centre	Yelverton	0822 854250	481

THE INVITATION SERIES
by
Joy David

The following titles are currently available
in this series:

Invitation to Lunch, Dine, Stay & Visit:

Devon & Cornwall (2nd edition)	❏	£8.20 inc p&p
Somerset & Avon (2nd edition)	❏	£8.20 inc p&p
East Anglia	❏	£7.20 inc p&p
Mid-Shires	❏	£7.20 inc p&p
Heart of England	❏	£7.20 inc p&p
Southern England	❏	£8.20 inc p&p
Wales	❏	£8.20 inc p&p
Somerset, Avon & Gloucester	❏	£6.20 inc p&p
Yorkshire	❏	£8.20 inc p&p
An Invitation to Devon	❏	£7.20 inc p&p

(A very readable, gentle meander through Devon)

An Invitation to Plymouth	❏	£9.20 inc p&p

(A contemporary, easily read book covering all aspects of the city)

To order please tick as appropriate:

NAME ....

ADDRESS ....

....

....

Tel: No (daytime) ....

Please make cheques payable to Leisure in Print
**Leisure in Print, 24-26 George Place, Stonehouse,
Plymouth PL1 3NY. Tel: (0752) 265956**

NOTES

NOTES

NOTES

NOTES

NOTES

NOTES